THOREAU'S IMPORTANCE
FOR PHILOSOPHY

AMERICAN PHILOSOPHY

Douglas R. Anderson and Jude Jones, series editors

THOREAU'S IMPORTANCE FOR PHILOSOPHY

Edited by
RICK ANTHONY FURTAK,
JONATHAN ELLSWORTH, AND
JAMES D. REID

FORDHAM UNIVERSITY PRESS   NEW YORK   2012

Library of Congress Cataloging-in-Publication Data

Thoreau's importance for philosophy / edited by Rick Anthony Furtak, Jonathan
Ellsworth, and James D. Reid. — 1st ed.
p. cm. — (American philosophy)
Includes bibliographical references (p.   ) and index.
ISBN 978-0-8232-3930-6 (cloth : alk. paper)
1. Thoreau, Henry David, 1817–1862. I. Furtak, Rick Anthony.
II. Ellsworth, Jonathan. III. Reid, James D.
B931.T44T46 2012
191—dc23
2011037076

Printed in the United States of America
14 13 12   5 4 3 2 1
First edition

Contents

THOREAU'S IMPORTANCE
FOR PHILOSOPHY

ONE

LOCATING THOREAU, REORIENTING PHILOSOPHY

James D. Reid, Rick Anthony Furtak, and Jonathan Ellsworth

To be a philosopher is not merely to have subtle thoughts, nor even to found a school, but so to love wisdom as to live according to its dictates, a life of simplicity, independence, magnanimity, and trust. It is to solve some of the problems of life, not only theoretically, but practically.

—Henry David Thoreau, *Walden*, "Economy"

The philosophical significance of Henry David Thoreau's life and writings is far from being a settled matter. Although his best-known book, *Walden*, is admired as a classic work of American literature, it has not yet been widely recognized as an important philosophical text. In fact, many members of the academic philosophical community in the United States would be reluctant to classify Thoreau as a philosopher at all. For decades, Stanley Cavell's book *The Senses of Walden* remained the only philosophical monograph on Thoreau written in living memory, and Thoreau's work is seldom taught or studied in most American philosophy departments.[1] The purpose of this volume is to address and remedy this neglect, and to provide a clear account of Thoreau's contributions to philosophy. Our aim is to encourage more readers to appreciate his writings in this light and to justify the inclusion of his work within the philosophical canon. In the process of doing so, we will revisit some fundamental questions about the nature of philosophy and of philosophical writing.

Henry David Thoreau was born in Concord, Massachusetts, on the 12th of July, 1817. He attended Harvard College and graduated, without distinction (as Ralph Waldo Emerson tells us) in 1837, and died on the 6th of May, 1862. From first to last his life was, outwardly considered, hardly a success story: He made pencils for a season with his father, fell in love (twice by some reckoning) but never married, surveyed land for his neighbors, squatted on Emerson's property near a pond in the woods for a couple of years, traveled a bit, served as a sort of local handyman, and made many excursions into what he reverently called Nature.[2] He published only two books during his own lifetime; and the first, *A Week on the Concord and Merrimack Rivers*, sold so poorly that its publication nearly left its author bankrupt. Although he lectured widely in New England, he was hardly as popular at public speaking or as interested in engaging in academic life as his famous mentor Emerson. Although he could enjoy taking part in the exciting intellectual community that was forming in and around Concord, he seems to have been more at home outdoors—sitting patiently for hours in the woods, measuring the depth of a pond, or recording in his journal a strange tint in the evening sky. If you knew next to nothing about him, you might have greeted Thoreau as a capable craftsman and land surveyor or a local naturalist, and thanked him for locating the boundaries of your property or for taking your children huckleberrying. If you never met him, you might still have heard about his brief imprisonment for tax evasion or learned of his vehement opinions on the cause of abolition and the fate of John Brown.

And yet such details fail to explain why Emerson could proclaim of Thoreau in his funeral elegy that the country did not yet know "how great a son it had lost." An explanation might begin with something that Emerson mentions earlier in the same address: Thoreau had "no ambition" for measurable success in the world, since he was entirely devoted to the art of living well.[3] For Thoreau, philosophy was not only a mode of reflective thought and discourse but also an embodied practice, a way of life that required constant and vigorous cultivation. If today we tend to regard a philosopher as someone who has mastered a sophisticated conceptual vocabulary, then we might ask ourselves whether we are working with a diminished conception of the discipline. Indeed, the little attention paid to Thoreau's work within academic philosophy could be *because of* his polemic about the nature of philosophy (and his demand to be understood *as* a philosopher) rather than in spite of it. We neglect Thoreau, in other words, not because he is small and insignificant but because he looms so large and asks so much of us.

Beyond the example of Thoreau's life are the issues of the philosophical makeup and reception of his writings. When *Walden; or, Life in the Woods* was finally published in 1854, seven years after Thoreau abandoned his cabin by the pond and after many substantial revisions of the earliest manuscript, its author was still living in relative obscurity. And although his new book was greeted with some favorable reviews, it was not generally acknowledged as a work of philosophy in any modern sense of the word. Although a few readers saw in Thoreau a distant and quirky descendant of ancient philosophical traditions (George Eliot, for instance, called its author a "stoic of the woods," and others interpreted *Walden* as a latter-day defense of Cynicism), there was little offered to the public in the way of detailed philosophical weighing of what the book had to offer. Emerson's posthumous tribute to Thoreau, published in the *Atlantic Monthly* in 1862, hardly mentions his former friend's philosophical significance (and not because Emerson lacked an interest in philosophy and in the philosopher as a "representative" of the human condition).[4] Other enthusiastic admirers were content to point to his "religious" importance without clarifying what this claim might more generally mean.

So the history of Thoreau's neglect among the philosophically minded begins at the very onset of Thoreau's reception. It's probably fair to say that Thoreau's earliest readers were not quite sure what to make of *Walden*, even when some of his more sympathetic commentators weighed in on the author's literary achievement and his place in the history of American literature. And the evidence suggests that we (philosophers) still don't know what to make of a book we can so easily place in time, at least, and from which it's so easy to quote out of context and without much thought. It may seem almost arbitrary to insist that Thoreau and *Walden* belong to the tradition of serious philosophy. However, as we suggested above, the fault may lie less with its author than with us. As Stanley Cavell has argued, Thoreau is an embarrassment to "what we have learned to call philosophy," since his work embodies "a mode of conceptual accuracy" that is "based on an idea of rigor" foreign to the prevailing standards of the academy.[5] Thoreau is not alone, especially among American philosophers, in deviating from those standards: At least, major American thinkers from Ralph Waldo Emerson to William James did not assume (as some nowadays do) that an engaging style, or a concern for the broader human relevance of one's ideas, should raise doubts about one's philosophical merit.[6] Furthermore, the belief that

Walden is lacking in philosophical substance will not stand up under any careful reading.

In fact, it would be only a slight exaggeration to say that *Walden* takes a stand on every broad philosophical issue we've embraced, if not in the compartmentalizing way the professional philosopher tends to take them up. The metaphysician will find suggestive remarks on the nature of reality and our fascination with appearances; Kantians will discover an idealist who praises the life of the knowing subject and her conceptual contribution to the perceived world; social and political thinkers will find substance in *Walden*'s record of dissatisfaction with the polis of Concord and the marketplace more generally, reminiscent of Rousseau and Marx; aestheticians and philosophers of language are likely to find a wealth of material that is well worth pondering; and, of course, the moralist will come face to face with either an ally or an eloquent and quarrelsome foe. There are some passages in *Walden* that seem to speak in favor of foundationalism and others that strike a gleefully relativistic chord. It is possible to read *Walden* in the light of Aristotle's quarrel with Plato over the reality of ideas and where to find them, and to wonder where the author stands, or to see in Thoreau a disciple of Kant's moral philosophy in the battle of spirit against flesh in the chapter "Higher Laws." The exaltation of human potential in *Walden* is as rousing as anything to be found in Pico della Mirandola, and the book as a whole stands as a prescient critique of dehumanizing technology and of merely instrumental reason. It not only bears the mark of Thoreau's extensive knowledge of ancient Greek, Roman, and Asian texts, but it also seeks to renew the classical notion of philosophy as a way of life.[7] If we look beyond *Walden* to some of Thoreau's other writings, as many of the essays in this volume do, we discover influential contributions to radical political thought, along with extensive discussions on the nature of science, including Darwin's account of biological evolution in *On the Origin of Species*, which Thoreau read carefully and with admiration in the last years of his life. And Thoreau's voluminous *Journal* is filled with observations that anticipate what we now call environmental ethics, among countless other topics.

What is evident from the opening pages of *Walden* is that Thoreau is a polemical writer, taking critical aim at many targets. As E. B. White has pointed out, *Walden* opens like a Western in which the hero "rides into the subject at top speed, shooting in all directions."[8] What is more subtly hinted is that *Walden*, like all of Thoreau's work, was deeply informed by a variety of philosophical sources. Its author was well versed in ancient Greek and Roman philosophy, ranging from the pre-Socratics through the Hellenistic schools, and he was an avid student of Asian thought at a time when it was still uncommon for the Western philosopher to show any awareness of non-Western traditions.[9] He was familiar with the main currents of modern philosophy, extending from Descartes, Locke, and the Cambridge Platonists through the German Idealists and their heirs in England and America. It's fair to say that Thoreau was steeped in the history of philosophy, and the bulk of his most important work is unthinkable without it. Why, then, don't we take *Walden* at its philosophical face value? Why does it remain on the periphery of the discipline?

One answer is unlikely to arouse suspicion, although it has far-reaching implications: *Walden* is on the margin of philosophy not so much because of *what* comes to voice in it (we've seen already if only briefly how untenable that suggestion is) but because of the manner in which it is written. We've come to expect the philosopher to offer a certain kind of argument and to defend his position in a certain way. Perhaps we imagine Thoreau accosted by a modern-day Socrates who wants to know more precisely what it means to say that the mass of men lead lives of quiet desperation, and why Thoreau believes that this statement is true. Or we may think of the "Transcendental Aesthetic" of Kant's first *Critique*, which begins with a series of definitions and proceeds to argue rigorously that space and time are transcendentally ideal and empirically real, and find nothing of the sort in *Walden*. Or maybe we've been taught to be mistrustful whenever a piece of philosophical prose *moves* us, as though what we think and what we feel flow along separate streams, and feeling is obviously what the philosopher should silence.[10] Or perhaps we are ill at ease when an author tells us, unabashedly, that he's not quite sure what he has to prove or why he did what he's now telling us about. We've grown accustomed to the journal essay that informs its reader right away what its overarching thesis is and how the work to come is structured: "In what follows, I intend to argue that . . . ." The philosopher, we think, should assemble and organize the relevant material, weigh the evidence for and against, and offer his most convincing arguments. If you're not doing this much, whatever else you might be up to, then we're tempted to conclude that you're not doing anything recognizably philosophical.

It is, in short, its *style* that forbids easy philosophical access to Thoreau's account of his experimental life and sojourn in the woods: There are few straightforward arguments in *Walden*; the author is happy to refer to himself and his own personal experiences, quarrels, and ecstasies; and when he does say something about a subject other than himself, much of what unfolds seems to belong to the history of nature poetry, more in line with Virgil, say, than a descendant of Plato, Descartes, or Kant. His prose often soars to poetic heights, combining abstract speculation with close observation of a concrete place. If *Walden* is responsive to philosophical problems, it responds to the tradition of philosophy in an underground and unusual way, more like the work of a disgruntled son who refuses to play the game according to his father's rules than the product of a professional's sensitivity to established conventions. When this author renders his account, then, he is departing from what many philosophers might view as moving about soberly and sanely in the space of reasons. In this sense, *Walden* takes up again the ancient quarrel between the philosophers and the poets, this time on the side of the philosophizing or thinking poet.

Thoreau's mode of writing is, perhaps, enough to make some philosophical readers uncomfortable. But there are other difficulties that stand in the way of a truly philosophical appropriation of Thoreau. As we have already indicated, the academic reader of *Walden* is likely to be struck by the absence of any clear-cut boundaries between various philosophical disciplines. Thoreau offers no clear and distinct contributions to metaphysics and epistemology, aesthetics, ethics, social and political philosophy, and the theory of value. The answer to the question "Of which branch of philosophy is *Walden* a member?" seems to be "All or none." (Its very title is something of a philosophical embarrassment. Imagine Kant's *Critique of Pure Reason* bearing the alternative title *Königsberg, or Life in the University*. What would we expect to find in it? Perhaps Kant walking about in the afternoon, as his neighbors set their clocks, after lecturing on logic or physical geography, or hosting a small gathering where the number of companions is somewhere near the number of Graces,[11] on a Saturday evening; in short, we would expect anything but a patient account of the nature of human reason, its scope and limits, a "transcendental deduction" of certain concepts, grounded in a faculty of a priori "apperception," and a lengthy critique of the metaphysical tradition.)

According to one conception of what it is to make a contribution to the philosophical conversation, Thoreau's project is likely to seem confused.

He's happy to make *moral* claims when he's talking about beauty, for instance, and to interpret aesthetic experience in metaphysical terms; or to read our political failures ontologically; or to wax epistemological when he's apparently discussing our values. Here's a well-known and pregnant example, from the chapter "Where I Lived, and What I Lived For":

> Shams and delusions are esteemed for soundest truths, while reality is fabulous. If men would steadily observe realities only, and not allow themselves to be deluded, life, to compare it with such things as we know, would be like a fairy tale and the Arabian Nights' Entertainments. If we respected only what is inevitable and has a right to be, music and poetry would resound along the streets. When we are unhurried and wise, we perceive that only great and worthy things have any permanent and absolute existence,—that petty fears and petty pleasures are but the shadow of the reality. . . . By closing the eyes and slumbering, and consenting to be deceived by shows, men establish and confirm their daily life of routine and habit every where, which still is built on purely illusory foundations.[12]

In this dense passage we have, it seems, an opening *metaphysical* discourse on appearance and reality; a burgeoning epistemology and philosophy of *perception* that quickly collapses into an *aesthetic*, bordering on the philosophy of *value*; a reference to the *virtues* (patience and wisdom), and thus what appears to be a stance in *ethics*; a *political* view, rooted in a philosophy of *right*, which is itself cast in ontological and aesthetic terms. Later on in the same passage, Thoreau employs a *theological* vocabulary as well ("God himself culminates in the present moment . . .").

The impatient reader, accustomed to the practice of thematic segregation, is likely to dismiss passages like this as too *compressed*; the topics that Thoreau bundles together in one long paragraph the meticulous thinker will be more anxious to distinguish. And with each area crisply delimited, she can go on to argue fully for each of her separate claims. If she's a charitable reader, she may simply lament the fact that Thoreau was writing before the days of more specialized academic labor, as if *Walden* would have been a better book, philosophically speaking, had it been written more recently, with contemporary standards in mind. Then again, Thoreau's final sentence alone employs unmistakable Platonic and Cartesian metaphors for reality and knowledge, announcing its author's intention to avoid being deceived by illusions and to find solid foundations: What could be a more central philosophical theme than this?

Thoreau's example poses a challenge to what has become a standard way of thinking, reminding us that the compartmentalized approach to problem solving is by no means a perennial and essential feature of philosophy. If the different areas of philosophy are interdependent—that is, if (for instance) some general conception of the world is required in order for us to guide our conduct rationally—then we cannot understand any area of philosophy in isolation from all others, and the pursuit of ever-greater specialization is a mistake. As another critic of this trend has recently observed, the "principal weakness of Anglophone philosophy" may be "not that it is too narrow or analytical, but that it is too specialized."[13] Yet we should nevertheless bear in mind that Kant dealt separately with metaphysics and epistemology in the *Critique of Pure Reason*, ethics in the second *Critique*, and aesthetics and the philosophy of biology in the two major divisions of the *Critique of Judgment*; likewise, the *Metaphysics of Morals* is divided into a *Rechtslehre* (political philosophy) and a *Tugendslehre* (moral philosophy). When Thoreau began work on *Walden*, philosophy was already professionalized, at least in Europe, and demarcated into fairly discrete subdisciplines. If we want an ancient model of Thoreau's project, we should probably look back to Plato's *Republic*, which touches on almost every conceivable topic, including the theory of knowledge, psychology, politics, virtue and the good, art and the beautiful, the nature of education, and the philosopher's mode of existence. So even if Thoreau's method has at least some philosophical antecedents, it is decidedly unfashionable in the modern period.

We may be inclined to embrace the more sympathetic excuse for *Walden*'s apparent failure to work within the boundaries of the philosophical profession, but this approach is also ultimately inadequate. It mistakenly assumes that disciplinary confusion was simply an aspect of the "spirit of the age" (as some have maintained regarding the pre-Socratic philosophers) and that Thoreau *would* have compartmentalized his problems if he only *could* have done so, when the truth seems to be that he deliberately chose to ignore the usual ways of classifying philosophical tasks. It is more plausible to conclude that *Walden* sets itself against the "divide and conquer" mentality that shapes the practice of philosophy today, and that was already working itself out in the academic climate of Thoreau's time.[14] And, like Nietzsche's work, Thoreau's philosophy has an aphoristic quality, the form of which is arguably well suited to its syncretic, exploratory, "experimental" content and emphatically first person style. The challenge to the reader is to see the coherence of the entire philosophical outlook that is contained in his pages and condensed in rich, intricate passages such as the one quoted above.

If we find it hard to overcome a bias against the idea of a philosopher who is also a literary author, then we should remember that it is only a parochial assumption that disposes us toward believing that there exists a single way of writing philosophy and that this happens to be "a style remarkably flat and lacking in wonder," as if technical rigor were "a kind of all-purpose solvent" appropriate for all philosophical problems.[15] By taking a slightly broader or longer view, we can recognize that there is an astonishing diversity of style in those texts that are generally accepted as works of philosophy. In the Western philosophical canon, we find not only essays, treatises, and aphorisms, but also autobiographies, letters, dialogues presented in dramatic form, meditations written to oneself, narratives, lecture notes subsequently published, numbered series of propositions, geometric proofs, and poems.[16] Whatever category of writing *Walden* falls into, then, can hardly be designated as a genre in which philosophical works *cannot* be written. As for Thoreau's refusal to engage with philosophical subject matter in a more specialized fashion, this can be interpreted as one way of calling our attention to the way things appear in everyday life, where we are at once lovers of beauty, aspiring knowers, political animals, and natural metaphysicians,[17] concerned about the value of being in the world and the importance of our pursuits, before we develop any explicit theories of the distinct objects that stir us. Thoreau was clearly eager to establish philosophy as a way of life and to root our philosophical, conceptual affairs in "practical" existential concerns. *Walden* is, among many other things, a sustained meditation on the appropriate *conduct* of life, and on the importance of living our lives with integrity, avoiding what he calls "quiet desperation" and unhappy resignation.

Of course, this still leaves open the possibility that when we *think* about the content of our lives, we do well to move in distinguishable spheres.[18] The intellect, on this view, introduces welcome clarity and distinctness, in place of life's manifold confusions. But Thoreau seems to be making the provocative suggestion that our thinking is impoverished when we fragment the intellectual universe into utterly distinct classes of objects, and that we thereby run the risk of overlooking important connections between the disciplines we've come to pursue in isolation. Philosophers sometimes assume, for instance, that aesthetic questions (concerning beauty and form, in art or in nature) *can* be answered adequately without having to take a stand on the nature of human knowledge; or that the epistemologist can do his job without worrying about what the philosopher of art or the theorist of value might be doing; and we often take it for granted that the task of analyzing our moral obligations and duties, or defending a list of virtues, should not be infected by aesthetic considerations—as if, by taking the world apart and dismantling our experience in this way, we come to know each thing more precisely. As the progress of specialized scientific research seems to demonstrate, there's no better way of coming to know the world around us. It is, however, this pervasive assumption that Thoreau invites us to reconsider.

According to an older and now less popular conception, the philosopher is concerned about the *whole*—being, or what you will; if the objects that compose the universe can be sorted out and separately analyzed up to a point, it is the philosopher's responsibility to show how all things manage, despite obvious differences, to hang together, and to render a complete account of what there is.[19] This need not be construed as an expression of befuddled enthusiasm for the undifferentiated, or as a celebration of the proverbial night in which all cows are black; it may instead be the only way we can begin to sort things out meaningfully, and to see the elements of the world as they truly are. Anything less than the fruit of this ambitious quest may prove to be a distortion of the phenomena. An adequate philosophy of mind, for instance, should be able to account not only for the bare data of raw sensation, but, perhaps more important, for the mind's ability to appreciate form, the desire to understand, the perception of value and the capacity to judge, and experiences of anger, jealousy, resentment, and being in love. And these "mental experiences" themselves cannot be fruitfully considered without taking into account their intentional *objects*, as Brentano and other phenomenologists often remind us. In a more compelling account of what mind *is*, these sorts of *Erlebnisse* (in the phenomenological way of speaking) are not merely examples to be used for the sake of illustrating some general point, but primary phenomena that help define the area of inquiry. If you never get past the consciousness of sensible qualities in your account, you may not have *mind* sufficiently in mind.[20]

To the complaints just canvassed we should probably add another, related concern, one that was already intimated above: Namely, Thoreau's writing unabashedly gives voice to the *person* who lived in Concord and who experimented with words and life during his time of relative seclusion in the woods. The author of *Walden* is constantly reminding his readers that every work, however abstract and apparently impersonal, is always written from *someone*'s point of view: "We commonly do not remember that it is, after all, always the first person that is speaking."[21] As he argues at great length throughout the *Journal*, the phenomena of nature and human society appear most fully and become significant because someone in particular cares enough to attend to them, and to write or speak out lovingly or quarrelsomely—in either case, with concern—about them. Like Kierkegaard and Nietzsche, and anticipating Heidegger's early moral ontology of authenticity, Thoreau urges his readers to care about the quality of their own lives and the objects that have come to matter to them, before the abstract intelligence begins its work. Sometimes his project involves taking issue with political conventions and the soporific routines of everyday social life; at times it calls for protest against scientific descriptions and explanations that impoverish the phenomena and seem to speak about the world anonymously, as if from nowhere. (Speaking of impersonal trends in natural science, Thoreau writes, "Modern botanical descriptions approach ever nearer to the dryness of an algebraic formula, as if $x + y$ were = to a love letter.")[22] More subtly, it displays itself in careful poetic transcriptions of things in the world that the philosopher finds significant: "Wherever I sat, there I might live, and the landscape radiated from me accordingly."[23]

This doesn't have to involve obsessive, morbid preoccupation with one's own inner states and their incessant fluctuations at the expense of attending to the world—the sort of hypochondria that Goethe associated with modern philosophy as a whole, whether unjustly or not.[24] (*Walden* is very much about the world its author experienced and the various objects he encountered and attended to, carefully and vigilantly, for the two years and two months he spent in the woods.) It does, however, imply that there is only a world worth talking about, and a philosophical or scientific vision worth considering, because someone somewhere cares.[25] The most abstract and impersonal explanation of material reality in theoretical physics is possible because the scientist is moved by a *desire* to understand and to explain and to share his results with his fellows.[26] If his account of reality leaves no room for the interest that brought it into being and for the impulse to communicate, then so much the worse for the theory. As Kierkegaard would have agreed, there is something conspicuously lacking in a philosophical conception of nature that fails to account for one's own desire to understand, which is the basis for the whole enterprise. The world is *for us* what it is because we inhabit it, because we are bound to it and responsive to it in our various cares and concerns. We do, after all, take an interest in scientific personalities—the worldviews of Newton, Darwin, and Einstein continue to matter to us, even if today's scientist leaves the life of his predecessor aside in his strictly scientific research. And we take an interest in the life because we want to know how the person came to view the world as he did, and to explain its phenomena in a way that came to seem, for a while at least, convincing. We care about the human beings because of their passion for universal, scientific explanation. Those who are apathetic and indifferent are not better situated to perceive things as they truly are by virtue of their extremely impersonal perspective; we normally, and rightly, view them as lacking something essential, as tragically incapable of perceiving more accurately and feeling more palpably what the world has to give. We are, irreducibly, creatures for whom things matter.[27] This peculiar "fact" about us, and our shared failure to care passionately enough, and often eccentrically, about the life each of us is called upon to live—our tendency to take refuge in the way *one* does things and what *they* say, at the expense of what *I* think and experience in my own more imaginative flights and designs—are among *Walden*'s starting points. By inviting us to consider how we spend our lives, Thoreau issues a distinctly philosophical provocation.

Walden tells us that it is "never too late to give up our prejudices."[28] For those of us who are devoted to philosophy, one tempting yet deplorable variety of narrow-mindedness consists in limiting ourselves to an artificially small frame of reference, excluding other sources that might speak to our concerns—as if the ethicist could learn nothing valuable from the metaphysician, the contemporary philosopher from the history of ideas, or as if the philosophy of mind could safely ignore both psychology and phenomenology. Succumbing to this temptation makes our intellectual life easier, but less interesting—and it may supply a partial answer to what Stanley Cavell characterizes (in this volume) as the "soul-boggling and heartbreaking" question of why Thoreau has not yet been appreciated by philosophers in his own country. Yet we also know how rewarding, and even transformative, it can be to encounter a thinker who shows us how to approach familiar philosophical questions in a new and unique way. One of the tasks of the present volume is to make this encounter possible, by opening up the lines of communication between Thoreau's project and the central areas of philosophy. This is a many-sided task, and the essays that follow therefore cast light from different angles and on different aspects of Thoreau's work. Drawing in various ways on Thoreau's *Walden* and his other writings, they show how numerous interpretations combine to provide us with a fuller sense of reality; they explain how we might develop a point of view that is imaginative, yet accurate, and which would enable us to "meet more fragrant worlds"; they illuminate the nuances of embodied consciousness and the links between the search for knowledge and the development of personality. They encourage us to consider whether the spiritual meaning of nature is truly "there to be understood," and whether the philosopher can proceed critically without adopting skeptical doubt as his or her primary orientation toward the world. They clarify Thoreau's project by locating it in relation to earlier philosophical authors and traditions, ancient and modern, and they note the ways in which he either anticipated or influenced later thinkers and schools of thought; they also situate his well-known political views in the context of his often overlooked record as a committed activist, a critic of his society, who was not by any means a dropout from it. Most importantly, they show how Thoreau returns philosophy to its roots as the love of wisdom—providing an inspiring source of guidance for those who wish to confront the deepest problems of life, both theoretically and practically.

TWO

THOREAU AND EMERSONIAN PERFECTIONISM

Stanley Bates

What is at issue in deciding whether to call Thoreau a philosopher? One could employ Heidegger's distinction between thinking and philosophy, and concede "thinking" to Thoreau but not "philosophy."[1] This, however, would require some considerable reflection on Heidegger's distinction and in particular on the *relationship* between thinking, so conceived, and philosophy. If such thinking can be understood as a response to philosophy, or as an attempt to overcome philosophy-until-now by understanding it, and by responding more deeply to what originally aroused that philosophy, then such thinking simply is philosophy. In any case, the issue is not simply about the propriety of applying a word to a particular case; it is about what philosophy is—which has always been an issue for philosophy itself. The nineteenth century saw the professionalization of philosophy; as what we call science ceased to be called natural philosophy, philosophy became an academic specialty. Thoreau himself famously characterizes the situation with his own account of "philosophy" in "Economy," the first chapter of *Walden*.

There are nowadays professors of philosophy, but not philosophers. Yet it is admirable to profess because it was once admirable to live. To be a philosopher is not merely to have subtle thoughts, nor even to found a school, but so to love wisdom as to live according to its dictates, a life of simplicity, independence, magnanimity, and trust. It is to solve some of the problems of life, not only theoretically, but practically.[2]

In giving this characterization, of course, Thoreau was returning to an ancient tradition of considering philosophy to be a "way of life." It is the conflict between conceptions of philosophy, outlined in the above quotation, which lies at the heart of the issue of how Thoreau relates to "philosophy." As an academic specialty, philosophy courts the danger of becoming "academic" in the pejorative sense that has now become common—roughly meaning irrelevant to "real" life. In what follows, I shall refer to "academic moral philosophy," I hope nonpejoratively, by which I mean the way in which the nature and history of moral philosophy have been presented within the dominant philosophy department curricula in the English language tradition since the nineteenth century. Thoreau has had no place in such curricula.

Indeed, it seems to me that most of the thinkers and writers in Western culture of the last couple of centuries whose work has most affected how people actually live their lives have not been a part of academic moral philosophy.[3] This would seem to be a topic worthy of reflection. Why did John Stuart Mill believe that he had resolved a crisis in his mental life by reading Wordsworth and Coleridge? Why have figures such as Emerson, Kierkegaard, Thoreau, Nietzsche, Dostoevsky, George Eliot, Sartre, Camus, Simone Weil, Levinas, Adorno, and Marcuse not been a part of academic moral philosophy as described above? I don't here mean to be privileging so-called continental philosophy over the analytical tradition. Many of the figures I've listed have become part of academic philosophy (though not of its core as conceived by the analytical tradition) but have not entered into the subdiscipline of moral philosophy. However, entering Thoreau's name on a list such as I have given does not yet deal with the particularity of his thought. I want in this essay both to look at some of the ways in which Thoreau fits with a number of nineteenth-century thinkers responding to the post-Kantian period in the history of philosophy and to try to articulate something about the difference of Thoreau from those other thinkers.

Thoreau has been a continuing influence on how some in succeeding generations have lived their lives, but that was not sufficient to interest philosophers in his work until relatively recently. The work crucial for raising these issues, of course, was Stanley Cavell's *The Senses of Walden*— work that was extended in his subsequent explorations of Emerson.[4] In this essay, I want to draw on Cavell's reading of Thoreau and to expand his further discussion of what he called Emersonian perfectionism in an attempt to understand it in relation to the development of academic moral philosophy.

Perfectionism

The tradition of moral perfectionism extends throughout the history of philosophy, and many of the major philosophers of the West are associated with it, for example, Plato, Aristotle, the Stoics, Aquinas, Spinoza, Leibniz, Kant, Hegel, and Nietzsche.[5] It is important to say something about this tradition in order to understand the way in which what Cavell calls Emersonian perfectionism must differ from it as well as draw on it. There are certain features common to both ancient and modern (meaning here seventeenth- and eighteenth-century) perfectionism.[6] The supposition is that there is a transcendental or divine source of objective value—God or a logos—and that the task of a human being is to perfect himself or herself by coming to an understanding of that source of value. This will also be a process of self-understanding, since this understanding will establish one's place in the divine plan, and allow one to live in harmony with it. Jerome Schneewind, in contrasting perfectionism to a natural law tradition that includes Locke, puts it this way: "The major seventeenth-century alternative to modern natural law theory rejected both its empiricism and its refusal to tie morality to a divinely supervised universe."[7] Susan James summarizes Schneewind's account of these perfectionist writers: "Morality, as these authors saw it, is not just a matter of obeying an externally imposed law. Rather, we become virtuous by acquiring non-empirical knowledge of our place in a divinely governed universe, of a kind which transforms our characters."[8] Schneewind has given a beautiful account of the seventeenth- and eighteenth-century

THOREAU AND EMERSONIAN PERFECTIONISM

versions of perfectionism, which often begin from a revival of some forms of ancient perfectionism, especially Stoicism and Platonism.

In my view, this perfectionist strain of moral philosophy culminates in the work of Kant. From the point of view of academic moral theory, this would seem surprising. Kant has usually been presented as the exemplar of deontology, an advocate of rigorism about duty and a formalist about morality. (The work of Kant's most commonly read is *The Foundations of the Metaphysics of Morals*, and his other works of moral philosophy, though not neglected by Kant specialists, are neglected by most moral philosophers.) Perhaps Kant's version of perfectionism has been neglected because at a number of points Kant presents himself as a *critic* of perfectionism.[9] However, as Paul Guyer points out, "What Kant really rejects is not the abstract concept of perfection as the goal of morality." Rather, "what Kant really does is to replace the perfection of our intrinsic and extrinsic condition as the ultimate goal of virtue with the perfection of the quality of our will itself—the good will."[10]

However, even the most acute critics of academic moral philosophy in the past half-century (I am here thinking of Elizabeth Anscombe, Alasdair MacIntyre, and Bernard Williams as examples) tended to think of Kant as a kind of rigorist, formalist moral philosopher.[11] Hence, after the long detour of academic moral philosophy in the early twentieth century into "metaethics," the most usual way of presenting substantive moral theory was to contrast teleological (especially utilitarian) moral theories with Kant as the representative of deontology.[12] (Only in the latter part of the twentieth century, with the emergence of a revived virtue ethics, did we begin to get a broadened view within academic moral theory of possible moral views. Thomas Hurka, writing in 1993 in his book *Perfectionism*, says that the important perfectionist tradition has been "largely neglected.")[13]

I think the perfectionist element in Kant's thinking emerges most clearly in two places. The first is in the *Critique of Practical Reason*, when Kant argues that the immortality of the soul is a necessary postulate of pure practical reason.[14] His argument is that it is a condition for the achievement of the highest good that there be a fitness of the will to the moral law.

> But complete fitness of the will to the moral law is holiness, which is a
> perfection of which no rational being in the world of sense is at any

time capable. But since it is required as practically necessary, it can be found only in an endless progress to that complete fitness; on principles of pure practical reason, it is necessary to assume such a practical progress as the real object of our will.[15]

Kant here gives a picture of our lives as necessarily involving a striving for a perfection of our will (or, we might say, an endless attempt to realize our nature as rational free beings) that cannot be brought to a conclusion in our earthly lifetimes. His conclusion is that there must be a life beyond this one, but if one were persuaded that we are indeed earthlings, one would draw a different conclusion. Certainly the romantic thinkers who followed out this idea of an infinite striving as the essential nature of human being took it in a different direction. Their problem was to give some characterization of perfectionist striving that made it independent of the "divinely supervised universe" (as least as that notion is understood by the traditional, historical religions).

The second place where Kant's perfectionism is most clearly stated is in the second part of *The Metaphysics of Morals*, where Kant takes up "The Metaphysical Principles of Virtue." In a section of the introduction titled "What are the ends which are at the same time duties?" Kant answers, "They are these: one's own perfection and the happiness of others."[16] In explicating his idea of one's own perfection Kant adds, "It can be nothing but the cultivation of one's capacities (or natural endowments)." Hence, in addition to the striving for moral perfection, we are to attempt to realize ourselves in the development and expression of our nature as free, rational beings. This Kantian problematic sets the stage for a great deal of nineteenth-century thinking about how to live one's life well.

Stanley Cavell says of his conception of Emersonian perfectionism that it is not a competing moral *theory* but, rather, a dimension of moral life that must be considered in any complete understanding of how we should live our lives.[17] Let me elaborate on why it is not a theory. When one ceases to believe in the traditional conception of a divinely supervised universe, or a logos, which would be available to ground an account of the ideal end point of a perfectionist quest, one faces a new kind of problem. Even for Kant, who continued to believe in the moral law, and who argued that our recognition of the moral law could ground a belief in God, there could be no specific blueprint for which of our natural endowments we should cultivate (though, of course, there could be an imperfect duty to oneself to engage in some such cultivation). This is a more specific instance of the general problem faced by those nineteenth-century thinkers who believed that the traditional philosophical theories about the foundations of epistemology, metaphysics, and ethics could no longer be accepted. Nietzsche sees it as the problem of how to avoid nihilism. Of course, from the point of view of the traditional philosophical theories, any attempted solutions will look like nihilism because these "solutions" will have, ex hypothesi, given up those traditional foundations. No wonder that there is an issue from the point of view of modern academic philosophy as to whether thinkers such as Marx, Kierkegaard, Emerson, Thoreau, and Nietzsche are to be counted as philosophers. But we can now see why this version of perfectionism is not itself a theory. It is based on a characterization of us as human beings that precludes there being a formulable rule or principle about exactly how we should seek to develop as we move along on the path to the "unattained but attainable self."[18] It is, crucially, about the particular, actual, individual—not the ontologically isolated Cartesian "I" but the individual who lives in a natural and social world. It might seem paradoxical to call it a perfectionist view since, from the beginning, it is clear that there is no point during a human life at which one can expect that some perfect state will have been achieved. (This is, roughly, the same paradox inscribed in Carlyle's phrase "natural supernaturalism."[19] Romanticism had to try to accommodate the necessarily endless striving of human life, of which Kant wrote, to the condition of human finitude.) In the absence of the Christian salvational narrative, one must explore "the possibility of self-transformation according to an ideal that is internal to the self's constitution rather than one that comes from without."[20] Here we speak of the individual self, not an abstract conception of the human self based on some general account of human nature. Of course, any such ideal must be formulable within the limits of human forms of life, or (one might say) the necessities endemic to our condition. One of Thoreau's tasks in *Walden* is to explore such necessities.[21]

Need it be said that such a perfectionist path must be constrained by morality, by justice? Indeed, it needs to be said, and Cavell does say it: "If the perfectionist position I adumbrate is incompatible with . . . attention of and to justice, the position is morally worthless."[22] It is an old charge against Emerson, and an occasional charge against Thoreau, that their positions are simply antinomian, though both strove to avoid that charge.

Cavell calls the perfectionism he finds in these thinkers both secular and democratic. The latter term is used to counter the claim that perfectionism is necessarily elitist. No doubt some forms of perfectionism could be elitist, but not one that begins with the recognition that there is no single destination of "perfection" to which a map can be given. (Here we see the beginning of an account of why the specifically American setting of Emerson and Thoreau is relevant, and why their thought is relevant to a reading of what America is. I can't pursue such an account here, but others have.)[23] I hope this makes clearer why Cavell writes that this type of perfectionism is not a *theory*, although it is a crucial part of any comprehensive thought about how we should live.

Responding to the Kantian Problematic

The philosophical settlement proposed in Kant's critical philosophy proved to be unstable (as has been true of all such philosophical settlements), but it set the terms for the major thinkers of the nineteenth century.[24] We might see an aspect of this instability in the possible answers to the question of whether Kant is a skeptic. One might be tempted to answer "No" because Kant claims to refute idealism and to establish empirical realism. One might be tempted to answer "Yes" because Kant claims to show that there is indeed something that we human beings cannot know. Kant, of course, founded his critical philosophy on the distinction between things as they appear to us and things as they are in themselves, the phenomenal/noumenal distinction. Almost all of the major thinkers of the nineteenth century reject some aspect of Kant's conception of the distinction between the transcendental (or noumenal) and the empirical (or phenomenal). The connection of the thought of the greatest of American transcendentalists, Emerson, to Kant's thought has long been obvious (as the name "transcendentalism" would indicate). Yet, until the work of Stanley Cavell, I don't think it was often taken seriously as an important *philosophical* response to Kant and to the entire course of modern philosophy from Descartes to Kant.[25] Cavell considers Emerson, along with figures such as Marx and Nietzsche, to be engaged in a project of understanding our actual experience as living, acting, human beings, after the failure of modern philosophy to find the rational foundations of knowledge and morality that it had sought. In the case of all these thinkers, the crucial first move is to acknowledge that our primary relationship to the world is not one of knowing (as philosophy had conceived of knowing) but of living/acting/working—of being *there*. The skeptical problematic of modern philosophy itself needs to be accounted for philosophically. Skepticism is not to be refuted, as the foundationalist philosophers had attempted, but rather to be understood as itself arising from our capacity to reflect on our relationship to the world, a capacity that must be understood within an account of our actual being in the world.

It would not be difficult to show the relationship of Emerson to Nietzsche, since Nietzsche himself acknowledges it, yet there persisted a strong reluctance among both philosophers and students of American literature to think of Emerson as a philosopher (rather than a lecturer, essayist, or sage). Cavell writes:

> Something of this same sheer vision of, or unrelenting insistence upon, Emerson's inability to think and write rigorously has meant that, for all Nietzsche's explicit praise of Emerson, and for all the practically uncountable allusions to (I often call them rewritings of) Emerson in Nietzsche's writing, this relationship is forgotten as often as it is discovered.[26]

Given what we know of Emerson's relationship to Thoreau, it would be interesting to think of Thoreau in relation to Nietzsche. However, I won't attempt that here. I do want to consider the relationship of Emerson's thought to Thoreau's, but before doing so, I want to pursue a comparison of Thoreau to the young Marx. I think this will support my claim that the general philosophical climate of the post-Kantian nineteenth century is crucial for Thoreau.

Marx and Thoreau

Thoreau is not often thought about in conjunction with Marx, for obvious reasons.[27] Thoreau accords a value to the individual that Marx seems to deny. Marx wants a revolutionary politics, whereas Thoreau concentrates on the possible revolution within individuals. However, different as their responses are to the social and political conditions of the 1840s, there are fascinating points of agreement between the Thoreau of *Walden* and the early Marx (especially in the "Economic and Philosophic Manuscripts of 1844," written in the year before Thoreau began his sojourn at

Walden Pond). This is perhaps less surprising when we remember that the first and longest chapter of *Walden* is called "Economy" and is indeed a philosophical reflection on human economy. Both Marx and Thoreau begin from a judgment that something has gone wrong in the social/political/economic life of contemporary Europe/America. Thoreau says, "The mass of men lead lives of quiet desperation."[28] Marx identifies this condition as "alienation" (*Entfremdung*, estrangement).[29] Both go back to a reassessment of *economy* as a necessary starting point for understanding what has gone wrong with human life and how we might recover a fully human way of living in the world. We can juxtapose their remarks on a number of topics to compare their analyses.

Marx begins his material conception of human history from what he calls "real premises": "They are the real individuals, their activity and the material conditions under which they live, both those which they find already existing and those produced by their activity. . . . The first premise of all human history is, of course, the existence of living human individuals."[30] This could be a general characterization of what Thoreau explores in an individual case in *Walden*—the "material conditions" that he found and that he produced by his own activity. Marx adds, a little later, as an expansion of this premise, "that men must be in a position to live in order to be able to 'make history.' But life involves before everything else eating and drinking, a habitation, clothing and many other things."[31] These reminders were deemed necessary in an age when philosophers had, as Kierkegaard put it, forgotten what it is to be a human being. Thoreau's way of giving a similar reminder in "Economy" is to give an account of what he calls the things *"necessary of life."* "The necessaries of life for man in this climate may, accurately enough, be distributed under the several heads of Food, Shelter, Clothing, and Fuel, for not till we have secured these are we prepared to entertain the true problems of life with freedom and a prospect of success."[32] He then, of course, proceeds to discuss the application of all of these heads in relation to his life at Walden Pond. (I'll return below to my interpretation of an aspect of the significance of his opening chapter.)

Marx writes, "We have seen that the amount of necessary labour crystallized in a commodity constitutes its value."[33] Thoreau puts it that "the cost of a thing is the amount of what I will call life which is required to be exchanged for it, immediately or in the long run."[34] This "labor theory of value" arises for both of them within what Nietzsche calls "the perspective of life." A crucial factor for both Marx and Nietzsche is the division of labor. We can see Hegel's account of history as an adaptation of the Christian narrative of salvation. In Hegel's version, self-consciousness corresponds to the Fall, the various stages of history are steps toward the overcoming of the alienation of spirit, and the final moment when alienation is overcome is the goal and end of history. Marx's inversion of the Hegelian scheme replaces the development of the Idea (its coming to self-consciousness in *Geist*'s development through history) with the history of the material conditions of humanity. The Fall into history for Marx is the division of labor (and, even for him, that could figure as a felix culpa, a fortunate fall, since it will lead to the paradise of the realized humanism of communism). Marx writes that "the existing stage in the division of labour determines also the relations of individuals to one another with reference to the material, instrument, and product of labour."[35] Thoreau's moral perfectionism is different, but the division of labor plays a crucial role in it. He writes:

> It is not the tailor alone who is the ninth part of a man: it is as much the preacher, and the merchant and the farmer. Where is this division of labor to end? And what object does it finally serve? No doubt another *may* also think for me, but it is not therefore desirable that he should do so to the exclusion of my thinking for myself.[36]

And surely he is reinforcing this point when he observes, "I think the fall from the farmer to the operative as great and memorable as that from the man to the farmer."[37] The contemporary result of this division of labor for Marx is the capitalist society with its class divisions.[38] Thoreau observes the same thing when he comments, "The luxury of one class is counterbalanced by the indigence of another. On the one side is the palace, on the other are the almshouse and the 'silent poor.' "[39] For one final point of comparison, both men believe that the role of money in contemporary society is both a symptom and a cause of human alienation or quiet desperation. Marx, famously, claimed that "money is the alienated essence of man's work and existence; this essence dominates him and he worships it."[40] He also claims that "money is . . . the general overturning of *individualities* which turn them into their contrary and adds contradictory attributes to their attributes."[41] Thoreau's final word on money in *Walden* is "Money is not required to buy one necessary of the soul."[42] It follows from that observation that the postulated motivation of economic man, in the standard economic theory of the nineteenth century, represents a perversion of human nature.

I present these parallels in the writings of Marx and Thoreau, not to argue that their views are the same, but to point to the differences between their forms of perfectionist thought. Marx continues in the totalizing tradition of Hegel. He does believe in the arrival at a perfected state of society in which the individual/social opposition is overcome (though he is notoriously sketchy in his description of such a state both in his early and in his late writings). "This communism, as fully-developed naturalism, equals humanism and as fully-developed humanism equals naturalism. . . . Communism is the riddle of history solved, and it knows itself to be this solution."[43] If we read Thoreau as a perfectionist in *Walden*, it would be as an Emersonian perfectionist—that is, as someone who believes that we can do better in how we live our lives, and that seeking the better is an unending process that does not require achieved perfection to give it meaning. Thoreau obviously shares many positions with Emerson. However, I would like to concentrate on what differentiates Thoreau's presentation of his perfectionism from Emerson's various accounts of his own view.

Emerson and Thoreau

The relationship of Thoreau to Emerson was vexed both personally and intellectually. The biographies of both men have difficulty in describing a relationship that was so close and so important to each of them, but that was often strained. The essay Emerson wrote about Thoreau after his death offers a moving description of, and a heartfelt tribute to, the younger man. Still, even in this essay a querulous note surfaces. One senses something of the difficulty of being Thoreau's friend, when Emerson writes:

> He wanted a fallacy to expose, a blunder to pillory, I may say required a little sense of victory, a roll of the drum, to call his powers into full exercise. It cost him nothing to say No; indeed he found it much easier than to say Yes. It seemed as if his first instinct on hearing a proposition was to controvert it, so impatient was he of the limitations of our daily thought. This habit, of course, is a little chilling to the social affections; and though the companion would in the end acquit him of any malice or untruth, yet it mars conversation.[44]

Emerson had been his mentor, had advised him to keep a journal after his graduation from Harvard, had had him living in his home for extended periods, had secured the land at Walden Pond for him to build his habitation, and, to the end of Thoreau's life, Emerson had regarded him as his best friend.[45] Despite all of this, there were strains on their relationship. Each seemed to feel that in some way he had not met the standards of the other. Emerson, as the quoted passage illustrates, found Thoreau's instinctive opposition difficult. He also seems to have felt that Thoreau should have made himself more important in the town of Concord, rather than always being ready to lead a huckleberry party. Emerson wrote in his journal, "I fancy it an inexcusable fault in him that he is insignificant here in the town."[46] However, Emerson also wrote, "Thoreau gives me, in flesh and blood and pertinacious Saxon belief, my own ethics. He is far more real, and daily practically obeying them, than I; and fortifies my memory at all times with an affirmative experience which refuses to be set aside."[47] This is wholly admiring, but also somewhat chilling, as though one were to encounter daily a standard he could not meet. Thoreau may have had something of the same feeling about Emerson. He wrote in his journal, "If there is any one with whom we have a quarrel, it is most likely that that one makes some just demand on us which we disappoint."[48] Each spurred the other, but each was also conscious of falling short of the "just demands" of the other.

In terms of their philosophical views, we could find many similarities between Emerson and Thoreau. That this is so would never have been thought surprising. Their personal intimacy has always left them paired in intellectual history. Still, Cavell's comparison of their responses to the Kantian problematic will be surprising to any who are reluctant to think of them as philosophers. I won't attempt to summarize this comparison, which he makes in the first of his Emerson essays in his attempt to claim the name of philosopher for both Emerson and Thoreau.[49] What I would like to do here is to discuss some differences between the writings of Emerson and of Thoreau, especially between Emerson's essays and Thoreau's *Walden*. I'm not going to argue that, where they differ, one is right and one is wrong. Too often we assume that any account of difference must carry an implied judgment of superiority and inferiority. This is especially true in philosophy, perhaps because philosophers have wanted to make comprehensive, sometimes universal, claims. This is not the logic of my comparison. If we investigate the differences between Mozart's and Beethoven's music, it doesn't follow that one must eclipse the other. If we look at the difference between Jane Austen's novels and George Eliot's, that does not imply that either is unnecessary to us. Difference is what we want, among artists, among works of art, and among lives. Complementarity is possible as well as contradiction. If philosophy were a kind of literature, this would be true of it too. At any rate, my discussion of the difference between the writing of Emerson and that of Thoreau is not meant to suggest that he somehow surpassed or displaced Emerson.

I take it for granted here that Cavell's characterization of Emerson as a new kind of perfectionist is correct. (A quick rereading of, for example, "Self-Reliance" should be persuasive on this.)[50] Is this also the correct characterization of Thoreau? When he is directly formulating his beliefs, it certainly seems correct.

> I know of no more encouraging fact than the unquestionable ability of man to elevate his life in a conscious endeavor. . . . Every man is tasked to make his life, even in its details, worthy of the contemplation of his most elevated and critical hour. . . . I went to the woods because I wished to live deliberately, to front only the essential facts of life, and see if I could not learn what it had to teach, and not, when I came to die, discover that I had not lived.[51]
>
> I learned this, at least, by my experiment, that if one advances confidently in the direction of his dreams, and endeavors to live the life which he has imagined, he will meet with a success unexpected in common hours.[52]

It would not be difficult to cite more passages similar to these. However, if we reduce Thoreau to these brief excerpts, we shall have difficulty in distinguishing him from the more mawkish contemporary self-help books. (Consider, for instance, the motivational poster that contorts Thoreau's formulation by instructing business executives to "advance in the direction of [their] dreams.") We need to locate these Thoreauvian sentiments in both the philosophical background that I have sketched and also in *Walden*—that is, in what *Walden* is. Many of the general claims that are here being made can, indeed, be found in Emerson, but they are presented in a quite different setting there. Emerson was the master of the essay—in the tradition rooted in Montaigne and Bacon. Thoreau is not an essayist in the same way, despite the possible reading of

Walden as a series of essays. Emerson tells us *about*, for instance, narrative structure, in essays that are ordered not by narrative but, most often, by mood—or by what might at first appear to be an arbitrary set of headings. We need to think about Thoreau's perfectionism in *Walden* not just as presented in the quotations above but also as the structural principle of the book.

What is the "structure" of *Walden*? It is a narrative account of Thoreau's building of a dwelling at Walden Pond and inhabiting it for two years. Already this misdescribes the book, since in it Thoreau has condensed the time into one annual cycle of the seasons. Moreover, the particular cycle he has chosen begins in the summer. Perhaps this is natural enough, since he moved into his house "by accident . . . on Independence Day, or the fourth of July, 1845."[53] Nonetheless, it gives the book a particular structure to navigate the passage from summer to autumn through winter to spring—rather than, say, going from spring to winter. It means that there is a huge underlying structure of the rebirth of the earth being invoked. After an investigation of the idea of the necessities of life, there is a particular account of Thoreau's building of his house, what the materials were, where he got them, and what they cost. There follows an account of how he lived and what he lived for, and a detailed account of the plants, the animals, the pond, and so on, through the seasons. All of this is familiar enough, but we are apt to lose sight of one aspect of Thoreau's existence at Walden in our enjoyment of these scenes in the woods. As Cavell puts it, "*Walden* is itself about a book, about its own writing and reading."[54] Of course, Thoreau tells us of his daily hours of writing (and of his hours of reading), but these fade from the reader's imagination when compared to the scenes of the bean field, the pond, the countryside, the animals and the birds, the intruding industrial civilization of the railroad, and so on. The book is, however, a narrative of what its author's self-cultivation was that made it possible for him to write this book. In this way it is comparable structurally to Wordsworth's *Prelude*.

Thoreau is entirely open about this. "In most books, the *I*, or first person, is omitted; in this it will be retained. . . . We commonly do not remember that it is, after all, always the first person that is speaking."[55] He added that his first and last requirement of every writer is "a simple and sincere account of his own life." Can we doubt that he attempted that in *Walden*? Of course the book is not exactly an autobiography; it is an autobiography inexactly. It is at least in part a *Bildungsroman*.

The qualification is necessary because it is not simply an account of Thoreau's subjectivity but rather of the necessary interrelationship of self and world. Every development of a human being occurs in the context of an already given place and time and language and culture. That is our fate as human beings. But, after sufficient *Bildung* (education, enculturation) at the hands of others, we become responsible for our own self-cultivation. If we do not take this step, then our seeming fate is taken for necessity, and we lead lives of quiet desperation.

It is no secret that Thoreau literalizes the metaphor of cultivation in his account of the bean field. He is also perfectly open about this. After admitting that he didn't grow the beans in order to eat them, "but, per-chance, as some must work in fields if only for the sake of tropes and expression, to serve a parable-maker one day."[56] Almost immediately, the tropes come into play with a certain amount of irony, when he writes that his experience of cultivating the bean field led him to decide that "I will not plant beans and corn with so much industry another summer, but such seeds, if the seed is not lost, as sincerity, truth, simplicity, faith, innocence and the like." The twist comes with the result of this experi-ment: "Reader, . . . the seeds which I planted, if indeed they *were* the seeds of those virtues, were wormeaten or had lost their vitality, and so did not come up."[57] Nonetheless, *Walden* is an epic of self-cultivation but with no taste of the egotistical sublime.[58] This is Thoreau's great achievement. Emerson is a superb writer; he delineates and conveys views about human beings, religion, politics, and art in wonderful, exhortatory prose. Thoreau mostly shares those views, but he approaches them differently. The this-sidedness of the world is always there. "No ideas except in things" might be a motto for him. Thoreau in *Walden* presents a view of Thoreau in Walden. He sets before us an exemplary, individual life, in one stage of its development. (Can we doubt that he thought of the writing of it as having occurred in "elevated and critical" hours?) He is attaining the next self, which is not a final self. We should reflect further on the sense in which his life at Walden is exemplary. Thoreau is quite clear that he is not advis-ing each of his readers to go into the woods and build a dwelling.

> I would not have any one adopt my mode of living on my account,
> for, beside that before he has fairly learned it I may have found out
> another for myself, I desire that there may be as many different persons
> in the world as possible; but I would have each one be very careful to

find out and pursue *his own* way, and not his father's or his mother's or his neighbor's instead.[59]

Rather, he is showing us what it meant to him to live deliberately. Recall Thoreau's characterization of philosophy as a "way of life" that I quoted at the beginning of this essay—that being a philosopher is "so to love wisdom as to live according to its dictates, a life of simplicity, independence, magnanimity, and trust. It is to solve some of the problems of life, not only theoretically, but practically." (I cannot resist comparing that to "The question whether objective truth can be attributed to human thinking is not a question of theory but is a *practical* question. Man must prove the truth, that is, the reality and power, the this-sidedness of his thinking in practice.")[60] So Thoreau is making the claim that, in this book, he has portrayed a very serious attempt to live philosophically. It is the courage to advance in the direction of his dream that is exemplary, but each of us should have her or his own dream.

Let me return to the issue of Thoreau as a philosopher. Thoreau was an intellectual—a serious student of philosophy and religion. In *Walden*, he presents his reading as a crucial part of his experience. Thoreau read deeply in philosophical texts, and this reading was a central part of the self-cultivation of Henry Thoreau that produced the author of *Walden*. Even if one adopts the view of philosophy as a way of life, that way of life will necessarily be deliberate and reflective. The thinking about his life in the woods is central to his life in the woods, but it tends to be hidden from us in the beauty of his description of his activities. Thoreau, like a number of other philosophers of the nineteenth century, could not accept a philosophical view that seemed to entail a denial of the conditions of human finitude. Thoreau does not begin from the Cartesian self—the self in isolation from the world for whom the existence of the world is problematic. The real problem, masked by the Cartesian formulation, is whether *I* will exist fully. I see *Walden* as his attempt to redo the foundationalist project that Descartes undertook in the *Meditations*, only this time with the right foundation.[61] The "I" from which he begins is a human being on the earth whose human condition requires food, shelter, and clothing.[62] We are always already in this position, but we can only become conscious of it as we gradually form our identities. This identity formation is not completed once and for all while we live. Returning to Cavell's characterization of Emersonian perfectionism as a dimension of moral life, we might call it an aesthetic dimension. Recall that "every man is tasked to make his life, even in details, worthy of the contemplation of his most elevated and critical hour." This would not be an aestheticism that repudiates genuine morality, but it would mean that the judgment of what is "genuine" morality is ultimately the individual's (and of course someone can make a wrong judgment). The source of the moral law is one's own will. Thoreau wrote the following to a young admirer: "Do what you love. Know your own bone; gnaw at it, bury it, unearth it, and gnaw it still. Do not be too moral. You may cheat yourself of much life so. Aim above morality. Be not *simply* good—be good for something."[63] Given Thoreau's character, this is not an injunction to immorality but rather a reminder that what most people think is "morality" is not the sole determinant of the value of one's life.

It is not surprising that Thoreau's experiment at Walden Pond concluded with him leaving behind his house. "I left the woods for as good a reason as I went there. Perhaps it seemed to me that I had several more lives to live, and could not spare any more time for that one."[64] The seeming paradox of Emersonian perfectionism is that, as long as we live, we cannot stop the perfectionist quest. We don't want a final stasis; that would be the equivalent of death in life. Hence, Thoreau's conclusion is necessarily a beginning, "Only that day dawns to which we are awake. There is more day to dawn. The sun is but a morning star."[65]

THREE

THOREAU AND THE BODY

Russell B. Goodman

The field of our experience can . . . endure only so long as we, by responsive action, can make it habitable: habitable, as our habitation or dwelling place, where we live. . . . It is only through being active that we first have a single world of experience in which particular experiences can occur.

—Samuel Todes, *Body and World*

1

For some time now I have been interested in philosophers in whose writing the body plays a major role. I note, for example, that in the essays of Michel de Montaigne there is a strong sense of the earth and our animal nature. He talks of his kidney stones, of horseback riding, of the way he bites his tongue when he eats greedily. So it was with a certain sensitivity to the body that I returned to *Walden* recently, hoping that something new and worth writing about for this volume would come to my attention. Rather than begin at the beginning of the book, I started in the middle, with the chapter on "Solitude." Here is how that chapter begins:

> This is a delicious evening, when the whole body is one sense, and imbibes delight through every pore. I go and come with a strange liberty in Nature, a part of herself. As I walk along the stony shore of the pond in my shirt-sleeves, though it is cool as well as cloudy and windy, and I see nothing special to attract me, all the elements are unusually congenial to me. The bullfrogs trump to usher in the night, and the

note of the whip-poor-will is borne on the rippling wind from over the water. Sympathy with the fluttering alder and poplar leaves almost takes away my breath; yet, like the lake, my serenity is rippled but not ruffled. These small waves raised by the evening wind are as remote from storm as the smooth reflecting surface. Though it is now dark, the wind still blows and roars in the wood, the waves still dash, and some creatures lull the rest with their notes. The repose is never complete. The wildest animals do not repose, but seek their prey now; the fox, and skunk, and rabbit, now roam the fields and woods without fear. They are Nature's watchmen—links which connect the days of animated life.[1]

This is a vision of unity, of correspondences between the human and the rest of nature—animal, vegetable, wind, and water. With its emphasis on life, pleasure, and sympathy, it is a romantic passage, which bears some relation to Samuel Taylor Coleridge's poem "The Aeolian Harp."

> And what if all of animated nature
> Be but organic Harps diversly fram'd,
> That tremble into thought, as o'er them sweeps
> Plastic and vast, one intellectual breeze,
> At once the Soul of each, and God of all?[2]

The differences as well as the similarities are instructive, for whereas Coleridge speaks of an intellectual breeze, Thoreau's breeze is of air, and although Thoreau is a religious writer and like Coleridge in this poem something of a pantheist, he does not mention God or a world soul at all in his vision of himself as a part of nature. Most notable for our purposes, however, is that Coleridge's poem is entirely general or even abstract, whereas Thoreau's passage is concrete and particular, and not just concrete but bodily.

In the first place and most obviously, Thoreau employs the word "body" in his first sentence. It is a body that, unlike Montaigne's, imbibes delight (a Wordsworthian word) "through every pore." This is romanticism, after all. Notice that the word "delicious" immediately modifies "evening," already a metaphor then because we cannot literally taste the evening as we might an apple, but adding the ideal of sensory delight through every pore, as the entire body incorporates and registers or tastes the wider world of nature.

The second sentence of the paragraph does not mention the body, though the body is implied by the going and coming it reports. The phrase "strange liberty" marks this as a special, not normal, occasion. What is the nature of this "liberty" and how is it strange?

Passing to the third sentence, we have first of all the phrase "I walk." It's first person, and it requires a body. Now consider the thought that "I walk" occupies the same position in Thoreau's registration of his existence that "I think" does in Descartes's *Meditations*, or, to give the claim a Kantian reading, that it occupies the same position in the constitution of the world that the transcendental unity of apperception plays in Kant's *Critique of Pure Reason*. Thoreau, one might say, constitutes himself, organizes his experience, in his walk. This is a thought to which I return when I take up Samuel Todes's book *Body and World*.[3]

Let's go back to the third sentence. The body is implied not only by Thoreau's verb "walk," but by the verb "see," by the noun "shirt-sleeves"—for only human bodies wear shirts—and by the adjectives "cool," "cloudy," and "windy"—for he doesn't know of these features of nature on this evening from any weather report but from his own experience. That he is in shirt-sleeves on a summer evening allows him to feel the cool, windy weather with his upper body. Notice also the phrase "I see nothing special to attract me." He is paying attention to things, but he is not grasping them, manipulating them, trying to figure them out. He is tasting them, as he suggests, in a kind of walking meditation that allows him to register his own finely tuned responses—like Coleridge's Aeolian harp—to the breezes, sounds, and sights of nature. Is he enacting the free play of the imagination specified in of Kant's analysis of aesthetic judgment?

In the fourth sentence, Thoreau writes of the bullfrogs and whippoorwills, and in the fifth of his own "sympathy" with nature in a manner that again brings his body explicitly into the picture, for he states that "sympathy with the fluttering alder and poplar leaves almost takes away my breath"—there is no need to see this as a mere metaphor rather than a report of his bodily response to the nature of which he is a part. Thereafter, the paragraph moves away from the scene of liberty in nature to reflections on nature, the animal world, and the human place in nature's daily rounds. Thoreau does not begin with reflection or thought, but with movement, with his walk. The concrete evening is the occasion for his thinking, perhaps even, its ground. The paragraph as a whole is the record of a successful search for bearings.

2

In one of those happy coincidences that dot the scholarly life, I was reading last term a work of phenomenological philosophy originally written as a 1963 dissertation at Harvard, Samuel Todes's *Body and World*. Todes, who taught at Northwestern before his death in 1994, published his dissertation with Garland Press in 1990 under the revealing title *The Human Body as Material Subject of the World*. It was reissued in 2001 by MIT as *Body and World*, with introductions by Hubert Dreyfus and Piotr Hoffman.

As in the epigraph to this essay, Todes writes explicitly in the Kantian and phenomenological tradition of Husserl, Heidegger, and Merleau-Ponty, and his book contains both a series of criticisms of pre-Kantian philosophers such as Descartes, Leibniz, and Hume, and a Kant-inspired deduction of the central importance of the body in constituting the world that we experience. In Kant's *Critique of Pure Reason*, unity or unification is a central concern: For example, the categories synthesize the manifold of intuition, and behind them lies the mysterious "transcendental unity of apperception = x," which is both at the root of the unified self and world that we find in our experience, and unavailable for knowledge.

This sketch is enough to introduce the basic move Todes makes. Although agreeing with Kant that experience requires or presupposes a unifying function, he finds that function not in an activity of mind but of the body, and moreover not as something postulated behind the scenes but as something that we know in concrete detail through our own absorbed coping with the world. In the passage from *Walden* with which I began, and in others to which I shall soon turn, it seems to me that Thoreau enacts and recovers the unifications, settlings, and orientations that, according to Todes, are necessary features of human experience. As Dreyfus puts it in his introduction to *Body and World*, Todes shows how "we make ourselves at home in the world by moving so as to organize a stable spatiotemporal field in which we use our skills to make determi-n*ate* the determin*able* objects that appear in that field" (xvi–xvii). Making himself at home in the world through determining the specific character of this cool breeze, these bullfrogs, this evening light is just what Thoreau does in his evening walk on the shores of Walden Pond.

Consider some of Todes's main points in more detail, beginning with his claim that Hume and Leibniz eliminate the active body from experience. Regarding Hume, he states:

> Our familiar situation is that of being in some sense identified with our active subject-body in the midst of circumstances whose givenness implies that our body is also an object. . . . Hume's view, on the other hand, distorts the familiar situation by, in effect, shrinking our active body down to the vanishing point of our visual point of view as a pure spectator with an inactive body. The familiar relation of "having an active body" is eliminated from experience. We are conceived to "have" our body much as we in fact "have" our experience. (T, 6)

For Hume the body attenuates to a mere idea.

Todes argues that Leibniz objectifies the body as a foreign object that we seek to control. We do sometimes take such an objective attitude toward our body, as when one's foot is wedged under the airline seat in front of one, and one seeks to extract it by pulling on it sideways. This, however, is a special case as, where we operate, as Todes puts it, "by will but not by desire." Our normal relation to our body is quite different: "What Leibniz 'forgets' from the point of view of ordinary experience, is that *to live as an animal is to live not in one's body but in one's nonbodily circumstances*, which one has to make habitable as best one can. These circumstances in which we live as animals are given to begin with as precisely *not* fully governed by us, in the way our bodies *are*. That is why our embodiment is our *danger* as well as our opportunity" (T, 38).

I have been quoting from the second chapter of *Body and World*, titled "Critique of the World-Subject of Leibniz and Hume," and I want now to examine a crucial concept that Todes introduces late in the chapter in a section titled "The actual a priori of poised response." Poised response is a priori, Todes argues, in the sense that it is necessary for there to be a world at all. He states that "without poise no determinate perception is possible" (T, 79). What then is poise? It is the command and directed movement of our bodies in the world, by our desire and not, as in the case of the foot stuck under the seat, by will. Here is Todes on poise:

> Poise is always a way of responding to, of dealing with, objects around one. . . . Poise does not, when successful, "coincide" or "agree" with its

later "effects," as does will with its achievements. Rather, when successful, poise *is* its own effect. The success of poise it not in its execution, but in its very existence by which the body is, to begin with,
knowingly in touch with the objects around it. . . .To be poised is to be
self-possessed by being in touch with one's *circumstances*. (T, 65–66)

Todes mentions catching a baseball as an example of poise (T, 63–64),
and Dreyfus talks about dribbling a basketball. In each case, the agreement is not with later effects but rather with *present* effects; or rather, the
catching or the dribbling *are their own effects*, to adapt Todes's expression. They are not something following upon some act of balance or
achievement but the very act itself. In Todes's Kantian terms, the body
contributes not forms for the possibility of objects but "forms of actuality
satisfied by the kind of object that distinctively presents itself as actually
existing" (T, 265). Thoreau's walk is such a form of actuality, a poised
achievement of objects—the frogs, the leaves, the wind—that present
themselves to his delighted sensibilities. He is knowingly in touch with
the stones on which he walks, the cool wind that blows across his shirt-
sleeves, the sounds of the pond's life.

Poise—what Dreyfus calls "absorbed coping"—allows us to form both
the world and the self.[4] As Todes puts it, we "*make our self by discovering
our world*" (T, 124), a discovery that is accomplished through our poised
responses. In this sense, as Todes puts it in the sixth chapter of his book,
"the human body is the material subject of the world." The a priori character of the human body is brought out in Todes's claim that "we can
have an object in perception only by becoming circumstantially self-
aware. And we become circumstantially self-aware by becoming aware of
the existence of our active body in the center of our perceptual field of
objects." The unification achieved by our active body, Todes continues, is
synthetic, "a unity of separable parts in replaceable objects in different
locations, all comprehended in the same world" (T, 206).

In his walk around the lake Thoreau becomes "circumstantially self-
aware," that is, aware of his particular circumstances. He depicts himself
not from a god's-eye view and not from a merely particular point of view,
but from an embodied point of view. Many great scenes in *Walden* depict
his goings from place to place, his work at discerning the "determinate
character" of each thing, while also experiencing "the felt unity of body-
activity" (T, 206).

Todes's claim that we know ourselves by our poised responses to the world runs counter to the rationalist tradition that one finds in Plato and Descartes. Plato's Socrates argues in the *Phaedo* that it is precisely by freeing oneself from the body that one knows who one is, and Descartes conducts his meditations in his study away from nature, seeking a completely intellectual knowledge of a self that turns out to consist only in thinking and not at all in extension. For Todes, in contrast, "the body progressively fleshes itself out, determining not merely things but also itself as a being together with them in a common world" (T, 265).

3

Let us now return to *Walden* with these remarks from *Body and Mind* in hand, if not entirely under our control, and consider the chapter titled "The Village." The opening of the chapter is as follows:

> After hoeing, or perhaps reading and writing, in the forenoon, I usually bathed again in the pond, swimming across one of its coves for a stint, and washed the dust of labor from my person, or smoothed out the last wrinkle which study had made, and for the afternoon was absolutely free. Every day or two I strolled to the village to hear some of the gossip which is incessantly going on there, circulating either from mouth to mouth, or from newspaper to newspaper, and which, taken in homoeopathic doses, was really as refreshing in its way as the rustle of leaves and the peeping of frogs. As I walked in the woods to see the birds and squirrels, so I walked in the village to see the men and boys; instead of the wind among the pines I heard the carts rattle. In one direction from my house there was a colony of muskrats in the river meadows; under the grove of elms and buttonwoods in the other horizon was a village of busy men, as curious to me as if they had been prairie-dogs, each sitting at the mouth of its burrow, or running over to a neighbor's to gossip. I went there frequently to observe their habits. (*W*, 167)

Let us first of all recount the verbs in this passage that indicate bodily activity: hoeing, reading (with the eyes), writing, bathing, swimming, washing, strolling, hearing, walking. Thoreau's body is also directly mentioned by the phrase "my person," indicating that from which the dust of labor is washed in the pond. This is a record of days spent doing things and, one might say, reorienting oneself through these doings: through the labor of hoeing or of writing, the bracing pleasure of a bath in the pond and then, when "absolutely free," the stroll into town to hear the gossip of the day, which, if we are not constantly occupied with it, turns out to be "as refreshing in its way as the rustle of leaves and the peeping of frogs." The word "stroll" indicates the relaxed and receptive manner in which Thoreau walks, and it chimes both with the walk around the pond described in "Solitude" and the later essay "Walking," which opens with a discussion of what he calls "sauntering." Once again Thoreau depicts himself as a practically engaged person—with the beans, his paper and pencil, his swim, his walk, his observations of prairie dogs and village inhabitants.

Walking back home from the village is the subject of Thoreau's second paragraph.

> It was very pleasant, when I stayed late in town, to launch myself into the night, especially if it was dark and tempestuous, and set sail from some bright village parlor or lecture room, with a bag of rye or Indian meal upon my shoulder, for my snug harbor in the woods, having made all tight without and withdrawn under hatches with a merry crew of thoughts, leaving only my outer man at the helm, or even tying up the helm when it was plain sailing. I had many a genial thought by the cabin fire "as I sailed." I was never cast away nor distressed in any weather, though I encountered some severe storms. It is darker in the woods, even in common nights, than most suppose. I frequently had to look up at the opening between the trees above the path in order to learn my route, and, where there was no cart-path, to feel with my feet the faint track which I had worn, or steer by the known relation of particular trees which I felt with my hands, passing between two pines for instance, not more than eighteen inches apart, in the midst of the woods, invariably, in the darkest night. Sometimes, after coming home thus late in a dark and muggy night, when my feet felt the path which my eyes could not see, dreaming and absent-minded all the way, until I was aroused by having to raise my hand to lift the latch, I have not been able to recall a single step of my walk, and I have thought that perhaps my body would find its way home if its master should forsake it, as the hand finds its way to the mouth without assistance. (*W*, 169–70)

Thoreau feels the trees like someone catching a baseball; he's been through this routine before. Those who haven't, like some evening visitors to his cabin, may spend the greater part of the night trying to find their home in the dark even when it is "close by." Thoreau presents a compilation of evenings here and not just one, as in his solitary walk around the lake, but the body is equally present. Terms indicating his body include "shoulder," "hand," "feet," "mouth," "walk," and "body." Thoreau speaks of feeling the path with his feet or hands, looking up through the trees, of waking up from his dreamlike genial thoughts by having to raise his hand to lift the latch of his cabin. In this passage his body, his "outer man," provides the foundation in action and absorbed coping for him to do other things. He can tie up the helm of his ship as he puts it in his maritime metaphor, letting the body take care of his direction and settling himself "under hatches with a merry crew of thoughts." The body is not everything, but it is essential for everything we do and are.

4

Even a brief survey of Thoreau on the body cannot neglect his late great essay "Walking," published in the *Atlantic Monthly* in 1862.[5] Reading it alongside the two passages from *Walden* we have examined, one is struck by the coincidence of themes of leisure and freedom. Walking in the sense in which Thoreau recommends it is "a noble art," and no "wealth can buy the requisite leisure, freedom, and independence which are the capital in this profession" (Wa, 598). As in the walk around the pond and the walk home from the village, Thoreau values a kind of losing of himself or reverie (and this marks an affinity with Rousseau's *Reveries of the Solitary Walker*). "Some of my townspeople," he writes with derision, "can remember and have described to me some walks which they took ten years ago, in which they were so blessed as to lose themselves for half an hour in the woods; but I know very well that they have confined themselves to the highway ever since, whatever pretensions they may make to belong to this select class" (Wa, 598–99). This losing of oneself is at the same time a return to the body and to the senses: "In my afternoon walk I would fain forget all my morning occupations and my obligations to society. But it sometimes happens that I cannot easily shake off the village. The thought of some work will run in my head and I am not where my body is,—I am out of my senses. In my walks I would fain return to my senses" (Wa, 602). This is a return, however, that allows for the merry thoughts that Thoreau has when he battens down his hatches on returning from the village, an idea he signals in "Walking" with his notion that "you must walk like a camel, which is said to be the only beast which ruminates when walking" (Wa, 601).

Thoreau is of course not just a philosopher of the body, as the essay "Walking," no less than *Walden*, makes clear. Near the end of "Walking," for example, he writes:

> My desire for knowledge is intermittent, but my desire to bathe my head in atmospheres unknown to my feet is perennial and constant. The highest that we can attain to is not Knowledge, but Sympathy with Intelligence. I do not know that this higher knowledge amounts to anything more definite than a novel and grand surprise on a sudden revelation of the insufficiency of all that we called Knowledge before— a discovery that there are more things in heaven and earth than are dreamed of in our philosophy. It is the lighting up of the mist by the sun. Man cannot KNOW in any higher sense than this, any more than he can look serenely and with impunity in the face of the sun: "You will not perceive that, as perceiving a particular thing," say the Chaldean Oracles. (Wa, 626)

Although he does not envision a complete break with the mist and sun of the world, this is clearly a discussion of something not "particular," something not only yet unknown but undreamt of, and something not so much knowledge as sympathy with a higher intelligence. Here we find Thoreau's Neoplatonic and Hindu streak, as indicated by his citation of the Vishnu Purana a paragraph later. Indeed it is striking how much of "Walking" concerns these themes rather than specific walks in specific natural settings.

5

In concluding this essay, I want to return to the body in Thoreau's work in a way that rehearses and takes us outward from some of the themes I have raised so far: of poised action as a way of orienting us to the world, of bringing order or unification to our experience, and of living or dwelling the world. I want to consider a well-known passage in which Thoreau is not walking but sitting. (I say parenthetically that Todes has a discussion of sitting and its relation to moving about that I cannot consider here.) This passage is in *Walden*'s second chapter, "Where I Lived and What I Lived For," and it is as much about imagination as about perception, but with the measure of the body at the center of its outlook on the world.

> At a certain season of our life we are accustomed to consider every spot as the possible site of a house. I have thus surveyed the country on every side within a dozen miles of where I live. In imagination I have bought all the farms in succession, for all were to be bought, and I knew their price. I walked over each farmer's premises, tasted his wild apples, discoursed on husbandry with him, took his farm at his price, at any price, mortgaging it to him in my mind; even put a higher price on it—took everything but a deed of it—took his word for his deed, for I dearly love to talk—cultivated it, and him too to some extent, I trust, and withdrew when I had enjoyed it long enough, leaving him to carry it on. This experience entitled me to be regarded as a sort of real-estate broker by my friends. Wherever I sat, there I might live, and the landscape radiated from me accordingly. What is a house but a *sedes*, a seat?—better if a country seat. I discovered many a site for a house not likely to be soon improved, which some might have thought too far from the village, but to my eyes the village was too far from it. Well, there I might live, I said; and there I did live, for an hour, a summer and a winter life; saw how I could let the years run off, buffet the winter through, and see the spring come in. The future inhabitants of this region, wherever they may place their houses, may be sure that they have been anticipated. An afternoon sufficed to lay out the land into orchard, wood-lot, and pasture, and to decide what fine oaks or pines should be left to stand before the door, and whence each blasted tree could be seen to the best advantage; and then I let it lie, fallow, perchance, for a man is rich in proportion to the number of things which he can afford to let alone. (*W*, 81–82)

This passage speaks of walking and alludes to Thoreau's sometime profession as a surveyor. Thoreau talks about tasting apples, talking to farmers, and, most unusually, about sitting, a bodily posture that, according to Thoreau's analysis, is essential for understanding what a house is. For what else is a house, he asks rhetorically, but a seat, better if a country seat, a seat in the country such as he has found in the course of his survey of his neighbors' farms. "Wherever I sat," Thoreau states, "there I might live, and the landscape radiated from me accordingly." Thoreau, in sitting, is the unifying center of his world. He lives both sensuously—as the landscape radiates from his sitting body in each place—and imaginatively—as he plots out the farms and the crops in the landscape that his eyes take in. And he introduces a new element with his sitting and his imagining and his surveying: the element of not doing, of what the Taoists call inaction or actionless activity: *wu wei*. One is rich, Thoreau ends the passage by stating, in the number of things one can afford to let alone. This receptive, abandoning element in his thought, lines him up with Emerson's "Experience," where Emerson warns against "too much hankering for practical effects" and urges us to practice patience in the realization of our romance with the world. Both writers may seem at times prototypes of pragmatism, but in this nonaction mode their argument runs counter to a simple pragmatism that values actions and lives only by their results. Thoreau, a philosopher of the body, asks us to let our possessions go, or to retain them by not grasping them, to let things "lie, fallow." Sitting is the posture of this release. It is potential motion, as Thoreau practices it, relying on prior experience with walking and laying things out, but it is also at the same time an image and a practice of forbearing, of nonaccomplishing awareness. Let us then leave Thoreau radiating outward, rich with what he imagines, remembers, and has not yet done.

FOUR

SPEAKING EXTRAVAGANTLY

Philosophical Territory and Eccentricity in Walden

James D. Reid

Am I being extravagant? I am speaking of a *too much*.

—Rainer Maria Rilke, "The Young Workman's Letter,"
in *Where Silence Reigns*

That so few now dare to be eccentric, marks the chief danger of the time.

—John Stuart Mill, "On Liberty"

I n a well-known polemical passage in *Walden*'s opening chapter, Thoreau complains that, in our era of specialized labor, the economic world justified in 1776 by Adam Smith in *The Wealth of Nations* and parodied in "Economy," there are more than enough professors of philosophy, but no true philosophers. And in an obvious challenge to prevailing priorities, and drawing from ancient conceptions of philosophy as a way of life,[1] he adds that "it is admirable to profess because it was once admirable to live."[2] In these lean days of wisdom, where everything weighty seems in danger of being reduced to a matter of taste and arbitrary opinion, and our more serious hours are devoted to "metaphysical" and "epistemological" problems having little to do with the overall quality of our lives and the importance of what we care about, our professors of philosophy practice and profess anything but "the art of life."[3] We have, at best, an abstract philosophy of value, with examples drawn from tennis and playing chess, or a moral philosophy that gets no further than the importance of feeding the hungry and why the selfish should care about the less fortunate; we don't ask what the well-fed should do with their freedom from want; and we don't give a rich and compelling account of an admirable way of being in the world.[4] The true economy of living, which is in Thoreau's view synonymous with philosophy at its best, is a sadly neglected discipline. We search in vain in recent philosophical tomes for insight into the essential facts of life and how to cope with our apparently difficult and despairing condition. Our philosophical problems have become matters of mere theory divorced from the urgency of a searching life, uncertain of what is still possible and available for those who wish to live more fully.

But as Camus has suggested, whether the mind comes equipped with twelve categories or merely ten or how many dimensions there are in space makes no mark on someone who wonders whether life is worth living and his pursuits worth dying for or not.[5] There'd be, perhaps, no need for existential teaching if we stood already upright and cheerfully or pessimistically resolved; but most are, Thoreau insists, curiously uncertain whether their life "is of the devil or of God."[6] If your way is darkening, you'll reach for anything but our meager academic fare. Viewed from the vantage point of a human concern as urgent as this, our ruling academic philosophy is drowned out by the echo of a puffball.

Thoreau clearly sees himself as someone in search of wisdom, a lover of *sophia* who wants to rethink what it is to be wise and, what amounts to the same thing, to live well. His principal complaint against newly established philosophical practice is that it fails to live up to philosophy's original promise to teach a better way of life and to word the world of human experience and experiment accordingly.[7] Philosophy in the highest and largest and most vital sense is, Thoreau appears to be saying, in danger of falling into triviality and darkening our way, just when we feel ourselves already groping in the dark; it is falling and has already fallen into the hands of impostors, "those who," in Plato's words, "imitate [its] nature," mostly out of pretension and vanity rather than vision.[8] *Walden* intends no dogmatic rejection of philosophy, but to recast and to rethink, with the help of neglected paradigms, what philosophy can be and what sorts of questions the philosopher is called upon to address.

When I Wrote the Following Pages . . .

I celebrate myself, and sing myself,
And what I shall assume you shall assume,
For every atom belonging to me as good as belongs to you.[9]

Philosophy commonly begins when the philosopher takes leave of her self. *De nobis ipsis silemus.* "Of ourselves we'll keep silent."[10] We may be personally amused or distressed to read of Alcibiades' infatuation and its painful history in Plato's *Symposium*, but his love of Socrates leaves the strict philosophical expositor and hard schoolmaster cold. He wants in our assumed name a fruit we all can taste and enjoy without the personal bite, the theory rather than the "lived experience" that seems to come first in the order of time. He's anxious to hear what Plato thinks about what love itself *is* without much reference to the lover and his beloved, as though one could express the *sense* of love without fathoming its personal depths and experiencing its peculiar shifts and shafts and mysteries. The protagonist in those texts we've come to think of as philosophical is curiously abstract: human reason, having a peculiar fate, or *Geist* as it comes gradually to self-awareness over historical time, or the timeless structure of our discourse, or the community of the enlightened, the ideal spectator or the disinterested inquirer, or, more recently, the neurological basis of human experience. And the antagonist is equally abstract: irrationality, skepticism, a conception of mind or matter, the emotions, unenlightened folk psychology.

Of course we can safely take it for granted that the speaker has come to find certain problems interesting, that a personal narrative could be written that includes reference to this particular philosophizing individual; but none of this is *philosophically* relevant, and the literary work of telling *that* tale is nothing philosophical. The author of *Walden* clearly thinks differently about what the philosopher ought to bring to light (about himself and his experiments) and in whose name philosophy is called upon to speak. "We commonly do not remember that it is, after all, always only the first person that is speaking."[11] This is, I think, the first serious challenge the defender of Thoreau's philosophical significance must take up. (And it is, I think, tied to the difficulties surrounding our author's style.)

We've already encountered several ways of accounting for the widespread sense that Thoreau is moving on territory that isn't yet philosophical; but it strikes me that another plausible way of dismissing *Walden* is to say that the story of your becoming interested in philosophy is not itself philosophically interesting or important. Why you came to think that there is a problem of other minds, say, is one thing, and it belongs to your personal intellectual odyssey that this issue came to matter; what you have to contribute to the debate, what your impersonal arguments are in favor of one view rather than another, is quite another matter, and this, and this alone, is what will matter to your peers. We all probably grant that, as teachers of philosophy at least, it is necessary to arouse a desire to participate in the conversation; but once we've got someone going philosophically, we've got the prephilosophical preliminaries out of the way and are now free to get to down to more serious business. How to get someone interested is an important matter of psychology or pedagogy, and it may prove helpful to start with the "existential situation" of the student, just as Plato's dialogues begin with someone about to prosecute his father for murder or someone trying to win the affection of his beloved. Philosophy itself, however, gets under way on the other side of the "framing narrative," when scrutiny of abstract definitions of *hosion* or *philia* begins.[12]

It is one of the more suggestive implications of Thoreau's way of going about things that this way of splitting things up (and of splitting ourselves up) is itself anchored in questionable *philosophical* assumptions, and that it is philosophically worthwhile to speak in ways that renew your own interest in what you're about. *Walden*'s task, on one reading of the work, is to point out how difficult but important it is, after all, to take an interest in your life, and how valuable are accounts of what moved you and kept you engaged. The human being is not only a reasoning animal but, in Harry Frankfurt's fine phrase, a creature for whom things matter,[13] and the only animal as far as we can tell susceptible to discouragement, apathy, and despair. If what drove you into the woods for a season of solitary philosophical reflection is dissatisfaction with your neighbor's way of doing things and disappointment with the life you've been living among your associates in Concord, it is *philosophically* worthwhile to clarify your unrest. If certain experiences helped you overcome resentment, and you think sincerely that this overcoming is a worthy philosophical task, your "argument" will involve and portray, in some shape, just those refreshing experiences, recollected, perhaps, in philosophical tranquility. And the *concepts* you go on to fashion and the categories you find yourself prepared to defend should embody something you've sighted in those very experiences or their fundamental conditions. Our concepts ought to give voice to things that move us; our concepts should be *gripping*.[14]

In this sense, then, Thoreau seems to stand squarely in the history of attempts to preserve and defend the first-person point of view against the

impersonalizing trends of modern industrial capitalism and those philosophical schools that leave the thinking, feeling, and perceiving subject
behind in the name of an abstract theory divorced from life.[15] And yet,
Walden gives, surprisingly, precious little insight into the personal life of
its author and is often enough happy to offer impersonal generalizations.
In the well-known passage we've had in mind all along, Thoreau does *not*
say "I've been so miserable lately; my brother died some years back, in
1842, and I've had a hard time of things." He tells us instead that the mass
of men lead lives of quiet desperation. Although he requires of every
writer "a simple and sincere account of his own life, and not merely what
he has heard of other men's lives,"[16] Thoreau launches immediately into
an extended account of the outward condition and circumstances of
those "who are said to live in New England."[17] His experiment in the
words, however personal, is supposed to help clarify the *essential* facts of
life and its gross necessaries, to give insight into what life itself is, whether
mean or not, and to make possible a knowing publication of the findings.
We search *Walden* in vain for information about the details of Henry's
daily life; how many times he woke up during the night, what he nightly
dreamed, whether he wiped himself with leaves or cleaned himself in the
pond and how often—these are matters about which the author chooses
to keep silent, or if they enter the picture, they are transfigured, crystallized, and condensed ("I enhanced the value of the land by squatting on
it," he says).[18] His visitors remain unnamed in favor of Types, animals
become Brute Neighbors; even Thoreau's interactions with Emerson are
reduced to a short, unrevealing reference. We can guess what books he
might have read, but only a few authors and titles are dignified with a
name. It seems that the writer's own path is meant to open onto a common
path after all, and the author's word to tell us something we are in danger
of overlooking about a world we take for granted more often than we
should and "level downward to our dullest perception."[19]

Wording a World: The Makings of a Poet

Art and nothing but art! It is the great means of making life possible,
the great seduction to life, the great stimulant to life.[20]
    I want to speak of the purity and dignity of an apple, the explosive
joy and sexuality of a strawberry. (I would have found this ridicu-
lously overblown once.)[21]

It is commonly assumed that the world is *what there is*, a vast tissue or body of fact, and that we *know* already, if roughly, what sorts of fact we can expect to discover within it, and that the poet's labor only adds to the world another, perhaps more interesting and obscure fact, the poetic statement.[22] And we take it for granted, too, that, unless asleep or insane, we know where we are in the world. Growing up means knowing your place, the place of your calling—in the hospital, or at a court of law, in the bank or office, or working and resting at home. If your calling is a poet's, your home is language, perhaps; but taking up residence in words leaves the world well enough alone. The world greets us ready-made.[23] Or so it seems. And its seeming thus is partly what the author must undo.

An essential aspect of *Walden*'s teaching, then, is meant to be unsettling, precisely because its author intends to rethink what it means to find "hard bottom" and to make some progress toward settling in the world.[24] "At last, we know not what it is to live in the open air, and our lives are domestic in more senses than we think."[25] The philosophizing poet must draw our attention to the world's having been ready-*made* for us, not by some divine being who in some remote era brought the world into existence out of nothing, although this may in some sense be an important truth for some, or gave shape to matter lying already at hand, but by what calls itself, celebrating itself, common sense. There is a world for us and a plain sense of things because our world has already been worded, if only commonly, or expressed in "heroic books" we've learned to read shallowly and meanly, if we still read them at all.[26]

This helps explain the reader's uncomfortable sense of Thoreau's ingratitude, especially in the more unforgiving and apparently uncharitable parts of "Economy," where the task of beginning something new seems to involve a constant struggle against "inherited encumbrances," as though we should wipe the slate clean and see things more clearly, without ancestral help, as if Thoreau himself could have experimented without the aid of Emersonian territory and precedents. "Old deeds for old people, and new deeds for new."[27] "Practically, the old have no very important advice to give the young, their own experience has been so partial, and their lives have been such miserable failures."[28]

But we also hear it said, in "Economy" itself, that it is difficult to begin anything without borrowing.[29] And it is hard for the knowing reader to ignore the obvious fact that *Walden*, and Emerson's lectures and essays, for that matter, owe much to the traditions of idealism and romanticism in Europe that the transcendentalists took up in their own homespun ways, even when the chosen topic is self-reliance and the promise of independence on American soil. Each of us inherits a language, a loose set of (philosophical) concerns, and an affiliated cluster of intellectual, moral, and social tasks, however far back or near in time we decide to trace our concerns. The point is to return the borrowed axe, call it *tradition*, if you like, to its first owner, the community of those with whom we share an inherited world worth questioning, sharper than we received it.[30]

For this it isn't necessary to coin new terms or visit unfamiliar, exotic places and see strange new sights. Going elsewhere, from the desperate city to the desperate country, say, is no guarantee that we will see anything differently.[31] We dissatisfied travelers hungry with a savage taste for novelty are more likely to discover what we complacently thought we already knew or place the freshest find in a musty mold or merely be excited by the novel vista without lasting consequence. The task is rather to assign new weight and value to our currency and, laboring in the very places we already inhabit and make our daily exchanges, to put, if we can, "a new aspect on the face of [those] things" we already own without having made them ours.[32] To be an essential poet and to write a newer testament, then, is to *re*make the world we have in common beyond the senses commonly received, or to delineate deliberately a *higher* and larger sense than we commonly conjecture in our dullest readings of a world that seems with time and experience to deliver less than it originally promised in our greener years.[33] And this the revolutionary poet cannot do without taking his "mother tongue" seriously, by refining and expanding his linguistic inheritance. But this is just a sketch of what's at stake in *Walden*'s way of wording the world; and what is meant more precisely and fully by the work's experimental primitivism "in the midst of an outward civilization" is what we must now consider.[34]

The poetic statement or testament brings nothing new into the world (i.e., no new thing) beyond an arrangement of words. In this respect the author of Ecclesiastes and the ancient Stoics were right: At a certain stage of our maturity, there *is* nothing new to be seen under the sun, nothing the world of things has to offer that hasn't already been tried and tasted and found pleasing or not. However shocking it certainly is when it happens so unexpectedly and violently, an attack of terrorists on American soil merely confirms that buildings, however robust and taken for granted as permanent features of our landscape and symbolic though they may be, can fall, that hatred is a powerful motive still, and that world peace remains a distant goal. A poem or an unusual description of an event or place or thing, however obscure or strange, records something familiar to its writer and its audience. *King Lear* speaks of filial piety and ingratitude, *Othello* of jealousy, *Hamlet* of uncertainty, *Romeo and Juliet* of true love's wayward course; we are able to hear what the playwright has to say because we know something about what he's chosen to probe and to voice. A pilgrimage to Walden Pond under the poet's influence reveals a body of water surrounded by trees, at least for now, and the plot of land where Thoreau built his cabin and chose to live for two years and two months. You are not better placed to understand and interpret *Walden* because you've seen Walden or even lived there for a season. Its scenery, in fact, "is on a humble scale" and unlikely to impress.[35] In *Walden* we hear of beans, brute neighbors, and human visitors, of farms and farming, the pond in winter, and the return of spring, among other common things.

In a sense the world *is* what it is; and only the misguided child in the adult longs for there to be something else, some new toy for fresh sport or some altogether novel task to undertake. Our first education is a matter of getting acquainted and learning to cope with things new *to us*; our education in adulthood is learning to place the old familiar and worn-out things in rejuvenating light. It is the voice of despair and misunderstanding that asks for another world than this. "One world at a time," Thoreau is supposed in extremity to have said.[36] The true life might be absent and the choice words addressed to our condition wanting, but we are in the world with others, speaking out about what it is and how it stands with us when speaking or keeping silent. (Keeping silent is sometimes as revealing as lending something our voice, especially when we have nothing important or fresh to share: "Silence is the universal refuge, the sequel to all dull discourse and all foolish acts, a balm to our very chagrin, as welcome after satiety as after disappointment."[37] We require time, in *Walden*'s words, to acquire "new value for each other."[38] In the light of current pressures to publish, or perish, this view alone is almost enough to account for the neglect of Thoreau in the philosophical profession.)

Those who come to *Walden* in search of fact won't be disappointed. They'll learn how many acres of beans the author planted, how much he spent on various things, how much he earned in return for his labor, how deep Walden Pond really is, in opposition to those who fancy it bottomless, and who lived where and when. That Thoreau gives us this much is his way of drawing attention to the actuality of the experience he describes and the reality of a world where one must eat and drink, build and calculate. Economy can be treated with levity, but it cannot be dispensed with. His is no romantic fantasy of escape. But a mere catalogue of facts, however exhaustive, does not amount to an accounting of the world, and it is such an account of a world that *Walden* has to render.

What matters in *Walden* is not *that* something occurred somewhere, near or far. This we learn well enough in reading the daily news: So and so was hit by a train late last night; the queen has a cold and won't appear at the benefit today; a dangerous convict escaped recently from the state prison. If you are acquainted with the principle, you can dispense with the endlessly reiterated example. The offerings of the daily press are poor in world, even when the narrative is rich in detail. You draw no closer to *Walden*'s world by learning more about the life and times of its author, although you may have other good reasons to get acquainted with these things.[39] A complete factual record of everything that happened to and around Henry David Thoreau and a daily account of what he did during his twenty-six months by the pond would, I suspect, expand over more volumes than we could read in a lifetime; but even if we could discover the time to scan every page to the last recorded syllable, we'd draw no nearer to the world of this comparatively short work. Our lives are frittered away in detail.

A world, however poor, is not composed of accumulating fact. The truth is pretty nearly the reverse: There is a fact at all because there is a meaningful world, a site where facts cross because they've been significantly placed.[40] The world of the carpenter, for instance, is the way certain things show up as tools arranged for the purposes of carpentry. A scholar's study is a meaningful placement of books and notebooks, desk, writing implements, paper or computer, each thing *being* what it is in relation to the significant work to be done. The fact that something falls somewhere in an objective framework of disinterested and detached observation tells us little about the world the worker daily inhabits. In the absence of a meaningful context (call it a "world"), things become, at best (or worst), mere clusters of sensible qualities distributed over distinct fields of sensation. The falling snow visible through a window in my study becomes wet, white flecks moving about soundlessly in a multicolored but dimly perceived background. But for a vision entangled in and guided by a sense of what things *mean* in the ongoing course of our experience, it is also (no doubt among many other things) an obstacle to be faced during the morning commute to work; the promise of good skiing; an inhospitable climate to the homeless; a chance for children to make sculptures and snow-huts; perhaps a reason for the authorities to cancel school; an example of "perspectivism" in the thoughts of a university professor; a symbol of emptiness in the poetry of Wallace Stevens; a wonderful manifold of geometrical forms; a natural object subject to the laws of physics; a cluster of atoms for the physical chemist; a mystery of God's creation in the mind of the pious.[41] We are tempted to say, with Heidegger, that the very reality of each item (or fact) is fundamentally decided by its meaning.

What matters in *Walden* is the *significant* fact, or the significance that underpins the selective perception of fact.[42] Mere fact, stripped of value, is what shakes out when significance has faded, leaving us with the news, what the philosopher calls and dismisses as mere gossip, worthless.[43] Or it's what we're left with in the abstract and impoverished imagination of the epistemologist. "How is it," Thoreau muses in his journal, "that what is actually present and transpiring is commonly perceived by the common sense and understanding only, is bare and bald, without halo, or the blue enamel of the intervening air?"[44] Mere fact is what's left when we have in a sense ceased to live or, if that sounds too extreme, when we no longer *care* about the world in which it is at least for now our lot to live. "If we respected only what is inevitable and has a right to be, music and poetry would resound along the streets. When we are unhurried and wise, we perceive that only great and worthy things have any permanent and absolute existence,—that petty fears and petty pleasures are but the shadow of reality."[45] We have a world, then, when we are "overflowing with life" and "rich in experience," when we are attentive and alert and tracking the worth of what there is.[46] When we are drowsy and dull, the world recedes. And this having world or not, this being awake or sleeping, decides our speech.[47]

But we might still wonder how best to voice the significance of the significant fact? There is, it seems, no way to word the world in *this* sense but poetically. (This is not to say that poetry decides the world: Thoreau didn't take his stand with Darwin against Agassiz because he *fancied* evolutionary theory superior to the doctrine of special creation, for instance, and we aren't being asked to see Wordsworth's *Prelude* as a compelling contribution to physical science, but the physicist asked to share with us the *reasons* why he came to value physics should become in some sense a poet. We'd rightly think it strange if he delivered a lecture on big bang cosmology in answer to the question "But why do you *care*?" Even the care for truth has its poetry.[48] That we take an interest in the truth is something we often don't discuss richly enough; and we know well enough how commonly we take an interest in the *suppression* or the ignorance at least of it.)

In a number of entries scattered throughout the journal Thoreau names his language without embarrassment *myth*; and it is explicitly set in opposition to the common, unheroic sense of things. "Common sense is not so familiar with any truth but Genius will represent it in a strange light. Let the seer bring down his broad eye to the most stale and trivial fact, and he will make you believe it a new planet in the sky."[49] "My facts shall be falsehoods to the common sense. I would so state facts that they shall be significant, shall be myths or mythologic."[50] What is mere noise in the hearing of the unpoetic ear becomes the chanting of vespers by whippoorwills or the "wailing hymns or threnodies" of the screech owl.[51] We have no need of city life and culture to hear celestial music; for the poetic thinker "all nature will *fable*, and every natural phenomenon be a myth."[52] "My profession is to be always on the alert to find God in nature, to know his lurking-places, to attend all the oratorios, the operas, in nature."[53]

You could call this view of the world *religious*, but this now colorless word hardly means much any more, and is stretched too thin. (My refusal to read *Walden* "religiously" will seem evasive, I suspect, to some; but I'm anxious to avoid more controversy than I've already possibly created. Thoreau, admittedly, uses religious language freely in the journal.) Perhaps we'd do better to speak of *epic*, keeping in mind the ancient sense of *epos* as a record of the heroic words and deeds of heroic individuals.[54] (Thoreau often complains in the journal that our principal failure is to live without a sense of the heroic.) We know that Thoreau was an avid and careful reader of the *Iliad*,[55] one of the few books named in *Walden* (if only, strangely, in a passage where we learn that other labor left little time for reading); and several prominent and memorable passages echo Homer. If Thoreau's work can be said to give expression to a "religious" attitude, it is far more Greek or Hindu, perhaps, or Native American[56] than it is Christian.[57]

Possibly the most famous of these epic tales comes in "Brute Neighbors." It opens: "I was witness to events of a less peaceful character."[58] Two large ants, one red, the other a large black warrior, were "fiercely contending with one another."[59] Looking more closely, he discovers not two combatants but two armies pitted against each other, "red republicans on the one hand, and the black imperialists on the other," fighting with superhuman resolve.[60] What the prosaic eye dismisses as the unimportant motions of an insignificant species of insect the poet sees as "some Achilles, who had nourished his wrath apart, and had now come to avenge or rescue his Patroclus."[61] It would hardly surprise the poet to find two "musical bands stationed on some eminent chip, and playing their national airs the while, to excite the slow and cheer the dying combatants."[62] Although he never found out who won, his feelings were "excited and harrowed by witnessing the struggle, the ferocity and carnage, of a human battle."[63]

It is easy enough to dismiss this as mock-epic, a playful dramatization of something otherwise not worth our while to notice, on a par with Thoreau's account in "The Bean-Field" of his long war with weeds, "those Trojans who had sun and rain and dews on their side."[64] "Many a lusty crest-waving Hector, that towered a whole foot above his crowding comrades, fell before my weapon and rolled in the dust."[65] We are ready, like a literalizing Gradgrind, to remind ourselves that an ant is not, after all, an Achilles, that ants don't wage war, at least not in our sense, and that they certainly don't make music. (If forced to decide, most of us would probably choose to listen to Bach or Bartok than to a monotonous chorus of endlessly chirping crickets.) But if we are unwilling to take descriptions of this sort seriously, then we must be prepared to dismiss most of what we read in *Walden* as highbrow jest, mocking seriousness. It seems pretty clear, at least to me, that *Walden*'s burden is to show us that we fail, culpably, to take events worded like this seriously enough, and invest too much capital in affairs and accounts that ought to leave us more indifferent.[66] (There's time enough for the plain statement of literal fact, and in certain settings, it is entirely appropriate to "level [our meaning] downward to our dullest perception."[67] If a fire breaks out in the classroom, and I want my students to head for the door, it won't pay to waste time reciting poems on the tragedy of our mortal condition or to remind my audience, anticipating death, that every loss and "all pain [are] particular: the universe remains to the heart unhurt."[68] The various uses of language have their seasons; to speak extravagantly in this situation, where life and limb are at stake, is to have one interest too many.[69])

As paradoxical as it sounds, I'm tempted to say that if we cannot take polemical ants and warlike weeds seriously, if we are unable to hear symphonic sounds in the call of birds and forget that "the same sun which ripens my beans illumines at once a system of earths like ours,"[70] we cannot take ourselves in earnest; reduced to its factual skeleton, every *human* life, even the grandest and most heroic, is an impoverished and unimportant thing.[71] You can read your own sexual experience in the light of Shakespeare's sonnets or express yourself in the language of *Penthouse Forum*; it isn't obvious that the pornographic account does greater justice to your erotic experience, unless you are convinced that the crassest account comes closest to unadorned reality; but then you may just be making a sad confession about yourself and the poverty of your own erotic encounters. (Be careful, our author seems to be saying, about what you think and how you speak about your life; you may just come to resemble a debased version of yourself.[72] I admit there's a fine line here: The person who *really* thinks he's Jesus Christ walking once again among us and preaching the Gospel is not the triumphant representative of the heroic imagination but very probably insane.[73]) No one is a hero to his valet, not because the hero isn't a hero, but because the valet is just a valet. "We meet at meals three times a day, and give each other a new taste of that old musty cheese that we are."[74] Our insipid dinner discourse on weather and soup is a standing reproach. (If there's anything to complain of in these Homeric passages, it is possibly that they are still too common, not original and extravagant enough. And as Thoreau will remind us in the opening paragraph of "Sounds," while we are reading "the most select and classic" books, "we are in danger of forgetting the language which all things and events speak without metaphor, which alone is copious and standard."[75] It is one thing to impose ancient forms on newly witnessed figures in nature, something else to look to nature "for the sake of [fresh] tropes and [living] expression."[76]

If you still have a taste for the noble and sublime, you'll possibly look for substance in meaningful old tales of ancient prophets and founding fathers and lament the passing of the Golden Age.[77] Why not search and sink here and now? "We are wont to imagine rare and delectable places in some remote and more celestial corner of the system, behind the constellation of Cassiopeia's Chair, far from noise and disturbance. I discovered that my house actually had its site in such a withdrawn, but forever new and unprofaned, part of the universe."[78] "In eternity there is indeed something true and sublime. But all these times and places are now and here. God himself culminates in the present moment, and will never be more divine in the lapse of all the ages."[79] You will not begin to live in Thoreau's sense of living, beyond the preparatory labor of making a living,[80] until you cast yourself in a heroic light, and are ready to acknowledge in what you say about the world of essential, significant fact as it bears upon your *mea res agitur*, "I am at stake in this." The worth of your life depends on an elevation of purpose and a higher quaking of your tongue. "You must live in the present, launch yourself on every wave, find your eternity in each moment. Fools stand on their island opportunities and look toward another land. There is no other land; there is no other life but this, or the like of this."[81]

Leafing through the World in Spring

> This is the frost coming out of the ground; this is Spring. It precedes the green and flowery spring, as mythology precedes regular poetry.[82]

The world of *Walden* finds perhaps its most suggestive and richest poetic expression in the astonishing account of thawing sand and clay in its penultimate chapter. Astonishing, I think, it is; and yet the occasion that prompts the poet's imagining of primeval beginnings and creative leafy paradigm, worthy of an ancient cosmogony, is nothing too remarkable and is, in fact, altogether dependent, at least materially and factually, on contemporary happenings. It's the unintended consequence of the railroad builder's work and the movement of impatient cars, passing quickly through Concord to more important business and destinations. If the Irishman had not done his job, if Thoreau were not sometimes hungry for the gossip of the village or in need of some service, there'd be nothing seen along the tracks worth telling. The farmer wending his way to market near the rails with an impending profitable sale uppermost in mind is likely to overlook the phenomenon. The poetic naturalist and aesthete accustomed to finding satisfaction in what more obviously elevates will probably look elsewhere for inspiration and support in nature, in the rocky mountain peak overshadowing a quiet lake or in the thundering cataract. A vast desert landscape would seem more promising material than what gives rise to the experience Thoreau describes. The jaded senses of the tired tourist call for a more inspiring vista than this.[83] And what the weary traveler expects to find on her vacation is not a *world* but welcome relief from one. "World" is the burden the worker longs to leave behind, knowing it refuses to be left alone and waits for her reluctant return.

What "Spring" and *Walden* more generally (as I've been arguing) have partly to tell is how a world forms around something you take to be significant, whether others find it so or not and whether or not you will find it so forever, or at least for what remains of your life. (*Walden* allows you to leave your current life behind for the sake of another. "I left the woods for as good a reason as I went there. Perhaps it seemed to me that I had several more lives to live, and could not spare any more time for that one.")[84] Every beginning is probably in some sense common and low, although it strikes you as prescient and promising. An exchange of dollars on the street is enough to stir a Rockefeller to larger designs; an early, rude, and trivial sexual encounter enflames a seducer or makes an ascetic; a sudden consciousness of depravity and possible redemption the eventual saint. The budding philosopher responds in class to an unknown teacher speaking in obscurity or finds inspiration in a book read in a lonely hour and imagines fruitful days ahead. A promising poet finds his calling in the behavior of a spider spinning her web on a deck and sitting in its center with the patience and *ataraxia* of an ancient stoic. The lover knows precious little about the beloved on a first meeting. The world of the cancer patient takes shape around a short exchange with the doctor in a vanishingly small portion of cosmic space. A world can "world" (in Heidegger's suggestive phrase) around "the milk in a pan" or "the glance of the eye" or the gait of an old man, perhaps more suggestively for you than what's doing in Italy or Arabia.[85]

Our lives acquire whatever meaning they can embody because we read fugitive events extravagantly and momentary encounters expansively, with valor and generosity even in despair.[86] (Our descending paths and darkening ways have their own eloquent poets and philosophers. There is a poetry of apathy as well as joy.) Insignificance comes in contractions, when we think we've said the last word on the importance of what we care about, or when our choicest words strike us in our more reflective moments as the stale repetitions of what we've said, perhaps freshly once, before. What makes a possible world in these humble beginnings is what expansions they promise and what unpredictable landings[87] they darkly but meaningfully prepare. Whether a world comes into being or not depends on what happens next in the life of an animal endowed with logos and what she goes on to tell herself about herself in solitude and voices in society. And this depends, at least in part, on the unrecognized power of poetry to give word to our world. As one philosophical theorist of the Romantic movement puts it, "Our sense of reality, and of the claims it makes on us, is inseparable from the creative imagination."[88] The difference between one world and the next is to be measured by the imaginative work, call it eccentricity if its product seems unfamiliar to you, which goes into its making; and we have no way of measuring imaginative power beyond the language it forges.[89] There is no direct and immediate experience of what we think of as the world. (This is one of Kant's deepest insights in the critique of rational cosmology in the Antinomy of the first *Critique*—the world is no object of possible human experience. We have merely an *idea* of it that serves as a regulative principle in the organization of our local and finite encounters and efforts to explain in causal terms.)[90] The wording of the world, its peculiar way of being for us, is always indirect and figurative, a matter of tropes and symbolic expressions.[91] (It's *like* a vast clock, for instance, or more like a living organism, in an alternative way of conceiving.)[92] What we call "reality" and acknowledge as *important* fact is partly dependent on the strength and pervasiveness of our calling and saying. Too often, however, it will depend on unthinking reverence for ancient names and what they've come commonly to mean—matter, mind, spirit, virtue, character, nature, force, and fact, Newton, Rousseau, Kant, Darwin, Smith, Jefferson, Franklin, Emerson, or even Thoreau.

Once you've come to inhabit a world, it's no large step to enumerate what there is in it. The objects that enter the world of the banker or the baker are easily catalogued. Thoreau can tell you without much ado how and when he came to see thawing sand and clay, how often he revisited the site, and when he decided to write about it. What matters is how the author takes it up, and what it reveals to the poet about the *world* he's come to inhabit. The poet's question is not what there is in the world but how it all hangs together and what, if anything, it can be said to *mean*. It is a remarkable fact about our experience of what there is in the world that the items we enumerate *make* a world; they somehow manage to cohere and to signify, even when they seem to be opposed and work, as far as we can tell, against apparent harmony. "Why do precisely these objects which we behold make a world?"[93] The reference to making seems to gesture toward a poetic solution. And the answer builds on the reader's having encountered the poet's objects, or objects and their circumstances very much like his.

From the hurried point of view, there's nothing astonishing about sand and clay thawing under the sun's influence along the sides of a deep cut in the railroad in the earliest days of spring.[94] The theme of spring as a whole seems common enough. Every schoolboy knows that this is the season of rebirth and renewal: The earth slumbering in winter comes back to life with the thawing rays of the sun, and we, too, are not immune to seasonal influences.[95] The material is unremarkable ("sand of every degree of fineness and of various colors, commonly mixed with a little clay");[96] the railway setting in Concord is now equally common and familiar; the circumstance is Thoreau's customary traffic to and from the village. The poet introduces no new fact to the tutored consciousness of human life and its world. So what is Thoreau up to here?

As a first approximation, we can say that what is coming to expression is a sense of the world as something fluid and, like the poet's own consciousness, a *flowing* or outpouring from a concealed source, as though we were in danger of forgetting and had to be reminded that things come to be and pass away and move within an allotted span. "A history of animated nature must itself be animated."[97] But this alone is nothing remarkable: Although Aristotle felt compelled to assert the fact of *kinêsis* against the Eleatic School, most of us are commonly ready to grant that we inhabit a world of moving images and things, where birth and death and transformation in between have their necessary places. Our sciences of reality are one and all organized bodies of knowledge about how and why things move: cultural and historical phenomena; physical objects in space and their underlying elements; the mind thinking and feeling and willing; the body growing, peaking, decaying, and dying; groups forming, stabilizing, propagating themselves, and eventually declining; and the like. What matters, then, is not merely *that* things come and go and move, a "fact" about the world no one's likely to deny, but how the movement of sand and clay thawing in spring affects the consciousness of the poet, how the phenomena arrange themselves and what this spontaneous arrangement, without apparent aim or consciously intended end, has to teach us about the structured movements that define the poet's world. (And perhaps the villager, dwelling in a world of fixed forms and rites and musing despairingly over patterns apparently etched in stone, does, after all, need this reminder of movement and becoming and the rites of spring against more fatal evidence.)

A *poet's* world—this means that the work of wording it will involve an act of bringing things we tend to separate in ordinary consciousness into peculiar sorts of unexpected *relation*; it is this establishing of moving relations, or this poetic recording of emerging correspondences, that the passage accomplishes, in what at first glance seems little more than a grotesque fantasy where all things blend curiously together, and we are left with nothing unrelated to anything else, no more solid and independent facts, the spontaneous dance of a fluid substance in response to newly discovered heat. "What is man but a mass of thawing clay?"[98]

The account begins in fancy humbly enough. Initially we are simply reminded of certain resemblances: The sand begins to flow *like* lava, and as it continues to flow it assumes the shape of sappy leaves or vines and comes quickly to resemble "the laciniated lobed and imbricated thalluses of some lichens; or you are reminded of coral, of leopard's paws or birds' feet, of brains or lungs or bowels, and excrements of all kinds" (*Walden*, 305). At first, the poet's work resembles the child's innocent and idle playing with moving clouds: There's a dog, now an elongated cat, perhaps a rabbit resembling your beloved pet, then a house or a leaf, each form emerging as the previous shape dissolves in a fantastical metamorphosis in an imagined world bent on *leaving* shapes behind. This frivolous enumeration of likenesses and transitions seems harmless enough and hardly substantial enough to give compelling voice to the difficult world with which we have daily to cope. (And of course the hard-headed realist will rightly insist that the forms are not *really* the things they resemble.) The difference between the child's labor and the poet's seems to lie merely in the range of things the poet sees taking shape and blending into one another and resolves in *Walden* to relate.

And yet, the fact that the poet *ranges* as he does is, I think, central to the passage's larger design, for it turns out to be no random inventory of unrelated items, no mere catalogue of indifferently emerging forms in unchained fancy. Look more closely, and you'll discover most of the general sorts of things that make up our world: inorganic material, coral, plants and animals, geological phenomena (strands and streams and riverbanks), cultural artifacts (sculptures in bronze and buildings, language, and books), the human body and its organs; even excrement makes its appearance alongside our more sublimating moral aspirations ("that we may turn over a new leaf at last"),[99] a subtle reminder that what is springing up in spring and in these words of spring, after the long deathly blank of winter, is nothing less than the world, *our* world, after all, of things striving to accomplish and embody themselves, but newly minted and strangely reflected in these lively correspondences and vital analogies. And the poet ranges not arbitrarily, but rather in search of the visible evidence of a pervasive and enduring law of emerging form, crystallized around a marked perception of organic movement. "There is nothing inorganic."[100] The simplest inorganic transformation has, like the plant's unfolding in its element of soil and sun and atmosphere, its law of growth and development. This seems to be the underlying message: "The earth is all alive and covered with papillae."[101] Even the pond is said to be a thing sensitive and alive, responsive to changes in the weather imperceptible to us.[102]

Unlike the child's unfettered play, then, the poet's is methodical and organized, like the inspiring self-organizing sand itself, around a primal figure, an *Urphänomen*, so to speak, the prototypical leaf. This is its central, gathering image, an emblem of its author's world and the pattern of creative energy in nature and, by implication, in art. (The point of forsaking society for a season and getting back to nature is, after all, to find fresh poetic resources in the less cultivated scene. Working with beans and waging war against weeds in "the wild," or at least some distance from your neighbors in the village, is no end in itself, but for the sake of tropes and expressions, to serve a parable-maker someday.)[103]

The leaf is a pregnant symbolic form, mirrored in the "inorganic" phenomena below it, in the wonderful formation of ice crystals, for instance, and anticipating higher organic structure, the feathers and wings of birds, and, in one of Thoreau's more extravagant figures, human anatomy: "The ear may be regarded, fancifully, as a lichen, *umbilicaria*, on the side of the head, with its lobe or drop."[104] As the passage reaches its climax, the entire earth is envisioned as "living poetry like the leaves of a tree, which precede flowers and fruit,—not a fossil earth, but a living earth; compared with whose great central life all animal and vegetable life is merely parasitic."[105] "Thus it seemed that this one hillside illustrated the principle of all the operations of nature. The Maker of this earth but patented a leaf."[106] The world itself becomes in the poet's fancy a sublime work of art, the product of an ingenious Poet and the occasion of the human poet's extravagant dictum.[107]

In this apparently isolated and trivial phenomenon near the railroad, then, we are invited to see an epitome of cosmic law and the re-formation of a world in which each thing is what it is in complex relation to and in echo of everything else, mirrored in the poet's own visionary experience and expressed in fitting poetic form. The author of *Walden* seems to be saying that the poetic statement (broadly construed) is the only way we've got to disclose the world in comparatively unfamiliar ways; the worth of this sort of poetry dawns on us when we come to think that the familiar world is too much with us.[108] Only when you've lost the familiar world (as Thoreau points out in a memorable passage), where sand is just sand and a leaf is only one among many items we might enter into a growing catalogue of existing things, can you begin to find yourself in the infinite extent of your relations to a richer world of things, a world you only thought you understood because someone else bestowed upon the items you find within it what's become a common *name*.[109] In the poetic encounter, you'll discover no entirely new objects, but the same familiar things sporting in novel combinations a different face. (What this means for those of us who, by nature or upbringing, aren't cut out for poetry is another matter.)[110] "I ask not for the great, the remote, the romantic. . . . I embrace the common, I explore and sit at the feet of the familiar, the low. Give me insight into to-day, and you may have the antique and future worlds."[111]

An Immodest Defense of Poetry

But Poets . . . are the institutors of laws, and the founders of civil society and the inventors of the arts of life and the teachers, who draw into . . . propinquity with the beautiful and the true.[112]

> There comes a time when reason—not the grand
> And simple reason, but that humbler power
> Which carries on its not inglorious work
> By logic and minute analysis—
> Is of all idols that which pleases most
> The growing mind.[113]

It's easy to anticipate what the skeptic will make of all this. He'll speak in the name of Emerson's Materialist and "sturdy capitalist" respecting sensible masses, a clear-cut procession of fact, and measurable figures, and dismiss everything else that falls outside this picture's frame.[114] Thoreau himself often speaks in the skeptic's name: The voice of skepticism forms one strain in the chorus *Walden* sings, with its insistence on hard fact and pragmatic urgency, and its refusal to ignore the demand for one sort of figure; the author is no stranger to skepticism in the face of some pursuits: skepticism facing some ways of speaking, skepticism even about the worth of living.[115] And he is sometimes skeptical about the "poetic" fancies of unscientific reverie: "In sane moments," he writes in the Conclusion, "we regard only the facts, the case that is. . . . Any truth is better than make-believe."[116] There are those who think Walden Pond bottomless, but he's sounded its depths and knows better. Some things can, after all, be measured in the usual ways. "The greatest depth was exactly one hundred and two feet; to which may be added the five feet which it has risen since, making one hundred and seven."[117] If you wish to build a house or a cabin near the woods, it pays to know your material resources and your climate, answering to unchosen fact. The aspiring gardener must know what seeds are available and what the soil will allow to grow; it is essential to get to know beans. One misguided farmer, mentioned in "Economy," is taken to task for thinking that meat is required to make bones, while his oxen "with vegetable-made bones, jerk him and his lumbering plough along in spite of every obstacle."[118] The point of *Walden*'s celebration of an experimental approach to life is partly to draw attention to the importance of getting your facts right and fronting them squarely, especially the "essential facts of life,"[119] about which we seem so often to be in doubt. (There's one form of skepticism *Walden* does not take too seriously, skepticism regarding the reality of the external world. I suspect that, like Heidegger, Thoreau would happily dismiss it as a silly aberration of the abstract intelligence.[120] For both thinkers the question is not whether the world exists but what it means to inhabit one, how we take it up, and what our world makes possible and possibly rules out and why; and, just as important, whether we are right to place our boundaries where we do.)

One sort of scientific reader of *Walden* will almost certainly object. If Thoreau's fantasy is meant to capture the lawful organization of the world, as its several references to law may suggest, then it won't stand upright alongside the work of patient scientific research and cosmological speculation—which, however bold, is grounded in the rigorous language of mathematics and supported by the findings of repeatable experiment. Thoreau's account of thawing sand and clay in spring sticks to the visible surface of things, works by analogy, and offers nothing like precise causal analysis of events in nature. As a "theory" of biologic form, even, it pales next to Darwin's elaborate account of natural selection in *On the Origin of Species*.[121] What's worse, it lays before the reader no testable hypothesis, nothing that can be exactly formulated and empirically refuted. In the progress of scientific thought, it is sure to be cast aside, like Goethe's *Farbenlehre*, as the work of an amateur.[122] (Add to this that its ruling image isn't even original but borrowed from the German poet. *Walden*'s fate among the scientists is likely to resemble its fate among the philosophers.)

But life is not lived in the depths of a scientific theory; we live out our lives, if you like, on the surfaces of things, in response to qualities displayed in a world that organizes itself around a perceiver. The lover may very well be moved by chemical events in her brain; but from her own point of view, she's responding feelingly to form. We don't deliberate about what to do and with whom by consulting our neurotransmitters. The neurophilosopher's deeper explanation is, from the concerned agent's point of view, if not inaccurate (it may be true enough that oxytocin is a necessary chemical condition of attachment and trust, as experimental work with prairie and montane voles suggests),[123] at least a subtle way of changing the subject; that she has anything to explain at all she owes to the scientifically untutored experience and folk psychology she officially dismisses. If you take a drug to alleviate depression, it's only so that you can resume an interrupted response to form; you won't be spared the labor of sorting out how to go on again and how to express the importance of what you care about. You'll still need a subtle language that captures the *significance* of the phenomena you're now better placed to perceive, in a world you've come to inhabit again. "After all, the truest description, and that by which another living man can most readily recognize a flower [even], is the unmeasured and eloquent one which the sight of it inspires. No scientific description will supply the want of this, though you should count and measure and analyze every atom that seems to compose it."[124]

As the archaic phrenologist knew, it is hard to separate the qualities that captivate us in human souls from what we see, admire, and love in the visible world. No outside, nothing on the surface, and there's no way of knowing what's inside. Even the rarefied world of the thinker can find its outward shape. Rodin conveyed in shimmering surfaces of bronze the invisible, concentrated labor of thought—thinking is a tilt of the head, a gesture, a certain way of holding the arms and positioning the legs. The fiery speaker who would share with us his best thoughts is a moving image of lips and eyes and muscles, a sequence of sonorous impressions that overtakes and overwhelms us, a tangible performance. A culture that admires the athlete and the fashion model above all other figures of human excellence knows at least this much—that the body is where the soul appropriately spreads itself out and for now finds itself at home. As Heidegger in this spirit put the point in a course of lectures on the philosophy of religion, " 'World" is where one *lives* (you cannot live in an object)."[125]

We often forget, I think, that the significance of what we commonly experience is largely built up out of analogies and resemblances, some now stale and common but still circulating, others fresher and, at least for now, vital. What we call the language of plain, literal fact is, as Nietzsche reminds us, composed largely of dead metaphors.[126] Nothing in the world of everyday life *is* simply what it is: Everything is in some sense like every other thing. Our thinking is in analogy, a *reading* of the world. There is something perceivable at all because mind is ever gathering and responding to what's gathering itself. The world is partly what we conceive it to be: "The universe constantly and obediently answers to our conceptions; whether we travel fast or slow, the track is laid for us. Let us spend our lives in conceiving then."[127] This is Thoreau's way of lending his voice to the cause of transcendental idealism.[128]

It isn't just the perceived world of the contemplative poet, then, that displays itself in analogy. And it could be argued, further, that the healthy and "natural" development of a moral point of view is inseparable from seeing, beyond brute fact, certain correspondences—that grimaces are no mere modifications of meaningless facial matter but *mean* pain,[129] that many nonhuman animals, however unlike us in so many ways, are, like us, the experiencing centers of a life,[130] that the bizarre rituals of another culture are not altogether unlike some of our own practices, which would seem equally strange from an outsider's vantage point. However we choose to describe, ground, and defend it, as the development of a sort of virtuous character or as the awareness of rational law or in terms of some art of reckoning with possible and measurable utility, moral consciousness is born, it seems, of what we might call imaginative eccentricity. It's been said that the sociopath and psychotic immoralist live too much in an overheated imagination, divorced from reality and the healthy consciousness of plain fact; but I'm tempted to say that they imagine too narrowly and obsessively and not enough.[131] It isn't imaginative richness that explains, but the impoverishment of what gets seen that partly accounts for moral deviation and depravity and the ravings of lunacy. However unlike our own, the world of the immoralist revolves about an unimaginative and easily attainable self, unhappily narrowed. In this respect, the immoralist resembles the despairing fatalist who passes for normal among the infirm.

Our thoughtful making, too, is inconceivable without this work of finding resemblances. There is innovative artifice and technological advance because we discern novel forms and create new combinations in well-known material, often in creative imitation of what already exists: A tree is not *merely* a tree but a possible table; a carefully constructed winged artifice can, like nature's own avian produce, translate the traveler more speedily than the horse-drawn carriage and beat the bird to Boston; more astonishing still, pieces of etched plastic carry music to the masses at home in a living room without the benefit or need of a living orchestra. (It's worth remembering that the maker and the poet go by one name in an earlier tongue.) In our ancient and seemingly endless love affair with technology, at least, we are often most hopeful and convinced of the tremendous power of analogical thinking.

Science itself expands or, in Kuhn's terms, becomes revolutionary, ever by analogy and reconfiguration. Copernicus's model attracts because of its "aesthetic" qualities, because the equations describing a system with a central sun are more elegant and simpler than their geocentric counterparts, with unwieldy epicycles. It's a happier way of modeling what we now call, thanks to this triumph of the scientific imagination, the solar system.[132] The subatomic physicist finds one model, one way of shedding light on the dimly known, in the solar system, another in smears of probability. Nature, in Darwin's potent image, is "daily and hourly scrutinizing" every one of her products, "rejecting that which is bad, preserving and adding up all that is good; silently . . . working . . . at the improvement of each organic being."[133] What we call a bold scientific generalization is often a matter of reshuffling the available material in a fresh combination.[134]

Philosophers, too, have their favorite guiding tropes and metaphors. Plato bequeathed a potent image of the soul, composed of warring powers, and its health as a sort of *harmonia*, and was perhaps the first to figure wisdom in terms of light and enlightenment and significant spiritual change as turning around (conversion), compelling symbols still.[135] Kant's conception of the autonomous moral agent builds on the ancient Stoic's pregnant image of the inner citadel, where reason reigns supreme. Hegel's *Phenomenology* often reads like a sequence of expanding metaphors of *Geist*. Even the reductive materialist, working with hard scientific fact, is modeling what we call mind and mental activity on something else which it resembles: The movement of thought is *like* an electrical current traveling along a neuron; memory is *like* the modification of ribonucleic acid; fear is *like* the agitated outpouring of stress hormones.

Although its lessons and language should remain somewhat strange (if fully domesticated, the work will cease to matter; there should always be "some obscurities" and secrets in the poet's trade),[136] what *Walden* accomplishes is not as eccentric as we were wont at first to believe—no more so, at least, than human life itself in its finer and more elevated moments is. Its wayward path merely draws attention to what we've been doing all along, for better or for worse, as good poets or bad, without full awareness of our own eccentricity or failing, perhaps, to acknowledge the waywardness of our deviant ancestors (Socrates or Jesus, a favorite poet, Kant, Newton, Einstein, or whomever you will) who dared to read the stale prose of the world extra-vagantly,[137] and ventured to put new aspects on the face of ancient things: In the depths of our most creative thought, *Denken* is a sort of *Dichten*—the thinker in Thoreau's sense is a sort of poet.[138] There is only a world *for us*, and one worth inhabiting, "forever new and unprofaned"[139] and worthy of our most wakeful hours, because the human being, thinking, feeling, acting all at once, is inventive, is at bottom and above all a poetizing animal: "Dichterisch wohnet der Mensch. . . ." "Only that day dawns to which we are awake. There is more day to dawn. The sun is but a morning star."[140]

FIVE

IN WILDNESS IS THE PRESERVATION
OF THE WORLD

Thoreau's Environmental Ethics

Philip J. Cafaro

Environmental ethics asks how people should treat the rest of nature. In the words of a leading environmental philosopher, it seeks to specify "duties to and values in the natural world."[1] Over the past few decades, environmental ethics has emerged as an important area within philosophy, its growth spurred by our immense environmental problems and the sense that a change in values will be needed to successfully address them.

In helping us develop a strong environmental ethics, no thinker has more to offer than Henry Thoreau. He was one of the earliest and strongest critics of anthropocentrism: the view that only human beings have rights or "intrinsic value" and that other creatures may be used in any way we see fit. Perhaps even more important, Thoreau shows us how to lead happy, flourishing lives while still treating nature with respect.

There is a great practical need to develop positive arguments for environmental protection. Environmentalism is sometimes seen as intolerably limiting, spawning an endless string of "thou shalt nots." Often, the general public views environmentalists as killjoys and misanthropes, willing to countenance any trade-offs of human freedom or happiness in pursuit of our aims. Partly this is unavoidable. In defending nature, environmentalists are necessarily proscriptive. Recognizing intrinsic values in nature *does* limit its morally permissible use. Yet the writings of the great naturalists—and our own experiences—tell a story of joyful connection to nature. The artist, the scientist, the poet, the hunter, and the fisherman—all pay attention to nature and "capture values" that enrich their lives. This suggests that recognition of nature's intrinsic value brings rewards to go with environmentalists' proscriptions.

As I have argued elsewhere, in *Walden* Thoreau writes as a virtue ethicist.[2] I contend that *Walden* and Thoreau's other writings provide a philosophically deep and inspiring *environmental* virtue ethics, linking environmental awareness and protection to human flourishing and the pursuit of excellence.[3] Thoreau thus points the way toward a comprehensive, life-affirming environmental ethics.

By recognizing nature's value, we enrich our own lives. By restraining our gross physical consumption, we are more likely to lead healthy and enjoyable lives, and promote conditions in which future generations can do the same. By devoting ourselves to higher pursuits than money-making, we act in our enlightened self-interest—with great benefits for the many other species with which we share the Earth. These arguments need to be made—along with intrinsic value arguments—if we hope to persuade people to take the steps necessary to protect the natural world.

Fishy Virtue

Thoreau challenges conventional ethics in many ways. One of his most important challenges involves locating value directly in the nonhuman world, a theme made explicit in *A Week on the Concord and Merrimack Rivers*. Early in *A Week*, Thoreau gives a detailed account of the various species of fish in the Concord River. This is one of those digressions that have annoyed so many readers. "We come upon them like snags," wrote James Russell Lowell, "jolting us headforemost out of our places as we are rowing placidly up stream or drifting down."[4] Thoreau might have integrated this account more smoothly into the narrative, of course, but another alternative would have been to ignore the fish entirely: to glide downstream without noticing them, or to carelessly populate the deeps and shallows with generic or imaginary fish. This is the way of most boaters and most writers. This Thoreau will not do.

Instead, he describes the fish, accurately and in detail: their appearance, behavior (nesting, feeding, migrations), habitat preferences, relative abundance, and more. These fish have many fine qualities: The bream "assiduously" guards its nest; the pickerel is "swift and wary." Thoreau plays up both their otherness and their closeness to us: The fish are at once "fabulous inhabitant[s] of another element, a thing heard of but not seen," and "our finny contemporaries in the Concord waters."[5] These wonderful creatures are part of the same landscape as ourselves. We may know them if we will look.

Much of this section of Thoreau's book has little explicit ethical content. At first there are no ethical arguments, just descriptions continually bubbling up into little assertions of goodness: the "grace" of the bream; the "scholastic and classical" beauty of the chevin. Finally, however, Thoreau comes to the plight of the shad and other anadromous, migratory fishes. Formerly found in great numbers in New England's rivers, they are now mostly blocked by dams. Here the definite "ought" of moral concern flows out.

> Poor shad! where is thy redress? . . . Still wandering the sea in thy scaly armor to inquire humbly at the mouths of rivers if man has perchance left them free for thee to enter. By countless shoals loitering uncertain meanwhile, merely stemming the tide there, in danger from sea foes in spite of thy bright armor, awaiting new instructions, until the sands, until the water itself, tell thee if it be so or not. Thus by whole migrating nations, full of instinct, which is thy faith, in this backward spring, turned adrift, and perchance thou knowest not where men do *not* dwell, where there are *not* factories, in these days. Armed with no sword, no electric shock, but mere Shad, armed only with innocence and a just cause, with tender dumb mouth only forward, and scales easy to be detached. I for one am with thee, and who knows what may avail a crow bar against that Billerica dam?[6]

Our treatment of the shad is unjust. The fish obviously cannot "petition for redress," but they would be justified in doing so. The dams are not merely inconvenient or inexpedient for fishermen, downstream farmers, or other human beings—they are wrong, immoral, because of their effects on "mere Shad." One hundred and thirty years before the EarthFirst!

movement, Thoreau suggests that this injustice is grave enough to justify a new kind of civil disobedience. We have here not the monstrous injustice of making a mere tool out of a man or woman, but the equally monstrous injustice of extirpating whole species, whole forms of life, from the landscape.

Thoreau goes on to provide one of the earliest explicit calls for a nonanthropocentric ethics. The passage quoted above continues: "Away with the superficial and selfish phil-*anthropy* of men,—who knows what admirable virtue of fishes may be below low-water mark, bearing up against a hard destiny, not admired by that fellow creature who alone can appreciate it!" Reserving all love and concern for humans—phil-*anthropy*, emphasis in the original—is both superficial, based on ignorance of what is below the surface, and selfish, an excuse for unjustified self-partiality. Thoreau neatly brings his point home with the "fish" puns.[7] He argues that fish may have virtues of their own.

Thoreau's suggestion that certain piscine qualities are genuine *virtues* parallels recent attempts by environmental philosophers to justify the intrinsic value of nonhuman beings: to argue their basic goodness independent of their instrumental value to humans. These philosophers' arguments typically ground intrinsic value in various natural qualities, such as sentience, intelligence, goal-directedness, complexity, or an ancient and unique genealogy. Beings who have these qualities, it is argued, are good-in-themselves, regardless of what further good they may be to *us*. Recognizing their intrinsic value does not preclude all human use of these nonhuman beings, but it does set moral limits to that use. In the same way, Thoreau moves from facts to values, as his mostly descriptive account concludes with an explicit assertion of fish virtue and the demands of interspecies justice.[8]

Does Thoreau undermine his case for fishy virtue by speaking of the "humility" and "bravery" of fish, qualities that we typically associate with some degree of intelligence, and thus largely or exclusively with humans? Can fish be "innocent" if they cannot be guilty? Thoreau writes "perchance" the shad do not *know* where rivers still run unobstructed by humans, but of course they do not have conscious knowledge that may be formulated into propositional statements or communicated in scholarly lectures. If Thoreau's argument rests on an inaccurate picture of what shad actually are, it necessarily fails to justify their rights, or any after-hours crowbar work on the Billerica dam.

There are several ways a sympathetic expositor might respond here. We might argue that shad *do* possess literal, nonmetaphorical knowledge, perhaps as populations rather than as individuals. Through some combination of genetic programming and environmental cues (of which we are almost as ignorant as Thoreau) they do return to their native spawning grounds. They do "loiter uncertain" until some "intelligence" passes to them from the land or water, some cue which sends them up one particular river or another. They may fail to "know" of any undammed streams, if all the streams have been dammed, just as they "know" of home streams that have "proven" themselves good habitat in the past.

Alternately, we might question the notion that other beings have value only to the degree that they resemble us. Maybe we should value them for their *own* essential qualities, which might be very different from ours. Typically, those skeptical of nonhuman intrinsic value argue that rationality, or the related ability to act morally, define and limit who counts morally. Thoreau's admonition that we are "fellow creatures" who "alone can appreciate" the varied diversity of nonhuman life, suggests the following counterargument: If a true humanity involves the use of reason, that should lead to knowledge of the world around us, and thus to appreciation, and thus to restraint. If we truly value reason, it will show us a world where much besides reason has value. If we truly value diversity, we will have to jettison theories of value centered so firmly in our own nature. Those who argue that we are free to use the rest of nature any way we see fit, because we are rational and able to restrain our natural selfishness, show, ironically, their own poorly developed knowledge and capacity for altruism.

Thoreau sees a genuine heroism in the shad's efforts to spawn. It is a great story, but different from human greatness. The shoals of fish do not come armed with lance, or consciousness, or the human sense of personal importance. The shad, the philosopher will tell you, do not *act* at all, since they do not have conscious purposes. Yet we may watch them migrating upstream or hold one gleaming in our hands, imagine the vast distances they have traveled, and marvel. They truly are "reserved for higher destinies": higher up New England's rivers and streams, to spawn.[9] The shad's whole destiny is here on Earth, in this life. The same may be true for us, of course. In *Walden*, Thoreau will suggest that this is no reason to despair, for "heaven is under our feet as well as over our heads" (283).[10]

Thoreau's discussion here shows some of the difficulties of moving beyond an anthropocentric value system. We must steer the course between an uncritical anthropomorphism that gives other beings bogus honorific qualities and a hypercritical reductionism that denies other beings all qualities that we cannot yet detect in them and undervalues those qualities that we *do* detect. Our ethics should be based on accurate knowledge of the world. Yet perhaps engagement is even more important than accuracy. Thoreau argues that we should work to know nature, however imperfectly, and thus move beyond the "superficial" views with which most people content themselves. Whatever lives of excellence—or mere complexity and strangeness—fish or other nonhuman beings can achieve, humans alone can fully appreciate them. We should do so, Thoreau says, for their sakes and ours. For if the Billerica dam and similar developments unjustly obstruct fish, they may also ruin the fishing, and limit possibilities for human knowledge, poetry, and fulfilling contact with wild nature.

"Thou shalt ere long have thy way up the rivers," Thoreau cries, "up all the rivers of the globe, if I am not mistaken. Yea, even thy dull watery dream shall be more than realized. If it were not so, but thou wert to be overlooked at first and at last, then would I not take their heaven. Yes, I say so, who think I know better than thou canst."[11] Was this the passage that jerked James Russell Lowell out of his boat, rather than the long description of the Concord River's fish species, or Thoreau's other digressions? Certainly it bears a marked resemblance to a passage that Lowell, as editor of the *Atlantic Monthly*, later censored in "Chesuncook": "It [a pine tree] is as immortal as I am, and perchance will go to as high a heaven, there to tower above me still."[12]

It is ironic that Lowell fastened so thoroughly, early and late, on Thoreau's derivativeness in condemning his literary achievements, given his own public suppression of Thoreau's nonanthropocentrism, one of the more striking and original aspects of his work. Here was certainly one area where Thoreau pushed far ahead of his mentor Emerson. Here was a realm where, as he said, he looked toward the West and the wild, while Lowell and most of his civilized readers remained committed to the conventional anthropocentrism espoused on both sides of the Atlantic.

The Bean-Field

Walden represents a searching, sustained attempt to specify a nonanthropocentric ethics. Thoreau repeatedly asserts the intrinsic value of nonhuman nature—whether in trees (201), woodchucks (166), or Walden Pond itself (192–93)—and tries to justify these assertions. But *Walden* also discusses the benefits to *people* of recognizing nature's value and living accordingly.

The chapter "Higher Laws" develops a detailed and sweeping critique of hunting, fishing, and meat eating generally. As in *A Week*, Thoreau's wordplay identifies a key issue.

> No humane being, past the thoughtless age of boyhood, will wantonly murder any creature, which holds its life by the same tenure that he does. The hare in its extremity cries like a child. I warn you, mothers, that my sympathies do not always make the usual phil-*anthropic* distinctions. (212)

The "usual distinctions," of course, are between *human* suffering and the suffering of other sentient beings, which we discount and between ending *human* life and nonhuman life. Here Thoreau equates a true humanity with greater sympathy for all nature's creatures, and with a deep appreciation of their existence. If causing unnecessary suffering or ending a life unnecessarily are prima facie wrong, then we should avoid killing animals, since we arguably get no important benefits from killing them, or at least no benefits that outweigh *their* losses.

The chapter "The Bean-Field" moves beyond a concern to avoid directly killing individual animals, to a concern for preserving animal habitat and the wild landscape generally: in contemporary terms, from an animal rights ethics to a true environmental ethics. Recall that in order to feed himself and earn a little cash, Thoreau planted beans on two and a half acres of Emerson's lot. "This was my curious labor all summer," he writes, "to make this portion of the earth's surface, which had yielded only cinquefoil, blackberries, johnswort, and the like, before, sweet wild fruits and pleasant flowers, produce instead this pulse." As elsewhere in *Walden*, simplification and attentiveness to his experience allow Thoreau to see ethical issues where others might see only questions of economic expediency. For he knows this landscape well, as a locus of beauty and value independent of his own uses. This complicates things.

"What shall I learn of beans or beans of me?" Thoreau continues. For one thing, he learns the farmer's and gardener's common experience of dividing the world up morally, based on its effects on whatever he is trying to grow.

My auxiliaries are the dews and rains which water this dry soil, and what fertility is in the soil itself. . . . My enemies are worms, cool days, and most of all woodchucks. The last have nibbled for me a quarter of an acre clean. But what right had I to oust johnswort and the rest, and break up their ancient herb garden? (155)

The chapter's point becomes clearer when we realize that Thoreau takes this "rights" question seriously—he believes that a woodchuck and a person can each have rights—and that he attempts to answer this question over the course of the chapter.

What justifies appropriating part of the landscape and displacing other intrinsically valuable beings? Perhaps the only convincing answer, once we have fully awakened to the moral issue, is necessity. Thoreau suggests this answer, and the Bible's well-known story of how this necessity came about, when he asks, early on: "But why should I raise them?" and immediately responds: "Only Heaven knows" (155). It is simply our human lot here on Earth. Thoreau must "produce this pulse" to keep his own pulse going. We are also intrinsically valuable beings, who need to eat in order to live. This justifies *some* displacement of nature, which can be minimized by taking only what we need.

For those who feel the force of nature's intrinsic value, this is the most important part of a responsible answer. Take what you need, but *only* what you need. Live simply, so that *nonhuman* others may simply live. The directness of Thoreau's situation—clearing land to plant a crop, trapping out woodchucks he knew personally in order to protect his beans—forced him to confront the issue starkly. By fronting the problem on his own sacred ground, he was more likely to come up with a generous answer. And by attending to his own experience and distinguishing true needs from superfluous wants, he was *able* to answer generously.

"Only Heaven knows" why we must take life in order to live. But if it is natural to do this, it is also natural to put up our hoes sometimes and simply appreciate nature as it is. Working in his little field, Thoreau heard brown thrashers singing in the trees, saw nighthawks circling overhead on sunny afternoons, and disturbed "outlandish"-looking salamanders in their rocky hiding places. "When I paused to lean on my hoe," he writes, "these sounds and sights I heard and saw any where in the row, a part of the inexhaustible entertainment which the country offers" (159–60). This is the moment, when we pause in our own work, when we can appreciate nature's intrinsic value. This is also the moment when we can recognize the higher uses of nature: those of the poet, the painter, the scientist, or any of the others who put aside economic activity for a time in order to know, create, or experience the world in a richer way.

If cultivation leads us to count our yields and value agricultural improvements, *pausing* in our cultivation may lead to a different sort of accounting. "And, by the way," Thoreau asks:

> Who estimates the value of the crop which Nature yields in the still wilder fields unimproved by man? The crop of *English* hay is carefully weighed, the moisture calculated, the silicates and the potash; but in all dells and pond holes in the woods and pastures and swamps grows a rich and various crop only unreaped by man. (157–58)

Who gives wild nature its proper value? The answer is: very few of us. We are mostly too busy about our beans. As we come to recognize nature's value, we will be more likely to protect her. Just as important, we will begin to "reap" wild "crops" that we have hitherto let go to waste, through the methods of appreciation modeled for us in *Walden*.

This suggests a further way in which some human appropriation of nature may be justified. We are the only creatures who can understand and celebrate what we see. Through poetry, art, natural history, and science, we can be nature's storytellers. We can also consciously choose to allow these stories to continue. Even at work in "The Bean-Field," Thoreau continues to note the plants and animals around him, and in other chapters they rightly take center stage. This, he suggests, justifies his own presence at Walden Pond. Rather than justifying the unlimited human appropriation of wild nature by appeal to our superior reason, Thoreau indicates that only such *higher* uses of reason justify its *limited* appropriation. Reason in service to unnecessary consumption is no longer a superior faculty, and justifies nothing.

John Locke, in a famous attempt to justify the institution of private property, felt compelled to argue for the relative unimportance of nature's contribution to human wealth and sustenance.

> I think it will be but a very modest Computation to say, that of the *Products* of the earth useful to the Life of Man, nine-tenths are the

> *effects of labour*: nay, if we will rightly estimate things as they come to our use, and cast up the several Expenses about them, what in them is purely owing to *Nature*, and what to *labour*, we shall find, that in most of them ninety-nine hundredths are wholly to be put on the account of *labour*.[13]

This is hardly a "modest computation," and not just because it casually leaves nature's contribution vague by a factor of ten. But in its reliance on a particularly narrow criterion of use to define value, Locke's statement well reflects standard anthropocentric attitudes in his time and ours. We and our work are all-important.[14]

Thoreau, looking out the door of his shack and across his bean-field on a rainy day, comes to a different conclusion concerning the works of man and nature.

> While I enjoy the friendship of the seasons I trust that nothing can make life a burden to me. The gentle rain which waters my beans and keeps me in the house to-day is not drear and melancholy, but good for me too. Though it prevents my hoeing them, *it is of far more worth than my hoeing*. If it should continue so long as to cause the seeds to rot in the ground and destroy the potatoes in the low lands, it would still be good for the grass on the uplands, and, being good for the grass, it would be good for me. (131, emphasis added)

As our economic lives become more complex and specialized and our surroundings become more managed and humanized, Locke's attitude comes naturally, while Thoreau's recedes. Environmental ethicists may argue for nature's intrinsic value, but the experiential grounding for this belief fades. But when we eat food from our gardens, gather wood for the evening fire on a camping trip, or pick huckleberries, these actions both confirm and symbolize nature's goodness. We then know ourselves as inextricably dependent on nature, regardless of any calculations concerning relative contributions.

From this knowledge should come a belief in the rightness of nature's cycles of work and rest, growth and harvest, Thoreau believes, and happiness and even joy at playing one's part within these cycles. Finally, there should come a feeling of gratitude for the Earth's gifts and a willingness to share them: "We are wont to forget that the sun looks on our cultivated fields and on the prairies and forests without distinction. . . . These beans have results which are not harvested by me. Do they not grow for woodchucks partly? . . . Shall I not rejoice also at the abundance of the weeds whose seeds are the granary of the birds?" (166).

Between Thoreau's view of an intrinsically valuable landscape to be used lovingly and sparingly and a Lockean view of land ownership, with rights but no responsibilities toward the land, there is an unbridgeable gulf. Those holding the former attitude will have little interest in the "improved agriculture" that Thoreau mocks several times in "The Bean-Field" (158, 162); this attitude also leads naturally to efforts to protect parts of the landscape from direct economic uses. Locke's more aggressive, entrepreneurial attitude finds its natural limit in a view of nature solely as economic resource, in which we may modify the landscape any way we see fit so as to maximize yields and profits. This purely economic view has been written across hundreds of millions of monocultural acres of America, from the sugarcane fields of Florida and the cornfields of Illinois to the wheat fields of Kansas and the rice fields of California (not coincidentally, this view is also writing the family farm out of existence in America).

The Good Life and Wild Nature

Why follow Thoreau rather than Locke? I see two possible reasons. First, we might take Thoreau's path because we too love the land and value its creatures. Second, we might follow Thoreau because we believe environmental sensitivity will help *us* lead better lives.

We can divide ethics into two halves: the personal and the social. Thoreau wrote a fair bit about social ethics—our rights and responsibilities toward others—particularly in his antislavery lectures. But *Walden* focuses on personal ethics. There the main ethical question is: What is the good life, and how can a person go about living it? And it is striking how often Thoreau, in discussing the good life, defines human flourishing and excellence in relation to nature.

Some of this is quite basic. The simplest messages in *Walden* are to get outside, use your limbs, and delight in your senses. Run, walk, swim, sweat. Taste the sweetness of the year's first huckleberries and feel the juice dribble down your chin. It feels good to plunge into a pond first thing in the morning and *wake up*; or to float lazily in a boat along its surface, wafted we know not where by the breeze, looking up at the clouds. It is enjoyable to trundle through the snow on a cold winter night, and to warm up by a fire. *Walden* celebrates these simple, sensual experiences in nature (in addition to mining them for literary symbols or knowledge of deeper realities). Of course, "get out of the house" and "eat huckleberries" are not very profound messages. But then, who says ethics should be profound? What we need to know in order to live better lives may indeed be very simple.

At the other end of the spectrum, an enriched experience, the pursuit of knowledge, creative expression, and other intellectual goals are very important in Thoreau's conception of the good life. He draws clear connections between knowing nature, cultivating virtue, and enjoying life. *Walden* and Thoreau's journals contain many examples of vivid, accurate observations and descriptions of nature. These passages show how pursuing knowledge and cultivating the naturalist's virtues—patience, stillness, alertness, physical endurance, keen hearing, precise description, the ability to make fine distinctions—may enrich and intensify experience.[15] They show how access to a varied and partially wild landscape furthers the pursuit of scientific and historical knowledge, and how knowledge of nature furthers creativity and personal expression. After describing the screech owls and great horned owls living near his cabin, accurately and in detail, Thoreau remarks: "I rejoice that there are owls. Let them do the idiotic and maniacal hooting for men." And indeed they do, embodying moods or providing symbols for aspects of human experience that are difficult to convey. Similarly, a playful loon helps him convey the elusive nature of our search for knowledge, while a crumbling sandbank illustrates nature's creativity. Just as nature gives us many new experiences to ponder, so it provides the means to understand them and convey them to others.

Like Emerson's *Nature*—but more practically and with greater emphasis on *wild* nature—*Walden* teaches that nature is our greatest resource. It provides all that humanity needs to flourish, if we will use it wisely. I hasten to add, however, that wise use doesn't mean managing the whole of nature. A *genuine* wise use includes *nonuse* of nature, in places: the preservation of the wild.

These themes of love of nature, pursuit of knowledge, personal expression, and enriched experience all come together in *Walden*'s central chapter: "The Ponds." The plural in the title undoubtedly alludes to Walden's neighbors—Flint's, Goose, and White Ponds—which it also describes.

But the title also refers to the many Waldens that Thoreau experiences and describes for us here (has America produced a greater phenomenologist than Thoreau?). We are given the real pond with a certain depth and location, certain species of fish inhabiting it, particular bird species returning at particular times of the year. And we are given various imaginary ponds in the legends of Indians, settlers, Thoreau's contemporaries, and Thoreau himself. We are given the pond's varied inhabitants, from frogs and loons to fishermen and ice-cutters. But also: the pond as a harmonious whole, each ripple on its surface eventually smoothed out, no matter which unfortunate individual's end it speaks of. We are given the pond in time—personal, historical, mythological—and also a timeless Walden, symbol of nature's beauty, purity, and inexhaustible fecundity. We are shown "The Pond in Winter" (perhaps not accidentally *Walden*'s most abstract, analytical chapter), in "Spring," and indeed in all seasons. The pond as phenomenon (recall the brilliant description of the varied colors of its water) and as thing-in-itself (or as near to this as Thoreau can get; how near is a philosophical puzzle the pond puts to him). The pond as described by the poet, the aesthete, and the scientist; the fisherman, the hunter, and the ice skater; the visitor and the resident; the ascetic, the sensualist, and the home economist.

It is because the pond can be all these things to Thoreau that it is so important to him. If it were simply the scene of his own artistry and had no independent existence, it would have been much less important to him. Social constructionists, please take note! It is his recognition of Walden's independent existence and his sustained efforts to know and appreciate it that set Thoreau apart from the next half-century's flowery "nature fakers," on the one hand, and our own anemic postmodern literati, on the other.

Thoreau's journal recounts again and again his desire for a personal, fulfilling relationship with nature.[16] *Walden* documents his success in attaining it. "I experienced sometimes," he writes, "that the most sweet and tender, the most innocent and encouraging society may be found in any natural object" (131). Such personal, friendly, gentle acquaintance sustains him through his solitary days at the pond. "The poet," he had written earlier, "is that one who speaks civilly to Nature as a second person."[17]

At Walden, this personal affection and acquaintance broadens to include the river, the forests and fields, and the landscape generally. "The Ponds" gives Thoreau's respectful, loving, imaginative yet accurate description of Walden Pond, the second most fully developed character in *Walden*. Despite the many views taken and the variety of inhabitants described, Walden is portrayed as a coherent, harmonious whole, and repeatedly personified. The central moment in the chapter is Thoreau's thrilled assertion of this personality: its goodness, their relationship, and finally his union with it.

> Of all the characters I have known, perhaps Walden wears best, and best preserves its purity. . . . It is perennially young, and I may stand and see a swallow dip apparently to pick an insect from its surface as of yore. It struck me again to-night, as if I had not seen it almost daily for more than twenty years,—Why, here is Walden, the same woodland lake that I discovered so many years ago; where a forest was cut down last winter another is springing up by its shore as lustily as ever; the same thought is welling up to its surface that was then; it is the same liquid joy and happiness to itself and its Maker, ay, and it may be to me. It is the work of a brave man surely, in whom there was no guile! He rounded this water with his hand, deepened and clarified it in his thought, and in his will bequeathed it to Concord. I see by its face that it is visited by the same reflection; and I can almost say, Walden, is it you? (192–93)

He may *almost* use the second person singular to address Walden. Why "almost"? First, because as a naturalist he must love accurately, and a pond is not a unity or a person in the same sense as a human being or a woodchuck. Thoreau, observing the complex interconnections between its individual inhabitants and the creative force "welling up" within it creating these individuals, sees an ecological unity. His personification does justice to this insight, and to the beauty he sees and the affection he feels. Yet insofar as the pond as an entity is less unified or integrated than an individual organism, or less singularly directed in its purposes than a conscious actor, its personification is misleading. If Thoreau wants to love *it,* then he must take this into account. Overly insistent personification manifests either ignorance or a failure to appreciate the pond for what it really is.[18]

Second, it is because as a true lover Thoreau recognizes the power and the elusiveness of the lovingly spoken "you." We may describe a pond or a person in any degree of detail we choose, but the loving "you" moves beyond such descriptions. It is a personal *act.* Speaking this loving "you" is never merely an accurate description of our feelings for the beloved, or this, combined with an accurate description of her various qualities. Rather it involves an affirmation of her value and a taking on of responsibility for her. It is not something to be said lightly. The beauty of the beloved may call forth an effortless affirmation of our love. But to love well takes effort. Perhaps, then, Thoreau also means to say that he will not rest in a facile adoration of the pond and its myriad productions, but will continue to work to know them and publish their glories.

Third, Thoreau hesitates to say "you," because when we love truly, we love the beloved herself and not our own vision of her. The passage is followed and completed by this short poem:

> It is no dream of mine,
> To ornament a line;
> I cannot come nearer to God and Heaven
> Than I live to Walden even.
> I am its stony shore
> And the breeze that passes o'er;
> In the hollow of my hand
> Are its water and its sand,
> And its deepest resort
> Lies high in my thought.

For all their lyricism, this poem and the preceding passage suggest skepticism concerning the extent to which we can truly know the beloved. The surface of the pond is "visited by the same reflection" as the writer; is this Thoreau's own face reflected in the water? He might wonder to what extent his "reflections" on the nature of the pond are in fact projections of his own interests and desires onto it. Thoreau has visited Walden nearly every day since he was a child, but the many stories of his own he now associates with it may prevent him from seeing *it* and appreciating *its* stories. Hesitation here marks an acceptance that our knowledge of the beloved is never complete or perfect, and hence never does her full justice. Unless, of course, we are in love with love, like Agathon in Plato's *Symposium,* and more concerned to cultivate our own romantic feelings than to know and do right by our beloved.[19]

These are the ineliminable dangers of love. They all come down, in one way or another, to putting ourselves above the beloved. The great danger for the lover of *nature* is that he will put his own systems and creations above it. The greater his success—in understanding nature or creating new symbolic worlds which move beyond it—the greater the temptation to do so. In the prose passage above, the imagined "Maker" of the pond, who may be God or a logos within nature, is mirrored in the companion poem by Thoreau himself, the author of *Walden*. Both authors "deepen and clarify" the pond "in thought" and "bequeath it to Concord," making it available to Thoreau's neighbors and readers. This juxtaposition proclaims Thoreau's god-like achievement: Recall *Walden*'s preface, where Thoreau states his intention to "brag lustily" of his accomplishments. Knowledge of nature and nature's representation in a work such as *Walden* are divine—true second creations.

Three facts take the sting out of this presumptuous bragging and the anthropocentrism to which it might lead. First, Thoreau backs it up. He really does know Walden Pond, and he creates a great literary work. Second, as he says elsewhere, he is not bragging for himself but for humanity and to wake his neighbors up. These are possibilities for all of us, which we should actualize and celebrate. Third, and by far the most important, Thoreau believes that the representation of nature may be great *because nature itself is great*. The key words in the poem are:

> It is no dream of mine
> To ornament a line.

Walden Pond is not the creation of his own fancy, but a glorious reality. This is the source of his own greatness, Thoreau says, even as he insists on that greatness.

Thoreau places these two lines at the heart of *Walden*, because we are perpetually forgetting them and taking our own physical artifacts and mental constructions for the whole of reality. In a similar way, the plural in the title "The Ponds" reminds us that we necessarily have two ponds: the pond in the Earth and the pond in the book. Each of these fragments in its turn. The complex ecological system of the pond is imperfectly integrated; has uncertain, shifting, and overlapping boundaries; is the loci for many individual "personalities." The writer, strictly speaking, can never tell us *the* story of the pond, but only stories. New experiences and new experiencers create further stories, adding to the storied character of nature. The trick is to embrace this pluralism while remaining committed to the pursuit of truth and the goodness of nature.

Thoreau's position here is based on two axioms. First, that he does know Walden Pond, although that knowledge is incomplete. Second, that its stories are good ones that should be told and allowed to continue. Thoreau hesitates before saying "you" to Walden. But he does say it. He thus enriches his own life and (he may hope) helps preserve Walden's.

In getting to know Walden, Thoreau delved deeper into himself and swam further out into the great stream of life; articulated inchoate ideals and found his own voice; learned something of natural and human history and his own place within them. Thoreau's whole life—from his never-to-be-forgotten childhood exaltations to his mature artistic, scientific, and philosophical achievements—is thus intimately tied to Walden Pond and its environs. His goodness, such as it is, must be a function of *its* goodness. He went to the pond to pursue self-development and artistic achievement, but when he came to write a book about his experience he titled it *Walden*, not *I, Henry* or *A Portrait of the Artist as a Young Naturalist*. In an environmental virtue ethics, human excellence and nature's excellence are necessarily entwined.

Two Challenges: Gluttony and Tameness

Walden provides an inspiring account of one man living well in nature. It argues that we will be better, happier people if we take the time to know and enjoy nature. The many activities through which we do this will give our lives diversity and interest; performing them will help us develop virtues we might not otherwise develop. In these ways *Walden* suggests the rudiments of an environmental virtue ethics that is noble, challenging, and makes room for the rest of creation.

There are two main challenges to such an environmental ethics. First, there are those popular ideals that define happiness in terms of increased wealth and economic consumption. Modern life, especially modern advertising, provides a variety of such ideals, from the crude to the refined. Here a Thoreauvian response is clear: A satisfactory conception of human well-being extends beyond economic consumption and gross physical pleasure to encompass nobler human activities. If we value such higher activities, we must limit those economic activities that undermine them, whether they do so by taking over our lives or by harming that environment which makes all human endeavor possible.

Thoreau's criticisms of gluttony and acquisitiveness, which I discuss in detail elsewhere, are very much in the ancient virtue ethics tradition.[20] As he puts it, "The ancient philosophers, Chinese, Hindoo, Persian, and Greek, were a class than which none has been poorer in outward riches, none so rich in inward" (14). But these criticisms are also strikingly applicable to modern environmental issues. High levels of consumption deplete resources and generate excessive pollution, harming both wild nature and human beings. Americans' love affair with gas-hogging SUVs (hopefully coming to an end) translates directly into more asthma attacks and lung cancer deaths and more wild lands sacrificed for petroleum extraction. Here as elsewhere, our "vast abdomens" betray us (215).

In Thoreau's view, an excessively economic orientation also warps our understanding of the world, literally cutting us off from reality. The utilitarian "Farmer Flint," criticized later in "The Ponds," cannot see his namesake pond and the many plants and animals inhabiting it—both because he isn't interested and because the pond and its inhabitants are so vividly apparent to him as resources to be used or sold. A wild goose may be a tasty meal in the oven but not an animal with its own interesting habits or history, or a link with distant lands, or a symbol of spring. A wet meadow may be appreciated as the scene of two rich hay crops per year, but not as the site of dozens of plant species different from those in the adjacent uplands or of interesting patterns of ecological succession. Flint does not know these stories, and thus he cannot "interweave the thread of the pond's history with his own" (196). The idea wouldn't even occur to him. Rather, he would change the pond in any way that might prove profitable, wrenching its story abruptly out of past natural and cultural history and ending the stories of "old settlers" who do not fit his selfish economic regime.

The juxtaposition of farmer Flint with naturalist Thoreau suggests a radical choice in how we relate to nature. By focusing on the gross consumptive uses of nature, we miss out on the higher uses to which it can be put. By focusing on the landscape's monetary value, we miss out on the many other values it may exhibit or provide: aesthetic, spiritual, scientific, historical. Of course, Thoreau does not deny such monetary or consumer values, any more than he seeks to avoid economic life itself. The point is to put economics in its proper, subordinate place, in our lives and in the landscape.

Thoreau revisits these themes in his late manuscript *Wild Fruits*, where the marketing of huckleberries is contrasted with an appreciation of their beauty, knowledge of their natural and cultural history, generosity in dividing them up, and gratitude for their abundance.[21] *Wild Fruits* and Thoreau's other late natural history writings work to specify the correct mix between scientific and experiential knowledge, and between knowledge of nature and its appreciation and celebration. They stick up for those experiences and attitudes toward nature that a market-oriented society is in danger of forgetting. Although Thoreau remains as leery of money-love as in *Walden*, in *Wild Fruits* he seems to take a more positive view of appetite and at least some kinds of consumption, especially compared to the discussion in "Higher Laws." Approached rightly, consumption may be an important avenue for knowledge and pleasant experience. Like *Walden*, *Wild Fruits* tries to specify a good economics—healthy and uplifting for us, relatively benign in its effects on nature. Specifying such a proper economy might be the most difficult and important challenge currently facing environmental ethics.

We might call the second main challenge to an environmental virtue ethics the "artificial alternatives" challenge. A skeptic might argue that most if not all of what Thoreau finds in wild nature may also be found in the developed human environment—thus, that we need not preserve or explore wild nature. For example, a modern suburbanite can get his exercise by swimming at a health club or jogging around his neighborhood. He can improve his observational and descriptive abilities by painting still lifes, or studying architecture. Finally, the critic might say, human beings are themselves interesting and diverse, and we should know and celebrate this diversity. Not only can we develop "the naturalist's virtues" without wild nature, but Thoreau and his modern followers may cut themselves off from essential human contact, fail to cultivate the social virtues, and foreclose important avenues for knowledge and happiness.

In answering this challenge, we must first admit that cultivating good personal relationships and appreciating human creativity are indeed essential to our flourishing. We may also admit that any ways we get exercise, uncover diversity, or hone our powers of observation, description, and analysis are better than nothing. Still, failing to know and experience wild nature is a genuine loss, just as a complete insensibility to the history and diversity of human cultures and landscapes would be. The wild is essentially different from the tame. A person who does not experience and understand something of wild nature misses out on much of what this world has to offer, just as a person who never travels, or has friends of one sex only, misses out. But perhaps the wilderness ignoramus loses more than these others, because wild nature is so different from human culture, and because it is the crucible from which culture has emerged. To know nothing of wild nature is thus necessarily to fail to properly contextualize our own lives. As Thoreau puts it, "Our ancestors were savages. The story of Romulus and Remus being suckled by a wolf is not a meaningless fable."[22]

Hasty readers sometimes assert that *Walden* advocates a complete withdrawal from human society or the absolute superiority of nature over culture. But Thoreau's acts of settlement, the volumes of Homer, Plato, and Darwin by his bedside, and his return to the village at the end of his stay at the pond—all point to a different conclusion. Thoreau hopes that nature and culture may complement each other. He believes that the richest human life extracts from each sphere the best of what it offers. "In one direction from my house there was a colony of muskrats in the river meadows," Thoreau writes; "under the grove of elms and buttonwoods in the other horizon was a village of busy men" (167). Both are interesting and have much to teach him. Both deserve to be allowed to flourish. Thoreau's house is in between, nearby, but preserving a necessary distance from both.

What does wild nature specifically have to offer that the human world does not? A larger context in which to put our own lives, or to call them into question. New forms of beauty, mostly unseen and unappreciated by human beings. New stories and new kinds of stories, in which consciousness and individual control play a smaller part. Salutary reminders of our own unimportance (you will not break through the ice or get drenched by an unexpected thunderstorm at the mall). The revitalization of dead words and symbols. A sense of hope when our fellow human beings disappoint us. In *Walden* and in his other writings, Thoreau returns to these points repeatedly.

Just as *Wild Fruits* revisits important economic issues, the posthumously published "Walking" reiterates *Walden*'s claims concerning the need to engage wild nature. "In Wildness is the preservation of the World," Thoreau crows there. "From the forest and wilderness come the tonics and barks which brace mankind." An ethics centered on flourishing and the goodness of life cannot help but seek connection to wild nature, since "life consists with wildness. The most alive is the wildest. Not yet subdued to man, its presence refreshes him." We cannot tame the landscape without taming ourselves, Thoreau believes; a fully developed landscape will inevitably dull our thoughts and dim our hopes. "To preserve wild animals implies generally the creation of a forest for them to dwell in or resort to. So it is with man."[23]

In the end, those who seek to protect wild nature do so as much for their own sakes as for nature's.

> Our village life would stagnate if it were not for the unexplored forests and meadows which surround it. We need the tonic of wildness,—to wade sometimes in marshes where the bitterns and the meadow-hen lurk . . . and the mink crawls with its belly close to the ground. At the same time that we are earnest to explore and learn all things, we require that all things be mysterious and unexplorable, that land and sea be infinitely wild, unsurveyed and unfathomed by us because unfathomable. . . . We need to witness our own limits transgressed, and some life pasturing freely where we never wander. (317–18)

This passage captures the deep paradoxes involved in our attempts to know and experience the wild (can we "witness . . . where we never wander"? study nature without changing it? move beyond our own concepts and categories to understand things-in-themselves?). But crucially, it also asserts that we *can* draw back and limit our effects on the natural world, and that we can know *its* stories, rather than just projecting our own stories onto it.

Some critics of *Walden*—and of modern wilderness preservation efforts—assert that such judgments depend on specifying a single, sharp distinction between wild and civilized landscapes.[24] *Walden* instead develops a nuanced understanding of this ambiguous yet necessary distinction, as in Thoreau's description of his "half-civilized" bean-field (158) or in the repeated juxtaposition of the wild and the tame in the chapter "Sounds." Similarly, critics often present a stark dichotomy: Either we preserve the whole landscape completely with no human modification, or we use it in any way we see fit (the "do you want us all to live in caves?" argument). Thoreau instead suggests a flexible and contextual way of relating to a diversity of landscapes. He argues for fully preserving parts of the remote Maine woods as wilderness. But he also advocates protecting semi-wild areas closer to home—including a greenway along the river, the tops of hills, and the township's most extensive remaining forests—and an important part of his experiment at the pond involves using the land while minimizing his displacement of wild nature. In short, Thoreau's environmental ethics demands both preservation of wild nature and (genuinely) wise use of natural resources. It is eminently practical.

The proper mix of wildness and culture, in an individual or a landscape, is difficult to define. One reason to keep some forests uncut and rivers running free is so that the questions themselves do not disappear, as they have for many human beings and many regions of the Earth. We may be comfortable in our villages, but there may also be an excess of comfort there. We need the physical and intellectual challenges that wild nature sets for us. Nature may speak to us *piano* in individual flowers or birds, nonhuman beings who challenge us to know and appreciate them. Or it may thunder *fortissimo* with displays of power and vastness to overwhelm our understanding and destroy our sense of our own importance. Such experiences may lead to love, wonder, horror, awe, reverence—or to the renewed attempt to understand the order which we believe lies behind this complex world. These challenges to our intelligence and imagination strengthen them. Wild nature has been the source of great human achievements in science, poetry, religion, and philosophy. I share Thoreau's doubts that these highest human activities can thrive in its absence.

I believe Thoreau achieved something extraordinary in the history of ethical philosophy with his environmental ethics. Although there had been many discussions of vegetarianism and animal welfare in the Western ethical tradition, I know of no earlier attempts to set proper limits to the human appropriation of wild nature. Nor do I think the deepest of deep ecologists have bettered Thoreau's account of how to act on the recognition of nature's intrinsic value:

Satisfy necessities, avoid luxuries, and provide for a modest comfort in life.

Find happiness in knowing, experiencing, and being-with nature, rather than in consuming, owning, or transforming it.

Tell nature's stories to celebrate them and to convince others to allow them to continue.

Here is an environmental ethics that forthrightly asserts values and rights within the nonhuman world. This goes beyond a concern for individual animals—radical enough, in Thoreau's time—to a concern for endangered species, for how much of nature's productivity humans have a right to engross, and for preserving the wildness of the overall landscape. These concerns, in turn, are linked to Thoreau's ultimate goals of furthering genuine human flourishing and the flourishing of all life. It is a grand and a good vision, and deserves to prevail.

SIX

ARTICULATING A HUCKLEBERRY COSMOS

Thoreau's Moral Ecology of Knowledge

Laura Dassow Walls

In 1850, still simmering from the outrage of the Mexican War and the failed Revolutions of 1848, Emerson jotted in his journal, "The question of the Times is to each one a practical question of the Conduct of life. How shall I live? Plainly we are incompetent to solve the riddle of the Times. Our geometry cannot span the huge orbits of the prevailing Ideas . . . & reconcile their opposition."[1] His response to the riddle of the Times, published a decade later under the title *The Conduct of Life*, imagined the universe as a bipolar unity, a warring marriage of profound dualisms: Freedom and Fate, Power and Nature. The answer to his question, "How shall I live?," came in properly epic form: Use our intellect, our scientific knowledge of nature's laws, to convert every "jet of chaos which threatens to exterminate us" into "wholesome force." Convert our Fate into our Power.[2] It's a grand and potent answer, but just down the street, his friend Henry Thoreau was working through the same question not among books and papers but among forests and fields, and coming to a very different solution. Under Thoreau's influence Emerson found himself attracted to the "Practical Naturalist," a professional specialist every village should have, right alongside its doctor and its lawyer, whom one could ask, What is this plant? What is it good for? (*JMN*, 11:277–78). Emerson thought it important to localize science, for he had noticed how often "the scientific men of Cambridge & of London" failed to know anything about actual fishes and birds—why, the great Lyell himself proved unable to identify by sight the very shells he described in his *Geology* (*JMN*, 13:261, 8:250). Emerson was amused at "Henry's constant assumption that the science is or should have been complete, & he has just found that they had neglected to describe the seeds, or count the sepals, or mark a variety. The ignorant scoundrels have not been in Concord" (*JMN*, 14:278).

Emerson's affectionate amusement is just condescending enough to register their profound differences. Whereas Emerson is writing about Fate, Thoreau is describing seeds and counting sepals. One day while out walking in the woods, Emerson ran into Henry at Walden Pond, and the two had a little tiff. This time Emerson jotted in his journal,

> My dear Henry,
>   A frog was made to live in a swamp, but a man was not made to live in a swamp. Yours ever,
>   R.
>
>   (*JMN*, 14:204)

But as far as Henry was concerned, a swamp was just the place for a man. He wished he had a swamp for a front yard rather than flowerpots and borders, but since he didn't, he often walked out to visit one. After a day's tramp in Shadbush Meadow, where he gathered several quarts of *Viburnum nudum* berries, he marvels at "the pleasing variety which different bushes offer you, as you wind from one apartment or parterre of the swamp to another. It is a fairy-like garden. You will never see them till you *go* to see them."[3] If you don't see them, that is—if you don't *go* to see them—you haven't really lived. Any "conduct of life" is a pretty poor affair if it doesn't include a few days mucking around in a swamp with the frogs.

In his eulogy for Thoreau, Emerson famously went public with his regret that, "instead of engineering for all America, he was the captain of a huckleberry-party."[4] The man who wrangled with the "huge orbits" of Freedom and Fate, who had written that man was "a stupendous antagonism, a dragging together of the poles of the Universe" (*CW*, 6:12), had limited patience with Thoreau's stubborn antiheroism. But Thoreau might have rejoined that leading a huckleberry party was precisely *how* he was engineering for America. Instead of wrestling with planetary orbits and stupendous antagonisms, Thoreau was moving beyond them to construct not a polar but a hybrid politics, a moral ecology. While Emerson and his fellow architects of modernism were busy trying to reconcile the cosmic oppositions of Mind and Body, Man and Nature, subject and object, Thoreau planted himself just there in the space between them, that no-man's-land opened up by Emerson's grand polarities, to craft an alternative way of life. Thoreau sought to turn essences into events, eternity into history, representation into articulation. Given the riddle of their times, they both sought knowledge as a form of relation, but where Emerson looked for "the *metaphysics*" of botany, the place of reptile and mollusk in a "system" that would place it as an "inevitable step in the path of the Creator" (*CW*, 1:40; *JMN*, 13:261), Thoreau insisted that the important fact was the object's "effect on me." The space described by the relationship of an object to a subject—what he called the point of interest "somewhere *between* me and them (*i.e.* the objects)"—opened the perceptual middle ground that Thoreau spent the 1850s exploring.[5] It was there, after all, that the huckleberries grew. In asking, and in leading others to ask, what is the huckleberry's effect on me?, Thoreau sought not its place in a system but its—and our—role in an ecology. Thoreau was trading cosmic antagonisms for a livable cosmos.

Thoreau's work in bringing the cosmos down to earth is largely hidden because so much of it remained so long in manuscript. In particular, "The Dispersion of Seeds" and "Wild Fruits," the book projects that were to have culminated this thinking, were left unfinished at the time of his premature death, and have been edited and published only in recent years.[6] Thoreau studies are only beginning to incorporate this new material, though the crown jewel of *Walden* has been joined by several of the later natural history essays, now seen as gems in their own right. But the radically experimental *Wild Fruits* asks us not just to make room for more masterworks but to fundamentally rethink the arc of Thoreau's career, to see it not just as *about* ecology, but *as* an ecology—enacting, that is, an ecology of knowledge. That this is fundamentally a *moral* ecology goes back to Thoreau's acceptance of Emerson's question, "How shall I live?," as his own starting point. Moving to Walden Pond on the nonrandom date of 4 July 1845 was his own declaration of independence, giving him

the freedom to live out this question. To be sure, he built his house on
Emerson's land, a gesture that acknowledged their fraternity; the pond
was in fact just exactly that "point of interest . . . *between*" Emerson and
himself. Thoreau's liberation would be found not by breaking Emerson's
orbit but by planting himself at that orbit's focal point, exploring the very
ground Emerson's orbits circled around without touching.

The trajectory of *Wild Fruits* begins, appropriately, at the conclusion
of "Civil Disobedience," when Thoreau imagines a State that would allow
a few of its citizens "to live aloof from it, not meddling with it, nor
embraced by it," who yet lived as good neighbors—who, in effect, had
gone wild. As Thoreau continues, "a State which bore this kind of fruit,
and suffered it to drop off as fast as it ripened," would prepare the way for
a still more glorious State, imagined but unseen—the growth of the wild
seed from the ripened fruit of a true democracy.[7] *Wild Fruits* thus brings
together two deep strands of Thoreau's thought. His concern with "fruits"
began with his earliest writing, when he warned that we must not under-
rate the value of the natural fact, for it will "one day flower out into a
truth. The season will mature and fructify what the understanding had
cultivated."[8] Whereas *Walden* declared the value of the "azad" or "free
man," who, like the ever-green cypress, is liberated from the cycle of birth
and decay by refusing to bear fruit, Thoreau's work following *Walden*
concentrated instead on the seasons and pathways of fruits and seeds,
exploring the obverse of his generative metaphor.[9]

His concern with the "wild" responded to Emerson's suspicion that all
objects in nature are, like the stars, radically "inaccessible" (*CW*, 1:9). In
Nature, Emerson resolves this dilemma by offering both the ecstatic
image of the self as a "transparent eyeball" through which "the currents
of the Universal Being" circulate (*CW*, 1:10), and the quotidian ladder of
ascension from "Commodity," nature's lowest service to man, through
"Beauty" and "Discipline" thence to "Prospects," in which Nature disappears, once again, before the influx of Spirit. Thoreau, by contrast, figures
the inaccessibility of nature as "the wild," as on the slopes of Mt. Ktaadn,
whose sheer titanic and inhuman Otherness leads him to cheer for
"*Contact! Contact!*"[10] Instead of rendering either himself or nature as
transparent carriers of meaning, he wades barefoot in swamps, soaking
up the swamp-water and ingesting the wild berries. Indeed, in "Walking"
he figured the swamp as the "*sanctum sanctorum*" of the wild, "the
strength, the marrow, of nature." The decaying muck of the swamp

becomes the fertilizer that will grow "poets and philosophers for the coming ages" (*E*, 205–6). His image of the wild as mortality, decay, even predation—a "leopard" Mother (*E*, 213)—strops the backside of his celebration of the sportiveness of cows and the strains of the wood-thrush, sharpening it into the keen cimeter-edge of the "fact" that will, the sun glimmering on both its surfaces, divide us through heart and marrow (*W*, 98). "The wild" matters not because it is somewhere Out There, but because it is so keenly In Here, subtending life as the first condition of existence: "In Wildness is the preservation of the world" (*E*, 202). Without Thoreau's Trickster-Mother, Emerson's epic idealism would systematize the world to death.[11]

These two terms—the terror of the sublime that would divide us, soul from body; the comfort of the seasonal cycle that feeds us in soul and body—are yoked in *Wild Fruits* into metaphysical poetry. In a series of interlinked essays arranged by season from early spring's elm seeds to the evergreen fruits of winter, some still rudimentary and some quite developed and polished, Thoreau pursues the little, local, neglected fruits, berries, nuts, and seeds of New England, the overlooked weeds of yard, roadside, forest, and meadow that constitute our daily lived environment. The world-preserving wildness we need crowds in at our doorsteps, ignored and unseen, dismissed as "little things" of no value, neither commercial nor nutritional. The global marketplace that turns nature into commodity has so fully colonized our consciousness that we assign value only to the famous and exotic fruits we import from the tropics— "oranges, lemons, pine-apples, and bananas"—bypassing those in our own fields that would surprise by their beauty and sweetness. But, says Thoreau, "The bitter-sweet of a white-oak acorn which you nibble in a bleak November walk over the tawny earth is more to me than a slice of imported pine-apple" (*WF*, 3). "More," that is, calibrated not on the capitalist scale of value but on his own: "The cost of a thing is the amount of what I will call life which is required to be exchanged for it" (*W*, 31). By this standard, pineapples cost life, whereas white-oak acorns enhance life. One cannot import or export them but only go out to join them in the November air. Both the seasonal and the commercial cycles of production and consumption depend on making things—like seeds and fruits— mobile, but commerce cannot seize the seminal germ, only "the mere bark and rind": "This is what fills the holds of ships, is exported and imported, pays duties, and is finally sold in the shops." What commerce cannot seize is what Thoreau most values, "that pleasure which it yields to him who truly plucks it" (*WF*, 3–5). For pleasure cannot be mobilized, only experienced. White-oak acorns cannot be separated from bleak November days on the tawny earth.

The political stakes, which go back to "Civil Disobedience," are invoked as Thoreau completes the paragraph: "In short, you may buy a servant or slave, but you cannot buy a friend" (*WF*, 5). Where Emerson moved through nature as "commodity," its lowest use, to arrive at its highest use, Thoreau bypasses the ladder of hierarchical use-value altogether. "It is best to avoid the beginnings of evil," he wrote (*W*, 67): The logic of commodification begins by alienating value from being, labor from humanity, and ends by reducing all things natural and human to slavery. The man who began *Walden* with a long essay on "Economy" thus begins *Wild Fruits* by interrupting the circulation of global capital, invoking instead the reciprocity of exchange based on friendship. The logic that divides object from subject, nonhumans from humans, empties the one to make it serve the other; Thoreau counters by filling it back up, bringing the invisible back into view. The transparency that Emerson relies on to mobilize and integrate his system is in Thoreau refused: Everything will be opaque, visible, tangible. This means rewriting "economy" as "ecology."

Hence, huckleberry parties. Thoreau began, and remained, an educator, following Emerson's emphasis on "education" as the "educement" or drawing out of one's being and selfhood by action in the world. In "History," Emerson declared that "the world exists for the education of each man" (*CW*, 2:5); in "The American Scholar," he reminded his audience that the attractions of the world were "the keys which unlock my thoughts and make me acquainted with myself" (*CW*, 1:59). Thoreau, who felt the attractions of the world of nature so much more powerfully than Emerson, literalized his call to "action." Moving to Walden and getting himself jailed for nonpayment of taxes have become his two most iconic actions, but the way in which action educates or "educes" the self is most visible in *Wild Fruits*. Do not think, Thoreau warns, that the fruits of New England "are mean and insignificant while those of some foreign land are noble and memorable. Our own, whatever they may be, are far more important to us than any others can be. They educate us and fit us to live here" (*WF*, 5). Global networks of knowledge and commerce were disabling local knowledge and breaking down the reciprocity by which self and nature educed each other, together. By contrast, a child's "first excursions a-huckleberrying, in which it is introduced into a new world, experiences a new development, though it brings home only a gill of berries in its basket," were, Thoreau judged, of more absolute value than the most profitable pineapple expedition to the West Indies (*WF*, 4). In that sense, huckleberries "are of further importance as introducing children to the fields and woods" (*WF*, 54). Long after Thoreau's death, his students remembered how their teacher led them out of the classroom into Concord's wild landscapes. Thus the ending he chooses for the story of his night in jail should not surprise: "When I was let out the next morning, I proceeded to finish my errand, and, having put on my mended shoe, joined a huckleberry party, who were impatient to put themselves under my conduct; and in half an hour,—for the horse was soon tackled,—was in the midst of a huckleberry field, on one of our highest hills, two miles off; and then the State was nowhere to be seen" (*RP*, 83–84). He himself, he implicitly reminds us, was one of the State's wilder fruits, ripened, released, and busy preparing seed for that "still more perfect and glorious State" to come.

In one of *Wild Fruits*'s finest essays, Thoreau identified himself as a kind of New England wild apple, "wild only like myself, perchance, who belong not to the aboriginal race here, but have strayed into the woods from the cultivated stock" (*WF*, 79). Thoreau's playful autobiography centers on what it means to eat apples "in the wind," that is, outdoors as one comes upon them in all their delightful variety: the Wood Apple, the Blue-jay Apple, the cellar-hole apple, the Truant's Apple (which no boy can resist), the Saunterer's Apple ("you must lose yourself before you can find the way to that"), the Frozen-thawed Apple ("*Malus gelato-soluta*"), and so on (*WF*, 89). When Thoreau insists on eating a wild apple "in the wind" he is less interested in cultivating his Epicurean subjectivity than in educing a new and wholly hybrid entity composed of Thoreau and wild apple and wind and season all together, an entity only possible in the here-and-now experiential or phenomenal moment. This is what he means by wild fruit "educating" us, or living "in season," as he shows when he makes the mistake of biting into one of his favorite apples in his study. What in the woods had been "spirited and racy" tastes indoors "sour enough to set a squirrel's teeth on edge and make a jay scream." He must go back out into the November air to eat it, meet the apple on its own territory: "These apples have hung in the wind and frost and rain till they have absorbed the qualities of the weather or season, and thus are highly *seasoned*, and they *pierce* and *sting* and *permeate* us with their spirit. They must be eaten in *season*, accordingly—that is, out of doors" (*WF*, 85–86). At the end of the book, Thoreau pushes to generalization: "Live in each season as it passes; breathe the air, drink the drink, taste the fruit, and resign yourself to the influences of each" (*WF*, 238).

Thoreau recalls with pleasure his own education by huckleberries: Striking out across the fields with a pail and the whole day before him gave him "a sense of freedom and spirit of adventure . . . and I would not now exchange such an expansion of all my being for all the learning in the world. Liberation and enlargement—such is the fruit which all culture aims to secure" (*WF*, 57). But we have, he fears, fallen on "evil days" in which children are ordered out of the fields. Instead, professional pickers glean them to bring the berries to market, not for pleasure but for profit. "As long as the berries are free to all comers, they are beautiful, though they may be few and small," but bringing them to market strikes one more blow "at a simple and wholesome relation to nature." The market reinstates the divisions Thoreau has been trying to undermine, as the State invades and claims the huckleberry fields: "Such is the constitution of our society that we make a compromise and permit the berries to be degraded—to be enslaved, as it were" (*WF*, 58–59). Culture cannot secure liberation and enlargement by yarding up such fruits into barrels and sending them off to market. The opposite of the wild is the slave.

The essential fragility of wildness is represented by the bloom on certain fruits which cannot be touched without injury. This bloom, the breath of the artist, "is the handle by which imagination grasps it" (*WF*, 157). That "wild" handle by which imagination grasps the world is found, not by mounting Exploring Expeditions to the Far West, but by leading "comparatively cheap and private expeditions" by which we get, say, "the flavor of Gowing's Swamp and of life in New England," and thus by expansion, "the flavor of your life to that extent" (*WF*, 165–66). The theme of a phenomenal "bloom" that can be grasped only by the imagination is played out in *Wild Fruits* along sacramental, Eucharistic dimensions, as when Thoreau envisions man as a kind of higher animal invited to dine with nature for sociality rather than food: "We pluck and eat in remembrance of her. It is a sort of sacrament, a communion—the not forbidden fruits, which no serpent tempts us to eat. Slight and innocent savors which relate us to Nature, make us her guests, and entitle us to her regard and protection" (*WF*, 52). "Autumnal Tints," by contrast, plays out the visual dimension, as Thoreau imagines the reds and yellows of a New England fall as a ripeness intended only for the eye. Here, perception rather than ingestion is the gauge of one's aliveness to the world, but again, the experience, the partaking, depends on putting oneself there bodily. As in a certain season, for instance, standing before a scarlet oak with the sun behind it: "Every such tree become a nucleus of red, as it were, where, with the declining sun, that color grows and glows. It is partly borrowed fire, gathering strength from the sun on its way to your eye. . . . You see a redder tree than exists" (*E*, 254). The lesson here is that "objects are concealed from our view, not so much because they are out of the course of our visual ray as because we do not bring our minds and eyes to bear on them; for there is no power to see in the eye itself, any more than in any other jelly" (*E*, 256). Thoreau's phenomenology of the wild means that perception is a moral test. To register nature's phenom-enal reality means to be present, a participant, voting with one's whole body—to "cast your whole vote," as he said in "Civil Disobedience," "not a strip of paper merely, but your whole influence" (*RP*, 76). Such full and active mental and physical participation means doing more than "feebly" expressing your desire that right should prevail, but asserting your "own freedom" by your "vote" (*RP*, 69–70). How, then, can one live so as to vote with one's whole body, not merely a strip of paper?

The classic modernist move of exiling nature from humanity was effective because it opened up nature as an infinite reservoir of spiritual and material resources and an equally infinite dump for the toxins and by-products of human technologies. In both cases, nature exists by defi-nition as exterior to the human community, "outside" or "out of doors," not part of the dwelling space but its passive setting or backdrop. By set-ting up his own dwelling out of doors, Thoreau exteriorized his own house and interiorized nature, a figure he literalized when he turned his furniture out onto the grass for a housecleaning and admired it "standing amid the pines and hickories" in the sun and wind, blackberry vines run-ning round the legs of his writing table (*W*, 113). In "Walking" he imag-ined the setting sun shining into the hallways of "some ancient and altogether admirable and shining family" that had settled there in the woods, with the pines for gables, sunbeams for furniture, and a lichen for their coat-of-arms (*E*, 218). To live "in season" was, similarly, to turn oneself inside-out-of-doors, to inhabit the planet as if it were home, not outside the home, to walk the woods as if nature were human and humanity were natural. The lesson of "education" was that nature educes the human, and human educes the natural, into something new, a hybrid association that was not just a mosaic but a radically new and integrated whole. Once "outside" and "inside" disappear, so do reservoirs and dumps. Everything must come from somewhere and everything must evacuate to somewhere, here on the middle ground in plain sight: Not even the Amazon or the Arctic or the oceans are any longer "outside."[12]

The logic of this hybrid politics of nature is symmetrical with that of "Civil Disobedience," in which no nameless, faceless reservoir of labor exists which one may draw on endlessly, or dump on endlessly; all relations must be duly accounted for, and only reciprocal exchanges will balance the books. As Thoreau put it in his key statement, even if he does not devote his life to righting the world's injustices, he must withdraw from them his practical support: "If I devote myself to other pursuits and contemplations, I must first see, at least, that I do not pursue them sitting upon another man's shoulders. I must get off him first that he may pursue his contemplations too" (*RP*, 71). Philip Cafaro has observed that Thoreau here abdicates part of his responsibility—"morality cannot replace politics"—but at the same time, Thoreau's inability to see "a life-affirming political role, either for himself or others," points to a polity that is "out of joint. It suggests a lack of fulfilling roles for conscientious citizens within the existing political framework."[13] This restates Thoreau's dissatisfaction at the end of "Civil Disobedience," which reflects a State unable to incorporate, or even permit, those salvific "wild fruits." Thoreau sees a polity that is out of joint because, by excluding nature, it excludes that ground on which citizens might act.

The goal of *Wild Fruits* was to imagine an alternative polity, utopian insofar as it did not yet exist, but entirely realistic in that it operated not outside of or exterior to global capitalism (with its inescapable reach) but inside it, turning it, too, inside-out-of-doors. All the techniques Thoreau advances in *Wild Fruits* are perfectly ordinary and would not raise a ripple, though they might at first raise a few eyebrows: Take a walk; bring the kids; invite the neighbors. Share the work; share the pleasures, too. What kind of community will bring the world of *Wild Fruits* into being? What kind of community will those wild fruits in turn sustain? These were Thoreau's post-*Walden* questions. Yet the world that could make wild fruits possible is crumbling even as he writes. How few are attracted to nature! "How little appreciation of the beauty of the landscape there is among us! We have to be told that the Greeks called the world Κοσμος, Beauty—or Order, but we do not see clearly why they did so, and we esteem it at best only a curious philological fact" (*E*, 217).

Thoreau is verging here on what Bruno Latour has called "political ecology," a way to compose a common world "according to due process" rather than one "elaborated without rules," or "the right way to compose a common world, the kind of world the Greeks called a *cosmos*."[14] That two philosophers roughly 150 years apart would converge on the Greek word "cosmos" can be explained, at least in Thoreau's case, by recalling the immense popularity of Alexander von Humboldt, the German scientist who reintroduced the word into contemporary languages in his blockbuster best seller, *Cosmos*, which began appearing in 1845 and which both Emerson and Thoreau read avidly. Humboldt had chosen his title with great care, deliberately reviving the archaic Greek word as a calculated intervention in the day's increasingly polarized discourse. As he wrote, "*Cosmos*" should remind "the inhabitant of the earth" to look toward a much wider horizon: "the assemblage of all things, with which space is filled, from the remotest nebulæ to the climatic distribution of those delicate tissues of vegetable matter which spread a variegated covering over the surface of our rocks."[15] In the first two, and most popular, volumes, Humboldt outlined the two dimensions of this "assemblage": Volume 1 took up the self-subsisting physical universe apart from the human mind, from outermost space to the formation of the earth and the evolution of all life thereon, up to and including human beings. Volume 2 started at the threshold of mind to trace the development of the very idea of "Cosmos" through the millennia, in literature, painting, landscape design, sciences, and technology, through the global spread of commerce and the exchange of languages and ideas.

Humboldt's lifelong argument was that humans participate in the Cosmos both materially and intellectually: As he asserted in a later volume, "Man elaborates within himself the materials presented to him by the senses, and the products of this spiritual labor belong as essentially to the domain of the cosmos as do the phenomena of the external world."[16] The Greek word, he points out, meant both the "order of the world, and adornment of this universal order"—or in Thoreau's terms, "Beauty" and "Order."[17] Humboldt was no idealist. For him, nature, that "assemblage of all things," exists as an ordered universe quite apart from the human mind. But the *Cosmos*, the articulation of the universe as a beautiful and ordered whole, is a human achievement, and as such is as much its constituent as stars and lichens. All knowledge, he insisted, comes to us only through the active human mind, meaning that all knowledge (including scientific) lay not in the separation but the convergence of object and subject. Humboldt's Cosmos was the ultimate expression of that convergence, a vision of the entire known universe as the dynamic interaction of matter and mind, each "drawing out" or educing the other in a historical process as old as time, as wide as the stars, and as deep as human thought.

Thoreau's careful reading of Humboldt helped him draw out his own thoughts and, in particular, helped him articulate the philosophy he needed as the counterweight to Emerson's epic polarities. Humboldt was the progenitor of ecological thinking, and the more Humboldtian Thoreau becomes, the more ecological he looks. Perhaps the most important part of this genealogy is the light it sheds on Thoreau's blend of ecology and morality. For Humboldt, ecological thinking led not just to the science of ecology (which it did through his followers Charles Darwin and Ernst Haeckel), nor even just to the ecology of knowledge, in which human thoughts, words, arts, and technologies all become constituents of the Cosmos as an overarching ecological system. He also defined science, and knowledge more generally, within a large moral ecology: For Humboldt, nature was the realm of freedom, and the course of history, and hence of the Cosmos, was progressive because nature could be understood only by the free and cooperative development of all human faculties. This connected his German conviction in the importance of *Bildung*, individual self-cultivation, to the development of the progressive State. Humboldt measured civilizations not by the grandeur of their buildings or the greatness of their arts or technologies, but by the degree to which they allowed liberty to each human being.

This connects Humboldt's vision of "Cosmos" with the "Cosmopolitanism" he imbibed from Immanuel Kant, whose proposal for world peace maintained that just as no human being can be used as a means for another's end, so can no nation be used by another to its own ends; in the community of all nations on earth, a violation of law and right in any one place would be felt in all others.[18] When Humboldt sought to extend Kant's planetary physical geography to the universe at large, it was likely Kant's phrase that sent him back to its Greek root, "cosmos." Today, the debate over cosmopolitanism hinges on whether it places the whole world under a universal ethic of Western liberal humanism, or whether, instead of "universality," it can lead toward "a future critical and dialogic cosmopolitanism," or "'diversality.'"[19] Humboldt came through his wanderings across the Americas and Eurasia with an Enlightenment urbanity that refused to measure non-Western societies by the standards of Europe, but instead used the alternative worlds he experienced to criticize smug European imperial certainties—most especially the certainty that gave European men the power to conquer and destroy whatever and whoever got in their way. No country caused Humboldt greater grief than the United States, whose republican ideals embodied his own, carried forward from the French Revolution, but whose political economy betrayed those ideals into the hands of an expansionist slave-based populist democracy.[20]

Thus Humboldt's science always had a political edge and a moral dimension. He grounded his work in actual landscapes because for him the reality that mattered was outdoors, living and breathing, rooted and streaming through water, wind, and soil. Nature to him was that "assemblage," a whole not designed by a governing Intelligence but self-organized from below. Meaning emerges and grows as the mind traces the ramifying connections of each to each, learning to perceive and enact the whole they compose. Humboldt's science was thus radically historicist in approach (a legacy he bequeathed to his follower Charles Darwin), and his sense of history echoed that of his brother, Wilhelm von Humboldt, the foundational philosopher of history who wrote that the historian must not only investigate events with exacting impartiality but must also connect those events with the intuitive understanding of the poet. In justifying his method, Wilhelm reached in turn for a parallel from his brother's natural science: "Even a simple depiction of nature cannot be merely an enumeration and depiction of parts or the measuring of sides and angles; there is also the breath of life in the whole and an inner character which speaks through it which can be neither measured nor merely described."[21] In the work of both the Brothers Humboldt, natural history was cognate with human history, an unfolding of natural laws which yet could never be reduced to those laws. As nature unfolds—Darwin would say evolves—it does so as a contingent historical process, a sequence of causal events too full of accident and variation to be predicted. To study nature, one must turn oneself out-of-doors, open to the empirical surprises of the local. In this way, the Cosmos exists nowhere else but in the local, those myriad small constituent details, and the local becomes meaningful exactly insofar as we see in it another avatar of the Cosmos, here, now, heaven under our feet.

Thoreau's *Walden* was his passage to Humboldt's Cosmos, not a "microcosm" into which all nature folded up into a neatly packaged One, but more an exercise in navigation, "a good port and a good foundation" from which to mount an Exploring Expedition to the Celestial Empire. In his chapter on cranberries in *Wild Fruits*, Thoreau goes even farther, wading out into the swamp yet again with his pockets full of wild cranberries and his head full of wild thoughts.

> I see that not all is garden and cultivated field and copse, that there are square rods in Middlesex County as purely primitive and wild as they were a thousand years ago . . . little oases of wildness in the desert of our civilization, wild as a square rod on the moon, supposing it to be uninhabited. I believe almost in the personality of such planetary matter, feel something akin to reverence for it, can even worship it as terrene, titanic matter extant in my day. . . . How happens it that we reverence the stones which fall from another planet, and not the stones which belong to this—another globe, not this—heaven, and not earth? Are not the stones in Hodge's wall as good as the ærolite at Mecca? Is not our broad backdoor stone as good as any corner-stone in heaven? (*WF*, 168)

Here, he literalizes his call for "*Contact!*" as immersion in a cranberry bog, "my bare feet in the cold water beneath," filling his pockets with berries rejected by farmers. Wading into the heart of Middlesex County, Thoreau finds himself simultaneously at the heart of "planetary matter," the earth literally as star-stuff, right down to the stones in Hodge's wall and the backdoor landing. The near does not conduct to the far, it *is* the far, and the earth is scored with such transepts. Even the cars on the railroad tracks across from his Walden house move off "with planetary motion" (*W*, 116). There is no "Cosmos" out there, somewhere else: Thoreau, like Humboldt, places the Cosmos at our doorsteps, turns us inside-out-of-orbit so we find we are walking on aerolites. Thoreau scoffs at the botanists who send one westward for wild berries, "as if there were primarily and essentially more wildness in a western acre than an eastern one!" (*WF*, 169). Thoreau's life project was, as he put it, to "sail the unexplored sea of Concord," where "many a dell and swamp and wooded hill is my Ceram and Amboyna" (*WF*, 3).[22] The narrative of his expedition to Concord's own Spice Islands would show his neighbors the extent of their own cosmic relations.

Thoreau's laboratory for building this cosmic relationalism was his journal, which is filled through the 1850s with passages like this one, observing the particular date on which particular plants are found to bloom in a particular year:

> July 25 [1853]. Dodder, probably the 21st. Blue-curls. Burdock, proba-
> bly yesterday. . . . *Cerasus Virginiana*,—choke-cherry—just ripe. . . .
> *Cynoglossum Morisoni*, beggar's lice, roadside between Sam Barrett's
> mill and the next house east, in flower and fruiting probably ten days.
> (*J*, 5:333)

The journal is the bloodstream of his life in nature; moments like these are the oxygen-carrying cells that pump life and energy through the entire circulatory system. Humboldt asserted that "individuality of observation can alone lead to a truthful representation of nature."[23] Observations like Thoreau's, gathered and interlaced, start his cosmos aglow like the sun through the scarlet oak leaves.

As the details and the density of connections build, a deep qualitative shift takes place. Thoreau collated dates into massive phenological charts, and *Wild Fruits* was the next step, as tens of thousands of such data points accreted and fused into patterns, a kind of architecture of the middle landscape of Concord, a cartography of those unexplored seas. In this years-long longitudinal survey, Thoreau became increasingly sensitive to differences that he had before ignored; his nose and palate registered ever more subtle distinctions that struck him ever more forcefully. His allies in this painstaking survey were the books and instruments of science that helped him make such fine discriminations—the carefully keyed and collated plant species, the tree-ring counts, the temperature records, and stream depth measurements. Slowly, incrementally, gathering force and scope over the 1850s, the unexplored, unknown wild heart of Concord grew from vacancy into reality. Thoreau accomplished this not by trying to arrange language as a "representation" of observed nature, but by gradually filling language to capacity with the concrete until, supercharged, every material reference triggered the plenitude of being.[24]

This was Thoreau's method and goal. His enemy was not artifice, for what is more artificial than a plant press, a botany text, or a pencil?

His enemy was obtuseness. His townsmen's insensitivity, their indifference, was the single greatest threat to the reality of the wild nature Thoreau cared about so passionately. His weapon against their obtuseness was the poetry inscribed by this textual meiosis, which, like Shelley's azure wind of the spring, drove the seeds and buds of the real to feed like flocks in the air of the human imagination. First, through huckleberry parties; second, through *Wild Fruits*, where the nature that seemed so unreal and inexistent to Thoreau's townsfolk is made very real by Thoreau's ability to *articulate* it: to sketch or link up the hitherto invisible complex of natural, moral, and economic connections; to bespeak that complex of linkages into reality through language. Thoreau's goal was not to represent nature, but to articulate nature.

The paradox of articulation hinges on the book itself. Despite the insinuations of the title, there are no wild fruits in *Wild Fruits*. The reader holds not berries but cardboard and inked paper. Thus the volume that insists so emphatically on embodiment insists equally emphatically on disembodiment. However, what is lost in materiality is gained in portability: There are a whole year's worth of wild fruits in Thoreau's book, an annual harvest that can be held in one hand, and that can, unlike the fruits themselves with their delicate bloom, withstand packaging, transport, and rough handling. His book is also a gain in amplification. Only a few students and neighbors could share his Concord berries; the whole world can share *Wild Fruits*. Thus, while along one dimension the book is immersed in physical culture, Humboldt's "aggregate of all things" from elm seeds to aerolites, on another dimension it is equally engaged with the physicality of language and the agencies of words. When Humboldt wrote his volume on the "idea" of Nature, he meant not a single Platonic essence but a historical and many-sided gathering from innumerable cultures across the planet and the millennia. Emerson wrote that words are a form of action, and Thoreau's words are articulations rather than representations because he wishes them not to reflect a picture of his cosmos, but to do active work in the Cosmos. The words he records become vital to him as a form of consciousness embodied, and words for natural facts trace, in their etymology, a history of human consciousness of nature: a history of the composition of the Cosmos.

For example, one of the year's first fruits is the sweet flag, which Thoreau turns aside his boat to pick.

> As early as the fourteenth of May, such as frequent the riverside pluck
> and eat the inner leaf of the sweet flag and detect small critchicrotches,
> which are the green fruit and flower buds. The old herbalist Gerarde
> thus describes them: "The flower is a long thing resembling the cat-
> tails which grow on hazel; it is about the thickness of an ordinary reed,
> some inch and a half long, of a greenish yellow color, curiously check-
> ered, as if it were wrought with a needle with green and yellow silk
> intermixt." (*WF*, 7)

Thoreau relates how children especially love to go "a-flagging" in the
spring, as much as the muskrats, and so "we take our first course at the
same table with [the muskrat]. . . . He is so much like us; we are so much
like him" (*WF*, 8). Children begin with a muskrat's consciousness of
nature, but Thoreau's quotation from the herbalist Gerarde moves us
from nature into culture, evoking the history of knowledge as well as the
interlaced checkering of fine silk needlework. As Thoreau continues, he
expands into Gerarde's description of the Tartar's use of sweet flag tea,
the Cree's name for the plant—"*watchuske-mitsu-in,* or 'that which the
muskrat eats'"—and other Native American uses for the root infusion.
Thoreau's paragraphs thus interlink, into a single word, children's consciousness, antiquarian herbalists, women's needlework, contemporary
natural knowledge, Indian ethnobotany, and an afternoon's excursion,
making word into world. To carry "critchicrotches" into adulthood is to
know a more sweet world.[25]

   In writing, the process that threads experiences through language,
the physical interface of the written word partakes of some of the qualities of both mind and matter. Thoreau's scientific field notes of plant
bloomings and other natural phenomena were mediated as little as
possible, coming as close to the ground as the pen of the scientific illus-
trator who uses a nib to map the object's topography. Here Thoreau
called for another kind of space between, a pause or hesitation to give
time for the fact to come to flower: "But this habit of close observation—
In Humboldt—Darwin & others. Is it to be kept up long, this science,"
he asks himself. The answer is the poet's delay: "Do not tread on the
heels of your experience[.] Be impressed without making a minute
of it. Poetry puts an interval between the impression & the expression—
waits till the seed germinates naturally" (*PJ*, 3:331). This reflective interval opens up space to reflect, and to hear multiple voices, multiple
languages.

One was, to be sure, the language of science, which Thoreau never took for granted: He was ever alive to the way a scientific term might reveal an overlooked fact, like the rush he had passed for twenty years but never quite seen until he had the scientific name for it. "With the knowledge of the name comes a distincter recognition and knowledge of the thing. That shore is now more describable, and poetic even" (*J*, 11:137). As he added elsewhere after a similar moment of illumination, "Science suggests the value of mutual intelligence" (*PJ*, 5:444). But other languages were also important. Thoreau relished the medieval herbalist Gerarde because his plants "are green and colored and fragrant," their effluence intact, yielding "a man's knowledge added to a child's delight" (*J*, 8:29–30). He honored his friend, the Canadian wood-chopper Alex Therien, "cousin to the pine and the rock," for his flashes of true originality (*W*, 146–47). Or, most original of all, he celebrated the languages of Indians, with their "more practical and vital science." How much more "conversant" are their languages with wild animal or plant, as if their knowledge, instead of being dry and arranged like our science, were still in "conversation" with its object, proliferating with multiple names for "moose, or birch bark, and the like! . . . It was a new light when my guide gave me Indian names for things for which I had only scientific ones before. In proportion as I understood the language, I saw them from a new point of view" (*J*, 10:294–95).

Wilhelm von Humboldt, who in addition to philosophizing about history was a pioneering linguist, had argued that the "mutual interdependence of thought and word" was so great that clearly the various human languages "are not so much the means to represent truth once established but rather means to discover truth previously unknown." The differences between languages were not differences of "sounds and signs but ultimately of interpretations of the world."[26] Something like this notion—that languages are a means to discover truth and that each language reveals a different facet of truth—lies behind Thoreau's fascination with multiple languages, and in particular the great weight he put on Indian languages in his late natural history writings, composed at a time when he was filling eleven large notebooks with annotations about Indian words and customs. Thus *Wild Fruits* is filled with traces of Indian knowledge systems, as Thoreau draws together their words for wild fruits and, with their words, their world, their closeness to the wild that seems to recede westward as Europeans advance from the east. Indian words become the supplement and corrective to our own—as, for example, when he urges us to drop "the mean name of 'strawberry,' " assigned because the British spread straw under their garden kinds: "Better call it by the Indian name of heart-berry, for it is indeed a crimson heart which we eat at the beginning of summer to make us brave for all the rest of the year, as Nature is" (*WF*, 17). By moving from language to language—the scientist's, the medieval herbalist's, the woodsman's, the poet's, the Indian's—Thoreau multiplies subjectivities, expands his experience to include multiple new points of view, moving ever closer to that "effluence" that is the true essence of the whole human experience of nature. "Truth" is multiple, is approached fact by fact, but also word by word, language by language.

This is why Thoreau dedicates so much of *Wild Fruits* to calling up lost words and detailing disputed etymologies. When he invokes words from lost cultures, he is reminding us that to recall a vanished language is to glimpse a lost world: "Father Rasles, who was making a *Dictionary of the Abenaki Language* in 1691, says that their word for blueberries was: fresh, *Satar*; dry, *Sakisatar*—and the words in their name for July meant 'when the blueberries are ripe.' This shows how important they were to them" (*WF*, 48). Thoreau's digression into Abenaki words seems little more than an exercise in indigenous orientalism until one realizes his point: Words evoke a world, but here, that world has been destroyed. To gloss the words "*Satar*" and "*Sakisatar*" is to demonstrate that a linguistic world, an entire living cultural/natural environment, has vanished. The shadow side of this logic haunts Thoreau's text, which is so worried about the onset of the "evil days": To lose the words that articulate nature is to disarticulate, to unmake, to break our lived connection with our natural environment. Without words for sweet flags or blueberries, or for willows, oaks, pines, and prairie grasses, we have no way to see the "little things" that surround us—and remember, the Cosmos is *all* little things. *Wild Fruits* is thick with technical and antiquarian and Indian names because words are the key to the project of education, of educing self and nature together into an articulation, a gathering that fuses into a Cosmos. To lose the multiple languages of natural history is to lose nature, to dismember a culture that values nature; to kill words, to kill cultures, is to put out the eyes of the Cosmos.[27]

The shadow side of Alexander von Humboldt's writing, too, is the insight that so many languages have been lost during the growth of what he called "the contemplation of the Cosmos," the mind's ability to perceive the complex weave that threads all the local places, all the local names, all the points on all the maps, together into Cosmos. The lost word he excavated and revived, "Cosmos," was the culmination of his life's attempt to bespeak that concept into the consciousness of the nineteenth century, to replace blindness with insight. Thus Thoreau's resurrection of Abenaki words points directly back to Humboldt, who was one of the first to celebrate, and to struggle to preserve, the multitude of Native American languages the European invaders were encountering, and silencing, in the New World.[28] He forwarded his linguistic and ethnographic collections to his brother Wilhelm, who went so far as to suggest that the key to understanding language itself might lie in understanding the languages of Native North Americans.[29] Humboldt directs his keenest fury at the wanton destruction of cultures by the Spanish conquistadores, both in burning entire libraries of hieroglyphic paintings—and with them the historical records of millennia of human development—and in attempting to stamp out the remaining native languages that had survived the holocaust of first contact. But why should the loss of an isolated culture, a minor language, a single word like *Sakisatar*, matter? A hyperbole from Earl Shorris is suggestive.

> It is not merely a writer's conceit to think that the human world is made of words and to remember that no two words in all the world's languages are alike. Of all the arts and sciences made by man, none equals a language, for only a language in its living entirety can describe a unique and irreplaceable world. I saw this once, in the forest of southern Mexico, when a butterfly settled beside me. The color of it was a blue unlike any I had ever seen, hue and intensity beyond naming, a test for the possibilities of metaphor. In the distance lay the ruined Maya city of Palenque, where the glyphs that speak of the reign of the great lord Pacal are carved in stone. The glyphs can be deciphered now. Perhaps. Only perhaps, for no one knows what words were spoken, what sounds were made when Pacal the Conqueror reigned. . . .
>
> There are nine different words in Maya for the color blue in the comprehensive Porrua Spanish-Maya Dictionary, but just three Spanish translations, leaving six butterflies that can be seen only by the Maya, proving beyond doubt that when a language dies six butterflies disappear from the consciousness of the earth.[30]

Today, Humboldt's word "Cosmos" has been deflated to its lesser mean-ing: the stars beyond us, the universe apart from the world, as if when we turn our telescopes to the stars we could put the earth behind us. And when we turn our technologies to earthly nature, we still would turn our backs to the role of the mind and the agency of language, as if we could put our humanity behind us as well. This is not the path to a moral ecol-ogy of knowledge. As Thoreau asked, "Who placed us with eyes between a microscopic and a telescopic world?" (*PJ*, 8:13). For after all, "Science suggests the value of mutual intelligence," a linking of worlds through the mixing of languages. A lifetime spent in the study of nature taught Humboldt, and then Thoreau, that there could be no true progress until the reciprocal poles of the Cosmos—freedom and fate, nature and cul-ture, inductive reason and imaginative vision, the sciences and the arts— were conceived together, not as bipolar antagonisms, but as an interlaced whole, proving beyond a doubt that when this concept dies, the Cosmos disappears from the consciousness of the earth.

SEVEN

THE VALUE OF BEING

Thoreau on Appreciating the Beauty of the World

Rick Anthony Furtak

What is the relation between a bird and the ear that appreciates its melody, to whom, perchance, it is more charming and significant than to any else? Certainly they are intimately related, and the one was made for the other. It is a natural fact.

—Henry David Thoreau, *Journal*, 2/20/57

According to a common philosophical bias, the material world is devoid of value: Such axiological qualities as the beauty of a bird's song must lie only in the eye (or the ear) of the beholder. On this view, the color and scent of autumn leaves, the radiance of the sun, and the soothing voice of a friend, are alike false properties that do not actually reside in objective reality. If the world of appearance were stripped of its illusory tints, it would be "a dull affair, soundless, scentless, colorless: merely the hurrying of material, endlessly, meaninglessly."[1] No one philosopher or school of thought holds sole responsibility for this position, which has been represented in variations from the Greek atomists through the logical positivists. It generally arises from the desire to separate the observed properties that truly belong to objective reality from those that depend on peculiarities of the observer's constitution. This, in principle, would enable us to arrive at a description of the world that is free of all that is relative to our own experience. The "absolute conception of reality," as it has been called,[2] would be purged of all that is "arbitrary and individual" or otherwise subjective.[3] The charming significance of a bird's song can hardly be described without reference to the sensory responses of a particular creature: namely, the appreciative perceiver who is moved when he or she hears the bird. It would therefore have to be classified as illusory, so long as we assume that the vantage point of any particular sentient being must be transcended in order to arrive at "an undistorted view of the world as it really is."[4] This assumption leads John Stuart Mill, for instance, to characterize poetry as a description of "things as they appear, not as they *are*," which portrays them "not in their bare and natural lineaments" but in the "exaggerated colors" that appear to the observer whose imagination and emotions are excited by what he or she sees. Presumably, these colors are "not in the object itself," as it would be described by a naturalist.[5] Thoreau, however, had difficulty maintaining this distinction.

> I have a commonplace book for facts and another for poetry—but I find it difficult always to preserve the vague distinction which I had in my mind—for the most interesting & beautiful facts are so much the more poetry and that is their success. . . . I see that if my facts were sufficiently vital & significant . . . I should need but one book of poetry to contain them all. (*Journal*, 2/18/52)[6]

Elsewhere in his journal, Thoreau reports that his goal is to "state facts" in such a way that "they shall be significant," rather than allowing himself to be blind to "the significance of phenomena" (*Journal*, 11/9/51, 8/5/51). Those facts he records should not be "dry" and "stated barely," but "warm, moist, incarnated," and charged with meaning: "A man has not seen a thing who has not felt it" (*Journal*, 2/23/60). Clearly, he does not accept that whatever we register through our aesthetic and emotional responses ought to be viewed as unreal. In fact, Thoreau would argue that the person who is seldom moved by the beauty of things is the one with an inadequate conception of reality, since it is the neutral observer who is less well aware of the world as it is. When he states that the intimate relation between the bird's melody and the appreciative listener is a "natural fact," Thoreau is making a polemical claim. Poetic and naturalistic accounts of reality need not be at odds with one another. If we assume that they are, then we are guilty of either a philosophical error or, perhaps, a perceptual failure.

The philosophical error would be to believe that a list of insignificant facts might give us the whole truth about being; the perceptual failure

would be to lose touch with the significance of phenomena due to a defi-
ciency in our own mode of observation. Rather than imposing a sharp
division between facts and values, Thoreau urges his reader not to "under-
rate the value of a fact," since each carefully recorded fact may eventually
"flower in a truth." Later in the same essay, he writes that the "true man
of science" will "know nature better" by virtue of having disciplined and
refined his way of seeing: One "must look a long time" in order to see.[7]
Here Thoreau outlines an epistemological task that will occupy him for
the rest of his life, namely, to develop a method of attending to objects so
that they will be experienced as elements of a meaningful world. One of
Thoreau's most distinctive contributions to philosophy is "his discerning
naturalist's eye, informed by a scientific attitude yet committed to an
enchanted vision of nature."[8] He writes in *Walden* that each of us faces
the task of making his life, "even in its details, worthy of the contemplation of his highest hour," keeping in mind that "we are enabled to apprehend at all what is sublime and noble only by the perpetual instilling and
drenching of the reality which surrounds us."[9] The world is rich with
value that is not of our making, and "whatever we have perceived to be in
the slightest degree beautiful is of infinitely more value to us than what
we have only as yet discovered to be useful and to serve our purpose."[10]
For Thoreau, the most reliable observer is one who can "see things as they
are, grand and beautiful" (*Journal*, 1/7/57)—in other words, the beauty
and grandeur of the world really *are* there to be seen, even if we are not
always capable of seeing them. We can easily fail to perceive the value
of being if we do not approach the world with the appropriate kind of
emotional comportment. It is all-important, then, to cultivate our perceptual capacities—and a good part of Thoreau's work, from first to last,
is dedicated to this endeavor. He attempts to elaborate a vision of reality
as significant, and to identify the subjective conditions that enable us to
become aware of this significance.

If *Walden* is an "account of transformed understanding," as Stanley
Cavell points out, then "every word in it" might qualify as philosophical.[11] However, it is difficult to locate Thoreau's project within any one
area of philosophy. When he says that "the perception of beauty is a moral
test" (*Journal*, 6/21/52), he places an ethical imperative in the context of
aesthetic experience. Yet the reason why aesthetic perception carries such
weight is that our conception of reality will be inadequate if we are blind
to the world's beauty: So it is for ontological and epistemological reasons

that we have a moral obligation to develop our aesthetic sensitivity. Moreover, one could justifiably claim that the "central task" of Thoreau's philosophy is to articulate a "religious attitude" in which all of existence is regarded with wonder, reverence, and awe.[12] This "piety toward the actual," as John Dewey calls it, is an attitude toward phenomena that would allow us to experience "moments of intense emotional appreciation" in which the beauty of the universe is revealed.[13] "How sweet is the perception of a new natural fact!" Thoreau exclaims. It suggests "what worlds remain to be unveiled" and reminds us that the constitution or disclosure of reality depends partly on us. "When the phenomenon was not observed—It was not—at all" (*Journal*, 4/19/52). Such a passage indicates that Thoreau has anticipated some key insights of the phenomenological movement. He recognizes that the world is "known only insofar as our mental faculties allow," as Tauber points out.[14] Although the interdependence of subject and object has been noted by many philosophers since Kant, Thoreau is especially mindful of how the content of experience depends on the unique character of the individual's mind, defined by its own mode of vision. Because different "intentions of the eye and of the mind" are required to attend to different aspects of reality, it is useless to speak of "significant facts" without explaining the habit of attention that makes it possible for a person to perceive them (*Journal*, 9/8/58, 3/28/57). The world appears differently to us insofar as we approach it with differing orientations, since our perception is influenced by our beliefs about the qualitative nature of what we are perceiving. Our ability to experience things as meaningful, then, is predicated on encountering the world "as we best imagine it," with eyes that can find profound significance in the midst of everyday reality.[15] Self-discipline and purification are required in order to develop this kind of receptivity; according to Thoreau, it may also be necessary to bring simplicity and repose into one's life.

"We need pray for no higher heaven than the pure senses can furnish," Thoreau writes, suggesting that we can realize the sacred value of being through a discipline of our perceptual capacities.[16] Reality and value, knowledge and conduct, do not fall into separate domains of inquiry for Thoreau any more than they do for Plotinus. Even an essay on autumn colors must incorporate a theory of perception, for it "requires a particular alertness, *if not devotion* to these phenomena," in order for us to appreciate their distinctive beauty.[17] Because any change in our way of experiencing things will bring about a transformation in our understanding and an alteration in the quality of our world, the task of learning to see has an importance that cannot be exaggerated. Taking up residence at Walden, Thoreau claims, was an expression of his "wish to meet the facts," that is, "the phenomena or actuality the Gods meant to show us,— face to face" (*Journal*, 7/6/45). He wanted, he says, not to suppose or invent a case, but to "take the case that is," knowing that in those rare moments of sanity when we are truly awake and aware this is what we regard: "the facts, the case that is" (*Walden*, 318–20). And he uses the same biblical phrase ("face to face") as he portrays in a tone of mystical rapture what this encounter might be like.

> If you stand right fronting and face to face to a fact, you will see the sun glimmer on both its surfaces . . . and feel its sweet edge dividing you through the heart and marrow, and so you will happily conclude your mortal career. Be it life or death, we crave only reality. (*Walden*, 96)

Thoreau speculates that, if his habits of observation were adequate to the challenge, he could "improve every opportunity to wonder and worship" until he would be "elevated enough" to "dream of no heaven but that which lies about me" in common, "every-day phenomena" (*Journal*, 8/30/56, 3/11/56). It is impossible to tell whether he is describing a process of aesthetic education or of spiritual enlightenment. This shows how much is at stake for Thoreau in striving to find beauty in the world: To have a significant fact impressed upon us completely, he suggests, would leave us so fulfilled as to be willing to perish at once. Although it is a worthy accomplishment "to paint a particular picture, or to carve a statue, and so to make a few objects beautiful," Thoreau maintains that "it is far more glorious to carve and paint the very atmosphere and medium through which we look, which morally we can do. To affect the quality of the day, that is the highest of arts" (*Walden*, 88). Significantly, he refers to this as a *moral* enterprise: The perception of beauty is a moral test, a test of our character as embodied in our dispositions. Furthermore, the literary process of articulating a vision of the world cannot be detached from the practical task of inhabiting it. In other words, the project of envisioning and depicting a way of life is bound up with the discipline of living.

In the midst of a tirade about the decadence of modern culture, Thoreau remarks that he would like to count himself among "those who find their encouragement and inspiration in precisely the present condition of things, and cherish it with the fondness and enthusiasm of lovers" (*Walden*, 15). Yet contemporary civilization, with its obfuscating prejudices and its "restless, nervous, bustling, trivial" activity (*Walden*, 320), tends to instill a distorted sense of value. It threatens to prevent human beings from having the opportunity or the inclination to embrace the world in a spirit of grateful affirmation. For example, "If a man walk in the woods for love of them half of each day," he is regarded as a lazy person; but "if he spends his whole day as a speculator, shearing off those woods and making earth bald before her time, he is esteemed an industrious and enterprising citizen."[18] Going for a walk in the woods thus becomes not only a political act, but—as Thoreau provocatively claims in his late essay "Walking"—one that also carries a religious significance. It is when I go for a walk, for its own sake and with no other goal in mind, that I "return to my senses" and renew my acquaintance with the beauty of the woods.[19] The red color of an autumn leaf is a natural fact that is out there in the world "to be met with" by the appreciative perceiver, and the activity of going to meet with it is an end in itself. If the scarlet oak appears to possess a "more brilliant redness" than it does at other times, this "partly borrowed fire" may be due to the angle of the low sun in relation to the observer's eye.[20] As this sort of phenomenon shows, we need not escape into a realm of artificial fantasy in order to find our experience animated with sacred radiance. Rather, we need only adjust the lens through which we are perceiving things, in order to become less oblivious and more alert toward the intricate world that surrounds us. Nature will repay the closest investigation, continually disclosing new wonders for those who have eyes to see. And the "living poetry" that we find in the world of natural facts will not be exhausted by our best efforts to search for beauty in concrete things. Fact and value are deeply entangled, as Hilary Putnam has more recently argued;[21] therefore, we cannot embrace the notion that our aesthetic responses are untrue to reality. It is "by closing the eyes and slumbering" that people deceive themselves, but by steadily observing only what is real we can develop a clarified vantage point and come to discover that "reality is fabulous" (*Walden*, 94). Some of the most striking features of our surroundings are at risk of being missed due to avoidable limitations in our mode of vision.

The imagination, properly understood, is a faculty that gives us access to reality—not a means of taking flight from it.[22] Although our conceptions are answerable to how the world is, we have no access to the world except through the ways of apprehending it that are available to us. Between the extremes of dogmatic realism and subjective idealism, Thoreau stays on a middle path that is quite characteristically his own. The human mind is not a blank slate that simply mirrors empirical reality or an empty receptacle that simply takes things in. But neither is the mind a projector that casts its own fancies onto a blank screen without constraint, encountering only itself as it encloses us within a world of our own invention. Even if the imagination "half-creates what it perceives," what this means is that our receptive faculties are actively involved in interpreting the "significant facts" whose meaning is not self-evident to just any observer.[23] In order to read the "language which all things and events speak without metaphor" (*Walden*, 108), we must stretch our imaginations in the very process of coming to terms with material nature in its otherness. We must, for instance, figure out how to decipher the intonations of various birds, whose cadences carry their own connotations in a language that is (at first) foreign to us. If we attentively dwell on the essential facts of life, looking always at what is to be seen, then what we ultimately find will satisfy the most extravagant demands of our imagination. The great poet is simply a writer who is entirely occupied with "giving an exact description of things as they appeared to him, and their effect upon him." Thoreau continues:

> We can never safely exceed the actual facts in our narratives. Of pure invention, such as some suppose, there is no instance. . . . A true account of the actual is the rarest poetry, for common sense always takes a hasty and superficial view.[24]

We should worry only that our most rhapsodic and astonishing accounts of what we have experienced will fall short of the reality with which we have been acquainted. As far as his own experience is concerned, Thoreau attests that he "cannot exaggerate enough even to lay the foundation of a true expression" (*Walden*, 315). Although it would be naive to think that we have the power to construct our own world without any restrictions, it is nonetheless true that the lens through which we are looking goes some way toward determining what we see. As Thoreau says, the "boundaries of the actual are no more fixed and rigid than the elasticity of our imaginations" (*Journal*, 5/31/53). Reality depends on the attentive perceiver in order to be brought to articulation, since observation is a creative process in which the observer plays a decisive role in the taking-shape of what is observed. We take in only what we are morally and intellectually prepared to receive, seeing only what concerns us and comprehending "only what we already half know" (*Journal*, 1/5/60). If our life seems to be impoverished, this might be due to our own failure to attain a state of poetic awareness that would enable us to apprehend its true splendor. After all, "the fault-finder will find faults even in paradise" (*Walden*, 319), and what we see in an appreciative mood is different from what we see when we are looking at things more scornfully. Just as a skeptical bias condemns us to experience uncanny doubts, an attentive focus on the wondrous realities of the world allows us to perceive much that would otherwise be missed. "All the phenomena of nature need to be seen from the point of view of wonder," Thoreau claims, such as the lakeshore whose "poetic" beauty is visible only to someone who is looking at it with the eyes of a poet (*Journal*, 6/27/52, 8/29/58). Wonder, after all, is the emotion with which philosophical reflection is said to begin. It is the affective state in which we are struck by something of great but unknown importance that we wish to understand. A more prosaic, neutral, or disinterested attunement might lead us to assume that a landscape is objectively barren, and that it only later becomes colored by our imaginations.[25] For Thoreau, however, its beauty really is there to be seen: "All things are significant," he writes (*Journal*, 11/1/51), and yet we could not become aware of their significance from an apathetic or disengaged perspective.

If our "forms of feeling" are "as revelatory of the world" as other modes of experience,[26] then any substantial change in our affective receptivity will transform our sense of reality. By "looking at things microscopically," we shut out "a great part of the world"; when we take a wider view, on the other hand, we notice "a certain meagerness of details" as a result (*Journal*, 3/5/52, 7/2/52). What faces us in our historical moment is the challenge of acknowledging what actually exists: Whereas the Greeks "with their gorgons, sphinxes," and so forth, "could imagine more than existed," in our disenchanted era we have trouble imagining "so much as exists" (*Journal*, 2/18/60).[27] In order for an author "to defend nature's intrinsic value," as Thoreau certainly wishes to do,[28] he or she must find a way to amplify our awareness, making us see something that we are at risk of missing. This includes everything from the way a pond's colors vary under different atmospheric conditions to the hint of "holiness groping for expression" that can be discerned in one's neighbor as he labors outside on a spring day (*Walden*, 171–72, 303). Now, Heidegger would say that it is the poet's role to restore weight to things, opening up new worlds of tangible value rather than merely neutral facts.[29] But since it is also the goal of the phenomenologist to make us "see or experience something which otherwise remains hidden,"[30] Thoreau's representation of the world as emphatically *not* value-neutral can be viewed as a contribution to phenomenology as well. And yet, regardless of whether *Walden* is best viewed as a poetic narrative with philosophical significance or as a work of phenomenological philosophy, it clearly insists that a true account of reality must do justice to all the qualities that the human mind is capable of perceiving in the material world. Most of the time, "our vision does not penetrate the surface of things," and we assume that "that *is* which *appears* to be," according to an impaired way of seeing (*Walden*, 94). Lacking "sanity and sound senses," we are too often "comparatively deaf and dumb and blind, and without smell or taste or feeling."[31] As a result, we are monstrously obtuse, occupying "the heaven of the gods without knowing it."[32] In short, Thoreau suggests that many noteworthy properties of objects will be inaccessible to us unless we encounter them with a suitable attunement.

What he is gesturing toward is a disposition that can be deliberately cultivated, and which would enable us to perceive the beauty of the world. Due to his conviction that "the perception of beauty is a moral test," Thoreau often rebukes himself—or humanity in general—for failing at this task: "How much of beauty . . . on which our eyes daily rest goes unperceived by us?" (*Journal*, 8/1/60). He wonders if a child might pick "its first flower with an insight into its beauty and significance which the subsequent botanist never retains" (*Journal*, 2/5/52). And he adds that "the truest description, and that by which another living man can most readily recognize a flower, is the unmeasured and eloquent one which the sight of it inspires" (*Journal*, 10/13/60). As the pragmatists have underscored, our attitude toward the world is one element in the constitution of reality, and therefore the truth about the universe will vary to some degree depending on the disposition with which we approach it.[33] What we "meet with," as Thoreau might say, depends in part on our subjective comportment toward the world. The "objects which one person will see from a particular hilltop are just as different from those which another will see as the persons are different," since things are concealed from us "not so much because they are out of the course of our visual ray as because we do not bring our minds and eyes to bear on them."[34] Taking notice of another person's suffering, for instance, involves more than having the requisite physiological equipment and facing in the right direction: It also requires a certain kind of emotional receptivity. It is a mistaken way of thinking that allows us to speak "as if seeing were all in the eyes, and a man could sufficiently report what he stood bodily before," when in fact what we see depends partially on us (*Journal*, 1/12/52). This is not because the external world is merely a fund of inchoate matter upon which order is forcibly imposed by our mental powers: It is, rather, because our way of seeing affects what in the world commands our attention as well as how it appears.

Thoreau attempts to do justice to both the knower and the known, the lens of perception and the independently existing world that is shaped and highlighted by the mind's own categories. So he can consistently maintain that "the universe constantly and obediently answers to our conceptions" *and* that "the universe is wider than our views of it" (*Walden*, 64, 188). We meet the world halfway in the event of perception, and a satisfactory philosophical explanation will acknowledge both sides of this story, rather than exaggerating one at the expense of the other. The question of whether or not one perceives "the significance of phenomena," on Thoreau's view, is decided not only by "what you look at," but also by "how you look & whether you see" (*Journal*, 8/5/51). Accordingly, he argues that there will be "as much beauty visible to us in the landscape as we are prepared to appreciate," but "not a grain more."[35] An alert observer who has become emotionally attuned to the place where she is situated will consequently find herself "in a living and beautiful world" (*Journal*, 12/31/59). Hence it is impossible to overestimate the importance of "being forever on the alert," and of "the discipline of looking always at what is to be seen" (*Walden*, 108). As William James points out, a "rule of thinking which would absolutely prevent me from acknowledging certain kinds of truth, if those kinds of truth were really there, would be an irrational rule."[36] This is why the stance of the poetic observer, who is maximally susceptible to being impressed by the world's beauty, is rationally justified. Although we are always at risk of growing indifferent, Thoreau assures us that "the laws of the universe are not indifferent, but are forever on the side of the most sensitive" (*Walden*, 210). Remarking that it is only right for us to ascribe more reality to our visions of significance than to any other experiences, James comments: "Life is always worth living, if one have such responsive sensibilities."[37] Our convictions about the reality of the world are based on this affective awareness, and we are intimately bound to our environment by a sense of its meaning.

This, I think, is what Cavell has in mind when he writes that "our relation to the world's existence is somehow *closer* than the ideas of believing and knowing are made to convey."[38] Rejecting the ideal of neutral objectivity, Thoreau seeks "to preserve an enchanted world and to place the passionate observer in the center of his or her universe."[39] He also reminds us that "there is no such thing as pure *objective* observation" and asserts that all observation, in order "to be significant, must be *subjective*" (*Journal*, 5/6/54). The world cannot be accurately known or described, that is, except in terms that refer to a subject's possible or actual experience. And we have no good reason to base our overall conception of reality on experiences in which the world appears to be especially flat, value-neutral, and irrelevant to us. Even in his observations of natural phenomena, Thoreau finds that "the objects I behold correspond to my mood"; what is crucial, then, is to develop an attunement that keeps us from being "blind to the significant phenomena" that are always before us (*Journal*, 8/7/53, 8/5/51). In principle, a naturalistic approach to the world should be able to grasp its significance; part of Thoreau's motivation for measuring the depth of Walden Pond is to show that his appreciation of its beauty is not undermined by knowing this kind of quantifiable fact. Practically speaking, however, it may be "impossible for the same person to see things from the poet's point of view and that of the man of science" (*Journal*, 2/18/52). A maximally "objective" description, or one that aspires to reach this ideal, is bound to deliver an account of reality that is partial and incomplete, as it overlooks certain features of the world. Yet whether or not he ever succeeds at uniting the poetic and the scientific perspectives, Thoreau is confident that both of them are converging upon a single reality. Our various "points of view" on the universe, he proposes, correspond to the "infinite number of profiles" that a mountain displays as we glimpse it from a different angle on every step of our climb. Although it has "absolutely but one form," the mountain always has further aspects that we have not seen: Even if we tunnel all the way through it or cut it into slices, it will not be "comprehended in its entireness" (*Walden*, 281). The fact that there is a "subjective element" in the equation does not entail that objects have no actual properties; indeed, what we have apprehended of them is always only part of what they are.[40]

This is why we are not at risk of exceeding the facts in our most poetic descriptions.

Thoreau acknowledges that the axiological qualities of the natural world include the awesome, and the awful, no less than the beautiful: Nature is "untamed, and forever untamable," an autonomous power that we should expect neither to predict nor to control.[41] Moreover, the whole truth about the world cannot be apprehended from any one perspective— what has been imparted to each of us is necessarily only a partial view of a larger reality. Because every person's "view of the universe" is so "novel and original" (*Journal*, 4/2/52), it follows that if another human being "has lived sincerely, it must have been in a distant land to me" (*Walden*, 2). All of this suggests that Thoreau is trying to outline a kind of personal knowledge that depends to a great extent upon the interests and concerns that define our framework of observation. Recognizing that the thoughts of each perceiver are "part of the meaning of the world," he asks: "Who can say what *is*? He can only say *how* he *sees*" (*Journal*, 11/4/52, 12/4/46).[42] We have no transparent access to reality, in other words, and no vantage point from which to determine whether the world *itself* is somehow falsified by the categories of the human mind. Truth is radically perspective-dependent, and to the degree that our outlooks differ we will find ourselves living in different worlds.

Because all perception has a subjective aspect, the universe can be defined as a sphere centered on each perceiver: Wherever we are located, "The universe is built around us, and we are central still" (*Journal*, 8/24/41). "Wherever I sat, there I might live, and the landscape radiated from me accordingly" (*Walden*, 78). This does not imply that we are trapped inside of our own consciousness: The point is that it is only through the lens of our own subjectivity that we have access to the outside world. All of Thoreau's experience in the field enabled him to arrive at the realization "that he, the supposedly neutral observer, was always and unavoidably in the center of the observation."[43] It is the sympathetic encounter between mind and world that brings to light what is most wondrous in our existence, as when we see that "suddenly the sky is all one rain bow" (*Journal*, 8/21/51). Just as the "intense burning red" of the scarlet oak "asks a clear sky and the brightness of late October days" in order to be known in all its brilliance, the colors of a rainbow are disclosed only where there is a conscious observer to perceive them.[44] Claiming that "when the phenomenon was not observed," it "was not,"

Thoreau declares that "the philosopher for whom rainbows, etc., can be explained away, never saw them" (*Journal*, 4/19/52, 11/5/57). In the latter entry, he adds that "the point of interest" with such appearances "is somewhere *between* me and them"—that is, between the knowing subject and the object of knowledge. These words bring him very close to the position of another philosopher for whom the phenomenon of the rainbow demonstrates something about the nature of perception in general.

> Thus it is true, e.g., that when during a rain accompanied by sunshine we see a rainbow, we will call it a mere appearance, while calling the rain the thing in itself. And this is indeed correct, provided that we here take the concept of a thing in itself as meaning only something physical. . . . But suppose that we take this empirical something as such, and that—without being concerned about its being the same for the sense of every human being—we ask whether it presents also an object in itself. . . . In that case our question about the presentation's relation to the object is transcendental, and the answer is: not only are these drops mere appearances; rather, even their round shape, and indeed the space in which they fall, are nothing in themselves.[45]

To argue that a rainbow is a phenomenal appearance is not to dismiss it as a mere illusion—after all, the same can be said about the raindrops themselves—but to make room for it within an account of reality. To equate "reality" with "objective reality," however, would be a mistake. If Thoreau is "the American heir to Kant's critical philosophy,"[46] it is because his analysis of the observer's relation to what is observed leads him to explore and develop what is fundamentally a Kantian insight. We must account for the seer, one might say, in accounting for the scene. By doing so, Thoreau provides an original response to the problem of knowledge in modern philosophy. He stipulates that our comprehension of reality is limited by our capacity for seeing, and that the world as known is therefore "dependent on character."[47]

If Descartes had conceived of knowledge as embodied in our practical dispositions, he could not so easily have compared his beliefs to building blocks in an edifice that he could step outside of while it was being demolished and remodeled.[48] The project of pure inquiry must not be affected by the moral, aesthetic, or epistemic virtues of the particular human being who is carrying it out, since it relies on assuming an impersonal, disinterested vantage point. One commonplace of ancient philosophy that was largely abandoned during the early modern period is that a person "could not have access to the truth" without undertaking a process of self-cultivation that would render him "susceptible to knowing" it.[49] Descartes does not seek to develop and refine his individual point of view, but to arrive at a purified viewpoint that is not that of an individual person. Thoreau, by contrast, assures his philosophical readers that we should not go around "like true idealists, rejecting the evidence of our senses," and he entertains the idea of an evil demon for no longer than he imagines that he might be dreaming.[50] Yet he shares the Cartesian aspiration to get to the bottom of things and to find a solid grounding for knowledge, and he is interested in exploring how we might renew contact with the world that is lost to us when we doubt its existence. Furthermore, the "connection with things" that Thoreau wishes to recover will be insufficient if it includes nothing beyond the mere assurance that an external world exists.[51] He realizes that the philosopher who hopes to develop a convincing response to skeptical doubt must also explain how the perceived beauty and meaning of things are more than an illusion. As we have seen, this is above all a matter of examining how to develop eyes that are capable of appreciating the value of being.

Thoreau notes in a late journal entry that different frames of mind, even "morbid states," render us "peculiarly fitted for certain investigations," and thus "better able to deal with certain phenomena" (Journal, 7/18/59). Because there are "innumerable avenues to a perception of the truth," we must "reconsider our experience from many points of view and in various moods" in order to know the world more thoroughly (Journal, 9/4/51, 3/24/57).[52] According to Thoreau, the most desirable epistemic position is that of the person who sustains "a meticulous and discerning awareness of the particularities of nature," keeping in mind that "every perception bears an enormous weight of significance."[53] Since nature is not an inventory of dry facts, scientific knowledge may not have an exclusive claim to deliver the truth about the natural world. For Thoreau, the more important goal is to be "sensible to the finest influence" (Journal, 2/14/51) so that one can accurately perceive the beauty of the universe. As he is willing to concede, this aspiration might never be perfectly achieved.

> I do not know that knowledge amounts to anything more definite than
> a novel and grand surprise, or a sudden revelation of the insufficiency

of all that we had called knowledge before; an indefinite sense of the grandeur and glory of the universe. It is the lighting up of the mist by the sun. (*Journal*, 2/27/51)[54]

Thoreau laments his discovery that the "facts most astounding and most real" are often the "farthest from being appreciated." We "easily come to doubt if they exist," and yet "they are the highest reality" (*Walden*, 208). Whether or not these realities are lost on us depends on how we are oriented toward the actual world, and on whether we have succeeded at opening ourselves to a wider horizon of experience. As Thoreau wrote in his final journal entry, "All this is perfectly distinct to an observant eye, and yet could easily pass unnoticed by most" (*Journal*, 11/3/61). In other words, the alert and emotionally attuned observer will have access to many significant facts that would be invisible from the vantage point of dispassionate detachment. The world's beauty is not fabricated by the eye of the beholder, but it does require the right kind of eyewitness in order to be seen.

EIGHT

THOREAU'S MORAL EPISTEMOLOGY AND ITS CONTEMPORARY RELEVANCE

Alfred I. Tauber

Thoreau's practice of natural history and his understanding of science have been refracted from various perspectives and offer a composite intellectual portrait: an Emersonian transcendentalist,[1] an empirical naturalist,[2] a romantic naturalist,[3] an epistemologist reassessing perception,[4] a writer radically "writing nature,"[5] a hybrid Humboldtian postmodernist,[6] an early ecologist,[7] a pioneer conservationist,[8] and so on. To some degree, each of these characterizations holds true, but how might they be integrated? Indeed, given the complexity of Thoreau's character, the various cultural influences to which he responded, and the heterodoxy of his diverse studies, is there a common grounding for the extraordinary melding of his objective observations coupled with his self-conscious subjectivity? How might we characterize that venture that includes his nature studies, his transcendentalism, his poetry and other literary writings, and his social ethics? I argue that, indeed, Thoreau synthesized the divergent activities of his eclectic life into a coherent whole, one that I have previously characterized as a reaction to the ascendant positivism of his era.[9] Because he found his own way of "saving experience" and reenchanting a world that had been devalued, Thoreau's achievement holds much relevance for our own understanding of science and the objectification of the world.

In searching for a coherent theme, I have chosen to portray Thoreau as a "moral-epistemologist," a neologism that seeks to capture his particularly well articulated program of "encountering" nature in the context of a deliberately chosen set of values. A life *deliberately* lived included a recurrent assessment of his own place in nature. That appraisal occurred at a time when the subject-object dichotomy underwent redefinition as a reconfigured positivism confidently claimed its methods would achieve true knowledge and a comprehensive picture of nature. Thoreau rejected the ascendant scientism of his era and sought to "save experience" and reenchant a world that seemed devalorized. That achievement holds much relevance for our own understanding of contemporary science and its objectification of the world. Indeed, he could easily have written what Hugo Meynell writes:

> It seems to be rather widely held that the extension and application of the kind of "objective" knowledge typified by the natural sciences is somehow at odds with the "subjective" development and authenticity of human personalities. This leads to an effective contempt for human values in some quarters, and a hatred of science and of systematic reasoning in general in others. I hope to show that this whole conflict is based on a mistake.[10]

Here, I outline how Thoreau understood the "mistake" and how he approached its solution.

The Challenge of Coherence

At one level, modern science makes the most modest metaphysical claims and rests on its practical achievements. However, another agenda also beckons—the metaphysical wonder that drives scientific inquiry and the findings that must be translated into human meaning. In the modern period, the Cartesian construction of the mind-nature divide established the terms of philosophical discourse. From this perspective, modernist epistemology sought to discern the nature of human perception and the ability to derive mental "pictures" of the world. Science, with its apparent logic and universal methods, seemed to offer a model for understanding how those sensory findings are extended into scientific facts and laws, a project Descartes thought would result in the axiomatization of nature. David Hume abruptly interrupted that dream by arguing that causality was merely a psychological habit (or conceit), as opposed to a logical or inherent property of nature. This apparent artifice of mind awoke Kant from his "dogmatic slumber," and the entire transcendental project was designed to provide the conditions by which "mind" addressed the quandary Hume presented. Kant posited that *because* of reason's autonomy, the mind became the "lawgiver" to nature (i.e., it provided law as a product of human cognition and imagination), and, at the same time, mind patrolled and created its own human social and spiritual universe with a reason designated for that purpose. Kant thus directly confronted the human-nature divide with reason's own "division," and his formulation then demanded some understanding to reunify that which had been split.[11] He failed, and much of German Idealism, in combating the subjectivism he bequeathed, attempted to resolve the imbroglio.[12] But that project also floundered, and, with the rise of positivism in the mid-nineteenth century, the terms of debate shifted and the pursuit of radically objective science soon eclipsed Kant's enigma.

Although subordinated, the unification problem did not disappear. Whereas the nineteenth century posed the subject-object divide in opposition, the romantic complaint has still not been answered despite the failure of various positivist philosophies.[13] The "spectator gap" remains, as efforts to humanize science, namely bringing the objective world into closer proximity to the knowing subject, have yet to yield a harvest. Indeed, the very division of self and other makes unity *the* problem, for reason is not easily integrated, nor nihilism readily mended, given the power of those instruments that have so successfully conspired to separate and divide.

Always aware of separation, and appropriately so, since science would purge itself of subjective contamination, the "subjectless subject"[14] faces the metaphysical challenge of finding herself *in* the world defined without her. This refers to shifting the human "stare" *at* the world to human placement *within* it. Simply, Western metaphysics poses the challenge of how to mend the *res cogito-res extensa* divide, to make the world—humans and nature—whole again. Taking their lead from Goethe and Schiller, notable twentieth-century philosophers, for example, Weber, Husserl, Heidegger, Dewey, and Sartre, repeatedly addressed this quandary and provided commentaries about a reality depicted "ob-jectively," that is, a world in which humans self-consciously reside separated from that world.[15] From their descriptions, the challenges of defining meaning and the significance of human existence took diverse courses, but linking each voice is the overriding concern of finding a philosophical means by which to stitch together the subject and its object.[16]

To highlight this challenge as an existential issue, at the very least, one might seek a humane science that moves beyond mastery of nature to enlightening the metaphysical wonder that originally directed its exploration. Pulling science back from its steadfast aloof observation (and mastery) *of* nature would include its complementary function of framing meanings and significations to humans *in* nature. That project requires reconfiguring the knowing agent—outside observer/integrated participant—and discerning the values that would allow such a coupling. Thoreau clearly articulated this problem when he observed,

> I fear that the character of my knowledge from year to year becoming more distinct & scientific—That in exchange for views as wide as heaven's cope I am being narrowed down to the field of the microscope—I see details not wholes nor the shadow of the whole. I count some parts, & say "I know."[17]

Believing that humanistic values lie dormant in science's original enterprise, Thoreau offered a way of achieving an elusive coherence. That problem, and his answers, remain highly relevant today in the attempt to devise what others have called a "return to reason"[18]—a broad reason that allows for different faculties with different standards of knowledge to capture a spectrum of experience directed at different ends. This pluralistic, pragmatic endeavor not only identifies the dilemma of placing science in perspective but also asks the key question: How might reason serve various kinds of creativity to make the world meaningful? Below, I outline Thoreau's program, and then, in the concluding section, I present a précis of his approach in its wider philosophical context.

Thoreau's Moral Epistemology; or, His Moral-epistemology

Because Thoreau left a rich and detailed analysis of nature ordered by his unique interpretative faculties, he clearly illustrated how scientific inquiry is not necessarily at odds with the personal elements of knowing.

He exhibited a way by which splintered experience—objective and sub-jective—might be knit together by recognizing the full legitimacy of each. He arrived at this position by acknowledging the limitations of a singular rationality and instead championed various ways of knowing. In his view, the putative autonomous aloofness of the observer actually mirrors per-sonal fragmentation. He sought to mend the split by engaging and freely integrating the full panoply of various kinds of knowledge and thereby straddling the humanistic-scientific divide. His concern with becoming too scientific seemed to rest primarily on the fear of fragmenting experi-ence, of losing the whole. The challenge is clear: Unify the aesthetic, scientific, and moral universes.

Perhaps more than other contemporaneous artists, philosophers, psy-chologists, physiologists, and historians, Thoreau took steps to drive his epistemology toward a particular vision of himself. Indeed, he subsumed his epistemology to this vision. He thereby offered a *moral-epistemology*, a way of seeing that acknowledged both *the real* and its *value*. I mean *moral* as the task of finding value in the world that science presents, and, more specifically, *moral* stands for acknowledging the degree to which knowledge is value-laden. To view science from a moral-epistemological point of view, we highlight knowledge as structured by, defined through, and embedded in *diverse* values, and more to the point, these values are those established by lived experience and ordered by a personal ethic. Note, this terminology is not a characteristic usage, which addresses the epistemic status and relations of moral judgments and principles, for example, justification of statements or beliefs, in epistemology, or valida-tion of judgments of actions, in ethics. Instead, here, "moral" stands for acknowledging the degree to which knowledge is value-laden, and thus moral-epistemology captures the collapse of a dichotomous fact-value epistemology and substitutes a more complete formulation: When sci-ence is configured as a "moral-epistemology," the interplay of facts and values assumes primacy. Using Thoreau as an example, science may be construed as reaching deeply into the moral domain to find its respective *epistemological* footing, and beyond that domain a pervasive *ethic* guides and shapes practice and theory.

Studying nature objectively played a key part in Thoreau's project, but it was only a part. For him, nothing escaped penetrating ethical analysis. Ranging from social justice to the beauty of an apple tree, virtually any observation or occurrence became an expression of a value. Facts served as oils for a painter: He used them to create pictures of the natural and social environments much as an Impressionist painter would interpret a nature scene thirty years later. Individualized and unique, each appreciation reflected the unique vision of the observer. Thus facts required interpretation, and a value system structured that interpretation; the value system in turn was determined by the moral order of the individual; finally, character framed the moral order. In short, science provided a powerful tool for comprehending the universe, but the universe must become self-creatively his own. The distinctiveness of Thoreau's world was the appreciation that the borders between culture, nature, and the individual were moving boundaries that he imaginatively pushed in self-chosen directions. I refer to that enterprise as his moral (value-laden) project.[19] In that consideration, "personal" *value* and "objective" *fact* are synthesized.

This general problem has reemerged as a central concern of sorting out a postpositivist philosophy of science that seeks to understand the interplay of facts and the diverse values that support them. The so-called fact-value distinction has a long history,[20] and suffice it to note here that the positivist position developed in reaction to the subjectivity that compromised objective scientific pursuits. However, in the attempt to purge "subjectivity," the positivists failed to acknowledge the role nonobjective values play in the scientific enterprise. Instead of the various attempts to dissociate facts from values contaminating objectivity, we have come to understand that facts are facts because of the values that confer a factual status. And those values do not reside in some Platonic ideal domain from which their application confers the objectivity sought by investigators. The independent status of facts has been radically reappraised, that is, facts become facts *because* of the values attached to them, for their meaning and significance are determined by the context in which they are formed, appraised, and employed.[21] Most simply stated, facts cannot be separated from the values that embed them, and the understanding of science—from its institutional-political commitments to its various determinations of human comprehension of the world and human character—cannot be apprehended without some basic appreciation as to how values frame *everything*. In short, values are constitutive of facts, and more to the point, *different* values determine how facts are understood in various contexts.[22]

This philosophical issue did not absorb Thoreau's attention in a systematic fashion, but his commitment to synthesizing experience—the poetic and scientific—required that he articulate and thereby formulate a holistic composite in which diverse values—i.e., scientific, aesthetic, and moral—were in play. Note, Thoreau was not stating that we could not objectively perceive such reality as nature offered us, but each of us must engage it independently and directly. And that individual experience, because of its very character as *individual*, would be composed by different valences. The poet, naturalist, or scientist might offer guidelines or models, but ultimately we are responsible for our encounter, individualized and personal.

A derivative aspect of the scientific enterprise concerns the challenge of finding coherence in the synthesis of personal insights and intuitions with objective observations and rational dissection of nature. As I have already briefly discussed, Thoreau joined the metaphysical debate that had preoccupied post-Cartesian philosophers, and he would offer his unique response. For him, as for Goethe, the *synthetic* project becomes poetic: Facts "are translated from earth to heaven—I see that if my facts were sufficiently vital & significant—perhaps transmuted more into substance of the human mind—I should need but one book of poetry to contain them all."[23] In writing a single book containing facts *and* poetry, Thoreau addressed his greater concern, mending the divide between the self and his world, which ultimately relies on creative imagination.

The synthesis Thoreau sought would break the confines of solipsism and assert the authority of the self to know the world. He achieved that integration at times, but as the above journal entry acknowledges, his venture was never assured and not always successful. His life work was a labor with no end. This morally inspired project ultimately "succeeds" because Thoreau's epistemology "fails," by which I mean that he could not capture nature in his writings as he *experienced* it. At best, he might "present a scene in which the gap between man and nature will seem *virtually* closed."[24] But not quite. As beautiful and evocative as any of his descriptions might be, there was a gulf separating his unmediated encounter with the self-consciousness of reflection and composition. And even more fundamentally, no matter how deeply he sought correspondence with nature, Thoreau realized that "his [the poet's] thought is one world, hers [Nature] another. He is another Nature—Nature's brother."[25] But it was in the *doing*, in the exercise, in the pursuit of the vision he experienced, that we witness Thoreau practicing what he regarded as a virtuous life through what I call a "moral-epistemology."

Thoreau endeavored to capture a humanized worldview, one which employed the fruits of scientific investigation to create his *own* world. In this sense, I regard him as an exemplar of a scientist guided by a humanistic ethos. Indeed, Thoreau offered no apology that his natural histories (spliced with poetics and metaphors) might not conform to the standards of bona fide knowledge. Some passages did; others did not. But for him, the work was synthetic, an ongoing negotiation of melding the objective world with the personal. The detractor asserts, correctly, that although such elaborations may be important, one must recognize their true character: Perhaps holding relevance and revealing erudition within religious, literary, psychoanalytic, political, ideological, or historical contexts, such communications may never be confused with *knowledge*. Thoreau, however, engaged another project, albeit one that contained knowledge, yet hardly limited to that acquisition.

The "ethics" of *understanding* drove Thoreau's quest to know. His moral venture was a mandate of seeing—one developed, exercised, and pursued as an act of self-actualization, as an act of defining himself and his place in the cosmos. *Seeing*, of course, not only included mystical visions or waking dreams, but meticulous observation. He was cognizant of the limits of his role as epistemologist as one who could *know* the world as something real beyond his own efforts to see it in multiple dimensions. And, as a critical corollary, there were various faculties of seeing, each capturing an aspect of reality that must be forged into some unity through the mind of the beholder. So seeing was ultimately dependent on the individual's *ability* to see and create, and the world as known is thus dependent on self-conscious effort. When in the pursuit of nature, the project itself was informed by a self-conscious *doing* of those inquiries. As discussed below, he anticipated the later pragmatists' emphasis on the centrality of engaging lived experience. In this sense, the act of creation itself was a virtue.

To make the ordinary extraordinary became the moral endeavor Thoreau set himself.[26] The consequence? Thoreau possessed a unique view of nature, essentially creating, by means of an astute sense of detail and a poetic eye, the world in which he lived. This he accomplished as an act of will, asserting the primacy of his own knowing. *What* he saw was determined by *how* he saw and the value bestowed on the object of scrutiny. To see the world as beautiful and spiritual, Thoreau placed lenses of enhanced sensibility before his eyes, both to focus his sight and to filter it. Thus the very act of observing became a moral test, a test of his values and of his ability to live by them. He essentially composed nature in a personal format, taking what he required to compose a picture of the world, and of himself within it. The individuality he espoused was the sine qua non of the entire project. In short, instead of objectivity's "view from nowhere," Thoreau proclaimed the primacy of precisely his own vision. Accordingly, Thoreau's science thus became a *poiêsis*.

> Nature has looked uncommonly bare & dry to me for a day or two. With our senses applied to the surrounding world we are reading our own physical & corresponding moral revolutions. Nature was so shallow all at once I did not know what had attracted me all my life. I was therefore encouraged when going through a field this evening, I was unexpectedly struck with the beauty of an apple tree—The perception of beauty is a moral test.[27]

This journal entry (from 21 June 1852) resounds with *Walden*'s declaration that "Our whole life is startlingly moral,"[28] which may be understood as our placement on a set of coordinates defined by several axes. Just as space is geometrically defined by three vectors in simple geometry, so too might we draw a "space" by "vectors" which will analogously define the coordinates of Thoreau's experience: the first, the aesthetic imagination; the second, the imperative of attention; the third, the psychology of self-awareness. Their meeting, at the origin of the vectors that delineate this metaphorical space, is joined by a value-laden consciousness that guides each faculty as it probes its intention. Here, we find scientific thinking participating as one faculty among several to help form that composite we call "the world."

For Thoreau, that world was signified relative to himself through a moral-epistemology, one he forthrightly declared as a young man.

> How tremendously moral is our life. After all no man can be said to live much in the senses, but every moment is the product of so much character. What painters of scenery we are. We impart to the landscape the perfect colors of our mind.[29]

Nature could become meaningful only as knowledge of it became integrated into Thoreau's own experience. And experience, at least for Thoreau, was an imaginative and intimate encounter.

The true man of science will have a rare Indian wisdom—and will know nature better by his finer organization. He will smell, taste, see, hear, feel, better than other men. His will be a deeper and finer experience. We do not learn by inference and deduction, and the application of mathematics to philosophy but by direct intercourse. It is with science as with ethics—we cannot know truth by method and contrivance—the Baconian is as false as any other method. The most scientific should be the healthiest man.[30]

The world was thus integrated, as the scientific pursuit took its rightful place in the quest of reality, a reality of his own creative making. The world, just as Emerson had pronounced, would be built according to one's own dictates, directed by an inner compass: "Every spirit builds itself a house; and beyond its house, a world; and beyond its world, a heaven. . . . Build therefore your own world. As fast as you conform your life to the pure idea in your mind, that will unfold its great proportions."[31]

Thoreau employed scientific knowledge to fulfill that agenda, but science was only one of several tools to achieve the greater purpose of self-knowledge. The point is that he simply was dissatisfied with a false choice—knowledge *or* romance, science *or* poetry. Both modes of experience were crucial in fulfilling his quest for reality. Unified reason bequeathed unified experience. So in sum, I see Thoreau's venture as attempting to fully integrate the scientific worldview with human experience. His interpretations spanned a wide swath, of which "science" played a prominent role, and the challenge he faced, as do we, was how to find coherence among competing notions of knowledge.

From Thoreau to Dewey

Thoreau's "sentiment," for it can hardly be regarded as a formal philosophical position, serves as a prelude to more developed constructions, of which John Dewey's philosophy seems most consonant with the theme developed here.

All sciences are a part of disciplined moral knowledge so far as they enable us to understand the conditions and agencies through which man lives. . . . Moral science is not something with a separate province. It is physical, biological and historic knowledge placed in a human context where it will illuminate and guide the activities of men.[32]

Thus for Dewey, no firm demarcation between moral judgments and other kinds were possible, for "every and any act is within the scope of morals, being a candidate for possible judgment with respect to its better-or-worse quality." He thus widened the scope of "morals" to value judgments writ large: "Morals has to do with all activity into which alternative possibilities enter. For wherever they enter a difference between better and worse arises."[33]

For Dewey, morals are "objective" in the sense that consensus and considered judgment determine the better choice of dealing with the world or drawing inferences from it. A Platonic ideal of "objective" or "real" or "true" then is replaced with a pragmatic assessment adjudicated by the rules of human flourishing. Indeed, as Alasdair MacIntyre cogently confirms:

> To be objective, then, is to understand oneself as part of a community and one's work as part of a project and part of a history. The authority of this history and this project derives from the goods internal to the practice. Objectivity is a moral concept before it is a methodological concept, and the activities of natural science turn out to be a species of moral activity.[34]

And the entire enterprise directs itself toward a philosophy that would fully integrate the moral and epistemological domains.

> The problem of restoring integration and cooperation between man's beliefs about the world in which he lives and his beliefs about the values and purposes that should direct his conduct is the deepest problem of modern life. It is the problem of any philosophy that is not isolated from that life.[35]

Accordingly, for Dewey, "meaning is wider in scope as well as more precious in value than is truth,"[36] by which he means that "truth" (viz., science) was in the employ of *meaning*. Moral-epistemology redescribes and reasserts these tenets.

Using Thoreau as a case example of a moral-epistemology at work, three general precepts schematize this general attitude.

1. Following Dewey and later pragmatists, the only reality is "ordinary reality,"[37] and in that service, moral-epistemology then becomes a philosophical approach to the full panoply of experience. This attitude seeks to envelop all experience, from esoteric frontline science to the full personal

appreciation of a world so depicted. This final distillation of thought draws from diverse cognitive and emotional faculties and requires harnessing them into some integrated coherence. In short, moral-epistemology becomes an *integrative description* of the world and one's experience of it.

2. Moral-epistemology presents the world as an ongoing *dialectical exploration*, in which meaning, not truth, becomes the focus of interest. Not to demote the standing of truth, this configuration places truth in the employ of meaning. Truth-claims then constitute a stage on the way to some final synthesis, to meaning. On this view, truth functions in the service of meaning-seeking behaviors, which, of course, coincides with the integrative requirements of thought. Reality is thus experienced in an ongoing test of personal knowledge against the world that demands responses that invoke one kind of reason or another. This manner of constructing reality represents a synthesis of experience in the employ of meaning. Indeed, meaning becomes the end point of knowledge as the individual interprets the world as a product of the present moment within the context of prior experience.

In this fashion, meaning becomes the cognitive glue in which experience coheres. This attitude, developed by pragmatists and contemporary cognitive scientists, serves to capture human intention, because without the search for meaning, the motivation for integration and coherence would have no basis. Furthermore, experience would have no structure. Accordingly, a "foundational" epistemology has been replaced with a functional one, by which I mean the pragmatics of situating meaning-seeking ventures of ordinary experience.

3. Moral-epistemology embraces a *self-reflective attitude* about experience. In a sense, this becomes the heart of the project, where comprehension of an integrated world, created by the search for meaning in a dialectical exchange with the world, emerges as epistemology's object of inquiry. In the final analysis, meaning serves to focus judgment's function, an arbitration of experience to create human reality. The play of facts and values, interacting with varying valences assigned to each, serves as the métier of life experience, ordinary and otherwise. Following flexible (if not poorly defined) rules of navigation, moral-epistemology acknowledges that reality ultimately places humans within the reality *they* experience. The facts of the world—or more simply, the world—only

become factual with the values assigned by human evaluation. And thus reality becomes a product of mind and nature, as Kant first proposed— however, not constructed by a universal reason as he thought, but composed with varying rules, historical and culturally developed and thus contingent on time and place. Some cognitive rules may present themselves precisely, whereas others less so, and some remain seemingly nonspecific, their full character shrouded as the faculties of human explanation and understanding weave the threads of experience into whole cloth, all the while oblivious of analytic attempts to discern them. Giving up foundations may well require abandoning rigorous epistemological formalisms as well.

One last comment: The world so construed is fundamentally *moral*. Moral in the sense of human-valued, human-centered, human-derived, human-constructed, and human-intended. To segregate the self from the world—as some separate entity—defrauds philosophy's own quest, for a world without *human* value has lost human significance. The self firmly placed *in* the world constitutes the reality in which humans live. To fracture that fundamental unity not only distorts our understanding of ordinary experience, it misconceives it. In the end, moral-epistemology offers an integrative description, urges a dialectical exploration, and provides a self-reflexive attitude to *know nature as a meaningful experience.*[38] The goal of Thoreau's project is to oppose a disenchanted view of the world that leaves no room for the experience of meaning.

This approach can only serve as a platform to continue philosophy's unfinished business of confronting the Cartesian embarrassment of self-consciousness. Moral-epistemology's tools for insight and integration directly confront the ethical dilemma provoked by science. An epistemology that does not account for human value is laden with an unresolved irony, partly attributed to its historical development and partially due to its embedded precepts: That which masters also enslaves; that which provides also expends; that which enlightens also disenchants. This moral calculus emphasizes that the world picture science offers does *not necessarily* leave humans alienated. After all, science is a human invention for human use. The fruits of scientific labor may be harvested in many ways, and although the Faustian pact seems firmly entrenched, critical attempts to revise that contract remain possible, and, indeed, necessary. This is a cardinal Thoreauvian lesson.

Moral-epistemology is, in the end, a pragmatic approach to discerning, and fixing, epistemological malalignments. That it draws on a moral reservoir and points to a metaphysical problem simply acknowledges the coordinates of its function. And that function, accordingly, makes its commitments to casting science in its full philosophical rendering. A "reasonable" goal, to be sure, but one hardly endorsed by current fashions. Now that we have come to the *end* of positivism's demise, we might well ask in this postpositivist age, What is science's new philosophy? What epistemological precepts take the place of discarded dictums? If pragmatism has become our default resting place, what are its own philosophical limits? After all, the pragmatic rests in an ether of values, and the incredulous may well ask to what end does the pragmatist venture? Discerning and then establishing science's *philosophical* position on the coordinates of fact and value links the wide expanse of contemporary science studies, a project that on the reading offered here, finds Thoreau as a heretofore unrecognized forerunner and a worthy contemporary interlocutor.[39]

Thoreau's Relevance

Let me summarize: The value to be assigned to various forms of knowledge and their respective placement in a hierarchy of significance were key issues that underpinned the Romantics' reaction to science. *Meaning*, they insisted, must be sought outside an objective knowledge of nature. Thoreau sought a synthesis, where objectivity might be mixed with the personal and thereby achieve what Polanyi later called "personal knowledge."[40] On this view, science and *poiêsis* are only vehicles of knowing or expressing. One might assign them as tools of an interpretative faculty, which confers meaning. Since neither science nor poetry suffice, because, in a sense, they are appendages of a deeper cognitive function, a faculty Kant called "judgment." From this perspective, meaning cannot directly arise from epistemology or any of its branches, but rather arises from a dynamic synthesis—the moral vision (or orientation) of the knower who weaves facts into their fabric of signification. This is moral-epistemology at work.

And going beyond the particulars of Thoreau's life, his moral-epistemology speaks directly to our own challenges of how to integrate scientific findings with other kinds of knowledge and experience. Indeed, given the centrality of the ethics of how contemporary scientists govern themselves as truth-seekers *and* how the moral dimensions of the scientific worldview reflect the interpretation of scientific knowledge in a framework oriented by human need, science readily rests within a *moral* framework, one that antecedes epistemology proper.[41] I suggest that before facts, before theory, the values of science command the character of knowledge. This means, simply, that the values adopted to differentiate knowledge from opinion require certain "rules." These rules are fundamentally moral (as defined above), because they embed the values by which the exploration of nature becomes *science*. On this view, ethics is understood as establishing and guiding practice. So, just as values guide the behavior of moral agents, so too do values guide the practice of scientists. The rules, having followed a winding historical path, effectively establish the groundwork by which scientists proceed in their particular projects. These are not just conventions, but rather instantiate the lessons learned of how best to accomplish the local tasks at hand. Accordingly, without the particular values of scientific practice and assessment, scientific conduct could not be differentiated from other forms of inquiry, and, indeed, science has too often suffered a blurring of those boundaries.[42]

To conclude, Thoreau exemplified how objective findings might be incorporated into belief systems and insight, which drew from aesthetic, spiritual, and moral faculties and intuitions. On his view, knowledge became valuable not only for its application, but also for inspiring understanding of a complex, often hostile world, from various perspectives: the glorious creation of the divine; the beauty and order of nature; the rhapsodic intuition of cosmic wholeness. Whichever path is followed, each offers a more humane science, in which knowledge leads to human placement within the world studied. Accordingly, Thoreau's fuller appreciation and understanding of the scientific enterprise as part of a broad philosophical project sought to mend his fractured world. He would not abide alienation from nature, for he recognized that to say that a "disenchanted" universe is the inevitable product of scientific inquiry hardly resolved the imbroglio of the radical subject-object divide. The challenge cannot be dropped at the doorstep of "science" but rather rests more appropriately in another, broader context, namely, finding human meaning in a secularized world, whose values are no longer divinely revealed but arise instead in the throes of human life. Refracted with this lens, Thoreau becomes a moral-epistemologist.

The key question Thoreau posed, and which has still to be answered, concerns whether to leave science as a special sphere of study, employing a unique form of reason, or alternatively, to consider how science exhibits a peculiar, albeit powerful, means to study nature and seek to understand how it might be unified with other forms of interpretative reason. Thoreau chose the latter course, and this so-called moral-epistemology effectively embraces the melding of facts and values to produce an epistemology that better accounts for the value structure of knowledge, all knowledge, and more broadly, all experience. Indeed, this orientation points to a philosophy of science that again brings investigation of the natural world into the domain of a pluralistic reason, where various cognitive faculties receive their just deserts. His pursuit remains our own.

NINE

HOW *WALDEN* WORKS

Thoreau and the Socratic Art of Provocation

Jonathan Ellsworth

I was attached to this city by the god—though it seems a ridiculous thing to say—as upon a great and noble horse which *was somewhat sluggish because of its size and needed to be stirred up by a kind of gadfly.* It is to fulfill some such function that I believe the god has placed me in the city. *I never cease to rouse each and every one of you, to persuade and reproach you all day long* and everywhere I find myself in your company.

—Socrates, *Apology* 30e (emphasis added)

I do not wish to flatter my townsmen, nor to be flattered by them, for that will not advance either of us. We need to be provoked—goaded like oxen, as we are, into a trot.

—Henry David Thoreau, *Walden*, "Reading"

A present-day teacher of philosophy doesn't select food for his pupil with the aim of flattering his taste, but with the aim of changing it.

—Ludwig Wittgenstein, *Culture and Value*

Thoreau's *Walden* remains at the margins of philosophy today because we are still unsure what sort of book it is, and uncertain what we might do with it. And so it seems that, at most, *Walden* is regarded as a peculiar literary work that may lend itself to philosophical reflection but that probably ought not to be considered as a work of philosophy.

But what is it that we are really getting at when we wonder whether a given work of literature is a *philosophical* work? Whether it is generally regarded as such by professors of philosophy and taught in their classrooms? Whether it treats some cluster of concepts and concerns that still engage distinguished thinkers and writers? Or must a piece of writing make advances toward solving some intellectual problem if it is to be regarded as philosophical?[1] What if a work explicitly declares itself to be concerned with the pursuit of wisdom—will that suffice? But what if we find that work to be too simplistic or misguided? Is such a work, then, still a work of philosophy, albeit an unsuccessful one, or do its perceived shortcomings disqualify it? We might call a piece of writing a poor work of philosophy, but how bad—how unsatisfying, illogical, or poorly conceived—does it have to be before we simply don't recognize it as philosophy at all?

And what if, over time, our sense of what counts as philosophy shifts? What if certain works lose their appeal or their significance becomes hidden to us, apparently outdated, in our age of specialization? How are we to tell the difference between an irrelevant work of philosophy that we can afford to ignore and an untimely work of philosophy that could benefit us? If philosophy books, like philosophy teachers, should not merely flatter our taste but sometimes change it, then we are dismissive of unusual, difficult, or disturbing works at the potentially steep cost of our own advancement.

Of course, the problem of identifying whether a text qualifies as "philosophical" comes back to the difficulty of grasping what the discipline of philosophy is and what it requires of us. But this, in turn, at least presupposes the ability to recognize (and then, no less, the *willingness* to sit up and attend to) important philosophical claims and objectives when we encounter them.

The purpose of this essay is to make the case for the philosophical importance of *Walden* and to demonstrate that to neglect the philosophical concerns of *Walden* is not merely to miss part of the work's message—it is to miss the point entirely. Toward this end, I want to suggest that the book can be understood as a modern variation on the ancient literary genre of the *Sōkratikoi logoi*—that is, the Socratic discourse—and to show that the central aims of *Walden* are Socratic, for *Walden* is designed to serve as a catalyst for self-examination, and it employs a number of authorial strategies to assist the reader in this task. If we allow that a crucial component of philosophical activity is this business of self-examination, then those texts that successfully foster such work ought to be regarded as important philosophical resources. In this sense, *Walden* is arguably one of our greatest philosophical aids and deserves to be considered one of our most valuable philosophical texts.

Gadflies Ancient and Modern

The figure of Socrates, especially as depicted in Plato's *Apology*, casts a long shadow over *Walden*. Although this may not be immediately apparent to a reader absorbed in the vivid descriptions of the woods or focused on the details of his domestic arrangements, Thoreau inserts a number of Socratic allusions throughout his book. In the chapter "Reading," when Thoreau complains that "we spend more on almost any article of bodily aliment or ailment than on our mental aliment" and objects that his town of Concord "can spend money enough" on a parson, a sexton, a parish library, but not "for things which more intelligent men know to be of far more worth" (3.12),[2] we remember Socrates' admonition to his townsmen "not to care for the city's possessions more than for the city itself."[3]

Thoreau's fierce critique of our misunderstanding and misuse of wealth is Socratic in character and intent. When he writes, "Rather than love, than money, than fame, give me truth" (18.15), it is as if he is signaling his agreement with Socrates and pledging himself to a Socratic vocation: "I shall not cease to practice philosophy, to exhort you and in my usual way to point out to any one of you whom I happen to meet: Good Sir, you are an Athenian, a citizen of the greatest city with the greatest reputation for both wisdom and power; are you not ashamed of your eagerness to possess as much wealth, reputation, and honors as possible, while you do not care for nor give thought to wisdom or truth, or the best possible state of your soul?" (29d). Socrates continues, "Wealth does not bring about excellence" (30a), and we hear Thoreau reiterate, "Money cannot buy one necessary of the soul" (18.13). Thoreau's positioning of himself in a Socratic light becomes even clearer when we recall that Diogenes Laertius reports Socrates as saying, "Those who want fewest things are nearest to the gods";[4] and we find Thoreau stating, "My greatest skill has been to want but little" (1.93), and asking, "Shall we always study to obtain more . . . , and not sometimes to be content with less?" (1.52).

The underlying motive that drives both men's diatribes against those fixated with wealth and fame can be summed up by Plato's Socrates: "I shall reproach him because he attaches little importance to the most important things and greater importance to inferior things" (30a). Of primary value to Socrates is the health of the soul, and he worked to show that such health begins with the recognition and acknowledgment of the wisdom that one lacks: "Surely it is the most blameworthy ignorance to believe that one knows what one does not know" (29b). Thoreau echoes this conviction in the midst of his assessment of the consequence of excessive labor and too little freedom: "How can he remember well his ignorance—which his growth requires—who has so often to use his knowledge" (1.6). What Thoreau here calls "growth" is tantamount to what Socrates calls "the best possible state of the soul," and Thoreau sees the condition of possibility of this growth beginning with the recognition and acknowledgment that the current contours of our lives might make such health, such flourishing, impossible.

In another evocation of Socrates' mission and moral purpose, Thoreau reworks Socrates' claim that for his service to Athens, for "being such a man," he deserves to be given "free meals in the Prytaneum"—an honor usually reserved for victorious athletes—since, as he says, "the Olympian victor makes you think yourself happy; I make you be happy" (36d). Thoreau writes that his city, Concord, also failed to appreciate the valuable work he performs for it. Though he had not primarily traveled about Concord haranguing men as Socrates did (his harangues would mostly come in the form of *Walden* and other writings), Thoreau makes clear his belief that his public services of "self-appointed inspector of snowstorms and rainstorms," "surveyor . . . of forest paths" (1.28), and waterer of "the red huckleberry, the sand cherry and the nettle tree, the red pine and the black ash, the white grape and the yellow violet, which might have withered else in dry seasons" (1.29) deserved to be rewarded. However, "it became more and more evident that my townsmen would not after all admit me into the list of town officers, nor make my place a sinecure with a moderate allowance" (1.30). These apparently playful remarks nevertheless contain a serious (and Socratic) point: Socrates and Thoreau both wished to expand their townsmen's notion of public service, to increase their sense of what sort of life is admirable and worth supporting. "The life which men praise and regard as successful is but one kind. Why should we exaggerate any one kind at the expense of the others?" (1.31). The quote is from Thoreau, but the concern was registered long before by Socrates.

Plato's account of Socrates' life was occasioned by the charges raised against him by some of his fellow citizens. In another gesture to the *Apology*,

Thoreau opens *Walden* with the claims that he would not say so much about "my affairs," "my mode of life, which some would call impertinent," if "very particular inquiries" had not been made by his townsmen (1.2). Such points of contact with Socratic activity are difficult to dismiss as superficial given that, for Socrates and Thoreau, the obligation to account for oneself is not just a duty brought on by the demands of others but rather an internal requirement of a philosophical life.

Philosophy as Self-Examination

For Socrates and Thoreau, *apologia* is at the heart of philosophy. The ability to account for our actions is an essential component of philosophical activity and requires extraordinary vigilance. Stanley Cavell writes: "This is what those lists of numbers, calibrated to the half cent, mean in *Walden*. They of course are parodies of America's methods of evaluation; and they are emblems of what the writer wants from writing, as he keeps insisting in calling his book an *account*."[5] But these lists are also the necessary calculations of a deliberate life managed by a "rigid economy," which Thoreau identifies as the only hope mankind has to save itself from ruin (2.17). If this sounds extreme, it is certainly no more extreme, and in fact, is merely the upshot of the belief that "our whole life is startlingly moral. There is never an instant's truce between virtue and vice" (11.10). With the stakes this high, and the responsibility to account for ourselves at every instant, the half cent might just barely intimate how fine a standard of measure we are going to need. It would be comforting to interpret this claim as hyperbole, but Thoreau's purpose in *Walden* is not to comfort us but to wake us up, to sound the alarm. This list making and budget balancing is being offered as something like the first step toward salvation. In his essay "Life without Principle," Thoreau counsels us to "be fastidious to the extreme of sanity," in order that we would not "relax a little in our disciplines" and "cease to obey our finest instincts."[6]

But not only is it necessary to be able to give an account, it is important to call others to account. Socrates believed that his divine calling was to "live the life of a philosopher, to examine myself and others" (29a), and Thoreau charges each of his readers to "obey the precept of the old philosopher, and Explore Thyself" (18.3). What is remarkable about this quote is that Thoreau's most direct invocation of Socrates comes in the concluding chapter of a book that many seem to remember primarily as an extended advertisement for the great outdoors, and a book that certainly spends a lot of time detailing one man's experiences in nature, walking through woods, bathing in ponds, listening to the night, investigating chipmunks and loons and leaves. The staunch interior focus of the final chapter is a strategic attempt to emphasize the Socratic tenor of the book and prevent the misunderstanding that we too ought to rush into the woods. Instead he directs us to attend to our own *inner* natures: "If I were confined to a corner of a garret all my days, like a spider, the world would be just as large to me while I had my thoughts about me" (18.13). (We recall, too, that Thoreau writes that just because a man walks in the woods does not mean that his thoughts are free.) Thoreau's experiences and experiments in nature are an important part of his story, but not necessarily ours. For there is no place, no formula or program, that will automatically transform or awaken us. (Moreover, there is no exercise, no discipline, no set of texts that will automatically initiate reflection.) It does neither you nor me any good to measure the depths of Walden Pond, or to read about one who does, if we subsequently refuse to examine ourselves, to discern *our* needs, to accept our calling, to respond to that which we are summoned. "Let everyone mind his own business, and endeavor to be what he was made" (18.9).

Both men recognized how uncomfortable, how reluctant or unable, most of us are to give an account our lives. In fact, Socrates claimed that this is the true reason that he was sentenced to death, rather than the trumped-up charge that he was corrupting the youth: "You did this in the belief that you would *avoid giving an account of your life*" (39c). The resistance to account for ourselves that Socrates stresses in the *Apology* is a constant temptation away from the philosophical life. We do not wish to be roused, called into question, forced to admit our inconsistencies. (Thoreau asks, "Why is it that men give so poor an account of their day if they have not been slumbering?" [2.14].) We would prefer to "sleep on for the rest of [our] days" (31a), remaining, in Thoreau's words, in "the torpid state," our "present low and primitive condition" (1.58), unchallenged to "rise to a higher and more ethereal life" (1.58). Push us too hard, and we will push back: "You might easily be annoyed with me as people are when they are aroused from a doze, and strike out at me" (31a). Nevertheless, both men are ready to accept these consequences. Socrates will never "cease to rouse each and every one of you" (31a), and Thoreau will "brag as lustily as chanticleer in the morning, standing on his roost, if only to wake my neighbors up" (2.7).

The discomfort of accounting for ourselves is a primary reason why *Walden* often elicits vitriolic reactions from its readers. Many readers of *Walden* interpret their irritation as evidence of the book's deficiencies. But this is precisely the response that an author who aims to provoke and goad his readers is attempting to elicit. Our apparent exasperation with Thoreau is more likely the discomfort of being called out and confronted. It is the embarrassment of being caught asleep. *Walden* evokes such a strong reaction from its readers for the same reason that Socrates evoked such a strong reaction from his interlocutors: They are under interrogation. Thoreau, like Socrates, puts us on the defensive. In short, both force us either to defend our practices and our principles, or else change them—and most of us aren't prepared to do either. As Cavell has noted, these strong reactions are a crucial feature of the book, an occurrence that is so integral to the experience of reading (and reckoning) with *Walden* that it cannot be overlooked.[7] To read *Walden* without struggle, without uneasiness, is to fail to read it at all. It would be as damning as departing from a conversation with Socrates exactly as you were before. To be undisturbed by *Walden* is to be lost. Your annoyance or discomfort is at least the first sign that you are beginning to stir, that there is hope for you. To be infuriated, provoked, and then to begin to figure out the reasons for your infuriation, your unsettled state, is to begin to *think*—that is, to examine, to test, and to explore your beliefs and their consequences.

Philosophy and Autobiography

There are many traces of Socrates in *Walden* because *Walden* is a deeply Socratic work. But there are predominantly *traces*—suggestions, hints, and echoes of Socrates, rather than detailed analyses of his methods or thought—because of the specific *kind* of *Sōkratikoi logoi* that *Walden* had to be, given Thoreau's particular understanding of *apologia* and philosophical activity. *Walden* is a book that required its author (because its author demands it from *every* author) to render his account: "I, on my side, require of every writer, first or last, a simple and sincere account of his life, and not merely what he has heard of other men's lives" (1.2).

This remark stands as a particular challenge to those who would write of "Representative Men," as well as those authors of Socratic discourses, including, most famously, Xenophon and Plato. On Thoreau's view, a philosopher must eventually present his *own* account—and the failure to do this ultimately represents a personal philosophical failure, even for a writer of Plato's genius. Plato was good enough to give us Socrates, but was he good enough to have given himself?[8] In a lecture from the same year that *Walden* was published, Thoreau makes this issue plain: "Is it pertinent to ask if Plato got his *living* in a better way or more successfully than his contemporaries—or did he succumb to the difficulties of life like other men?"[9] Thoreau's questions may sound audacious, but they are more earnest than arrogant. He is far from scheming up some ego-driven takedown of one of the "heroic writers of antiquity." On the contrary, in *Walden* he expresses his desire "to be acquainted with wiser men than this our Concord soil has produced [that is, wiser men than Thoreau himself] whose names are hardly known here. Or shall I hear the name of Plato and never read his book?" (3.10). Thoreau then makes specific mention of Plato's Dialogues, and laments that they go largely unread.

> His Dialogues, which contain what was immortal in him, lie on the next shelf, and yet I never read them. We are underbred and low-lived and illiterate; and in this respect I confess I do not make any very broad distinction between the illiterateness of my townsman who cannot read at all and the illiterateness of him who has learned to read only what is for children and feeble intellects. We should be as good as the worthies of antiquity, but partly by first knowing how good they were.[10]

The strongest inference to draw here is that while Thoreau vigorously praises Plato's "heroic literary labors" (3.6), he cannot know whether Plato was a philosopher because he does not know how he lived. But this is simply to acknowledge that, in the words of Pierre Hadot, "*Discourse about philosophy* is not the same thing as *philosophy*."[11] For even the most penetrating thinkers and writers might still "make shift to live merely by conformity," but the philosopher "is in advance of his age even in the outward form of his life. He is not fed, sheltered, clothed, warmed like his contemporaries" (1.19). For Thoreau, as for Socrates, the philosopher is *atopos*, "unclassifiable," with respect to his contemporaries, and his way of life is not defined by conventional social and political categories. The philosopher is a "progenitor of a nobler race of men," and "maintain[s] his vital heat by better methods than other men" (1.70). The term "philosopher" is not merely an intellectual compliment or an honorary title, but an assessment of a distinctive and exceptional way of life.

Depending on how you look at it, Thoreau is either lowering the bar for who it is that might be a philosopher (after all, it is no longer necessary to hold a Ph.D., or secure tenure, or write books), or raising the bar to nearly impossible heights (after all, it is no longer sufficient to hold a Ph.D., or secure tenure, or write books). "Only one in a million is awake enough for effective intellectual exercise, only one in a hundred millions to a poetic or divine life," Thoreau tells us. "To be awake is to be alive" (2.14). But if the awake and alert individual is rare, it is not due to an uncommon lineage or exceptional innate qualities (such as being born beautiful, or tall), but because the desire to change, to elevate ourselves, to become better than we now are, is rare, and is not fostered by our art (1.54), our routines and habits (2.21), our reading (3.8), or our political arrangements.

If we are never prepared to show what we have made of ourselves, or what the discipline of philosophy has made of us, then our philosophical work remains unfinished. *Walden*, then, can be inspired by Socrates, but Thoreau cannot hide himself behind the figure of Socrates. *Walden* must testify to Thoreau's own mode of life. He must write his own *Apology*. And the second chapter of *Walden*, titled "Where I Lived, and What I Lived For," may be viewed as Thoreau's expansive translation of the word *apologia* itself. *Walden* is a Socratic discourse that must necessarily displace Socrates from the center. Socrates must be emulated, but not imitated. "We should be as good as the worthies of antiquity," and so must strive to equal or exceed their virtue, "but partly by first knowing how good they were" (3.10). If our lives are to be heroic, we will need the example of heroes. "The student may read Homer or Aeschylus in the Greek without danger of dissipation or luxuriousness, for it implies that *he in some measure emulate their heroes* and consecrate morning hours to their pages" (3.3). Our philosophical progress will be assisted by biography—since we need to first learn how good the good have been—but further progress will mean that our biographical studies of Odysseus and Prometheus and Socrates must lead us to write our autobiographies—that is, since we need to *become* as good as they were, and demonstrate that we live more wisely and by better means than others. For once one has cultivated an admirable life, it is now admirable to profess. Philosophical writing requires the turn from the biographical to the autobiographical.

Authorial Strategies of Provocation

Walden is a new type of Socratic discourse that employs certain authorial strategies to accomplish the task of waking people up and inciting self-examination. In what follows, I look more closely at some of the specific ways in which *Walden* attempts to do this and highlight its concerns to distinguish genuine philosophical activity from potential intellectual distractions.

> There are nowadays professors of philosophy, but not philosophers. Yet it is admirable to profess because it was once admirable to live. To be a philosopher is not merely to have subtle thoughts, nor even to found a school, but so to love wisdom as to live according to its dictates, a life of simplicity, independence, magnanimity, and trust. It is to solve some of the problems of life, not only theoretically, but practically. (*Walden*, "Economy," para. 19)

> What youthful philosophers and experimentalists we are! There is not one of my readers who has yet lived a whole human life. These may be but the spring months in the life of the race. (*Walden*, "Conclusion," para. 16)

These two quotations from *Walden* are taken from the first and last chapters, respectively. Thoreau opens with the claim that there are no longer any philosophers, and closes with the assertion that we are all philosophers. It is the purpose of the sixteen chapters that lie between these statements to direct us to this resuscitation of the philosophical way of life.

Acknowledging Ignorance, Becoming Disoriented

> For manifestly you have long been aware of what you mean when you use the expression "*being*." We, however, who used to think we understood it, have now become perplexed. (Plato's *Sophist*, 244a, and the epigraph to Martin Heidegger's *Being and Time*)

A philosophical question has the form: "I don't know my way about."
(Ludwig Wittgenstein, *Philosophical Investigations*)[12]

In the chapter titled "The Village," Thoreau writes of his return trips
from town to the pond: "It was very pleasant, when I stayed late in town,
to launch myself into the night, especially if it was dark and tempestuous"
(8.2). Thoreau tells of the deep darkness of the woods, and of his ability
to navigate the course home, guided by the stars, or familiar trees, or the
path that he himself had worn. In contrast to his own remarkable orientation in the woods, Thoreau reports of the disorientation of the townspeople who attempted to make their way home through the woods, and
he notes how easily they became lost. "Not till we are completely lost, or
turned round—for a man needs only to be turned round once with his
eyes shut in this world to be lost—do we appreciate the vastness and
strangeness of Nature. Every man has to learn the points of compass
again as often as he awakes, whether from sleep or any abstraction. Not
till we are lost, in other words, not till we have lost the world, do we begin
to find ourselves, and realize where we are and the infinite extent of our
relations" (8.2).

Walden is a book that attempts to diagnose and treat disorientation,
perplexity, and confusion. Thoreau is doubtful that dispositions can be
changed,[13] but he is confident that *confusions* can be resolved. To be per-
plexed is to be entangled and unable to grasp something clearly, and this
is the state in which Thoreau sees many of his contemporaries and his
readers.

Thoreau addresses numerous types of confusion: the confusion of the
individual who labors in vain, and who calls this labor a necessity (1.5);
the belief that things cannot or will not change—i.e., fate; the confusion
over what is truly necessary to subsist and to live richly; the "illusion"
of "'modern improvements'" (1.71); the confusion over what it is that
constitutes philosophy and the life of a philosopher (1.19), what it means
to live freely, and what it means to be philanthropic (1.98). He claims
that "shams and delusions are esteemed for soundest truths" (1.21),
and, finally, he notes confusion as to what constitutes true intimacy or
community (5.5, 6.17).

Thoreau (like Kierkegaard and Wittgenstein) is interested not just
in clearing up confusions, but in the question of how it is possible to
disabuse someone of an illusion. To suffer under an illusion is a very

particular problem, quite different from the problem of holding a false belief on account of false information. To come out from under an illusion requires that I see things anew—or that I resist certain impulses (perhaps perceptual or psychological impulses) that grip me.

In *Walden*, Thoreau does not wish to subsume the imagination to reason. He offers a litany of examples and perspectives that work to jar the reader from his or her myopic view. His philosophical work places heavy emphasis on these pictures rather than the formal arguments typical of the Western philosophical tradition. After all, we might ask: Are prejudices best shed by way of logical syllogisms, or by drawing someone into a familiar experience, creating an impression of being lost in a dark forest at night, fostering a sense of disorientation, and suggesting that this is how most of us live out our days?

Of course, Descartes's *Meditations* begin with a confession of confusion and doubt, and the call to "demolish everything completely and start again right from the foundations if I wanted to establish anything at all . . . that was stable and likely to last." So Thoreau is by no means unique in addressing these particular philosophical problems; but, perhaps, the manner in which he attempts to convey and solve these problems is unconventional. What Thoreau shows is a sensitivity to the fact that the proper *articulation* of certain philosophical problems is crucial, if the proposed solution to these problems is to be effective.

I would be willing to wager that most readers encountering the Cartesian *Meditations* feel little empathy with the scholar, sitting before the fire, claiming to question all. Conversely, who has *not* felt disoriented, anxious, and alone in the dark? It is an essential philosophical strategy of *Walden* for Thoreau to lead the reader both *by* example and *with* examples: with stories and analogies that seek to bring clarity and change.

The aim of Thoreau's authorial strategy, here, is to call our lives into question and bring us to the point where our lives (and what it means to be-in-the-world) become a question for us. So the philosophical importance of the experience of disorientation is that it brings us to the point of self-examination. And this moment—the moment when our lives become an issue for us—is the condition of possibility for philosophy.

Another unmistakable feature of *Walden* is that it is full of contradictions. Thoreau writes that "most men . . . through mere ignorance" can't pluck life's finer fruit (1.6), but he adds that our growth requires that we "remember well" our ignorance. He claims that "the old have no very important advice to give the young" (1.10), then states that the ancient authors offer "such answers to the most modern inquiry in them as Delphi and Dodona never gave. We might as well omit to study Nature because she is old" (3.3). He proclaims, "Old deeds for old people, and new deeds for new" (1.10), then implores us to harken back to ancient examples of what it looks like to live well (1.19). And he declares a reverence for "a primitive rank and savage" instinct (11.1), then acknowledges that this primitive instinct (in this case, to dine on animals) should be overcome (10.5–6). In order to make sense of this, it is important to recognize that, in *Walden*, Thoreau does not always mean exactly, or only, what he says: "The heroic books, even if printed in the character of our mother tongue, will always be in a language dead to degenerate times; and we must laboriously seek the meaning of each word and line, conjecturing a larger sense than common use permits out of what wisdom and valor and generosity we have" (3.3). As we shall see, to hurry through *Walden* is to ensure that the point of the book will be missed.

The abundant contradictions and paradoxes of *Walden* represent a purposeful authorial strategy, namely, to counteract two connected temptations that forestall philosophical progress: first, the temptation to stop thinking about a subject once we have puzzled out the *author's* position on the matter; and second, the temptation to simply imitate rather than emulate an author's principles or practices. Ultimately, *for us,* for *our* advancement, what Thoreau personally thinks about an issue is as unimportant as how he behaves. Thoreau knows this, and so he sets about making sure that we will get tripped up if we try to simply copy or mimic his behavior or his beliefs.[14] He moves us to reflect on a particular issue, but often, via contradiction and paradox, he forces us off his trail, not allowing us to rest in the satisfaction that we have figured out *his* position or merely adopted his habit. What he wants, instead, is to provoke in us an awakening of consciousness, as well as the courage to live by our principles.

Perhaps, then, *Walden*'s primary philosophical value lies less in the originality of the philosophical positions it puts forward than in its capacities to force us to think for ourselves. One of *Walden*'s significant philosophical achievements is that it resists our efforts to pin it down to a frozen perfection and be done with it. In short, our failures to master its positions—the near impossibility of such mastery—means that our repeated efforts to think through it ought to throw us back into the work of self-examination, back into reflection on ourselves, our thoughts, and our practices.

If we are to make philosophical progress, we ought not to get side-tracked. But Thoreau is aware that our philosophical pursuits can go awry in a number of ways. *Walden* takes up the perennial concern that the discipline of philosophy will devolve into the production of endless commentaries on earlier books. Furthermore, it is possible to view *Walden* as a critique of speculative philosophy, as defined as theoretical reflection that does not arise out of our lived concerns or does not help us organize our lives. In "Economy," Thoreau offers a wonderful image of "the broad, flapping American ear" (1.71). We indiscriminately try to catch even the most trivial news, and we would rather fixate on someone else's work or condition than attend to our own work or condition. (This point is reiterated in 2.17, where we are cautioned "to stay at home and mind *our business*.") If we solely concern ourselves with the history of philosophy, we may never get around to reckoning with our own lives, ideas, and concerns. This would be one way to speak of the difference between the scholar and the historian, on the one hand, and the philosopher, on the other: For the former, the aim is a thorough understanding of historical events; the latter is interested in these historical events primarily for the sake of coming to a better understanding of himself. It is a sign of trouble, then, when we become so invested in defending a particular interpretation of some thinker, mastering a historical epoch, or getting caught up in work on "interesting" problems or questions raised by others, that self-understanding and self-transformation are either set aside or come to be seen as concerns for when we aren't studying or *doing* philosophy.

By settling ourselves, by minding our business and remembering our real needs, Thoreau believes that we recover a perspective that better positions us to discern reality. Hence, philosophy becomes distinguishable from sophistry, and we become less likely to confuse aimless abstraction with anchored reflection, enervating luxuries with the "necessaries of life." We might, then, define sophistry for Thoreau as that which doesn't truly concern me or demand my attention. This, of course, makes both the concepts of sophistry and philosophy subjective insofar as their content will depend on what I most need and, consequently, most need to attend to.

In the Conclusion to *Walden*, Thoreau vividly depicts actions—even the so-called noblest of actions—as evasions. He dismisses exploring new worlds, undertaking exotic voyages, hunting game, or fighting for one's country. "Our voyaging is only great-circle sailing, and the doctors prescribe for diseases of the skin merely." (We are reminded of Socrates' comment in Plato's *Charmides* [156e] about the Grecian doctors who fail to treat the individual holistically.) Thoreau continues, "One hastens to Southern Africa to chase the giraffe; but surely that is not the game he would be after. How long, pray, would a man hunt giraffes if he could? Snipes and woodcocks also may afford rare sport; but I trust it would be nobler game to shoot one's self" (18.2). Rather than target animals, Thoreau admonishes us to approach ourselves with courage, patience, stillness, and focus, all attributes that he has offered as foundational to a philosophical life.

Of course, as noted earlier, Thoreau also enjoins us in his Conclusion to "Explore Thyself," and it might not be too much to say that if we ever did cultivate the courage to do so, we might soon discover that we deserve to be shot. Perhaps this is why, regarding this business of self-examination, he writes, "Herein are demanded the eye and the nerve. Only the defeated and deserters go to the wars, cowards that run away and enlist" (18.2).

Harold Bloom has said that we read great writers because they help us accept ourselves, or show us that we are unacceptable. This remark is an apt expression of the experience of moving from Emerson's "Self-Reliance," where we are helped to accept ourselves, in part by showing us what it means to be a "self," to *Walden*'s first chapter, "Economy," where we are shown to be unacceptable, where Thoreau's searing searchlights are trained squarely on our frivolity, our cowardice, our laziness, and our desperation.

Of course, at times, the only way that we *can* come to accept ourselves is to first be shown that we are unacceptable, so that we can identify and confront that which is unacceptable within us. This is the demanding, unending business of self-examination, the work of self-recovery, the first step toward our best selves. Thoreau's goal in *Walden* is not to produce irrefutable arguments for a handful of philosophical theories, but to goad the reader to clarify and account for his or her own principles and practices. Put in Emersonian terms, the intent of *Walden* is not so much to instruct, but to provoke and inspire. Let us hope that we will soon be able to recognize and be willing to acknowledge such aims as essential to the discipline of philosophy, and to our own advancement.

TEN

WONDER AND AFFLICTION

Thoreau's Dionysian World

Edward F. Mooney

Tragic undercurrents, figured both as primal sufferings and as literary coping with sufferings, course through Thoreau's writing, especially in some of his lesser-read works, and prominently in his *Journal*. "If it is not a tragical life we live, then I know not what to call it."[1] These dark currents surface in his first book, *A Week on the Concord and Merrimack Rivers*, written as a memorial to his older brother. John had died in Henry's arms, suffering a tortured death from lockjaw. This tragic strain also surfaces in his description, in *Cape Cod*, of approaching a partially buried and decomposed corpse abandoned in the sand after a deadly wreck, a body we take to be Margaret Fuller's.[2] We find it also in his impassioned defense of the martyred antislavery militant, John Brown.[3] Attending to these tragic undertows gives his steady affirmations a higher pitch of accomplishment and urgency, and also gives a new angle on his concept of the wild. Thoreau's theme of the wild is pluriform, but one of its dimensions is related to tragedy and to what Nietzsche calls the Dionysian. Thoreau's writing is a way to resist tragedy as raw suffering and to redeem the world through art, making life sufferable, as the

Nietzsche of *The Birth of Tragedy* claims it can. From the midst of inescapable afflictions, writing can open into the sublime and the sacred.[4] If
not in the style of Cartesian meditations, Thoreau gives us recognizable
philosophical writing nevertheless, heard now as the voice of Aurelius
or Levinas, now reminiscent of Nietzsche, Rousseau, or the German
Romantics.[5] But this waits to be shown. Starting with Thoreau in stride
with Nietzsche's Dionysian wild, I end with Thoreau in stride with
Kierkegaard's philosophical and religious explorations. The upshot is
that just as Emerson should be read with Kant and Nietzsche, so should
Thoreau be read alongside his forebears, say Aurelius or Socrates, or
alongside his continental contemporaries, say Kierkegaard and Nietzsche.

Tragedy and Dionysian Religion

In the first instance, tragedy is not a theatrical performance or literary
genre, still less a philosophical *theory* of the human condition. It is a condition of terrible suffering. A person is or persons are at the center of
affliction, which spreads out in waves to afflict others who witness.
Tragedy on stage feeds on our knowledge of offstage tragedy and gives us
a culturally shared scenario of life at the limit. It is a condition suffered
viscerally, pressing the senses to the point of radical incapacity. We are
struck dumb, blinded. The world is present with intensity so explosive
that it simultaneously verges on total blackout, loss of self *and* world. We
are not ourselves, but become the very pain of our affliction.

Oedipus rips out his eyes because he cannot bear what he has seen, but
it is also true that there is no more left to see, given pain's saturation of
his bodily consciousness. His world *is* his suffering, and he doesn't need
eyes to know that. He remains the intense living site of pain's demonic
power even while his suffering wipes out any other world. Yet Oedipus
and Hamlet and Lear are not utterly stripped of speech, mad though that
speech may become. Tragic suffering in these cases occasions eloquent
lament, the affirmation of human expressive powers, an insistence on
dignity in circumstances that undermine it. "The need for dignity arises,"
Fred Beiser writes, "when tragic circumstances put a strain on our human
nature, on the normal human constitution."[6] To achieve tragic dignity is
to become more than a defeated victim of harsh fate. As Nietzsche put it
in *The Birth of Tragedy*, to attain a tragic dignity is to defeat the so-called
wisdom of Silenus: *Better to die early; best never to have been born.*[7]

Whatever tragedy Oedipus or Hamlet endures, and whatever tragic circumstance Thoreau endures, a measure of dignity can supervene. Thoreau
will embrace what Nietzsche identifies as the inversion of Silenus, the
heroic wisdom of Achilles: *Better to live long, but best never to die.*[8] Thoreau
enacts that wisdom in writing, and also in walking, building, and speaking. Each enactment is a fundamental way of sustaining affinity with
our landscape and place and with other of its inhabitants, modulated by
ever-more perceptive senses and by a range of vibrant sensibilities.

Nietzsche sees the roots of tragic drama in Dionysian religious rites
that enact great suffering and sacrifice. A performance of violence and
sacrifice preempts and forestalls raw annihilation by giving affliction a
ceremonial voice. Recurrent enactments become a celebration not only
of cycles of death but of connected cycles of rebirth. Participants survive
to enact lives and deaths once more and again, accompanied by music,
dance, and intoxication. Dionysus is ripped apart and then reborn.
Celebrants undergo cruelty and its metamorphosis in eloquent rebirth.
Nietzschean invocations of Dionysus can model the sort of suffering and
survival Thoreau describes and lives out.

Through the eloquence of words and walking, Thoreau articulates and
lives out the ephemerality of pain and its transformations as death yields
to life and life yields to death. In the swamp outside Concord in what he
calls a hell before the coming war, he smells paradise in a lily.[9] There is
inescapable hell to undergo, even Dionysian dismemberment, which
was Margaret Fuller's fate. This young and greatly gifted philosophical-
literary companion of Emerson's and Thoreau's drowned in shark-filled
waters off Long Island, returning by sea from the Italian Revolution.
Thoreau was sent to the Fire Island beach to find in the wreckage the
body and what might remain of her personal effects. Yet in the pages of
the journal that finally make their way into *Cape Cod*, Thoreau can bring
wonder and majesty to that desolate site.[10] If there is inescapable affliction, there is also metamorphosis. Dismemberment does not disappear.
Yet for the moment it is denied an *enduring* or *unmitigated* dominance.[11]

As Nietzsche sees it, tragic theater grows out of Dionysian rites. In
early theater, a tragic hero emerges who suffers yet eloquently *resists*. The
Dionysian wildness at the archaic heart of tragic drama is wiped out, as
Nietzsche sees it, with the triumph of rationality, ascetic intellectualism,
and a rage for order. Athenian Platonism (or as he would call it, Socratic
religiousness) is a stance that denies death *and* life. Nietzsche valorizes

wildness as a necessary counterforce to orderly, Apollonian aspects of life and art. Both Thoreau and Nietzsche disavow any theoretical *onlooking* that sunders a person from immersion in the senses and in embodied life.

The Dionysian sets a context for Thoreau's affirmation of a many-faceted wildness that engenders and preserves the world. Other aspects of the wild, each pulling in a slightly different direction, are linked to the tragic or Dionysian. For instance, there is Thoreau's sense of the woodland or forest wild celebrated by present-day conservationists.[12] There is also wildness in all life in its strivings and declines, of trees and insects as well as of salmon and hawks, a biocentric view of creation. There is the alien, forbidding, even horrific wild that Thoreau finds atop Mt. Ktaadn as well as the lethal wild that wipes out Margaret Fuller, Emerson's young son, and Thoreau's older brother. Each of these contrasting facets of "the" wild can be threaded through the primal theme of a Dionysian wild.

"The Dionysian" is not a Thoreauvian term of art, though it weaves unnamed throughout his work. Take his intoxicated pursuits through woods and mountains, his wild desire to devour a woodchuck in his path, his joy in tasting fermented and wild frozen apples, his rebellion against Apollonian stasis in business-as-usual Concord, his tracking cycles of death and rebirth in plants and all life (a Dionysian centerpiece), his affinity for the wildness of John Brown (who, on Thoreau's rendering, dies and becomes immortal),[13] his sense of impending apocalyptic destruction, laid out at the biblical close of his essay "Wild Apples"—not to mention his thoughts on music: "There is something in a strain of music [which] reminds me of the cries emitted by wild beasts."[14] And "It is the wild thinking in Hamlet . . . that delights us."[15] In *A Week on the Concord* he alludes to archaic Corybantic rites.[16] Only half tongue-in-cheek, in "Walking," Thoreau says he might prefer that life be "a divine tragedy" rather than "this trivial comedy or farce."[17] And his treasured fields become "a Dismal Swamp."[18] There is a recurrent Dionysian sensibility breathing beneath the deceptive quiets of Walden Pond and daily pastoral saunters.

Even in writing *Walden*, Thoreau acknowledges what Nietzsche would recognize as the haunting presence of the Dionysian (not to mention the measured and serene Apollonian).

> [I] find an instinct toward a higher . . . life and another toward a primitive rank and savage one, and I reverence them both. I love the wild not less than the good.[19]

The fires of the tragic feed the prophetic outrage of his political essays and burn slowly even under the more meditative tone of his *Week on the Concord.* We should not overlook, in this account of a trip with his brother, the sobering, even silencing, presence of another wild story of the river from a century and a half earlier, inserted quite unexpectedly. It is the story of Hannah Duston's escape down the Merrimack after her capture in an Indian raid in 1697. Her still-nursing child was ripped from her arms and savagely killed. Later she killed and scalped her captors in their sleep, carrying her bloody trophies downstream in her canoe. This is far from Apollonian classical orderliness (or Christian Paradise, or the New World "City on a Hill").[20]

Plato says philosophy is a rehearsal for death.[21] Thoreau had no rehearsal for John's death, suffered at close quarters. He was violently invaded three days later as death hollowed him out and took up residence. Thoreau took on all of John's dying symptoms. Philosophy, nestled in the narrative of *A Week,* became a kind of retrospective account of his love for his brother, his "friendship" (though that's too weak a word) with John, disrupted by death, and became an account of the violent story of Hannah Duston.[22] He had translated the violence in Aeschylus and Homer. He would later be spiritually eviscerated high on Mt. Ktaadn.[23] Through the mist he sees the top to be the workshop of indifferent gods. He feels his spirit fly outward from a crack between his ribs. But this Ktaadn-based anxious death and recovery was a minor skirmish next to John's dying.

Death's insistence calls us to life and to moods that are counter to death: joy and exaltation (among others). Philosophy can be a preparation by recuperating a sense of place and aliveness as a counterweight to devastation.[24] It is an arc rising from sadness and grief to lamentation and on toward ever-stronger affirmations in (and of) an anomalous, wonder-saturated world. Thoreau presents a wry and exuberant resistance lived out in walking, moving upriver, skating, tasting fermented cold apples, writing through and over all of these. His walk into life reanimates the movement of limbs and the movement of pencil over and through his *Journal.* It is a crescendo toward acknowledgment of a Dionysian, musical pulse of life and death, of a god of disorder, drunkenness, and night.

Searching for Fuller's personal effects, Thoreau returned to Concord having found nothing but scraps of clothing. Bones in the sand, never precisely defined as hers, were still on his mind days later when he reports a "lurid" and "blood-stained" sky. Not insignificantly, he also called that sunset "glorious."[25] Writing a monument to Fuller's majesty was, as we will see, an imaginative achievement. From the middle of Dionysian wildness, he preserves and redeems the song of Achilles: *Better to live long; best never to die.*

Thoreau needs to find the knit of things against threats of unraveling. Writing through and over wilderness and death let him face unraveling while knitting composure. *A Week on the Concord* is a liturgical week, starting on Saturday, the day Christ enters the underworld to rescue the dead.[26] Thoreau's holy Saturday would bring John up from the dead. He would be more than a corpse or a body in death's spasm.

Redemptive Writing and Reading

A glimpse of heaven is occasion for deep joy at just being alive. It is a renewable redemption from otherwise dark desperation. Thoreau's words of gratitude and attentive praise, his hymning and love of the world, leave desperate circumstance tactfully aside—or *nearly* aside—or on the best days, *and when possible* . . . aside.[27] As he glides across the frozen pond in pursuit of a scampering fox there's no denying his lively delight. His exuberance places him in momentary heaven. We are redeemed from our darkest hours by joining his gliding pursuit. This is affirmative joy, but it does not just spring spontaneously from the brute luck of a cheerful disposition. Consider how Thoreau works to *achieve* redemption of (and for) Margaret Fuller.

Here he is—along a bleak strip of beach off Long Island's Atlantic shore, some miles from Manhattan. A distant splinter marks the place he hopes holds Margaret Fuller's bones. This must be a place of grief. Yet as Thoreau approaches he sees the inconsiderable stick become a ship's spar, and then become a rugged cairn, a monument holding the place of her reign and majesty.

> Once . . . it was my business to go in search of the relics of a human body, mangled by sharks, which had just been cast up, a week after a wreck. . . . I expected that I must look very narrowly to find so small an object, but the sandy beach . . . was so perfectly smooth and bare . . . that when I was half a mile distant the insignificant sliver which marked the spot looked like a bleached spar, and the relics were as conspicuous as if they lay in state on that sandy plain, or a generation

had labored to pile up their cairn there. . . . [T]hey were singularly
inoffensive both to the senses and the imagination. . . . That dead body
had taken possession of the shore, and reigned over it as no living one
could, in the name of a certain majesty that belonged to it.[28]

This passage is imported from Thoreau's *Journal* (31 October 1850). It was
written three months after he returned from Fire Island, having traveled
down from Concord on hearing of the shipwreck and that Fuller had
perished. There he found spectators, scavengers, and those looking for
friends or relatives. He learned of an unidentified body given a shallow
burial five miles up the beach, marked by a stick. Arriving, the body was
too decomposed to identify. Thoreau wrote to Charles Sumner that there
was such decomposition that his "poor knowledge of anatomy" left him
not knowing if it were male or female.[29]

A spar displaces a stick, and a cairn displaces a spar. The wide sweep of
the shore displaces any offense the remains might have held: The scene is
one of metamorphosis in an anomalous world, a world that doesn't hold
still. And the place of Fuller's reign becomes the place of her communion
with endless surf that brings her a kind of immortality. It is a rapport that
leaves him out: He is this side of death. Thoreau lets the site be illuminated, "clarified" in his writing, lets it assume its rightful majesty. It is as
if the *Journal* or *Cape Cod* accounts show what *might have been* his discovery of Fuller's bones. Kierkegaard calls this sort of metamorphosis the
transfiguration of experience: "All poetry is life's glorification (i.e., transfiguration) through its clarification (through being clarified, illuminated,
'unfolded,' etc.)."[30]

> [The] bones were alone with the beach and the sea, whose hollow roar
> seemed to address them . . . as if there were an understanding between
> them and the ocean which necessarily left me out.[31]

Strips of flesh yield to rolling communion with the sea. Blinding sorrow
is deflected by somber exaltation.

Poetry and philosophy can deflect the cruelest of realities without
becoming only an illicit cover-up or an avoidance of truth. Recapitulation
of experience in a mode that deflects can be a healthy defense—say, as
we deflect a blow aimed at the head.[32] It allows us to live and move
on. Similarly, sublimation is not always a refusal to face up to difficult
reality. Thoreau's art deflects or sublimates, not as *denial* of trouble or
affliction, but as activity that transfigures it in the service of restoring and

redeeming life. He writes to redeem tragic conditions, as in his "Plea for John Brown," where we witness his achievement of immortality for Brown.[33] He works to redeem Brown and Fuller, and works toward his *own* redemption from the wounds inflicted by the loss of his brother and the hell of an approaching civil war. He redeems readers by giving them a sense that *his* transforming resistance can be *theirs*.

The wisdom of Achilles, *best never to die,* is a counterweight to the dismal adage of Silenus, *best never to have been born.* We could think of Thoreau's redemptive writing as effecting a shift from Silenus to Achilles as he faces the dismal evidence of Fuller's death. In "Slavery in Massachusetts," he sees nothing but hell along his meadows and water-ways, aware as he is of increasingly violent clashes over slavery and the dark approach of war. Yet as he walks the edge of a malodorous swamp, a fresh-smelling lily appears, a promise of purity and hope that offsets the political stench.

There are also moments of heaven in *A Week.* Having slept the night at the top of Mt. Greylock in the make-do comfort of a ramshackle coffin, he awakens to look across three states, surveying a heavenly expanse of good earth.[34] Returning to the Merrimack, an old hell obtrudes. The now and again turbulent river that Henry and John take upward toward New Hampshire's White Mountains is the river that carried a desperate Hannah Duston back down by Indian canoe, with scalps, to her burned-out home in Haverhill, thoughts of her slaughtered infant fresh in mind.[35] Thoreau links the upstream journey toward a source of light and life-giving waters to the downstream memory of a bitter fall for humankind in the cameo of Duston's capture, forced march, retaliatory slaughter, and downriver escape. Some years after the recapture of Anthony Burns in Boston in 1856, Thoreau laments that his usual sojourns in meadows are bringing no relief. "I cannot persuade myself," he writes, "that I do not live wholly within Hell."[36] Then a lily brings paradise.

Sensing Heaven in Hell

Thoreau elicits imagined yet not unreal moments of the best, forestalling inundations of the worst. He boils this down to the aspiration for prin-cipled action and for an increase of fragrance in the land—delivered by lilies, for instance. In a mock-Kantian twist, he gives us his categorical imperative: "*So behave that the odor of your actions may enhance the general sweetness of the atmosphere.*"[37] A phoebe darts against the fragrance of a meadow, moist earth slippers our feet. These saving perceptions can be turned over in hindsight and memory, playing a crucial role in the refinement of perception, and in expanding our capacity to meet more fragrant worlds. Reflective memory is the space where Thoreau's *Journals* take shape, where his perceptions mature in a fertile marinade of imagination. Perception is *philia,* a companionable relation, an ongoing duet of perceiver and perceived, achieved and at risk, moving always (despite hell and its stench) toward a glimpse of heaven, even as a moon glimpses us.

Heaven can appear as the wildness of a woodlot calling for attentive praise in poetry or prose. The wildness of apples calls for tribute. There is the global wildness of all life—from leaves and flowing sands[38] to the life of rivers and soaring hawks. To say these are heaven-like is to picture them unfolding under something like the glance of a divinity—as if a fine creator were appreciating the wonder of her work. Such an image underwrites a confidence that *here* a glimpse of heaven is achieved (when it is).

And there are less salutary wilds to tally, closer to hell than to heaven. There are the often wrenching lives and deaths of ordinary folk, and a terrifyingly cruel wild so vivid in the deaths of Fuller or Brown, in the heartless blotting out of Thoreau's brother, John, or of Emerson's son, or in the loss of American Paradise haunting the capture and flight of Hannah Duston. As woodland wilds become heartening, lethal wilds are accordingly muted; and when the focus is death and dismemberment, woodland wilds lose salience. Yet again, there is a contrasting register, neither explicitly lethal nor warmly reassuring, the indifferent and vaguely hostile wild atop Mt. Ktaadn. As the time of woodland wilds arises to hearten, lethal wilds retreat, evermore discreetly muted. As the time of wildly cruel death and dismemberment obtrudes, the time of nurturing woodland wilds for the moment is lost. The gentle wild of Walden wanes as the menacing wild of Ktaadn intervenes. All wilds, whether gentle or horrific, diminish under the baleful indifference of a pervasive mere habit and narrow technical or bureaucratic efficiency.

At the more desolate reaches of the wild, Thoreau shows us eloquent resistance equal to the aspirations of redemption. The very sea that kills Fuller sings to her undying spirit. Perceptual metamorphoses deliver such saving moments. Eyes *see* the spar and the cairn that memorialize

Fuller, and ears *overhear* her whispered communion with the sea. Writing raises the dead though effecting sensory transformations, while the world delivers an ever-changing range of prompts for lyric perception. This ongoing three-way exchange—writing, perceiving, and incoming sources—never leaves the awakened senses behind. They are modified by writing, and writing is informed by sources that in turn feed senses and writing. Thoreau declares near the end of *A Week*, "*We need pray for no higher heaven than the pure senses can furnish.*"[39]

A sentimentalist could believe that senses can furnish a heaven, but even the rigorous Kant succumbs, as his friend Wasianski reports.

> [Kant's] face radiated [a] kind of grave charm when he told with intense delight how he had once held a Swallow in his hands, peered into its eyes, and felt as though he had looked into heaven.[40]

In a strange parallel, Thoreau imagines himself looking through the eye of a bittern, a bird contemplating water, which "may have wrested the whole of her secret from Nature." Despite its veils and secrets, Thoreau would know nature through a liquid eye attentive to waters.[41] In *A Week*, Thoreau asks wistfully (and not altogether hopelessly), "Might I not *see* God?"[42] Perhaps seeing God is seeing a bittern who "wrests all her secrets from Nature." Perhaps seeing the bittern seeing nature is the closest we'll come to seeing God.

For Kant, mind is not an empiricist's passive, empty basket where impressions arrive for inspection or sorting or joining.[43] It is more like a construction site or processing site where experience and judgments are shaped or produced. Kant asks what the mind must be like if the world is as it seems. Thoreau asks what the world *can* be—can it be *better*?—if we but see and hear more of its wonders. Kant asks what makes ordinary perception of ships or spoons possible. Thoreau asks why perception sinks so easily toward the dull and deadening. Kant wants to *explain* perceptions and experience whereas Thoreau wants to *expand* the range and depth of our experience. He wants to reform waning capacities for tasting apples, seeing heavens, sounding ponds that cannot be fathomed. We have hardly begun even to desire to perceive.

Kant can only *hope* to see heaven in the eye of a swallow. The official system of his first *Critique* does not allow glimpses of heaven. The third *Critique* might do better. The theme of the sublime and the positing of aesthetic ideas can expand imagination to a world beyond the pale objecthood of ships or spoons. Aesthetic ideas include love, envy, fame, death, and vice.[44] If these open to the sublime, in dramas of yearning, beholding, and despair, we might imagine them also open to a glimpse of heaven in the eye of a sparrow, and a glimpse of vice in a profligate's eye; a glimpse of love in the eye of a friend, and a glimpse of Hades in the visage of a slave-catcher.[45] In any case, in the first *Critique* Kant does not linger with the role of affect, desire, or mood as affording access to the beauty or vice, the terrors or redemptions of our worlds. Nor does he linger to consider educating senses and imagination, as these afford access to better attunements to worlds perceived, and to better capacities to voice our worlds, and to voice who we are in them.[46] In the *Critique of Practical Reason*, he pauses in a famous moment, to bask in awe under starry heavens. But this is an uncharacteristic break in an otherwise puritanical work.

Achieving Perception and Affinity

Thoreau does not give us an explicit theory of perception, but it is clear that he would have rejected both the classical empiricist model of mind (a receptacle for impressions) and the Kantian model (a bustling multi-storied processing plant). Thoreau gives us a variety of perceptual attunements to the world across an expansive range of possibilities and notes our recalcitrant distance from those attunements that could be redeeming. The implicit lesson of his examples, as I read him, roughly follows the lines of a Stoic model of perception. To perceive well is to attain a learned affinity with one's embodied action with others in a surrounding habitat and an inherited milieu. One learns adjustments, culturally, if one is a cultural animal, that attune one naturally to one's needs, desires, physicality, sociality, sexuality, place, family, and history.

Oikeiosis is the Stoic term of art for the acquired fit between a fox and its world, for instance its capacity to bound naturally through snow; for the acquired fit between a bird and the location of nonpoisonous berries; and between a duck's awareness of its wing alignment and the look of the pond as it descends in an easy water landing that gracefully confirms its fit to its world. This perceptual fit of creature to itself and world, this *oikeiosis*, might translate as attunement, affiliation, or affinity. As a network of such protective and nourishing affinities, the term is sometimes rendered in modern parlance as "economy."[47] We can speak of an ongoing perceptual economy of connectedness, or, more poetically, of an unfolding dance of the senses with others, with oneself, with things, with remembered previous perceptions, with anticipations of our next perceptions. We assume this connectedness as a matter of course in the animal and vegetable world. For human animals, even when smooth affiliation or connectedness is admitted as a goal, achieving it is often excruciatingly difficult (and, at other times, so easy that we hardly notice). When perceptual affinities are lost or damaged, we are misfits to ourselves and our milieu and others. We undergo estrangement, disenchantment, objectification, a despairing loss of meaning. How can we picture, not the failure of fit, but a successful fit-to-world?

My touch on your shoulder (as we move into a turn) gives a perception to you. But your shoulder touches me at the same time. Our successful attunement rests on a mutual fittingness of perceptions exchanged. We learn of the aptness of fit from response of the other. Perhaps your flinch tells me my perceptual delivery has misfired. I learn thereafter to better modulate my tactile communication. My perception of you is modulated by your perception of me, as you return a responsive perception to me (a kind of flinching, or a kind of gentle yielding). Such is our dance-like access to the world, and the world's significant echo of us.[48] Thoreau imagines the roar of the sea addressing Margaret Fuller, calling to her scoured bones, establishing a communion—her ear (as it were) alert to the endless whisper of waves. Thoreau addresses us, gives us a concatenation of perceptions and words that are the moving communion between Fuller and the sea that seems to exclude him. We receive (or reject) his perception of intimacy between bones and sea, and his sense of exclusion. We flinch or are warmed by the perceptions delivered.

The world and others advance and recede, and our receptive capacities are ever in growth and decline. We can hear better (or worse), feel more (or less) of the subtlety afoot in a touch delivered. A sound has a pitch, extension, and rhythm not immediately evident. A look has a density. How much do we sense it? The press of a hand has insistence or gentleness. Narratives emerge as my touch meets your shoulder, and your shoulder touches back, this way or that. The dance of mutual perceptions can weave into ever-expanding narratives of approach and avoidance, lordship and bondage, embrace and exile, love of the world, and suffering its refusals.

Thoreau works to modulate touch, better to receive the subtleties of the world. The touch of the eye elicits response. With the sight of a bounding fox, Thoreau bounds in response. Under a silent sky he's patient with silence. As whippoorwills whistle from across the lake, he sings back. Seldom if ever does sensory input arrive completely unfit for a dance, inert like an accidental shop-window manikin, strewn with dust, unsmiling, not scowling, not even dressed. Things of the world and their absence greet us, surprise or annoy us, pique our curiosity or raise our ire, prompt a song or lament or a bounding, mimicking celebration. Learning to modulate our perceptions, attunements, and responses is an ongoing, educational affair. It is learning to hear and see better, more aptly, catching the drift of promising affinities with ever more subtle attention to all that impinges.

Philia begins as a register of *oikeiosis,* as part of our elemental perceptual fit-to-world. It can be as evident as the moves of a dance couple on ice, or the moves of a sloop tacking into the wind—hearing (and seeing) the flowing warnings and invitations of a breeze and a chop. Alternatively, this perceptual fit can be less dramatically displayed, and easily overlooked. As I stride, I'm given the sense that a mild unevenness in the floor threatens to upset my poise and calls for correction. The bump calls for an adjustment from me, and I make it effortlessly—thus restoring and maintaining filial exchange between my body and world. We are smoothly in stride so much of the time. Through infancy and beyond, perceptual fit is continually refined as part of ongoing initiations into various aspects of physical and social life (an ability to balance in snow, an ability to apologize). Refinement in perception allows me to see burdens (are they shame?) in my friend's halting glance.

Interweaving mutually exchanged, imagination-saturated perceptions over time makes possible all that I see in my friend's glance. Our best perceptions are founded on kinship, on what Cavell calls love of the world (and acknowledgment of others).[49] This is not to say that such love won't be crushed by the intrusion of evil or of indifference or of natural catastrophe, or by our own insufficiencies of heart. Thoreau figures our best perceptions as *achieved*—often something still *yet* to achieve, as our elemental nature develops ever toward more complex second nature.[50] Perceptions initially *Thoreau's* achievement can tilt *our* developing perceptions toward preservative, redeeming love (if we will).[51]

With its own generous inspirations, the world meets Thoreau's generously inspired pen. Margaret Fuller delivers majesty—and Thoreau's eye
and pen receive and convey it. She is received as majestic in death, which,
in Thoreau's rendering of the beach, is a startling imaginative achievement. This is perception at risk, not guaranteed. It is not data-reception,
but a dance full of stumbles and miscues and meaningless diversion—
while also full of wonder (and terror) and fulfillments. Philosophy can
start and end there, in perceptual achievements and also with disappoint-
ments and struggles with miscues. As Thoreau has it, we are perennially
tempted to digress and divert and insistently explicate or defend, which
in crucial cases is to forgo contact for the trappings of byplay. "Could we
for a moment drop this by-play—and simply wonder—without reference
or inference!"[52]

Wonder-wounded Hearing

Thoreau's genius is his perceptual range, depth, and acuity, made possible by keen imagination that modulates his affinities to the world through
all the senses. Its fulfillment rests on his success in passing on his perceptions and on the expressiveness of a *world* that delivers all that is *worth*
perceiving. The unfolding of the world is like a face-to-face encounter
where meaning intervenes and flowers. Thoreau opens a hand to a world
that extends *its* hand to him. At its best, a creative expression of self is
completed, at least momentarily, in the unfolding reality of an expressive
world—and an expressive world is completed, at least momentarily, in
the dance of the self's perceptions and responses, attuned to the expressiveness and receptivity of the world.

Co-creation is the mutual implication of self and world.[53] Thoreau is
receptive to the movement and whisper of wind and to the gaze of stars;
in turn, he is polyphonically expressive in his address to them. Each can
be in better or worse attunement to the other. Blinding snow can repel
our walk and sight. Our approach and gaze are repelled by fetid scatter-
ings of flesh. A striking melody can fall on deaf ears. We wonder if a finer
attunement can be achieved, and applaud if it can. Wonder-raising prose
depends on wonder-flowing worlds, and on what Hamlet calls "wonder-
wounded hearing."[54]

At its best, the world has an erotic appeal addressed to our capacities
for love. But *eros, philia,* and preservative love are always at risk—and

perceptual *philia*, a disposition toward friendly perceptions, is no exception. What lover walking the wreckage-strewn beach would *not* want to avert her eyes at the spot where Fuller's body is tossed and half-buried like old lunch? The bones can't be *only* discarded flesh. Thoreau tells us they are a *saint's relics*, nestled inoffensively in the sand. To see only their brokenness is to be false to the friend who walked with him in Concord before leaving to report on the revolution in Rome. Thoreau's cairn makes a place for her continuing life.

Thoreau responds to his friend's catastrophe in the perceptual registers of friendship and love (mixed with grief). He responds to the catastrophe of slavery in the registers of integrity that is outraged and of justice defiled, in shreds. In the case of less catastrophic troubles, say the need for shelter and the warmth of companionship, he would respond with simple hospitality.

In an underappreciated essay, perhaps best titled "The Inn Keeper," Thoreau elaborates a poststructuralist theme; yet, more important, a primal religious and ethical theme: unstinting welcome to the stranger and traveler. The inn and its keeper offer that humane and convivial refuge and succor in answering the knock of all who travel from home, who list between homes, or who are homeless. They are a momentary answer to the sense of placeless *Unheimlichkeit*. This is a vein we would do well to attend. This welcoming and generous host offers shelter to those of all faiths and walks of life.

> Methinks I see the thousand shrines erected to Hospitality shining afar in all countries, as well Mahometan and Jewish, as Christian, khans, and caravansaries, and inns, whither all pilgrims without distinction resort.[55]

His roof gathers in any who arrive to escape storms or the chill, giving haven to all to talk, eat, drink—share in good cheer. The tavern keeper also presides, if not over full Dionysian revelry, then over mild inebriation. (In "Wild Apples," as the very "nectar of the gods," Thoreau savors frozen but thawing and fermented apples.)

Of course, the needs of those caught in tragic ordeals or devastation exceed what hospitality can offer—though hospitality must always be welcome. Fuller, Hannah Duston, John Thoreau, and John Brown need more or other than shelter and good cheer. A more adequate response to their calamity would call on our capacities for outrage and deep willingness to witness *with* their suffering, in a kind of *philia* or love. E. M. Forster's "only connect" sounds against a world bent on destruction. Rick Furtak observes that when our connections with life are severed, *"it is as if an erotic bond has been broken."*[56] But what is broken can often be mended, or made sufferable, and it is worth the try. Thoreau writes: "There is no remedy for love but to love more."[57]

Thoreau and Philosophy

Thoreau gets shelved as literature, even when he's writing as a naturalist or comparative religionist or angry prophet or explorer of those anomalous zones where the stench of the swamps meets the fragrance of the lily, or where life is intermixed with death, or death with life. Those whose model of true philosophy is sustained and explicit argumentation won't quibble at shelving Thoreau there. And those whose model of religion is bound up with social institutions or denominations will want him shelved there, too, not with books on (or of) religion. But why should we assume that books must have but a single shelf-identity?

Philosophers dedicated exclusively to disciplined argumentation may block out moments of silence, quiet, or waiting, or moments of a particular beauty or terror, that so often appear in Thoreau. Of course, these moments might be reconstructed as moves within a subtextual argument, but it's as likely that Thoreau and other "literary philosophers" let their writing carry essentially nonargumentative impact. Often first on Thoreau's agenda is what John Austin would call the perlocutionary force of speech or writing—writing that may state something, but as important, may be an instance of experiential evocation, or an instance of performative utterance, say promising. If Thoreau bursts out, "I wanted to devour the woodchuck on the spot!," he might be asserting something about his desires, and also calling others to witness to an impulse they might have disowned or missed as their own, and be startled to find in Thoreau.[58] Wonder has its time in the pace of philosophical writing, a time of its own beyond quick comment or critique. Both wonder and, less commonly, its shadows—say, terror or outrage—are woven seamlessly through Thoreau's most detailed descriptions, into his most arching overviews, as well as his most sober critiques and his most explicit arguments.

His sentences give us what Stanley Cavell calls passionate utterance, words whose force and effect is a passionate intervention in "the disorders of desire," in that site of conflicted impulses and fantasies and aspirations that one could call the soul. A passionate utterance is "*an invitation to improvisation in the disorders of desire.*"[59] And Thoreau's passionate, intimate words cannot effect or cause change willy-nilly, but they can appeal movingly to our need for change, to our yearning or only half-acknowledged readiness for it, to our sensitivity to the improvising poetry of his appeals. And perhaps we will respond in a way that shows we are changed, in small or bigger ways. This sort of intersubjective exchange and change of view and comportment is far from the business of offering and accepting (or rejecting or amending) well-crafted arguments.[60]

Thoreau gives fragments of argument, and in his political essays, he makes extended and powerful argumentative appeals. But like the writing of Aeschylus and Homer, whom he admires and translates, his texts use narrative as the stream that carries arguments along; they don't have automatic pride of place. Socrates is irritated at the boys squabbling at his feet because they don't grasp the larger aims and visions in whose service Socrates interrogates. For his students, philosophy means intellectual swordplay, an amusing diversion, a byplay that deflects from a wondrous reality that needs to appear and sink in.[61] There is a way of writing philosophically, for instance in Montaigne or Aurelius, that doesn't end in a clear-cut propositional "therefore." Perhaps it evokes an appropriate mood for thinking—thinking in a way appropriate to life. In any case, such writing stalls or sidesteps the impulse toward smart rejoinder or counterargument. This is because what's being presented for philosophy, for wisdom or insight, is not a strikingly demonstrated conclusion, but wisdom or insight free and clear. What's presented can be a stunning or gentle emergent philosophical wonder or image, an alluring vision or event. Thoreau gives us sentences that are philosophical *showings*—of delight and affliction, for instance. His sentences say and also reveal and evoke. They can reveal as they deflect the worst of suffering and brokenness and as they open toward what Cavell calls love of the world.[62]

Plato teaches by argument but also with drama, myth, images, and *Eros,* making these essential to his task.[63] Rousseau presents arguments in his prize essays, but he also gives us, in *Reveries of a Solitary Walker*, evocative settings and moods and flashes of insight.[64] In his *Critiques* Kant gives us deductions, but in his essays he gives us his myth (or parable) of creation in which animal instincts are "that voice of God that all animals obey."[65] He gives no argument for this mysterious and unexpected claim. He knows that none could be given, yet he is not just indulging a foolish whimsy. We get a specifically philosophical conceit, a moment of wonder: Creatures, he confides, have access to the voice of God. God accesses *them*, and they obey naturally, instinctually. So instinct is not a hard-wired mechanical response but a wonderful *answering* to a call (or command). Animals are attuned to the divine; the divine is attuned to animals.[66]

Here we have Kant figuring an animal's place in creation in an emphatically non-Cartesian framework. And expanding his abbreviated gesture toward myth, we could take an animal's answer to a call or command from heaven as itself a form of speech. Hawks bespeak ease and power and grace in their flight. Instinct is the way animals voice an affinity with multiform creation, and with the divine—all this is implicit in an image from no less rigorous a thinker than Kant! Of course these are loose associations that *demonstrate* absolutely nothing. But to my ear, Kant's myth of creation provokes poetic-philosophical wonder that I would not want to censor or suppress.

Wittgenstein announced without elaboration, "If a lion could speak we would not understand him."[67] This oracular pronouncement belongs with his picture of language at play within forms of life, an image meant to displace the picture of language as a deracinated propositional system. Wittgenstein assumes that we share too little life with a lion to understand him, were he to speak. My initial observation is that Wittgenstein's point, whatever its worth, is uttered with next to *no* explicit argument about animal speech. We're left with a picture, as if from a children's book, of a speaking lion who can't be understood. The image is meant to persuade largely on its own—based on our willingness to improvise stories, as if to a listening child, that might (or might not) give the image more resonance. If such a rapid picture-remark works, Wittgenstein will have left us in philosophical wonder. This wonder can be pursued after it has sunk in, but it's clear that Wittgenstein is not offering a smart, doubt-stopping QED meant to cancel all further discussion. The remark is something like Kant's figure of animals obedient to God. If we are annoyed by such images or story-fragments in philosophy's sanctum, we will be left just plain exasperated: In Wittgenstein's case, what in the world are lions doing there!

Provoked by his gnomic remark, I'd add a second observation in the form of a trailer: "If a lion could talk, we wouldn't understand him *much more than we already do*." I propose by this gloss to shift us from a presumed *lack* of understanding across species to a plain *sufficiency* of understanding. Thoreau can bound across snow with a fox because he understands it—quite apart from speech. Likewise, I understand my dog's plea for a walk. We already understand the lion who (through instinct, as Kant would say) speaks, voices, gestures, roars: "*This turf is mine! Back off!*" We bipedal, speaking animals who read this page share ways of life with these felines, and so share understanding, in advance of what Wittgenstein conjures as a lion speaking and our failure to understand.[68] We too protect our food and our cubs and occasionally bask in the sun. Some, like Thoreau, will bound after a fox.[69] He enacts, thereby, a mutual understanding across species.

Now if these evocations of a shared form of life across species seem the least bit plausible, I've accomplished something philosophical with barely a shred of argumentation (though parts could be recast as an argument). Philosophical insight, if it's deepened at all, comes in this case and in others like it, through little scenarios and fantasies and imaginative prods, meant to make a new aspect of things come to light—not, for instance, by making the case for our affinities with animal life by arguing abstractly that animals have rights or minds, or can reason or suffer. Insight will arrive (if it does) in a glance of surprise or recognition.

These moments in Kant and Wittgenstein on animals (and my elaborations and friendly amendments) illustrate a place for wonder (and its shadows) in philosophy. They mark a place for the unargued and perhaps the unarguable, for the capacity of philosophy to reorient our perspectives and let us *see*. Thoreau gives us the sort of pictorial philosophical vision, assembled loosely piece by piece, that we find in Kant's essay or in Rousseau's *Reveries* or in Wittgenstein's strange assemblage of scenarios, questions without answers, images, and anti-pictures called *Philosophical Investigations*.[70] The upshot is that Thoreau cannot be excluded from the precincts of philosophy solely on the basis of his relative lack of interest in casting his reflections as sustained arguments. Let me continue with another instance of philosophy without argument, the instance of *Hamlet*.[71]

When Hamlet asks, "To be or not to be," he is not weighing arguments on the merits of suicide. He is letting dark truths flare out with unrivaled eloquence. He exposes his exposure to a world other than ordinary, or

ordinary but not ordinarily acknowledged. He exposes his exposure
to what Cora Diamond calls difficult realities.[72] Ordinary arguments
launched from a region where we are neither exposed nor find it apt to
expose our vulnerabilities are often ineffectual or beside the point or irk-
some. They are beyond the pale when one speaks and listens from the
domain of affliction and despair, taking that domain as the center of
the matter, and speaking to others in affliction or despair. Dispassionate
observations or arguments are outside any world Hamlet can, in his
time, inhabit. He is *witness* to his troubles, exposes his vulnerability to
them. He is not a meticulous accountant keeping track of malfunctions
in the world. The startle and wonder of it all is that his words of dark
exaltation fly wildly, elegantly, *above* and *through*, those troubles. "What
a pity," Thoreau exclaims, "if the part of Hamlet be left out,"[73] for his
words ought to stop us in our tracks—awaken us to terror, but also to
the wonders of the human voice and its capacity to mitigate and modulate sheer terror and despair. We are animals who can not only bound
through snow beautifully but who can also launch readily into registers of
eloquence.

Hamlet's voicing of terror, melancholy, doubt, and wonder should not
be lost—not lost for philosophy merely for lacking argumentation. Over
and over in Thoreau, there are moments of philosophical radiance, joy,
and exaltation. They do not stand to be confirmed or refuted, but are
exposed on their own to stand on their own for what they are. In the
moment, they quiet or arouse quite independently of supportive reasoning. Yet too extended a silence in their presence would fail them. As
responsive creatures, we're moved to speak in memoriam and celebration, in elaboration and repetition, continuing and renewing the moment
of their life. We bring words of commemoration and redemption again
and again onto this meager stage where they can speak, be heard, be
exposed and seen, once again.

Here again is Thoreau at that place of mourning he transforms through
commemorative evocation.

> When I was half a mile distant the insignificant stick or sliver which
> marked the spot looked like a broken spar in the sand. There lay the
> relics in a certain state, rendered perfectly inoffensive to both bodily
> and spiritual eye. . . . That dead body possessed the shore as no living
> one could. [The bones were] alone with the sea . . . whose hollow roar
> seemed addressed to the ears of the departed.[74]

Fuller's placement and aspect are changed. What Thoreau takes as her shark-scored bones yield to infinite communion with the sea's address. Sorrow and terrible loss are displaced. Against the pull of undertows, Thoreau through his writing inhabits the confluence of wonder, poetry, and philosophy.

Concord and Copenhagen

Let me round out the plausibility of Thoreau's full membership in the congress of philosophers by a quick comparison with another literary thinker, a Danish writer and walker as rich in philosophical insight as Nietzsche (with whom we began this essay). In December 1838, Thoreau wrote out in his journal a brief but striking philosophical desire:

> Could we for a moment drop this by-play—and simply wonder—without reference or inference![75]

Some eight months earlier, a literary philosopher from Copenhagen reported in *his* journal:

> This morning I saw half a score of geese fly away in crisp cool air. . . .
> They divided into two flocks arched like a pair of eyebrows above my eyes, which were now gazing into the land of poetry.[76]

We might be surprised that Thoreau bears comparison to Kierkegaard (yet we can read just that in the marvelous entry on Thoreau in *The Stanford Encyclopedia of Philosophy*).[77] Of course, once we think of it, there are intriguing parallels.

Each kept astounding journals. Thoreau started his at age twenty, in 1837, and Kierkegaard jotted his first entry at age twenty-one, in 1834. Both were poetic, ethical, political, and religious, and both skewered their fellow citizens with mordant wit. Both were philosophers of the place they inhabited. Although their reading made them global and brought the past to their present, Kierkegaard left provincial Copenhagen as seldom as Thoreau left Concord. From the mid 1840s on, Kierkegaard exposed the sham of his city's Christendom. Thoreau found the freedom won at Lexington and Concord despoiled when Mexico was invaded and slavery was enforced in Concord and Boston, the latter in the case of Anthony Burns. Kierkegaard dies disowned by the elite of his city at forty-two, and Thoreau dies almost uneventfully at age forty-four, his demise overshadowed by the Civil War. Yet he had his part in bringing on that cataclysm.[78]

There are differences, notably, of temperament. Thoreau was not sentimental enough to have written this: "No turtle-dove builds its nest in my branches."[79] And lacking Thoreau's marvelous animal exuberance, Kierkegaard could not have given us this:

> I saw a fox . . . making across to the hills on my left. As the snow lay five inches deep, he made but slow progress, but it was no impediment to me. So yielding to the instinct of the chase, I . . . bounded away, snuffing the air like a . . . hound.[80]

At a deeper level, there are a number of convergent philosophical motifs whose presence might surprise us. In no special priority, these five stand out:

1. Thoreau said one could find teachers of philosophy but no philosophers in and about Concord. He valued not just a *conception* of how to live. He valued its exemplary *enactment* in the detail of one's life. Kierkegaard mocked the strictly academic practice of professors of philosophy that had absolutely no bearing on expressing one's convictions in daily life.

2. Thoreau waits for new days to dawn, creation occurring ever and again, bequeathed to those with "eyes to see"; Kierkegaard's poetic "young man" awaits a new world delivered in a thunderclap, given in an *Augenblick* that he calls "repetition."[81]

3. For both, the *telos* of awareness is an *earnest openness*, a moment for responsibility, not just a moment of cognitive success or of self-interested or rational satisfactions.[82] Kierkegaard calls this *subjectivity*; Thoreau has no single term to catch this fertile slant of attentiveness.

4. Thoreau asks why George Washington, who never gave his life or word to rid the land of slavery, should be ranked *higher* than John Brown, who did. Kierkegaard asks why Abraham, who was ready to sacrifice another's life, should be ranked *higher* than a common murderer.

5. Maine's Ktaadn, at the top, is an indifferent, even hostile mountain: Spirit exits through a gap in one's ribs; a frighteningly "raw existence" forces Thoreau to cry out in uncharacteristic dismay, "*Contact! Contact! Where are we? What are we?*"[83] Kierkegaard calls this onslaught (and frightful *flight*) of existence dizziness or anxiety, and places it, like Thoreau, in a dark before the world is born.[84]

We have more than enough here to improvise (on another day) any number of extended conversations.

Great Moral Philosophy

There is a tragic undercurrent in much of Thoreau's writing, an undercurrent that travels with a Nietzschean concept of the Dionysian. Thoreau's writing as resistance to affliction is in part a transformation of a Dionysian wild. In bringing out these themes, I've simultaneously pursued a wider aim. Thoreau's writing belongs within a broad tradition of moral philosophy that flourishes in the work of Nietzsche and Kierkegaard, Hegel and Carlyle, and earlier in the work of Plato, Aristotle, and the Stoics. Stanley Bates characterizes that tradition as an exploration of human living aimed at seeing and living better.[85] This is a tradition more or less lost to twentieth-century moral philosophy. Accordingly, if Thoreau is to be woven into a tradition neglected or in decline, retrieving his presence for philosophy is part and parcel of retrieving that broader tradition of, and for, philosophy.

> It is a striking fact that since the latter part of the nineteenth century when academic philosophy divided itself into subdivisions and the specialty of moral philosophy was created, almost no one who has practiced that specialty has been a "great" philosopher.[86]

The occlusion of that older tradition occurs with disciplinary professionalization. Moral philosophy loses the stature of providing a grand vista on the person immersed in cultural, civic, and interpersonal life in the way that Aristotle or Plato, Montaigne or Seneca might provide. It shrivels or disappears in our time and becomes one of a number of specialized subfields. It is lost in the competition for curricula space among epistemology, aesthetics, metaphysics, logic, cognitive science, history of philosophy (in its many periods), and endless other proliferating subdivisions. The cosmos and soul, the city and forest, the garden and human are lost.[87]

Bates doesn't deny that there have been any number of philosophers concerned with the question of how one should see and live life better, but these thinkers, he says, fall outside what has become the restricted twentieth-century academic rubric of "moral philosophy."

> Since that time [the latter part of the nineteenth century], or a bit earlier, almost all of the philosophers who have been most significant

in helping general readers to understand how to live their lives would not be classified as "moral philosophers." I think of Hegel, Kierkegaard, Emerson, Thoreau, Marx, Nietzsche, Freud, Dewey, Heidegger, Wittgenstein, and Sartre (and of course not all of these would be allowed the name "philosopher" by analytical philosophy). These thinkers tend either to produce narrative structures or to reflect on the narrative structure of human existence, not in order to provide a formula, or a template, of human existence, but to deny the possibility of such a formula.[88]

Thoreau gives us narratives of domesticity (through writing and residing at Walden Pond, establishing a home) and narratives of travel, pilgrimage, or commemoration (*Cape Cod, The Maine Woods, A Week on the Concord and Merrimack Rivers*). He delivers narratives of ways of living with others ("Slavery in Massachusetts," "A Plea for Captain John Brown," "Resistance to Civil Government"). And he delivers narratives of ways of living with oneself (parts of *Walden*, "Walking," and "Wild Apples"). Furthermore, we find in Thoreau the haunting undertones of tragedy that intimate, as Bates puts it, the impossibility of any simple formula or template to guide seeing and living life in the midst of its ample vicissitudes and terrors.

None of this fits well with contemporary academic models of moral philosophy. There one seeks moral "action guides" and formulas, guiding principles, and constraining and enabling rights. It continues worthy—and often vibrant—debate about the capacity of utilitarian or Kantian or neo-Humean orientations to provide order and guidance. And there are debates about virtue theory and investigation of specific virtues (and vices): courage, compassion, and jealousy, for instance. But these efforts are seldom tied into larger understandings of the human, and they set aside questions about the tragedy or comedy or melodrama of human life. They tend to duck altogether what Diamond calls "the difficulty of reality," its sheer contingency and harsh interruptions.[89]

If Thoreau falls outside the ambit of contemporary academic moral philosophy, he nevertheless falls well within the ambit of moral philosophy in the sense of the term that brings in Schopenhauer and Kierkegaard, Nietzsche and Levinas, Camus and William James, and Thoreau's nearest neighbor, Emerson.

Bates finds in Stanley Cavell's discussions of Emerson, Nietzsche, and others, an interest in a dimension of moral life that "concerns what used to be called the state of one's soul" and "the possibility or necessity of the transforming of oneself and of one's society."[90] It takes little or no modulation to hear Thoreau voicing a concern for the soul and its relation to others, to the wild, and one's society. That is an interest more diffuse and elusive than Apollonian investigations, so characteristic of contemporary academic debates, of principles or lawlike frameworks, or of specific virtues, pulled from the flow of ongoing life. But if Thoreau is in fact working in (and out) toward his soul and the souls of others, toward the transformation of souls, and toward the resonance and impact of this work in reforming society, then this should secure his eligibility as a "great moral philosopher"—a thinker at home in the company of Kierkegaard or Nietzsche or the early Marx as they write, for instance, on suffering, alienation, and redemption.

Thoreau speaks to the state of one's soul, which is an implicit concession or promise to forgo technical, specialized arguments—say, epistemological ones that contest Kant or Hume on the issue of value-apprehension, or that explicitly contest Plato or Aquinas on the status of the transcendent. Thoreau addresses nonspecialists, bringing them to issues any person in an inquiring or contemplative or troubled mood might raise about orientations to a life, about what it is like to see life from unconventional perspectives in desperate or unanchored times. That sort of address is only minimally argumentative and relies on images, pictures, scenarios, narratives, untamed wonder, and a glimpse of release from terror. It is writing that lacks the closure of a "therefore" written on the blackboard. We see (or don't see), are overwhelmed (or worried or disappointed) by Thoreau's ability to mark a path through life—and to light it for another. He writes out an invitation to enter a setting, laid out with full justice to its complexity and allure, wherein a soul might find itself at home despite ineluctable ephemerality, pain, and incompleteness.

Thoreau gives us writing that lights up deficient life (or segments of it), that exposes constrictions and corruption in a life, that shows it to be shallow or full of quiet desperation—all this on display not for casual onlooking or entertainment, not for curiosity or bursts of shallow indignation, but for as much deliverance from affliction as the heart and the pen can provide. We do not destroy affliction through writing but work through its tragic lineaments. We can receive, listen, and see, in the face of that overwhelming devastation that lies outside the ambit of our immediate opportunities for action. We cannot undo past atrocities or cruel accidents of fate or the burdens of mortal being.

We listen, see, and then hope through new perception to acquire—if not untroubled delight, then at least a stance beyond indifference, outrage, or despair—if not exactly serenity, then at least affinity; and if not full affirmation and love, then acceptance and welcome, however mottled its intensity and eloquence.

ELEVEN

AN EMERSON GONE MAD

Thoreau's American Cynicism

Douglas R. Anderson

When Plato was asked what sort of man Diogenes was, he answered, "A Socrates
Gone Mad."

—Diogenes Laertius, *Lives of the Eminent Philosophers*, 6.54

I doubt if Emerson could trundle a wheelbarrow through the streets, because it
would be out of character.

—Henry David Thoreau, *Journal*, 30 January 1852

W
e sometimes forget that Emerson and Thoreau were hard-core, if
somewhat romantic, social reformers. They were also engaged in
the transformation of philosophy, ready to quit the old school British
empiricism and the tedious moral dogma of their Harvard professors.
Emerson, defiant of the schoolmen, explicitly identified Plato as "the philosopher" and focused on Plato's peculiar ability to be at once a poetic
and systematic thinker. "A philosopher," said Emerson, "must be more
than a philosopher. Plato is clothed with the powers of a poet, stands
upon the highest place of the poet, and (though I doubt not he wanted
the decisive gift of lyric expression), mainly is not a poet because he chose
to use the poetic gift to an ulterior purpose."[1] Thoreau, as was his wont,
found his own road into a Greek inheritance. Whereas Emerson took his
lead from Platonism, Thoreau seems to have been more inspired by
Socrates and another set of post-Socratic thinkers whose focus was not
solely on theoretical or intellectual excellence but on leading a philosophical life. Thoreau was, as others have noted, influenced by the Greek and
Roman Stoics.[2] But this influence was itself underwritten by a more direct

affinity with the ancient Cynics, who regarded themselves as the true heirs of Socrates.[3] Like them, Thoreau did not reject writing and intellectual endeavor; rather, he sought to reorient these by bringing them into line with a Cynic's sense of *eudaimonia* as a freedom through simplicity. One advantage of reading Thoreau as a descendant of the Cynics is that it helps make sense of traditional difficulties in reading Thoreau's work as whole. For example, there has been some debate concerning whether he was an anarchist. As a Cynic, he would be critical of the state's bad conventions and of his own habits acquired uncritically from the state, and he would favor the individual's independence from the state. However, the Cynics focused their resistance not on every cultural convention but primarily on those causing present harm. In this light, one can make sense of Thoreau's rejection of the state that legitimizes slavery but acceptance of the state that builds useful roads. In what follows, I want to explore some of Thoreau's inheritances from the Cynics with an eye toward how these might speak to our own current philosophical practices. If this exploration does not cause us to revise our ways, it might at least make us more self-aware of what we think philosophy is.

The lives of Antisthenes, Diogenes, and Crates became exemplary for many in the Hellenistic world—they were not only philosophers but also, like Heracles, cultural heroes. To others, of course, they were a social nuisance—the offspring of the Socratic gadfly. There is also evidence that Cynicism had some influence on early Christianity, another threat to the Roman social fabric. This was reason enough for the Emperor Julian to treat the Cynics as socially dangerous characters. Intellectual differences can sometimes be tolerated, but challenges to the ways we conduct daily life are always a threat to dominant regimes. When we look at Thoreau, we find that his habits closely fit the Cynic lifestyle. And we know that at least for a few important social reformers such as King and Gandhi, Thoreau's own practices were exemplary. It is of course well documented that Thoreau read widely and was influenced by various thinkers and traditions; my aim here is simply to show that the Cynics, whom he at least read about, serve as foundational role models for Thoreau's philosophical outlook.

Thoreau's philosopher is not an intellectual lawyer intent on besting others in scholarly contests. Nor is he a charlatan entrepreneur aiming for short-term fame and a cult following. Just as the Greek Cynics chastised those philosophers who lived in elite company and sought favor at court, Thoreau rejected the clerical professionals who led New England education. And, as I will suggest later, Thoreau would have been provoked by the tedious, logicized, and existentially incompetent philosophy that dominated the twentieth-century academy in America. Indeed, it would even be misleading to think of Thoreau as a proto-pragmatic thinker; the pragmatists too lived and continue to live under the sway of the professional philosophical academy. His own account of philosophy is, I think, better understood as an American Cynicism.

Nature with a Twist: Basic Affinities

As we noted, the Cynics were infamous for their resistance to unreasonable *nomoi* or cultural conventions. And they were noted for talking back. Speaking of Diogenes the Cynic, Diogenes Laertius says: "He was great at pouring out scorn on his contemporaries. The school of Euclid he called bilious, Plato's lectures a waste of time, the performances of the Dionysia great peep-shows for fools, and the demagogues the mob's lackeys."[4] This practice of critique and negativity, it is sometimes forgotten, was accompanied by a positive doctrine—that one lives and learns best in accord with nature. This is true in two ways. First, in living close to nature one simplifies life enough to live it reflectively. As Laertius suggests:

> Indeed what Diogenes proposed was to bring back to *man's* awareness that easy means of living, and to show that human beings always have at their disposal what they need in order to be happy *provided they know how to accept the real limits of human nature.*[5]

Second, to live in league with nature is to open the possibility for a good life—a philosophical life. "Nature," as Julie Piering says in describing Cynic ethics, "offers the clearest indication of how to live the good life, which is characterized by reason, self-sufficiency, and freedom."[6]

Thoreau adopted Emerson's dynamic Spinozism—we humans are both *natura naturata* and *natura naturans*. We are creat*ed* and creat*ing*; we can learn about ourselves, and we can create the world anew in some ways. Wherever we have been *made*, civilized, or what we now call socially constructed, we must remain wary and critical so that we don't abandon our creative abilities. We must keep wildness alive even as we live in the midst of cultural norms. As R. F. Nash argues, Thoreau's "ideal man" maintains a working middle ground "drawing on both the wild and the refined."[7] Here Thoreau follows a basic theme of the Cynics: "Conventions are not inherently bad; however, for the Cynic, conventions are often absurd and worthy of ridicule."[8] The point is that the focus is on revitalizing lives and cultures, not just tearing apart the social fabric. The harshest words of the Cynics were still aimed at improving lives. To accomplish this task, Thoreau's "ideal person" would have to draw on both Nature and on *her own* human nature.

To live with and through nature, we must be attuned to our own natures. We must engage our natural agency, and we must learn from nature itself. As Thoreau wrote in *Walden*: "However hard your life is, meet it and live it; do not shun it and call it hard names."[9] This was a persistent theme for the Cynics as well as their Stoic descendants; persons need to live with their own natures. As Piering remarks regarding the Cynics: "Life, as given by nature, is full of hints as to how to live it best; but humans go astray, ashamed by petty things and striving after objects, which are unimportant. Consequently, their freedom is hindered by convention."[10] Thoreau clearly embraces this dimension of the Cynics' thought; the Thoreauvian philosopher is not so much a naturalist as a "naturist," one for whom nature is an object of love and reverence. And, as William Desmond notes, "The Cynics stress that human beings are not immediately at home in nature, but must struggle to regain their rightful place in it."[11]

It is important to keep in mind that the Cynics were not in principle anti-intellectual, and neither was Thoreau. The naturist is fundamentally a learner, and believes we are so natured as to have "higher faculties" that can take us beyond everyday affairs. Thoreau would have us engage these faculties: "But the fact for the philosopher, or a nature loving wisdom, is that it is most important to cultivate the highest faculties and spend as little time as possible in planting, weaving, building, etc."[12] Despite the popularity of "back to nature" primitivism in his day, Thoreau was not himself a primitivist, though some have read him in that way. Rather, what primitivist features he endorsed, he defended on the basis of clearing space for the higher faculties. "I think that there is nothing," Thoreau said, "more opposed to poetry, to philosophy, ay, to life itself, than this incessant business."[13] This was a central theme for Antisthenes, Diogenes, and Crates. Diogenes Laertius put it as follows, speaking specifically of Diogenes of Sinope: "He would say that men strive in digging and kicking to outdo one another, but no one strives to become a good man and true."[14]

Thoreau's Naturally Reasoning Person

The aim of philosophy for the Cynics as well as for Thoreau was not to achieve academic recognition or gain control of the Academy but to live well. To carry out this natural philosophical task of living well, two general skills need development. First, we must, Thoreau argues, become good observers and perceivers. We must be able to learn directly from nature, our primary teacher. Second, we must be able to create and produce. To this end we must employ active imagination tethered by experience. Moreover, we must become students of reading and writing so that we can both learn extant wisdom and learn how to generate more of the same. The natural and the civilized, the wild and the tame, must work in concert.

It was in the interest of perception and writing that Thoreau went to Walden. These were central pursuits of his experiment in living deliberately. His encounters with "brute neighbors," with ponds, with seasons, were always learning experiences. Like the Cynics, he learned experientially nature's laws and the limits these place on us. At the same time, and perhaps even more than the Cynics, he pursued the particularities and contingencies in nature's lessons—he swam with an unpredictable loon and studied the pond's idiosyncrasies. The key for Thoreau, as for Emerson, was to learn metaphysical truths in an experiential way, and then to give them articulation in thought and word. "Unless Nature sympathizes with and speaks to us, as it were," he argued, "the most fertile and blooming regions are barren and dreary."[15] Again like the Cynics, Thoreau resisted philosophical theories that wandered astray from everyday experience. For both it was precisely in the everyday and the ordinary that truth was disclosed. It helped not to have royal or academic connections. Theories that were internally whole, intellectually elegant, and logically consistent were, for Thoreau, not nearly as significant as those that helped bring nature's reason into our own being—only in perceiving nature's laws could we come to live in harmony with them. "It is vain to write on the seasons," he warned, "unless you have the seasons in you."[16]

Our natural abilities to think and reason must always be constrained by our encounters with nature. Intellect must initially be receptive, as Emerson put it, and imagination must create our worlds in harmony with nature's reason if we are to live well. "Any truth," said Thoreau, "is better than make-believe."[17] The key, again, is that nature is a better measure of truth than are the *nomoi*; our civilizing conventions *can* be extremely useful and illuminating, but they also tend to become extreme, to age, and to outrun their usefulness. Thoreau's resistance to the conventional pedagogical practices of New England comes to mind. Living under the influence of dysfunctional conventions, we are led by our everyday habits into routine and desperation—our wild dimensions become overcivilized. Therefore, the philosophical life requires an openness to nature that civilization tends more and more to resist. The twist, again, is that nature is a better truth-teller than civilization, and that our encounters with nature help enliven our own wildness, without which we soon fail to learn from nature and therefore to creatively transform culture. The philosopher's life requires an attentiveness to wildness as a condition for creating a higher culture.

> I found in myself, and still find, an instinct toward a higher, or, as it is named, spiritual life, as do most men, and another toward a primitive rank and savage one, and I reverence them both. I love the wild not less than the good.[18]

Indeed, for Thoreau, without the wild, our attempts to cultivate the good will eventually fail, stifled by the dead habits of the past.

> A town is saved, not more by the righteous men in it than by the woods and swamps that surround it. A township where one primitive forest waves above while another primitive forest rots below—such a town is fitted to raise not only corn and potatoes, but poets and philosophers for the coming ages.[19]

The Primacy of Ethics

Against the tradition of "professional" philosophy, the Cynics and Thoreau aimed to make philosophy once again an ordinary, natural, human endeavor in which one attempts to live a reasonable, or a thoughtful, life. As Piering points out, "The Cynics neglect, and very often ridicule, speculative philosophy."[20] Thoreau too rejected the formality and dogmatic theoretical distance of his Harvard teachers, who "professed and practiced" anything "but the art of life."[21] Neither, however, rejected philosophy that led in the direction of living well. For them, ethics trumped metaphysics and logic—these disciplines must be instrumental to living wisely. As Laertius pointed out, the Cynics "are content then, like Ariston of Chios, to do away with the subjects of Logic and Physics and to devote their whole attention to Ethics."[22] Technical philosophical thought—theorizing and speculation—is itself a practice and needs to show its import in enabling us to lead a good life, not merely in advancing our careers. The question is how we spend our days and our human energies. Thus, for Thoreau, philosophy was synonymous with an "economy of living."[23]

In ancient Greece and in nineteenth-century America, however, mongers of technical philosophical analysis tended to look down on ethicists and political thinkers as second order. The case is much the same today. It seems to be "just the case that" only those who can hang with mathematical logic and its ontological upshots are included in the class of genuine philosophers. Philosophers seem to operate with an implicit "degree of difficulty" thesis, which maintains that the more technically clever and difficult an outlook is, the more authentically philosophical it is. Moral philosophy, especially poeticized philosophy, is "easy" and therefore should be discounted for its low degree of difficulty.[24] This makes it easy to exclude Cynics and American Transcendentalists from the philosophical canon. The Cynicism of Crates, for example, was charged with being "just a way of life."[25] But, as Emerson argued, "a long logic" can well be embedded in a moral and poetic philosophy, and it is more difficult to work with because it more closely engages the contingencies of experience. Logic, physics, and math, however technically subtle, tend to have fairly clear-cut answers; once one grasps the drift of the system, what was difficult becomes in another way easy. These disciplines produce "knowledge" in the sense of certainty. In dealing with living, with experience, and the reason of nature, however, ethicists do not achieve this sort of calculative knowledge. "The highest that we can attain to," says Thoreau, "is not Knowledge, but Sympathy with Intelligence."[26] Thoreau orients philosophy toward consummatory experiences that might achieve this sympathy. These experiences are not easy to come by, nor are their contents easy to grasp. Thoreau and the Cynics take discourse on the conduct of life, then, to be as difficult as logical analysis, if not more so. "How can one be a wise man," Thoreau asked, "if he does not know any better how to live than other men?—if he is only more cunning and intellectually subtle? Does Wisdom work in a treadmill?"[27]

Freedoms in Concert

For both the Cynics and Thoreau, a philosophical life was conditioned by freedom. As Thoreau directly put it, "The question is whether you can bear freedom."[28] Here, it seems, Thoreau drew directly on Cynic tradition, which argued that most of us are enslaved to cultural competition. As he writes in "Life without Principle": "There is no more fatal blunderer than he who consumes the greater part of his life getting his living."[29]

As Cynicism developed, three modes of freedom revealed themselves as requisite for a philosophical life: *eleutheria,* or what we would call negative freedom or liberty; *autarkeia,* self-sufficiency or self-reliance; and *parrhesia,* the freedom to speak directly and bluntly.[30] None of the three is sufficient on its own; instead, they work mutually to create the possibility of a thoughtful life. Achieving these three modes of freedom working in concert seems to me Thoreau's chief aim. And like Antisthenes, Diogenes, and Crates, he presented them not only in his writings but also in the life he lived. The isolation of philosophical thought from everyday life, as is common among contemporary professional philosophers, was fundamentally foreign to the outlook of Thoreau and the Cynics. Thoreau, like Diogenes and Crates, lived as an exemplar, but only in a generic way—the idea is not to be Thoreau, but to be self-reliant according to one's own nature. In *Walden* he explicitly reminded us that we are not each to do what he does; rather, he "would have each one be very careful to find out and pursue *his own* way, and not his father's or his mother's or his neighbor's instead."[31] We are each to take the measure of our own drummers and advance in the direction of our own dreams. A Cynic's life is lived according to her own nature, which is itself an expression of Nature's reason.

Eleutheria requires strength in resisting external controls; it involves toil and an ability to endure. An initial move in this direction is to seek solitude—to remove oneself from the social controls that abound in a civilized world. This was at least one of Thoreau's motivations for moving to Walden Pond. It was his attempt to begin to live deliberately by absenting himself from some of life's distractions. As he put it in 1840, "I can move away from public opinion, from government, from religion, from education, from society."[32] However, it was for an equally important reason that he eventually left Walden. Solitude is useful for initiating *eleutheria,* but it is not a permanent condition. This is one of those mistaken excesses occasionally attributed to Thoreau—he was not a recluse or a hermit. His experiment in solitude was instrumental to his philosophy, to his economy of life. After all, the other modes of freedom, especially *parrhesia,* are not well enabled by solitude; they have clear social dimensions. Although the writing and thinking of *Walden* may have taken place in solitude, the import and impact of the text are public and socially significant.

Solitude not only physically separates one from some of life's ongoing distractions, but it also sets one outside civilization and the law. In this much Thoreau shared with the Cynics a peculiar sense of cosmopolitanism. Their idea is not that all communities can be brought together in a global union, but that one living a philosophical life will be at home anywhere. Thus, Laertius was to say of Diogenes that "he used any place for any purpose, for breakfasting, sleeping, or conversing."[33] This cosmopolitanism helps establish a kind of outlawry inasmuch as one lives freely outside anyone else's jurisdiction. Thus Thoreau, for his part, echoing Diogenes' claim to be a "citizen of the world," stated, "I have a room all to myself, it is nature. It is a place beyond the jurisdiction of human governments."[34] This is the sort of liberation toward which Thoreau tried to lead his readers in "Walking," where the walker becomes an outlaw and a member of the fourth estate. Laws after all are constraining and lead us into habits of conduct—such as accepting the *Fugitive Slave Law*—that in a more deliberate or thoughtful life we might see to be dangerous, unreasonable, or unacceptable. As outlaws, we come to see laws as the *nomoi* that they are. These conventions are not *necessarily* problematic, but what is always problematic is our habituated inability to be critical, to be reasonable, in the face of conventions. We tend to become unfree in their presence, and it was toward the disclosure of this unfreedom that Thoreau aimed his jabs at American citizens who remained inactive in relation to a host of injustices in the early nineteenth century.

A second enabling condition of *eleutheria,* for Thoreau, was poverty. In a chosen poverty one is not constantly controlled by one's belongings; for Thoreau, "a man is rich in proportion to the number of things which he can afford to leave alone."[35] Diogenes' poverty was legendary and served as an embarrassment to those around him, as a judgment on their own modes of accumulation. The important thing for the Cynic was to avoid being controlled by things and manufactured needs, as we too often allow ourselves to be. Thoreau saw this happening in the industrious and relatively wealthy New England culture that grew out of Plymouth Plantation, and he made his own assessment of his hometown, Concord: "The town's poor seem to me often to live the most independent lives of any."[36] Only poverty deliberately chosen would reliably preclude our enslavement to "ownership" and consumption, since, for Thoreau, things come to *own us*. Thoreau often remarked on the various meanings of "owning." To own by way of payment and deeds is to own only in an external way. This sort of materialistic acquisitiveness, when it is habitual, can come to dominate our lives, and in this way it comes to "own" us. As Desmond remarks, "The rich are deluded by a million unnecessary 'needs.'"[37] In order to genuinely own something—a sunset, for example—we must embrace its meaning for us and develop an internal ownership. If we succumb to our culture's measuring of success by way of how much wealth we acquire, we will likely miss the importance of living. "I must not," Thoreau reminded himself, "lose any freedom by being a farmer and landholder."[38] Similarly, Diogenes declared the love of money "to be mother-city of all evils."[39]

As a condition of *eleutheria,* poverty can be part of a useful economy. However, an unchosen poverty is no guarantee of freedom. The choosing of the poverty is a way of augmenting one's freedom; the economy becomes one's own experiment and not a function of some social necessity. Choosing poverty is a first step into a working self-reliance, which is why, I believe, it appears at the outset of many of Thoreau's writings.

The life of Thoreau's American Cynic is to be one of reflection aimed at a right orientation and attitude for body and soul. His constant harping on the goal of simplicity is an attempt to attain freedom and to bring himself into a world he *can* control, where he can govern himself. The self-sufficiency required by the Greek Cynics must be underwritten by a manageable economy as well as by self-reliance and self-trust. We see here another of those perplexities surrounding Thoreau brought into focus by the lens of Cynicism. Thoreau's simplicity is not driven by an attempt to be a Luddite; rather, as we will see, it is a feature of *autarkeia* that will enable one to pursue one's higher abilities.

Interestingly, in following the Greeks Thoreau foreshadowed the emphasis on embodiment that is found in some recent continental, feminist, and American thought. "Our soul," he wrote in his journal in 1840, "is but the Soul made known by its fruits, the body. The whole duty of man may be expressed in one line—make to yourself a perfect body."[40] A year later, he developed this point further: "We should strengthen and beautify, and industriously mould our bodies to be fit companions of the soul—assist them to grow up like trees, and be agreeable and wholesome objects in nature."[41] As commentators on the Cynics routinely point out, the physical training (*askêsis*) in which they engaged was aimed at just this end. The Cynics trained the body to work and endure in a variety of situations. "Instead of training the body for the sake of victory in the Olympic Games, on the battlefield, or for general good health," Piering points out, "the Cynic trains the body for the sake of the soul."[42]

Self-reliance thus develops itself. As we make the body fit, we enable our souls to exhibit their simplicity and to take more control of themselves, to live more deliberately. "I know of no more encouraging fact," Thoreau wrote in *Walden*, "than the unquestionable ability of man to elevate his life by a conscious endeavor."[43] This, for example, is the aim of Thoreau's simplified diet—in strict imitation of the Cynics, some of whom were vegetarians and who ate "for nourishment only" and who drank "cold water only."[44] On the one hand, it frees us from the so-called *necessities* of hunting and husbanding and from the desire for gourmet meals, but it also makes our bodies simpler, purer, and hence more governable. We need spend little energy on food preparation and the social conventions of dining. Thus, as we noted earlier, we find the Cynics eating wherever and whenever its meets their bodies' actual needs. They did not eat meals at conventionally appointed times and places. Indeed, pushing this bodily economy to its extreme, Diogenes opted for his tub dwelling and Thoreau suggested it might be "better not to keep a house."[45]

Such background situational and bodily choices, for Thoreau, both enact *autarkeia* and provide the conditions for more. The soul's natural ability is reasoning broadly construed, and this is what it needs to be free to do. "None," remarks Thoreau, "can be an impartial or wise observer of human life but from the vantage ground of what *we* should call voluntary poverty."[46] Again, the philosopher's energies are therefore best directed at moral and political aims, not at physics and mathematics except insofar as these are instrumental to living well. As outlaws, philosophers must learn to be self-legislators. Moral and political conventions are not *necessarily* wrong, but they are always potential sources of blindness, and they provide the basis for a moral and philosophical laziness.

This brings us to the aporia in reading Thoreau that we noted at the outset—his supposed anarchism. As a Cynic he sought self-government instead of an external governor, but he did not reject all normative restrictions. The clear aim of "Civil Disobedience," for example, is not anarchy but *autarkeia*. Persons are *awakened* to the need to make judgments both on the state's laws and on the state's actions enabled by those laws. This was in large part also the lesson of Thoreau's experiment at Walden Pond. If one lives "through obedience to the laws of his being," he

> will put some things behind, will pass an invisible boundary; new, universal, and more liberal laws will begin to establish themselves around and within him; or the old laws be expanded, and interpreted in his favor in a more liberal sense, and he will live with the license of a higher order of beings. In proportion as he simplifies his life, the laws of the universe will appear less complex, and solitude will not be solitude, nor poverty poverty, nor weakness weakness.[47]

In the absence of constraint and with self-reliance, we achieve a life that enables the third moment of freedom, *parrhesia*—our freedom to speak truly and authentically. It is crucial to note that this is not merely the negative freedom of free speech. The speech must also be driven by living through obedience to the laws of one's own nature. Here, I think, is the central difference between a Cynic and a cynic in our contemporary sense. The latter speaks without a well-crafted *autarkeia* and is merely a complainer. At this juncture, the Cynic exploits her ironic "cosmopolitanism" and makes the conduct of life a public and philosophical endeavor. The Cynic's task is to speak the truths of our social conditions, to bring them into focus such that others will be able to contest them. As Michel Foucault reports, "the main types of parrhesiastic practice utilized by the Cynics were: (1) critical preaching; (2) scandalous behavior; and (3) what I shall call the 'Provocative dialogue.' "[48]

The first of these we know Thoreau enjoyed in Concord and the surrounding towns. As he reported in "Life without Principle" concerning his local preaching, "I am determined that they shall have me, though I bore them beyond all precedent."[49] Thoreau's "scandalous behavior" was legendary but generally tolerated by his community—the same can be said of both Diogenes and Crates. Thoreau quit school teaching in resistance to the pedagogical *nomoi* of Concord; he held no "real" job; he failed to pay a poll tax; he went to stay at Walden for two years.

These were the acts that Emerson could not perform—these were what made Thoreau "an Emerson gone mad." It was, however, the last of Foucault's parrhesiastic modes where Thoreau best found his stride. He was an essayist provocateur. In his significant works he invariably introduced himself as chanticleer, as an awakener. He was akin to the musician whom Diogenes praised as "chanticleer" because his song "makes every one get up."[50] His aim was to bring readers to an encounter with their own living conditions, and in this much he was a clear inheritor of Cynic wisdom. "Cynic preaching," Foucault remarks, "had its own specific characteristics, and is historically significant since it enabled philosophical themes about one's way of life to become popular, i.e., to come to the attention of people who stood outside the philosophical elect."[51] Thoreau addressed Concord and New England as a way of addressing the human cosmos. In *Walden* he aimed explicitly to say something about their "condition, especially [their] outward condition or circumstances in this world, in this town, what it is, whether it is necessary that it be as bad as it is, whether it cannot be improved as well as not."[52] Poetry, experience, irony, sarcasm, and humor (light and dark) become Thoreau's philosophical tools; they are more penetrating, more provocative, and ultimately more effective than the tools of math and logic employed by the heavy-handed moderns and, in our time, by mainstream Anglo-American thought. The American Cynic philosopher is thus engaged in learning how to live well in achieving a radical form of freedom that involves provoking others to consider the possibility of their own freedom.

Philosophy, from Thoreau's angle of vision, needed to move from tedious abstractions and conventions back to experience and the conduct of life. "How can a man be a philosopher," he asked rhetorically, "and not maintain his vital heat by better methods than other men?"[53] The practitioner of candid speech must reawaken folks to their own wildness, to their own possibilities for living well under their own legislation. Philosophy needs to move from dogmatic assertion of doctrines to an ongoing creative conversation. Only through such a conversation can the lives of individuals and cultures be improved. In this conversation, Thoreau, as chanticleer, is an exemplary awakener and liberator in the tradition of Diogenes and Crates. His speaking out is a public behavior that others might emulate in general. I say "in general" because, as we noted earlier, Thoreau did not want others to do *specifically* what he did.

Rather, others should pursue their own freedoms, the beat of their own drummers, according to their own natures.

American Cynicism

Let me return to some things I said at the outset. Reading Thoreau as an American Cynic has, I think, the virtue of making sense of a number of the excesses with which he is occasionally charged: anarchism, antisocial behavior, escapism, naive idealism, being a Luddite, and so on. But I think it also reveals Thoreau's rejection of *our* philosophical practices. Diogenes and his followers were critics of social norms gone awry or become outmoded, but they were likewise critics of philosophers who never found the human highway. Crates notably remarked of the Megarian Stilpo: "Endlessly did he dispute, and many a comrade was round him. They wasted time in the verbal dispute of Virtue."[54] Appropriating Cynicism was, in part at least, Thoreau's attempt to revise philosophy.

Nevertheless, there were American additives in Thoreau's Cynicism that we should not overlook. First, he was addressing a culture in which the church and the academy had quietly merged into a seamless whole. And it was one in which academic life was beginning to become its own sphere. In this milieu he was led to criticize both religious dogma and scientistic certainty.

> There are nowadays professors of philosophy, but not philosophers. Yet it is admirable to profess because it was once admirable to live. To be a philosopher is not merely to have subtle thoughts, nor even to found a school, but so to love wisdom as to live according to its dictates, a life of simplicity, independence, magnanimity, and trust. It is to solve some of the problems of life, not only theoretically, but practically. The success of great scholars and thinkers is commonly a courtier-like success, not kingly, not manly.[55]

The similarity of these lines to the critiques Diogenes and Crates leveled against the philosophers of the Academy of their day is striking. And like the Cynics, Thoreau well knew that his American Cynicism would be met with condescension and dismissal. It is not accidental that Emerson and Thoreau were left out of the American philosophical canon for well over a century and that they remain, at best, on the margins of our current

American philosophical schools. But "making it" on the professional scene was never their aim—the narrowness and, we might say, blindness of the professional scene has been and remains the problem. This is something for us to consider as we open the twenty-first century. Regardless of their intellectual subtlety, Donald Davidson and Robert Brandom have little if anything to teach us about the art of living. Even in the field of ethics, Thoreau might say that the writings of Henry Bugbee and Edward Abbey would bring us closer to a philosophical life—and to nature—than the overly schematized rationalizations of Tom Regan and Peter Singer.

Philosophy in our century remains on a long slide into irrelevance. It is actually in many ways a reasonably easy life to become a professional philosopher—one learns to read and write according to the conventions and then disseminate the results in a highly scholasticized set of venues. Nevertheless, we take up very little cultural space. The "Gourmet Report" that purports to rate our graduate programs in philosophy would have provided a feast for the *parrhesia* of Diogenes and Thoreau—such radical, courtier-like silliness from folks self-identifying as philosophers would have made an easy and important target.

Thoreau's Cynical philosopher, however, was not a cynic. The aim was not merely to tear down ugly conventions and expose self-aggrandizing behavior. The aim was always to find improved economies for our own lives. And here we find, I think, the second American additive: an experiential joy in consummatory experience. As we noted earlier, Thoreau appeals to us to live our higher and lower faculties—to be cultivated and wild at once in living. Theoretical philosophy brings to life our higher faculties; for Thoreau as for Emerson it brings into use both our logical and our poetic abilities. Recall, however, that Thoreau finds us achieving "Sympathy with Intelligence," not "Knowledge." Our strictly philosophical abilities must be turned again toward a yet higher endeavor. For Thoreau, that higher endeavor is a living mysticism—an ability to grasp the world directly in intuitive embrace and to see what truths we might live. "The fact is," he wrote in his journal, "I am a mystic, a transcendentalist, and a natural philosopher to boot."[56] Such mysticism does not appear squarely within the frame of the Greek Cynics' suggestion that we learn directly from nature; however, I think Thoreau's American angle of vision enabled him to think that it was implied in that suggestion. Moreover, the Greek Cynics project little in the way of joy in the philosophical life; as with the later Stoics, life seems to be suffered more than enjoyed. Thoreau's American Cynic, however, embraces nature's presence with hope and possibility.

> So we saunter toward the Holy Land, till one day the sun shall shine more brightly than ever he has done, shall perchance shine into our minds and hearts, and light up our whole lives with a great awakening light, as warm and serene and golden as on a bankside in autumn.[57]

Whether we professional philosophers of the twenty-first century have any hope for or faith in such an aim, we should at least hear clearly Thoreau's provocation as an avenue for assessing our own chosen vocation.

TWELVE

HENRY DAVID THOREAU

The Asian Thread

Robert Kuhn McGregor

For the early stages of his writing career, Henry David Thoreau might be characterized as an intellectual man-of-all-trades. Certainly Thoreau found himself drawn to an almost impossibly broad array of subjects, ranging from local history and archaeology through ancient mythology and modern languages to the esoteric and at times contradictory world of transcendental philosophy. He also sought to act for the moral good while confronting the great political and social issues of his day. Often writing in a moralist vein, Henry Thoreau ranged over a multitude of subjects in his early writing efforts, enthusiastically addressing pretty much every imaginable subject except natural history, eventually his métier. Thoreau's initial interest in Asian thought, the subject of this essay, must be viewed in this context. As the years passed, Thoreau more firmly shaped his interest in Asian materials to enhance his understanding of the themes characterizing his mature career. Drawing on Asian images and ideas, Henry Thoreau found deeper expression for his understanding of the natural world. His interest in the subject waxed and waned with the passing years, but remained always an essential element in his intellectual foundation.[1]

Thoreau's engagement with Asian ideas began in his association with Ralph Waldo Emerson. This is no surprise. Emerson and his fellow transcendentalists provided the root inspiration for essentially all of Thoreau's initial interests. The first question, then, is: What drew Emerson to Asian writings? The answer lies in the intellectual quest Emerson undertook following the death of his first wife, Ellen Tucker Emerson, in 1831. Searching for answers in his grief, Waldo embarked on a vigorous and searching program of reading, which came to include the work, encountered in May 1831, of the French philosopher Victor Cousin. Cousin wrote admiringly of the subtleties of Indian scripture, the Bhagavad Gita in particular. Emerson was intrigued, and eventually concluded that the Gita stood at a par with the Christian gospels. Subsequent readings stretched his interests to include Chinese, Persian, and Hindu literature. By the time Emerson was prepared to place his ideas on paper, Zoroastrian, Confucian, and Hindu doctrines had woven themselves into his text, eventually published as *Nature* in 1836.[2]

Henry Thoreau's initiation to Emerson's increasingly pantheistic worldview derived from a reading of *Nature* during his senior year at Harvard (1837). Thoreau read the book a second time that autumn and met the author at roughly the same time. Waldo was not yet the famous author and orator we recall—his wealth and social position came largely from Helen Tucker's estate. A close circle of like-minded friends recognized Waldo's intellectual drive and acumen, and he sought to inspire others. Emerson quickly recognized Thoreau's talents and encouraged them, drawing him into profound intellectual exchanges, clarifying ideas, critiquing writing efforts, suggesting that the young man keep a journal. Asian thought was just one thread in this broad-based exchange, but an important one. By this time, images from the Bhagavad Gita had found expression in Emerson's lectures. In 1840, Waldo echoed the concept of the Krishna's *atman* in discussing the concept of the Oversoul, his expression of the wholeness of all things.[3]

Thoreau's first recorded reading of an Asian text is dated to 1840, when he studied a copy of the William Jones translation of *The Laws of Manu*, a Hindu text loaned to him by Emerson. At this early stage, Thoreau, guided by Emerson, focused largely on the ethical aspects of the scripture, mirroring the transcendental quest for a more wholesome and universally pure model of moral behavior. Thoreau's interest in this and related subjects deepened, and by 1841, he had moved into Emerson's house, exchanging his services as handyman for bed, board, and above all, access to Emerson's expanding library.[4]

It may as well be said at this point that the range and quality of Asiatic literature available to Thoreau and Emerson were nothing like the vast resources at our fingertips today. At best, Thoreau glimpsed the rich potential of Eastern scripture through a swirling mist created by time, distance, language barriers, and, safe to say, religious and ethnic prejudice. In his youth, Thoreau had expressed the standard Western dismissal of "Indian superstition," as had Emerson. What was unusual in the 1840s was their willingness to look past such unheeding assumptions, to see for themselves what was there. This was by no means easy. In the early nineteenth century, just a small portion of the vast literature was available in translation. Its quality was uneven. The earliest texts came from missionaries determined to demonstrate that Hindu, Zoroastrian, Buddhist, and Confucian texts were horribly un-Christian and therefore in error; the translations tended to support that intent. More literal and unbiased translations began to appear with the founding of the Asiatic Society of Bengal in 1784. Several scholars, fascinated by the richness of Asiatic texts and determined to provide them a fair reading in the West, produced translations of some merit. Sir William Jones published The Laws of Manu in 1825, and Charles Wilkins had unveiled an English translation of the Bhagavad Gita in 1785. The process was still in a pioneering state in Thoreau's time; much of his understanding derived from dubious texts. More important, there were vast libraries of material the transcendentalists never saw. Zen was literally a closed book to Emerson and Thoreau, and Taoism too. Nor did Thoreau ever peruse any edition of the Dhammapada, the most immediate of all Buddhist texts.[5]

Ironically, Thoreau's own skill in modern languages, developed at Harvard, stood him well in his quest for Asiatic readings. Several Hindu and Buddhist writings came to the West not in English translation, but in French, most importantly the Mahabharata, published by M. A. Langlois. Thoreau was able to read such works with profit, and at times produce secondary English translations for American publication. In retrospect, Thoreau's work with these texts represented significant contributions to the exposure of Asian thought in America.[6]

Tragedy came to both Emerson and Thoreau in early 1842. Thoreau lost his brother John to tetanus on January 11; Emerson saw his five-year-old son succumb to scarlatina on January 24. The deaths haunted each man for years afterward, deepening their needs for greater spiritual understanding than the standards of their own culture could provide. One expression of this search came to fruition through their work on the *Dial*, the transcendental journal begun in 1840. Originally edited by Margaret Fuller, the journal initially addressed a broad spectrum of the arts. After two years of unpaid aggravation, Fuller threw up her hands and turned over responsibility to Emerson, who focused his editorial efforts on literature. Included was a feature titled "Ethnical Scriptures," highlighting excerpts from various sources of Asian literature. The series began in July 1842, with passages drawn from the Hindu work Vishnu Sarma. In January 1843 came material from Wilkins's translation of *The Laws of Manu*. Works from Confucian, Zoroastrian, Hindu, and Buddhist sources followed in every issue until publication ceased in April 1844. Although many New Englanders had previously shared in some vague recognition of such writings, the materials presented in the *Dial* stood as the first real effort to present Asian thought sympathetically. The choice of scripture and the accompanying tone underscored the essential transcendental idea that all religion, all philosophy at its most profound, wrestled with the same ethical dilemmas, and arrived at much the same resolution, regardless of culture or history.[7]

Henry Thoreau was intimately involved in the "Ethnical Scriptures" series, working closely with Emerson to identify appropriate passages from *The Laws of Manu*, "The Sayings of Confucius," and *The Chinese Classical Work commonly called the Four Books*. Thoreau also took part in a most intriguing effort for the *Dial* edition of January 1844. He had spent considerable time examining a collection of Buddhist works "discovered by M. Hodgson, the English resident at the Court of Katmandou, and sent by him to the Asiatic Society of Paris." Eugene Burnouf translated the works, "a great part of the canonical books of the Buddhists," into French, producing a volume that Thoreau (presumably) translated into English as "White Lotus of the Good Law." Nine pages of excerpts appeared in the *Dial*, the first introduction of the Lotus Sutra—truly one of the most essential of all Buddhist texts—to America.[8]

Thoreau titled his translation of the Lotus Sutra "The Preaching of the Buddha." Even a brief perusal of the piece is enough to suggest his struggle with the writings in front of him. He quoted extensively from an article by Eugene Burnouf to preface the quotations and provides a few explanatory footnotes to illuminate the text. But it is plain he is struggling with the more esoteric concepts and that he possessed almost no reliable sources to draw on for help. Buddhism was so poorly understood in America that both Thoreau and Emerson—two men who truly sought to understand—believed it to be a form of Hinduism. Neither was ever dis-abused of this critical misunderstanding. The mistake is ramified in Thoreau's studies of Asiatic thought throughout his career—in consider-ing the Buddha's thought and the implications of the Bhagavad Gita, Thoreau honestly believed he was considering two aspects of the same philosophy. American studies of the Asiatic contained a considerable margin of homespun.[9]

Much of Western religious thinking is characterized by ethical posi-tioning—there is a knowable and perceptible difference between right and wrong, and Heaven responds in accordance with the path human beings choose. Virtually unacquainted with the very different nature of Eastern thought, Western students such as Cousin and Burnouf (and, by extension, Emerson and Thoreau) assumed that "The Preaching of the Buddha" concerned itself with similar questions of black and white. In the essay the *Dial* employs as a preface to "The Preaching of the Buddha," Burnouf argues that the Buddha's doctrine was "more moral than meta-physical." To Burnouf, the Buddha's path of escape from the Great Wheel of Transmigration lay in "the knowledge of the physical and intellectual laws, and the practice of the six transcendent perfections, of aims, of morality, of science, of energy, of patience, and of eternity." Behavior is what matters, in Burnouf's construction. That behavior was a by-product of transcendence—enlightenment, as we now understand the concept—was poorly grasped, at best. To Burnouf, the Buddha was some kind of Hindu moralist preacher and reformer.

It is instructive to compare the *Dial*'s translation of Burnouf's Lotus Sutra excerpts to a comprehensive modern rendering. The last portion of "The Preaching of the Buddha" comes from a chapter in the Sutra titled "The Parable of the Medicinal Herbs." The *Dial*'s version presents a metaphor for humankind based on three kinds of plants, each repre-senting a stage of moral development. The piece has the Buddha des-cribing his teaching as a "homogenous water" poured from a cloud, a "single law" that will nourish each kind of plant according to its nature.

The great trees, "the rank of heroes among men," will inevitably benefit most. "Exclusively occupied with this work," states the Buddha, "I explain the law."[10]

There is nothing inherently wrong in this translation; the alert reader can trace the essence of the words in the more recent version. But the modern translation offers a perspective lacking in the *Dial* rendering. "Having heard the law," the Buddha advises further, "they will escape from obstacles and hindrances, and with regard to the various doctrines will be able to exercise their powers to the fullest, so that gradually they can enter into the way." In the fully rendered Lotus Sutra, the law—the definition of right moral behavior—matters very little. Right moral behavior is simply the removal of an impediment, a first step in the way, the path of enlightenment. If Henry Thoreau ever comprehended this, the knowledge did not derive from the verses Burnouf provided.[11]

The close of the *Dial* with the April 1844 issue left Thoreau without an outlet for further print exploration of Eastern literature. It was a difficult moment in his life, as he had earned very little money in writing after seven years of effort. School teaching and tutoring proved equally unrewarding, so he determined to undertake a combined experiment in minimal living and sustained writing. With Emerson's permission, he built a cabin on Waldo's land close by Walden Pond, living and writing there for two years, two months, and two days. To fully understand Thoreau's life and work—and the role of Asian thought in his development—it is critically important to separate the historic event of Thoreau's Walden stay (1845–47) from *Walden*, the book he wrote re-creating those years, published in 1854. Thoreau's view of the world changed profoundly *after* he left Walden, and his use of Asian ideas shifted in consequence.

A Week on the Concord and Merrimack Rivers, the book Henry Thoreau fashioned while actually living at the pond, is best viewed as a summary of the work and focus of his early career. Thoreau intended the book as an elegy to his deceased brother, and shaped the narrative as a river journey the brothers share. As in all elegies, the voyage takes place at two levels—the literal journeying through a rapidly changing New England landscape and a spiritual journey through a world of challenging ideas. Thoreau draws on his Asiatic studies in discussions of religious values and ideas in two of his chapters.

Thoreau spent five years drafting, editing, reorganizing, supplementing, and expanding *A Week*. His struggles to construct a coherent and sustained narrative are evident in a comparison of his initial draft, entered into a journal known to scholars as "The Long Book" while living at Walden, to the eventual product released in 1849. From the first, he drew heavily on his early essays and publications in the *Dial* for material, as well as journal entries. His initial draft of the "Monday" chapter included segments mined from his essay "The Laws of Manu," which he employed to impart a sense of timeless and everlasting truth. "The true India is neither now nor then—east nor west," he observed. Like so much of *A Week*, this discussion retained its essential place in the narrative as published, though the interpretation and use changed considerably.[12]

In the published version of the book, Thoreau developed his use of Asian ideas to include long passages in the "Sunday" as well as the "Monday" chapters. Embarked on a most New England journey, he sought to expand the narrowness of the landscape for his readers, help them to recognize the spiritual unity he saw in a much larger world. In effect, he used Asian spiritual concepts to counterweight the Christian insularity he witnessed along the Concord and Merrimack Rivers. "In my Pantheon, Pan still reigns in his pristine glory," Thoreau advises. He admits a value in pure Christianity but finds the same values expressed just as cogently by the Buddha. "I know that some will have hard thoughts of me, when they hear their Christ named beside my Buddha, yet I am sure that I am willing they should love their Christ more than my Buddha, for the love is the main thing, and I like him too. Why need Christians be still intolerant and superstitious?" A few pages on, Thoreau speaks of the "true flavor" of the New Testament—a flavor shared (by implication) with the Hindu scriptures.[13]

"My Buddha." Most of the very few of Thoreau's readers found such pantheism abhorrent, a sacrilegious combining of the True Word with Eastern heathenism. That aside, Thoreau's choice of expression remains fascinating, as his discussion of Eastern belief suggests almost nothing of Buddhist thought or belief. Thoreau seized on the Buddha as a symbol for the larger spiritual realm he wished to comprehend—he aspired to some essence of Buddhism he sensed far more than he understood.

When he returns to the subject of Eastern thought in the Monday chapter, Thoreau focuses primarily on the Hindus, and it is well to remember that he understood his Buddha as a Hindu messenger. Again he reaches for the spiritual center he believes common to all religious thought, and again he labors under a misapprehension. He begins by praising the great religion of the East: "The wisest conservation is that of the Hindoos." He finds in both the Laws of Manu and the Bhagavad Gita a "pure intellectuality," an "inevitability and unchangeableness of laws"— a fatalism that modern scholars would label determinism. Thoreau finds much to value in an approach that emphasizes careful contemplation of universal truth. Then comes the criticism, a complaint born of Thoreau's still patently Western sensibilities. What the Hindu scriptures lack, he believes, is a call to action. Christ is the "prince of Reformers and Radicals," those willing to accept the moral responsibility to set the world aright. Thoreau is struggling mightily to apply a Western belief in moral absolutes to an Eastern philosophy that does not share in that belief. "The Brahman never proposes courageously to assault evil, but patiently to starve it out." That the "evil" Thoreau wishes so valiantly to fight may not exist to the Hindu way of thinking never occurs to him. Thoreau remains trapped in a world of ethical choices, where the individual must choose. He is unavoidably disappointed in the climax of the Gita. "No sufficient reason is given why Arjoon should fight. Arjoon may be convinced, but the reader is not." The Western reader is not convinced, perhaps, even if his name is Henry David Thoreau. The Eastern reader would see the thing differently, understand that Krishna has shown Arjoon the world that truly exists, rather than the ephemeral world of the material we commonly perceive. Good and evil are relative concepts distracting human beings from a comprehension of the real. Thoreau constructs his criticism on a baseless premise, in the Hindu way of understanding.[14]

No matter. No more than a couple hundred people read *A Week on the Concord and Merrimack Rivers* in 1849, and no one got to grips with the larger aspects of Hindu thought. The simple charge of pantheism was enough. For Thoreau himself, it is difficult to gauge whether his comprehension of Asian thought underwent any great change while he lived at Walden. The material in *A Week* grew directly from his early work for the *Dial*; there is no growth to be found. It is possible that Thoreau kept a copy of the Bhagavad Gita while living at Walden, as he later pictured. It is even possible that he read and reread this essential work with joy and profit. But the discernible change in Thoreau's approach to Asian thought begins late in the 1840s, after the work on *A Week* had reached conclusion. The shift derived from two very different and unrelated events.

By far the more significant of these events was Thoreau's determination to distance himself philosophically from Waldo Emerson, a decision made on intellectual and professional grounds. As he began his writing career in the late 1830s, Thoreau adhered very closely to Emerson's dualistic view of the universe, derived from Neoplatonic thought. Waldo saw two planes of reality but placed all his emphasis on the higher, spiritual realm he eventually labeled the Oversoul. Nature, the material world, was merely emblematic of the higher plane, and might not exist at all—Emerson had only the poor evidence of his own senses to demonstrate its presence. His limited comprehension of Hindu philosophy lent credence to this view of the duality.[15]

For all his willingness to cast himself into the higher realm of the spiritual—fully emphasized in *A Week*—Henry Thoreau was a most practical man. Throughout the 1840s, Thoreau spent a lot of time in the outdoors, even if he did not write much about the experience. Climbing mountains, trekking vast forests, boating wilderness streams, Thoreau risked his life and sanity enough times to reach a critical conclusion: Nature was real. Not simply real, but important, essential to understanding his place in the universe. The first inkling of this change in view came with the publication of the essay "Ktaadn" in 1848. He then decided to pose the issue directly in the closing pages of *A Week*: "Is not Nature, rightly read, that of which she is taken to be the symbol merely?" he asked. The proper reading of nature Thoreau now found necessary might also call for a different, more careful reading of the Asian texts.[16]

The second event to set Thoreau down a different path with respect to Hindu thought was an essay published by James Elliot Cabot in the September 1848 issue of the *Massachusetts Quarterly Review*. Cabot served as an assistant to Louis Agassiz at Harvard's Department of Comparative Zoology; Thoreau collected botanical specimens for him in the Concord woods during 1849. Like many scholars of his time, Cabot entertained wide-ranging interests. His reading of the ancient texts resulted in a far more subtle and comprehending analysis of Hindu thought than Emerson and Thoreau had achieved. In "The Philosophy of the Ancient Hindoos," Cabot reprinted extensive quotations from the translated scriptures to illustrate what he perceived as the "main principle of the Hindoo Idealism—that Reality is equivalent to pure abstract Soul or Thought, unexistent, and thus simple and unformed; in a word, pure Negation,—is presented especially under the aspect of the unity and identity of all things in the Deity." In short, all the world that truly exists is God; there is no separate identity. Cabot saw through the ethical criticisms brought by Thoreau and countless others, demonstrating that such moral distinctions "belong merely to the sphere of Nature, which it is the aim of every wise man to transcend." In the Hindu view of the universe, "material existence is possible only so far as it is established by the soul." Cabot is unable to keep himself from a few expressions of Western chauvinism before he is finished, stating that while Hinduism was certainly the first bold attempt at philosophical speculation, it could not be called a system. Still, his reading of the ancient texts provided a fundamental interpretation far more sound than its American predecessors. Hinduism was not a pale and lazy version of Western ethics-based religion, but something very different.[17]

Here was an elaboration of Eastern thought that provided new inspiration for Henry David Thoreau. He probably read Cabot's essay in September of 1849, the autumn of what had proved a very bad year for Thoreau. He had published *A Week* to mostly bad reviews and very poor sales that put him deep in debt, personal tragedies dogged him, and he had strong words with Emerson. His career had reached a critical, potentially fatal juncture, and he needed a new direction. For a brief while he stopped work altogether. When Thoreau regathered the threads, he committed himself to two demanding projects: a closer study of the natural world and a reworking of a long essay begun at the pond, one he had titled "Walden." Not coincidentally, the first work he did to revise and enhance the quality of the "Walden" manuscript was to add a carefully considered series of quotations from Asian literature, together with his own inventions and commentaries on the texts.[18]

In his search for new direction, Thoreau seems to have begun a new and more systematic study of Eastern doctrines, maintaining that "the Hindoos by constitution possess in a wonderful degree the faculty of contemplation," so different from Westerners who thought "only with ruinous interruptions & friction." In September 1849, he borrowed a two-volume French translation of one of the key works of Hindu religion, the Mahabharata, from the Harvard Library, along with a history of Hindu literature. Thoreau examined the Mahabharata—which collected a wide assortment of vedas, prayers, cautionary tales, laws, and other material—most carefully, even taking the time to write out an English translation of one story, "The Transmigration of the Seven Brahmins."

By October he had concluded, "Why should we be related as mortals merely—as limited to one state of existence—Our lives are immortal, our transmigrations are infinite—the virtue that we are lives ever."[19]

In the next year and a half, Thoreau borrowed the Vishnu Purana and the Sankya Karika, both works devoted largely to the proper living of one's life; the Sama Veda and other Vedas; the Sakoontala; and a collection published by the Asiatic Society of Bengal that included the Upanishads. The reading confirmed in his mind that the "Hindoos are more serenely and thoughtfully religious than the Hebrews." In 1851 he extended his studies to include Chinese works, specifically translations of Confucius and Mencius.[20]

On the surface, Thoreau's purpose in renewed study of these various texts was to obtain further insight into living a more perfect intellectual life, to discern the proper moral paths conducive to the achievement of higher, more spiritually pure, thought—the goals behind his initial studies ten years earlier. Quoting the Sankhya Karika, he noted that "by attainment of perfect knowledge, virtue & the rest become causeless; yet soul remains awhile invested with body, as the potter's wheel continues whirling from the effect of the impulse previously given to it."[21]

The moral element of Hindu thought was important to Thoreau, but given the conclusions he had reached in the "Friday" chapter of *A Week*— that the world of the spirit and the sensate world of nature were not separable—his interest in this aspect was muted. In "The Transmigration of the Seven Brahmins," the one portion of the Mahabharata Thoreau found instructive enough to translate, the story involves the spiritual quest of seven individuals who had committed indiscretions in their quest for greater spiritual attainment. In consequence, the Brahmins had to undergo several further incarnations. Those who remained most true to the quest for spiritual fulfillment lived the lives of stags, of geese, of swans before achieving transmigration. In short, they lived in nature.[22]

More important to Henry was a second, related aspect of Hindu thought, one that had attracted his attention quite early, but which he pursued carefully only in the early 1850s. This was the Hindu vision of the creation of the world. Several of the great Hindu works, including the Harivansa, the Bhagavad Gita, and Manu's *Institutes of Hindu Law*, relate the Hindu story of creation. Thoreau first took note of such stories in 1841, when he abstracted several portions of "The Laws of Manu" for publication in the *Dial*. Although he did not include the creation story in the published selections, Henry was impressed enough to copy the entire creation chapter into his literary notebook. In this version, Manu, speaking the words of the creator, related how God first created the water, in which he planted a protective seed which grew into an egg. BRAHMA, the primary incarnation of God, was born in the egg. For an entire year the egg sat inactive, then split into two equal portions, heaven above and earth beneath. Having thereby pervaded, "with emanations from the Supreme Spirit," all of the universe, "he framed all creatures." The chapter concludes with a verse noting that "all transmigrations, recorded in sacred books, from the state of BRAHMA, to that of plants, happen continually in the tremendous world of beings."[23]

Thoreau encountered the Hindu vision of creation again in January of 1850, when he read the Vishnu Purana. In this work, a student, Maitreya, questions his teacher, Parasara, regarding the origin and nature of the universe. Parasara then prays to Vishnu ("the preserver"), another version of Brahma, for enlightenment. In the fifth chapter of the work, Parasara explains that Vishnu made the universe in a series of six creations, beginning with the "developments of indiscrete nature," including intellect, elemental creation, and organic creation (the world of the senses). Then followed the secondary creations, the various classes of wild and domestic animals, the lesser divinities, and human beings. All were creations from Brahma's own body. For example, the fifth order of the animal classes, the birds, were formed from Brahma's "vital vigor."[24]

The Harivansa, which Thoreau took up in May of 1851, further considered the problem of creation. Henry studied the work at length, and in a journal entry dated "Monday May 6th 1851," abstracted several passages bearing on the presence of spirit in nature.

> The Harivansa describes a "substance called *Poroucha*, a spiritual substance known also under the name of Mahat, spirit united to the five elements, soul of beings, now enclosing itself in a body like ours, now returning to the eternal body; it is mysterious wisdom, the perpetual sacrifice made by the virtue of the *Yoga*, the fire which animates animals, shines in the sun, and is mingled with all bodies. Its nature is to be born and to die, to pass from repose to movement. The spirit led astray by the senses, in the midst of the creation of Brahma, engages itself in works and knows birth, as well as death. The organs of the senses are its paths, and its work manifests itself in the creation of Brahma."[25]

Two important themes emerge from these stories: first, that the universe, in both its spiritual and sensual aspects, emanates directly from God; and second, that the physical world is in a state of constant flux.

Henry had previously encountered commentaries on the spirit in nature in his studies of the Bhagavad Gita, the work he had criticized so misleadingly in the "Monday" chapter of *A Week*. The story continued to intrigue him nonetheless; he drew heavily on the Gita's images in crafting the revisions of *Walden*. The Gita was written as a folk story intended for the instruction of all Hindu peoples, and its messages are plainly written and direct. The book comprises eighteen lectures, each written as a dialogue between the warrior Arjoon and the God Kreeshna, another form of Brahma. Kreeshna, answering Arjoon's doubts about a great battle soon to take place, advises the warrior to seek asylum "in wisdom alone," and then explains the true nature of the universe. Mincing no words, the God states in the tenth lecture that "I am the soul which standeth in the bodies of all things." Three lectures later he elaborates, telling Arjoon:

> Know, O chief of the race of *Bharat*, that every thing which is produced in nature, whether animate or inanimate, is produced from the union of *Kshetra* and *Kshetragna*, matter and spirit. He who beholdeth the Supreme Being alike in all things, whilst corrupting, itself uncorrupting; and conceiving that God in all things is the same, doth not of himself injure his own soul, goeth on the journey of immortality.[26]

The Bhagavad Gita clearly argues that even a contemplative life must be an active life; the world changes, and even to stand still a person must work. The important thing is to understand the true purpose of this work, which is neither to achieve a specific goal nor to gain material reward, but merely to understand. By 1854, when Thoreau deemed his "Walden" manuscript complete, he had come to an understanding of the text considerably more subtle than the shallow moralist interpretation offered in his first book.

More important, the reading assisted Thoreau to develop a view of nature unique in the Western society of his time. The prevailing American and European view of nature was to hold that only God and humanity possessed a spirit, that nature was spiritually dead. This view, promoted by much of the Judeo-Christian tradition and reinforced by the science of Descartes, Newton, and others, promoted the objectification of the natural world. Emerson's heresy was to suggest that the world of God and the spirit did extend to plants and animals, but he had done so in a framework that denied the value of the objective, sensate world—the bodies of animals and people alike. Thoreau rejected Emerson's heresy—only to embrace a far more heretical view of his own: The spiritual and the natural world were inseparable and present all around him. Spirit not only existed in nature; its existence was there to be understood, if one was mentally prepared to do the work.[27]

Thoreau understood that he was not really saying anything new. His ideas were echoes of the Hindu sages, who had concluded that all the universe was simply the body and mind of God long before the birth of Christ. By reinterpreting these beliefs in a Western context, Thoreau challenged the notion that nature existed merely for the use of humankind. Out of this conclusion would come the impetus for a new way of looking at nature in Western society, one that eschewed utilitarian values and sought the presence of the universal spirit in animals and trees.

Henry's readings in Oriental literature did more than reinforce his belief in the presence of spirit in nature. By suggesting that all of nature was just one thing—each creature was really a part of Brahma's own self—these works encouraged Thoreau to look at the natural world in a profoundly unscientific way: as a complete and interworking whole rather than as a series of carefully delineated and discrete parts. If one God pervaded all of nature, then each animal, each plant, was a functioning part of a greater unity. As Thoreau came to apply himself more completely to the study of nature, he would retain the image of nature as an interrelated wholeness. His studies would combine minute examination of each part of nature he encountered with reference to the principles that held all the parts together.[28]

Hindu literature is broad, rich, and subtle in content. Thoreau read extensively in these works between 1849 and 1854, drawing any number of impressions, recording thoughts in his journals, and applying them to the various projects he developed. A passage from the Vishnu Purana on the liberating duty of discovering true knowledge found its way into his lecture "The Wild" in the winter of 1851. He worked many, if not all, of the quotations from Oriental literature into his "Walden" manuscript at the same time, practically the only work he did on the book between the autumn of 1849 and the winter of 1852. By the time Thoreau completed his seventh and last revision of the "Walden" manuscript in 1854, he had created a subtle tapestry of ideas woven from a truly rich selection of readings and personal experiences. One of the greatest testaments to Thoreau's skill lies in the seamless blending of so many disparate elements. Reading *Walden* for the joy of the experience, it is an easy thing to overlook the author's continued reliance on Asian thoughts and images. Quotations from the Hindu texts abound, as do images such as the Staff of Kouroo, obviously inspired by Asian readings.[29]

But what of Buddha? Despite Thoreau's confrontational embrace of "my Buddha" in *A Week on the Concord and Merrimack Rivers*, he makes no direct reference to the Buddha in *Walden*. At first glance, he seems to have given over this association, subsuming any specific interest in Buddhist teaching into his depiction of the Hindu understanding of the world. Thoreau's knowledge of Buddhism remained grounded in his translations of the Lotus Sutra from the French source; he still saw Buddhism as an aspect of Hindu belief. Thoreau knew nothing of Buddhism's history, and more important, he had little reason to pursue such knowledge. What was important was not the place of Buddhism in any Eastern religious philosophy, but the ideas themselves, and how he might apply them to his own experience. In that applied sense, Buddhist ideals are clearly visible in the *Walden* tapestry.[30]

Translated literally, the title "Buddha" simply means "the awakened one." Thoreau may or may not have known this from his reading of the French translation of the Lotus Sutra, but he had every opportunity to grasp this critical image while reading the text. To provide a single example, the Eighth Chapter of the Sutra celebrates the Buddha's message, stating that "the World-Honored One awakens us and makes us aware." The very core of Buddhist teaching is the knowledge that most human beings sleepwalk through life, unaware and unheeding of the greater reality that is humanity and all that surrounds humankind. The Buddha is a being awakened, seeking to awaken others. And that image lies at the heart of the picture Thoreau creates in *Walden*.[31]

Very early in the opening ("Economy") chapter of *Walden*, Thoreau portrays himself as a man determined to see the world as it is, "to stand on the meeting of two eternities, the past and future, which is precisely the present moment; to toe that line." In the chapter following (tellingly, "Where I Lived and What I Lived For") he proposes not "to write an ode to dejection, but to brag as lustily as chanticleer in the morning, standing on his roost, if only to wake my neighbors up." Here is the essence of the

Buddhist determination: to be awake to the world and to awaken others to that same consciousness.[32]

A long passage a few pages on amplifies the idea. Thoreau quotes the Vedas, observing that "all intelligences awake with the morning." Drawing on this theme, he writes:

> Moral reform is the effort to throw off sleep. Why is it that men give so poor an account of their day if they have not been slumbering? They are not such poor calculators. If they had not been overcome with drowsiness they would have performed something. The millions are awake enough for physical labor; but only one in a million is awake enough for effective intellectual exertion, only one in a hundred millions to a poetic or divine life. To be awake is to be alive. I have never yet met a man who was quite awake. How could I have looked him in the face?[33]

Nor does the thought end there; very soon Thoreau states that he "went to the woods because I wished to live deliberately."[34]

The image is sustained throughout the text of *Walden*, always implied if not overtly stated. The Henry David Thoreau the reader confronts living in Walden Woods is an individual embracing a world to which he is fully awakening at just that moment; from the sheer joy of hearing the quarrel of owls and geese to the puzzlement over humans and their habits, Thoreau is a witness awakened. And in the final paragraph of his text, he reminds the reader of this critical truth one last time: "The light which puts out our eyes is darkness to us. Only that day dawns to which we are awake. There is more day to dawn. The sun is but a morning star." Thoreau desired more than anything to be awake, and he wished as much for his readers.[35]

Henry Thoreau made his most profound, and essentially his last, use of the ancient Asian texts in writing *Walden*. As his devotion to natural history deepened and matured, he continued to view nature as a single system imbued with both a spiritual and a material reality, a view sustained by his understanding of Asian thought. But his actual study of Asian literature waned; there are essentially no meaningful journal entries regarding Hindu thought after 1854; no mention in the later manuscripts (*Cape Cod, The Maine Woods, Faith in a Seed, Wild Fruits*) that were published after his death. On the last day of November 1855, Thoreau received a shipment of forty volumes of Oriental literature and commentaries, sent from England from a new friend, Thomas Cholmondeley. He recorded the arrival in a most matter-of-fact entry in his journal, and extolled them as "a royal gift" in a letter. Presumably he derived pleasure from reading them, but they inspired no further literary explorations. By the mid-1850s, the Asian texts had become an essential thread in Thoreau's intellectual weave; he no longer felt the need to discuss at length ideas he had thoroughly adapted to his own uses. He saw nature as an organic whole; Asian thought provided foundational support for just that understanding.[36]

In the final analysis, it is impossible to say to what degree Thoreau absorbed the actual tenets of Asian thought—Hindu, Buddhist, or Chinese. He read extensively in the ancient Asian texts over several years, but for the greatest part, his comprehension was no more than a product of his eclectic primary reading. He had no knowledgeable teacher to help him; the few commentaries and analytical essays he encountered were often as much a hindrance as a help. But exact knowledge was never Thoreau's goal in his Asian readings; what he sought was an enlarged understanding of his world, a more encompassing framework for examining his own experiences. Asian thought was a vehicle to free himself from the conventions of Christianity and traditional Western thought— his universe was larger than the limitations those philosophies imposed. Thoreau's examination of the Asian texts was not so much a search for an alternative, but rather a quest for inspiration. He was not seeking the letter of Asian doctrines, but the spirit he found in their content, a spirit he could interlace into his own life and work. Henry Thoreau's voice was uniquely his own, an imagination conditioned by his searching explorations of knowledge in many forms. The Asian texts were one source among many, but an essentially important source. The voice of Walden Pond was a voice tempered by the anguish of Arjoon and the awakening of the Buddha.

THIRTEEN

THE IMPACT OF THOREAU'S POLITICAL ACTIVISM

Paul Friedrich

It is said that the British Empire is very large and respectable, and that the United States are a first-rate power. We do not believe that a tide rises and falls behind every man which can float the British Empire like a chip, if he should ever harbor it in his mind.

—Henry David Thoreau, *Walden*, "Conclusion"

In the Bhagavad Gita that Thoreau so admired,[1] the virtue of *bhakti*, or "loving devotion," is both a source of knowledge and a motive for action.[2] Believing that a contemplative life should also be an active one, Thoreau sought to follow the example of Arjuna, hero of the Gita. In the light of his view that the philosopher should also be heroically engaged in social and political activism, it is outrageous that Thoreau is often stereotyped as a lifelong recluse who lived in a hut like a hermit and was selfish and asocial. In this essay, I hope to set the record straight.

Thoreau lived on Walden Pond for two years as an "experiment," a model followed by many of his contemporaries: He walked into Concord several times a week to gossip, visit, eat his mother's pies, and hear the news. He also acted socially and politically as a writer, lecturer, and citizen of Concord and New England. Today he stands as fundamental and formative in the defense of civil liberties, in the cause of environmentalism, in opposition to war, and in condemning human exploitation of all kinds—not only of slaves but also, for example, indebted farmers. He stands as a champion of the higher laws of individual conscience in the face of state tyranny—an awesome catalogue for someone who was primarily a naturalist, pencil-maker, and lyrical prosaist. He seems relevant now, even prescient.

It would be difficult and unrealistic to disentangle concrete activism from activist writing, so let us consider them together in chronological order to see how Thoreau was involved in political activism all his life. First, in 1844, when Emerson was to give a speech on the emancipation in the West Indies, Thoreau rang the town bell to sound a cry of alarm that would bring public attention to this issue. This was in defiance of the town selectmen, who had prohibited such a gesture. Then, from 1845 to 1847, while he was sojourning in the woods at Walden Pond, Thoreau not only spent a night in jail for his principled and overt refusal to pay a poll tax, but he also took great risks as a link in the Underground Railroad. According to Emerson's son, "Slaves were sometimes brought to him there but obviously there was no possible concealment in his house . . . so he would look after them by day, and by nightfall get them to his mother's or some other house of hiding."[3]

During the 1840s and 1850s, Thoreau's writings were often punctuated by political agendas. The *Walden* chapter called "The Village" describes his night in jail and the reasons behind it, namely that he did not want to recognize the authority of a state that bought and sold men, women, and children "like cattle" at the door of its senate-house.[4] In "Baker Farm" he writes that "the only true America" is "where the state does not endeavor to compel you to sustain . . . slavery and war and other superfluous expenses."[5] His reference here is to the Mexican War, one of the most unjust wars in American history. These passages in *Walden* connect the fight against slavery with resistance to war and imperialism. During this same period of time Thoreau's family home, which was shared by his parents and two sisters, was "a nest of Abolitionists," as reported by a contemporary: "Rarely a week went by without some fugitive being harbored overnight in town and sped along his way before daylight. Henry Thoreau more than any other man in Concord looked after them . . . [by] purchasing their tickets, escorting them to the [train] station," and so forth.[6]

In 1848, Thoreau's essay "Resistance to Civil Government"—which has also become known as "Civil Disobedience"—was published for the first time. It advocated the idea that individual conscience was higher than any civil law; if the machine of government "requires you to be the agent of injustice to another, then, I say, break the law. Let your life be a counter friction to stop the machine."[7] Throughout "Resistance," Thoreau, again, linked antislavery with anti-imperialism: New slave states such as Texas would result from the Mexican War. "Resistance" and related speeches were delivered in many Massachusetts venues in the 1850s while civil war was raging in Kansas. On July 4, 1850, Thoreau lashed out with his fiery "Slavery in Massachusetts" at a meeting of radical abolitionists in Worcester that was protesting the Compromise of 1850 with its Fugitive Slave Act. This legislation soon resulted in the return in manacles of runaway slaves Anthony Burns and Thomas Simms. "Slavery," like the "Resistance" essay, spoke against the rule of "expediency" and "policy": "The law will never make men free; it is men who have got to make the law free."[8] The water lily emerges near the end of the essay as a symbol of political rectitude—thus resonating with the lotus of the Gita as a symbol for purity in men's thoughts and actions.

Between 1852 and 1854, Thoreau and his abolitionist compadres sided with and helped antislavery forces who were fighting with the proslavery "Border Ruffians." The abolitionists bitterly opposed the Kansas-Nebraska act of 1854, and welcomed John Brown, a leader of antislavery forces in Kansas, when he came to the Boston area in 1857 and 1859; he spoke in Concord in 1857 and collected money on both occasions. By 1859, when Brown and his twenty-one men were captured after seizing the munitions factory in Harper's Ferry, Thoreau went into overdrive during a uniquely agitated ten days of writing. His journal reveals the degree to which Thoreau was preoccupied with this event: In one of the few entries during this period that refer to anything besides politics, he notes that "there was a remarkable sunset, I think the 25th of October . . . but it was hard for me to see its beauty then, when my mind was filled with Captain Brown. So great a wrong as his fate implied overshadowed all beauty in the world" (*Journal*, 11/12/1859). On the 30th of October, Thoreau again rang the town bell in defiance of the selectmen, before delivering his rousing lecture "A Plea for Captain John Brown" to his fellow citizens. He also opposed the town authorities by holding a funeral service in Concord that December, on the occasion of Brown's execution by hanging. "A Plea" was delivered as a speech days later in Worcester and in the Boston Temple of Thoreau's abolitionist friend Theodore Parker. It was "reported, reprinted, and discussed in all the Boston papers."[9]

When the essay was published, it appeared through many outlets and enjoyed enormous distribution in the Northeastern United States. Its persuasive message was again consistent with the Gita: Violence is bad, but social evil is worse.

Thoreau viewed John Brown as a man who had "followed the voice within himself even though it led to opposition with the state."[10] Calling Brown "the bravest and humanest man in all the country," Thoreau appealed to the Christian values of his neighbors: "You who pretend to care for Christ crucified, consider what you are to do to him who offered himself to be the savior of four millions of men."[11] In defending this position, Thoreau set himself against most of his fellow Concordians, including (to some extent) Ralph Waldo Emerson; even against the great majority of other abolitionists such as William Lloyd Garrison; and, finally, against antislavery liberals such as Abraham Lincoln—all of whom saw Brown as a threat to law and order in civil society. Of the "secret six" who had supplied Brown with arms and money, three fled the country (one helped on his way by Thoreau), two were jailed, and one was put away in an asylum for paranoia. Thoreau, in collusion with a "band of felons" and also subject to prosecution for treason, was "in danger of his life," according to one scholar—not only from the government, but from mob action.[12] But he kept putting his spoken and written word into the fray and saw to its publication, assisted by his sister Sophia, Elizabeth Peabody, and other abolitionists. His lectures and his writings, during and after 1859, brought the meaning of John Brown to Thoreau's fellow Americans so that, as the hymn has it, John Brown's truth went marching on, all the way to Appomattox and the end of the Civil War in 1865. The passive resistance of Thoreau's essay on civil disobedience, and his advocacy of fighting a just war in "A Plea for Captain John Brown," although apparently divergent, are in accord with Thoreau's convictions as shaped by the Gita, where nonviolence *(ahimsâ)* and the imperative to fight are repeatedly recommended to Arjuna in contiguous passages.

The Hindu roots of Thoreau's political convictions, found especially in the Bhagavad Gita, mark a key area of common ground between Thoreau and Mahatma Gandhi. During the long years of struggle that culminated in Indian independence, Gandhi claims to have reread and meditated upon one stanza of the Gita per day.[13] His theoretical grounding in the Gita ran parallel with his study of Thoreau. "I read *Walden* first in Johannesburg in South Africa in 1906 and his ideas influenced me greatly. I adopted some of them and recommended the study of Thoreau to all my friends who were helping me in the cause of Indian independence. Why, I actually took the name of my movement from Thoreau's essay, 'On the Duty of Civil Disobedience' [sic], written about eighty years ago."[14] Gandhi also read Henry Salt, Thoreau's English biographer, "with great pleasure and equal profit"—which presumably includes profit from his anarchical, anti-authoritarian rhetoric.[15] After his second imprisonment in 1908, Gandhi explicitly compared himself to Thoreau, both in his principled resistance to the state and in his reasons for resisting it. As one historian has written: "There can be no doubt that Gandhi was deeply indebted to the Thoreau who defied society and government to follow his conscience."[16] After both Gandhi and Thoreau were cited as sources of personal and philosophical inspiration for Martin Luther King Jr. during the civil rights movement of the 1960s, Thoreau's political influence grew wider still. A few decades later, the prime minister of India could be heard declaring to the United States Congress that "Thoreau influenced Mahatma Gandhi tremendously," just as Thoreau's philosophy had been shaped in part by Hindu thought.[17] The internal "struggle" that Thoreau mentioned in his journal as early as 1840, between a love of contemplation and a life of action, would ultimately lead to him distinguishing himself in both the contemplative and the active life. Because Thoreau viewed philosophy as a way of life, it is only fitting that philosophical ideals would lead him into radical political action.

FOURTEEN

WALDEN REVISITED

An Interview with Stanley Cavell

Interviewed by Rick Anthony Furtak

One of the most prominent and accomplished philosophers in America, Stanley Cavell has demonstrated his appreciation for Thoreau's *Walden* in a number of his own books: *The Senses of Walden*, Cavell's most sustained engagement with Thoreau, was first published in 1972 and has remained continuously in print. It has been reissued three times (in 1974, 1981, and 1992) and is recognized as a classic and pioneering work of contemporary philosophy. Thoreau's influence on Cavell's thought is also shown in *Themes Out of School* (1984), *In Quest of the Ordinary* (1988), *Conditions Handsome and Unhandsome* (1990), *Emerson's Transcendental Etudes* (2003), and *Philosophy the Day after Tomorrow* (2005). Cavell has been honored with many awards and distinctions—including a MacArthur Fellowship—and his brilliant, idiosyncratic writings have earned him international acclaim. No other thinker of recent times has made such a compelling case for the enduring significance of Thoreau's work, and here Stanley Cavell reflects on *Walden* and philosophy almost four decades after *The Senses of Walden* first appeared.

This interview with Rick Anthony Furtak was conducted via e-mail between September and December 2008.

Furtak: Several of the contributors to this volume follow your lead in reading *Walden* as a response to Cartesian skepticism. Thoreau himself seems to invite this. In addition to his many remarks about finding a solid foundation, he alludes to Descartes in "The Ponds," noting that his axe once slid into a hole on the ice "as if some evil genius had directed it"; early in "The Pond in Winter," when he again takes up his axe and walks onto the surface of the frozen pond, he entertains the idea that he might be dreaming.[1] You have pointed out that the opening chapter of *Walden* is haunted by "a sense of loss," as if its author has been deprived of "a connection with things."[2] How would you characterize this acquaintance with the world that Thoreau seeks to recover, and how does it differ from the foundational certainty that Descartes wishes to find?

Cavell: Let's assume that Thoreau's invocation of "some evil genius" and the surmise that he might be dreaming are both allusions to Descartes's *Meditations*, encouraging the thought that the mood of loss and the project of recovery I find in the opening of Thoreau's *Walden* bears, or wishes to be seen to bear, some illuminating, if marginal, relation—whether of similarity or difference—to the haunting of doubt and the project of certainty in a central piece of Descartes's world-historical philosophical work. (This cannot, but I think need not, be proven one way or the other in order to provide serious food for thought—not proven, at any rate, before undertaking to ponder the matter. "Believe," Augustine advised, "and you have eaten.")

There is a further, equally specific, connection between these texts that suggests a practical route between them. I mean their each opening with a brief account of the cause of their writing here and now, and more particularly of how they have each arrived at the readiness for composing their accounts. Remember Descartes's opening paragraph of his *Meditations*: "It is now several years since I first became aware how many false opinions I had from my childhood been admitting as true, and how doubtful was everything I have subsequently based on them. Accordingly I have ever since been convinced that if I am to establish anything firm and lasting in the sciences, I must once for all, and by a deliberate effort, rid myself of all those opinions in which I have hitherto given credence, starting entirely anew, and building from the foundations up. . . . I waited until I had attained an age so mature that I could no longer expect that I should at any later date be able to execute my design. . . . I should now be failing in my duty, were I to continue consuming in deliberation such time for action as still remains to me." Descartes's second paragraph begins: "Today, then, as I have suitably freed my mind from all cares, and have secured for myself an assured leisure in peaceful solitude [nb],[3] I shall at last apply myself earnestly and freely to the general overthrow of all my former opinions." The third begins: "Whatever, up to the present [nb], I have accepted as possessed of the highest truth and certainty I have learned either from the senses or through the senses." And in the fourth: "But, it may be said, although the senses sometimes deceive us . . . there are yet many other things which, though known by way of sense, are too evident to be doubted; as, for instance [nb] that I am in this place, seated by the fire, attired in a dressing-gown, having this paper in my hands, and other similar seeming certainties. Can I deny [nb] that these hands and this body are mine, save perhaps by comparing myself to those who are insane, and whose brains are so disturbed and clouded by dark bilious vapours that they persist in assuring us that they are kings, when in fact they are in extreme poverty . . . or that their head is made of clay and their body of glass. . . . But they are mad; and I should be no less insane [nb] were I to follow examples [nb] so extravagant."[4]

Compare Thoreau's opening paragraph of *Walden*: "When I wrote the following pages, or rather the bulk of them, I lived alone [nb], in the woods, a mile from any neighbor, in a house which I had built myself, on the shore of Walden Pond, in Concord, Massachusetts, and earned my living by the labor of my hands [nb] only. I lived there two years and two months. At present [nb] I am a sojourner in civilized life again." (My life is my example. How does this happen? Thoreau had made his case clear as the presentation of something like the report of a narrative. Is this philosophy? Descartes makes his case by something that he recognizes to court madness. Is this nevertheless sane?) And Thoreau's second paragraph continues: "I should not obtrude [nb] my affairs so much on the notice of my readers if very particular inquiries had not been made by my townsmen concerning my mode of life, which some would call impertinent, though they do not appear to me at all impertinent, but, considering the circumstances, very natural and pertinent." He has made himself an example, a spectacle. As Descartes has done, but more clearly, more "naturally" motivated, than Descartes. The "circumstances" Thoreau refers to are that his "affairs" and the "inquiries" made about his affairs are both equally pertinent and impertinent. And further along: "We commonly do not remember that it is, after all, always the first person that is speaking. I should not talk so much about myself if there were any body else whom I knew as well. Unfortunately, I am confined to this theme by the narrowness of my experience."[5] The irony in this concluding remark, mocking the tendency of philosophy to be restive with human finitude, is quite classical.

Both of these writers and thinkers announce and expand upon the fact that they are alone (later Existentialists will make of this the metaphysics of an entire philosophy, arguably writing less distinctively). The sense is that what is being presented, call it philosophy, is a considered confrontation that accordingly requires as it were personal justification, unlike offering entertaining fictions or contributions to an established science. Both insist that their writing is made from their own, present experience, which is assured by their taking themselves as their source of examples— indeed one could say, taking themselves, in their greatly, even opposite, ways as their perpetual, unfolding example of philosophical curiosity and illumination. This would once upon a time have been the familiar condition of undertaking the making of a book called *Confessions*. The insistence here, however, is on the writing as proceeding from the most ordinary of human experiences (sitting, musing, in a chair before a fire; writing in response to a neighbor's inquiries). Neither of our writers is here obviously confessing sins, although like sins, what is being told of oneself is meant as common to, inescapable for, humankind. What is dramatized in such openings is the question of knowing when and how philosophy begins, and the answer discovered and proposed in each case is that philosophy has already begun, before you know it, in thoughts seeming to risk insanity and in behavior causing impertinence, or rather raising the question whether philosophy itself, the attempt to view and systematically examine one's life, is impertinent yet "very natural."

I would offer such a description of philosophy as fitting Wittgenstein's questioning in *Philosophical Investigations* at once of philosophy and of the ordinary.[6] But does this not beg the question whether the mode in which Wittgenstein conducts his investigations should be called philosophy? This does not beg the question in invoking Wittgenstein's writing; it is one of Wittgenstein's questions.

I note that Wittgenstein, in his *Investigations*, more than any other philosopher I am familiar, and can contend, with, since Descartes at the beginning of modern philosophy, perceives the impulses to philosophy and to madness as growing from the same stem. (Foucault and Derrida once held a prominent exchange on philosophy and madness out of conflicting readings of Descartes. I remember my fascination with it, but equally my sense, as with so much else going on in the opposite Anglo-American dispensation of philosophy, of similarities and differences with my sense of intellectual fruitfulness, that a coherent, finite, response from me would arise nowhere but from going on sitting in a corner with my slants on Wittgenstein and Emerson and Thoreau etc., mostly quietly, but sometimes, out of exasperation or sudden companionship, banging with a wooden spoon on the bottom of a kettle.) Riffling Wittgenstein's pages for a few minutes I find well over a dozen or more of what I take to be examples of this perception. Quickly sampling them: "There is no doubt that I now want to play chess, but chess is the game it is in virtue of all its rules (and so on). . . . Are all the rules contained in my act of intending? Is it experience that tells me that this sort of game is the usual consequence of such an act of intending? So is it impossible for me to be certain what I am intending to do? And if that is nonsense—what kind of super-strong connection exists between the act of intending and the thing intended?" (§197). "Why can't my right hand give my left hand money?" (§268). "What gives us *so much as the idea* that living beings, things, can feel? Is it that my education has led me to it by drawing my attention to feelings in myself, and now I transfer the idea to objects outside myself? . . . —I do not transfer my idea to stones, plants, etc. Couldn't I imagine having frightful pains and turning to stone while they lasted? Well, how do I know, if I shut my eyes, whether I have not turned into a stone? And if that has happened, in what sense will *the stone* have the pains?" (§283). "You think that after all you must be weaving a piece of cloth because you are sitting at a loom—even if it is empty—and going through the motions of weaving" (§414).

RAF: The two Descartes allusions I just mentioned are not direct references. They will be recognized by most philosophically literate readers, but they are likely to be lost on others. I wonder if you think that this kind of indirect allusion is exemplary of what we should expect from philosophical writing that has managed to "become literature," as you have suggested that philosophy possibly ought to (on the last page of *The Claim of Reason*).[7] Have you intentionally employed an allusive style in your own work? For instance, you sometimes allude to phrases from *Walden* without citing it directly, so that readers versed in Thoreau will catch your references and others are liable to miss them. In your essay on Heidegger and Thoreau, for example, you speak of Thoreau's mode of apprehending "whatever is culminating in the present," without mentioning that "God himself" is what "culminates in the present moment," according to *Walden*.[8] Should these methods be more common in philosophy insofar as it understands itself as a literary discipline? Or do they run the risk of being opaque to those readers who are not yet familiar with Thoreau's work?

sc: Have I suggested on the last page of *The Claim of Reason* that philosophy possibly ought to become literature? I mention the possibility there as a tendency or temptation, and in my preceding answer I record literary influence as a fact of the opening of Descartes's *Meditations*, at the origin, accordingly, of modern philosophy. One of my motives is exactly to get the question raised philosophically of philosophy's fear of literature, raised at the beginning in Plato's banishing of poetry from the *Republic*. By now, with the institutionalization of university philosophy, this banishment becomes automatic, a matter of insisting on philosophical writing as the provision of arguments. Nothing wrong, I trust, with providing arguments. But so uncontroversial is that requirement, that I would have thought it was recognizably time to go on to question whether we recognize that argument mongering runs dangers of what used to be called logic chopping, something preventing thought, encouraging us to forget what it is that moves us, justly moves us, to assertion and to argument. Plato, in our beginning, in his struggle for reason, for that reason has to struggle against sophistry (blatant or concealed), what he takes as a mockery of reason. It takes literariness up to the eyeballs to get us to take it as a reasonable reflection that in dreams "our hands perhaps, and the whole body, are not what we see them as being" (First Meditation, sixth paragraph). What else do we see hands and bodies to be in dreams other than hands and bodies? Nonexistent hands and bodies? Is that clearer or truer than calling them dreamt hands and bodies? You might as well say that the hands and bodies in the passing words of these questions are not hands and bodies. Is it informative to say that as words they are not literally hands and bodies? It seems to make better sense to say that within the stated sentences, they are *only and wholly* literally so.

You go on here to ask whether I have "intentionally employed an allusive style" in my work. What you seem to mean by this is that I leave some things inexplicit. I can't imagine either what it would be to make everything explicit (for example, Descartes does not reveal whether he was wearing underclothes under his dressing gown), or that leaving out matters that I expect readers to pick up constitutes the basis of a "style." That some things will not be picked up or not be clear to "those readers who are not yet familiar with [Thoreau's] work" is merely inevitable, but why say that they are "opaque"? That accusation, if true, seems to point to a fault of judgment in writing, like giving a poor set of directions or mishandling the art of paraphrase.

You seem to me to agree with others that there is something unexpected, even provocative, in the way I write, anyway in writing what I am pleased to claim as philosophy. Others call it my style, and generally express either contentment or contempt with and for it as a medium of philosophizing, sometimes allowing that it may be fit for some (other?) form of writing, sometimes called literature (implying that this, since Plato, continues to represent the most intimate risk of philosophy's claim to, or for, reason). Your suggestion, as I understand it, is that this tendency on my part is explainable as a certain studied inexplicitness on my part. And the fact is that I agree that there is something like an air of inexplicitness that my writing happens to create. Some, unkindly, may take this as a mark of my fear of drawing conclusions—suggesting that, while like others, I am bound to harbor conclusions, I nevertheless, out of some quirk or fear of my own (recognized or not by me) prefer to insinuate rather than state these conclusions. Not regarding myself as an excessively fearful or unprecedentedly eccentric writer, I look another way for an account of this intangible air, or air of intangibility.

The background is my understanding of Wittgenstein's protestation, in I suppose his most sustained sequence of meditations on what he desires for, or calls, or recognizes to be, philosophy, that "if one tried to advance *theses* in philosophy, it would never be possible to debate them, because everyone would agree to them" (*Investigations*, §128). I am not unaware that such a claim appears to deny what many teachers of philosophy nowadays would take as the heart and soul of philosophy. (I have seen a departmental document distributed to its students to explain the difficult matter of writing an acceptable term paper for philosophy courses which begins, roughly: "Clearly state, at the beginning of your paper, the theses you intend to provide arguments for and/or against.") My own understanding or appreciation of the shunning of theses in philosophy has philosophical authority behind it at least as old as that approving arguments, both views associated with the figure of Socrates. The view I am moved by is that, with respect to the collisions that motivate and define philosophy, neither side of the catastrophe knows anything the other side does not know. Yet we sometimes find ourselves inflamed, perhaps over whether one may inform against a father, or whether a father is entitled to demand a public expression of love in return for the gift of a third of the father's kingdom, or whether a daughter may be reasonable to withhold love as payment, or perhaps whether our senses address the world or at best representations of the world, or whether there is a world beyond the world of our senses and if so whether in that further world there exists the guarantee that our words find their power of mutual comprehensibility. To regard any of these assertions as *conclusions* (rather than perhaps as inflamed opinions) is untrue. To regard them as *theses* is to define them argumentatively, namely as requiring argument.

Philosophy of any serious stripe is bound to be moved to question what it calls opinions, which it takes perhaps as rumors presented as facts; or to examine what it calls beliefs, which it takes perhaps as unfounded conversational pastimes. Descartes describes what he is attempting to do as "[applying himself] earnestly and freely to the general overthrow of all my former opinions." What then causes him the threat of madness is evidently the route to this overthrow, whereas his being moved to call the objects of this overthrow something like his former "opinions" does not strike him so much as worth the whistle. When Wittgenstein remarks, "My attitude towards him is an attitude towards a soul. I am not of the *opinion* that he has a soul" (*Investigations*, part 2, p. 178), he may be taken as challenging the entire history of modern philosophy's self-understanding as bonded to searching for the epistemological grounding of our beliefs and claims to knowledge of the world.

To deny that I know the existence of the world and of others in it appears to be saying that I lack something I cannot readily imagine not having (unlike my still mostly negligent knowledge of the history of Boston, which waxes and wanes) rather than discovering a lack in what I seem to understand as constituting my relation to the existence of the world and others. Wittgenstein's German reads: "Meine Einstellung zu ihm ist ein Einstellung zur Seele. Ich habe nicht die Meinung, dass er eine Seele hat." I wonder whether the German "ein Einstellng zur Seele" in the former sentence rather has the sense "an attitude towards soul [or towards the soul]," constituting as it were a condition or *preparation* for the claim to have an attitude towards this soul which an individual other, I gather, has. The preparation for soul is, let's say, scattered throughout receding millions of experiences of things and others and places and exchanges of thoughts and perceptions and feelings, in and beyond or before language. My attitude toward particular others is, in contrast, centered on particular histories between us, brief or epic, remembered or distorted. I add that I am equally not of the opinion that I am here, dressed as I happen to be, and possessed of this body with, for example, these hands. But does it help to say here that my attitude toward myself is my attitude toward a (my) soul? I might sometimes wish it were (more consistently).

It is, I might say, out of a determination to shun the hubris or ignorance or distraction of attempting to inform my interlocutors of something they cannot simply not know, in which case I would be attempting to regard my position among others as intellectually or emotionally inherently superior to theirs, that I find myself proceeding indirectly, evocatively, suggestively, skirting the literary in order not to avoid or evade irresistible promptings to philosophy.

I hardly need to be informed that this is not the only way to proceed in philosophizing. I am more than content in being confirmed, rather more often lately than in the past, that it is one way. It is here that my lifelong tendency, from my first book onward, to include the reading of works of art among my philosophical inclinations and ambitions, must find its justification. I might take this as raising the question why the examples I invoke in philosophizing are apt not to confine themselves to things like a bit of wax or a drifting ship or a piece of paper or a hand or a man who believes his head is clay, but to include works of high literary art whose presentation of figures and events permit and reward and, for me, require a certain evocative, associative prose in detailing my relation to them. This taste, or determination, may be seen as my justification (if only successful to myself)—I wouldn't much mind seeing it called, if necessary, my excuse, though I would prefer thinking of it as my occasion— in my desire to find for myself such deliberately responsive prose as I come upon. How could the events of a life be discovered and conveyed otherwise? The shunning of this register of responsiveness helps account, to my mind, for the relative shunning, or subordination, in classical epistemology of our knowledge of others (let alone our nonhuman others, surely beginning with horses and dogs) as if they were afterthoughts. (If philosophy is solely a developing set of problems seeking solutions, and is not also inspired, let's say, by sets of solutions lacking satisfaction, then what leg of standing I have in philosophy is shakier than even I have imagined.)

RAF: I take to heart your reminder that laying out "problems resolved" is not the exclusive task with which philosophy ought to concern itself. The passages that I cited in my first question also show that Thoreau, by responding to Descartes, is acknowledging some kind of relationship with modern philosophy and its focus on problems of knowledge. Another link between *Walden* and the epistemological tradition is one that you have emphasized in claiming that a single line from *Walden* could be construed as a summary of Kant's *Critique of Pure Reason*.[9] You write, in *The Senses of Walden*, that the imagination has a priori status no less than other forms of knowledge, and that "human forms of feeling" are perhaps "as revelatory of the world" as the laws of physics.[10] In what ways do affective or emotional modes of knowledge reveal something true about reality? Might Thoreau's conception of the world, and our means of knowing it, be akin to the "epistemology of moods" that you detect in Emerson's work?

SC: Your formulations (you call them, nicely, "prompts")[11] in this question seem to me perhaps most clearly to express a certain exasperation with my ways of things and words. You pick up more or less provocative phrases from here and there in my work and ask how they go together, whereas in each case the question for me is what has prompted each of them, in the specific crossroads in which they are constructed. The crossroads are apt to be locales in which I find myself saying, even insisting upon, something obscure or even wretchedly banal, or in which I have missed something blatant, which for me is not a signal to argue my way into clarity, or to excuse my shortcomings, but rather to characterize the best way I can what has caused this obscurity or banality or unresponsiveness.

In speaking, for example, of Thoreau's "forms of feeling," I am not appealing to some well-known fact but to passages in his work whose presence I sense to be underestimated. An instance is my picking up in Thoreau's opening words his harping on the question whether philosophy (or meditation and description of his kind) is apt to give cause for impertinent interventions, or whether the interventions it invites are pertinent, even natural. I claim this is his way of identifying philosophy as apparently impertinent but essentially and simultaneously natural. What would it mean to provide an argument in favor of this claim? Yet I regard it as a formulation whose clarification of what philosophy is, or can be, is worth the expense of all the words of *Walden*, and all that may be brought in response to them, to establish.

Let's take the fairly obvious impulse in your question to question the unobvious intimacy of intuition I find, or claim, between what compels flowery Thoreau and what sustains monumental Kant. I cannot think this pairing would have made itself felt inescapably to me apart from my early work inspired by, made possible by, Austin and Wittgenstein, and by my soon linking of Wittgenstein with Kant and later with Emerson (hence with Nietzsche's intimate conversation with Emerson). I look up and quote two passages from my essay "Finding as Founding" in *This New Yet Unapproachable America*.[12] First, on page 87: "In claiming the *Investigations* as a Kantian work, I claim for it the work of extending Kant's categories of the understanding into the use of language and its criteria as such, Kant's achievement as invoked and summarized within the work of the *Investigations* in its paragraph §90: 'We feel as if we had to *penetrate* phenomena; our investigation, however, is directed not towards phenomena, but, as one might say, towards the "*possibilities*" of phenomena.'" Second, on page 81: "[In] Emerson's essay entitled *Fate*, . . . I find the *Critique of Pure Reason* turned upon itself: notions of limitation and of conditions are as determining in the essay 'Fate' as they are in Kant, but it is as if these terms are themselves subjected to transcendental deduction [Wittgenstein would say: subjected to grammatical investigation], as if not just twelve categories but any and every word in our language stands under the necessity of deduction, or say derivation."

I hope it does not seem inhospitable of me to answer a question about my writing by asking the inquirer to read further, or read again, a piece of mine. But, relying on good will here, I am just pointing, hoping to save the reader time, to specific moments in an essay of mine that I am fond of and feel grateful for, covering necessary ground that I cannot see how to improve upon relevantly now. I get the impression that sometimes what makes my work hard to take up, or take on, is that its occasional elaborateness is perceived as an effort to avoid making my meaning clear (hence presumably too easily dismissible as superficial), whereas it results, so far as I can determine, rather from trying to make as clear as I can that I am, to the best of my ability, insisting on meaning every word I say. I take it that this is no more or less what philosophy asks, and seeks to answer, in various, sometimes incompatible, ways.

RAF: What I meant to express was not exasperation, only a wish to hear you build on the suggestive thoughts you've already offered on the Kantian echoes in Thoreau's work. Your recognition of the link between Thoreau and Kant seems to me entirely apposite, and a handful of others have extended this line of interpretation in recent years.[13] So there's no need to offer an apologia for your own earlier recognition of the common ground between the project of *Walden* and that of the *Critique of Pure Reason*. If there's a single topic upon which I'd be most eager to pursue our conversation further, that would be it. For now, however, let me introduce one more theme.

You have remarked that Thoreau is a threat, or an embarrassment, to "what we have learned to call philosophy," and you have commented on what this indicates about the state of philosophy in America.[14] In the decades since you published *The Senses of Walden*, we have seen a modest increase in the amount of attention paid to Thoreau by American philosophers—yet this growth has been incremental, and his works remain on the margins of the philosophical canon (if not outside of it altogether).

This must be troubling for anyone who cares about Thoreau and the conception of philosophy that he represents. What signs can you point to, and which would you look for in the future, as promising evidence that Thoreau's legacy is being taken more seriously than it previously had been? If philosophers have come to acknowledge such vehement critics of the academic establishment as Kierkegaard and Nietzsche, then why should they continue to neglect the nineteenth-century American thinker who, in many respects, resembles them most closely?

sc: You suggest that the growth in attention to Thoreau's work, in recent years, on the part at least of American philosophers, however modestly incremental, may be attributable to my championing of that work. I would be glad if that is so, but I would not be surprised to learn that its larger effect has been further to question my own credibility as a philosopher. Your parting question, wondering to the air why philosophers who have grudgingly come to accept the philosophical pertinence of Kierkegaard and Nietzsche persist in turning deaf ears to Thoreau, strikes me not simply as puzzling but as soul-boggling and heartbreaking. I don't have answers, but I have given myself thoughts of the following kind to ponder. There seems to me to be some persisting, deep-lying assumption among philosophers, near and far, that the United States *cannot* be understood to make, is metaphysically debarred from making, an original contribution to philosophy. (This assumption, or deep-lying belief, will have constituted eating, but at the same time indigestion.) Of course, our American locale came to contain leading voices in international efforts of analytical philosophy, but only after Carnap, Reichenbach, Hempel, etc., took refuge here from Hitler and after their pedagogy of logical positivism became the spreading avant-garde of philosophy in major American universities.

But I feel that the United States has contributed to its own academic philosophical subservience, in two main, seemingly unrelated, ways. One way is represented in the emergence of John Dewey as the incomparably most famous and influential homegrown American philosopher we have produced, the voice to be imitated or deplored over so many decades, still in power and vogue as positivism was conquering. Dewey's attack on metaphysics was congenial with that of logical positivism, but its pedagogy, however permanently beneficial to childhood education, was to my way of thinking too shallow and repetitive for the education of grownups. His example, while a permanent reminder, to be grateful for permanently, of what philosophy should mean in the practice, say the living, of our lives, nevertheless left philosophically inclined intellectuals too often paralyzed by the sting of positivism in the realm of aesthetics and ethics and religion, and as often vulnerable otherwise to impatient philosophical fashion. (If you have to be as learned and as gifted intellectually as, say, Hilary Putnam, or one of his and my most distinguished students, to confront, largely on your own, exaggerated claims of philosophy to scientific status and diminishing interests in human culture beyond that, the cultural situation of philosophy would become largely hopeless.) Another contributing phenomenon to pragmatism's ineffectiveness is that of C. S. Peirce, whom everyone recognizes to be touched with genius but who could not produce extended and stable works to build from fruitfully. Like the positivists, Dewey's attacks on philosophy left the history and the cultural fact of philosophy almost empty of interest; even, I would say, mysterious. How could anyone take work seriously that repetitiously made such empty errors as those Dewey found in Plato and Descartes and Kant and Freud (if Dewey mentioned him) and who not? I recall no instance (but it has been a long time since I tried) in which Dewey confronts and probes an actual text of philosophy to determine its motive for its existence and its specific human bafflements in achieving its desires. Modern culture as a whole, beyond amateur thoughts of science, or rather beyond the invocation of "scientific method," is largely absent from Dewey's thinking. Every important philosopher has distrusted philosophy as s/he inherits it. But Dewey taught too many of us not to read; anyway, not to read philosophy. This is perhaps all right if you are Socrates (or conceivably, to an extent, Wittgenstein) and if you can talk as well as anyone is likely to write, and if you can talk to everyone in the world you consider you need to know, about anything in the world you want to know and to be known, and ones you imagine to be apt students of philosophy, drawn to self-examination. (I confess that I am rather surprised at the note of bitterness seeping into these memories of reading Dewey. I attribute this note at the moment to memories of how long it takes in philosophy to arrive at thoughts that begin to satisfy oneself are worth expressing and asking others to consider; and, relatedly, to endless reminders of the continuous energy that is demanded, in the long road of teaching philosophy, if one is to keep great and original work in the history of philosophy from lapsing into becoming parts of inert topics on a course syllabus. But of course these quests and energies are as inescapably internal to any good teaching as to what gives to philosophy its particular economy of preciousness.)

I said there were two (companion) ways in which American culture has worked to defeat its interest in philosophy. After Dewey's dominant reception, the second way is that philosophy is on the whole not offered as a normal subject or discipline in our (public) high schools. This seemingly trivial, all but unnoticeable, policy, or convention, assures that philosophy will on the whole forever seem foreign or intimidating or unyielding to most educated Americans. At an early stage philosophy, instead of being inviting, suddenly becomes embarrassing, discouraging, risking showing oneself a fool, a bar rather than a spur to one's sense of welcome expansiveness. (My thought is that even one year-long course the last year of high school, even taught inexpertly, but demanding the reading through of half a dozen philosophical classics, would distinctly change the odds in philosophy's joining the North American table of education.) How else could it happen that so many distinguished literary figures in America still treat philosophy as untouchable or forbidden? How else could, for example, the greatly talented founders of our New Criticism have left our literary culture so unprepared for, and helpless before, the challenges of so-called postmodernism? Perhaps my favorite among the ways I have wished to combat this loss of philosophy, a way less private than it once was, is to treat the worldwide admiration of Hollywood cinema as, in irreducible part, the attraction of a medium of philosophical prompting.

Sometimes ticklishness in facing philosophy is as discouraging as glibness with it.

Notes

1. LOCATING THOREAU, REORIENTING PHILOSOPHY
James D. Reid, Rick Anthony Furtak, and Jonathan Ellsworth

1. There may be a modestly growing number of American philosophers who recognize that Thoreau's ideas are worthy of attention in certain respects: See, e.g., *Emerson and Thoreau: Figures of Friendship*, ed. John T. Lysaker and William Rossi (Bloomington: Indiana University Press, 2010). Several of the contributors to the present volume have written in the past decade about Thoreau's philosophical significance, and insofar as this represents a small but increasing tendency we hope to encourage others to move further in the same direction.

2. For biographical details, see Robert D. Richardson, *Henry Thoreau: A Life of the Mind* (Berkeley: University of California Press, 1986), and Henry S. Salt, *Life of Henry David Thoreau* (Sussex: Centaur Press, 1993).

3. Originally published in the *Atlantic Monthly* in 1862, Emerson's elegy for Thoreau is reprinted, for instance, in Thoreau, *Walden and Other Writings*, with an introduction by Ralph Waldo Emerson (New York: Modern Library, 2000), xi–xxxi.

4. This omission might be due to Thoreau's many personal disagreements with Emerson, or it might have more to do with his philosophical iconoclasm. Thoreau has often been classified as a New England transcendentalist; and although he never rejected this label, it is, perhaps, somewhat misleading. A history of transcendentalism in New England that appeared in the late nineteenth century mentions Thoreau only once, in passing: See Octavius Frothingham, *Transcendentalism in New England* (New York: G. P. Putnam's Sons, 1886), 133. And a more recent history of the movement concludes that Thoreau had little in common with this group of thinkers, who were typically committed to some version of Christianity, to a dualistic understanding of mind and matter, and to the related idea that sense experience is unreliable. See Paul F. Boller, *American Transcendentalism, 1830–1860* (New York: G. P. Putnam's Sons, 1974), 29–35, 176.

5. Stanley Cavell, *In Quest of the Ordinary: Lines of Skepticism and Romanticism* (Chicago: University of Chicago Press, 1988), 14.

6. Taking issue with this assumption, Stephen Mulhall remarks that "nothing is easier than to write philosophy in a way which represses the fact of one's humanity." Stephen Mulhall, *Routledge Philosophy Guidebook to Heidegger and Being and Time* (London: Routledge, 1996), 33.

7. Thoreau's proficiency in the Greek and Roman classics has been documented by Ethel Seybold, in *Thoreau: The Quest and the Classics* (New Haven, Conn.: Yale University Press, 1951); his intellectual affinity with many of the ancient Greek and Roman philosophical schools has been noted by Pierre Hadot: "There Are Nowadays Professors of Philosophy, but Not Philosophers," *Journal of Speculative Philosophy* 19, no. 3 (2005): 229–37.

8. "A Slight Sound at Evening," in *Essays of E. B. White* (New York: Harper and Row, 1977), 235–36.

9. Leibniz and especially Schopenhauer stand out as noteworthy exceptions to this trend of neglect.

10. Typical in this respect is the distrustful attitude toward emotions shown by W. V. O. Quine in *The Time of My Life: An Autobiography* (Cambridge, Mass.: MIT Press, 1985), 476: "I am deeply moved by occasional passages of poetry, and so, characteristically, I read little of it." We thank Edward Mooney for pointing out this passage.

11. See Immanuel Kant, *Anthropology from a Pragmatic Point of View*, trans. Victor L. Dowdell (Carbondale: Southern Illinois University Press, 1978), 186–87. Whereas Thoreau gives an account of his dietary practices as part of his philosophical project, Kant tells us nothing about his inclination to eat cheese sandwiches, leaving such impure matters to his physician and his friends, and eventually to his biographer. See Manfred Kuehn, *Kant: A Biography* (New York: Cambridge University Press, 2001), 420.

12. Thoreau, *Walden*, "Where I Lived, and What I Lived For," 21st para.

13. Roger Scruton, *Modern Philosophy* (New York: Penguin, 1995), 12. He continues: "When someone can call himself a philosopher, while entertaining *no views whatsoever* on aesthetics, political philosophy, morality or religion, something has gone wrong with his conception of the subject."

14. In this respect, Thoreau anticipates some of Heidegger's stated dissatisfactions with disciplinary boundaries within the university. For more on this topic, see James D. Reid, "Ethical Criticism in Heidegger's Early Freiburg Lectures," *Review of Metaphysics* 59 (September 2005): 33–71.

15. Martha C. Nussbaum, *Love's Knowledge: Essays on Philosophy and Literature* (New York: Oxford University Press, 1990), 3–20. Nussbaum's appeal for "a different sort of precision, a different norm of rationality" is remarkably similar to Cavell's description of what is provided by Thoreau's prose: "a mode of thinking, a mode of conceptual accuracy," that is "based on an idea of rigor" unfamiliar to academic philosophy in its present form. See also Cavell, *In Quest of the Ordinary*, 14.

16. See also Alain Badiou, *Theoretical Writings* (London: Continuum, 2004), xiii–xiv. At the end of a similar list, he states in summary that the category of "philosophy" contains just about "anything whatsoever that can be classified as 'writing.'"

17. On the idea of metaphysics as a natural disposition (*metaphysica naturalis*), see Kant's *Critique of Pure Reason*, B21–22.

18. Habermas has argued for this view, against Heidegger. In the Anglophone world, when a thinker such as David Wiggins proposes that the concept of truth is inexorably related to questions of meaning or value, he is arguing for a departure from the currently prevalent way of separating things. See David Wiggins, *Needs, Values, Truth* (Oxford: Clarendon Press, 1998), 140.

19. This is clearly the task of Aristotle's *Metaphysics*, as the philosopher argues famously, if obscurely, in book 4 (Gamma).

20. Similarly, what passes for aesthetics is likely to look spare and lean if it fails to ask whether, in the experience of the work of art, something like *truth* comes into play, whether we can be said to know something about ourselves and the world in aesthetic transactions, and what, if anything, the reception of beauty has to do with ethical life and moral experience. You may conclude, in the end, that aesthetic experience *is* utterly distinct (as some of Kant's remarks in the third *Critique* have been taken to mean), but in order to make that claim convincing, you'd better be able to answer in considerable depth and detail: distinct from *what*? It could be argued that every account of any one thing is, at least implicitly, an account of everything else; as Spinoza wisely noted, *omnis determinatio est negatio.*

21. Thoreau, *Walden*, "Economy," 2nd para. Here one might be reminded of Nietzsche's remark, in *Beyond Good and Evil* (§6), that every philosophical view is a personal confession and an involuntary memoir.

22. Thoreau, *Journal*, 16 December 1859. See *The Journal of Henry D. Thoreau*, ed. Bradford Torrey and Francis Allen (New York: Dover, 1962), 13:30.

23. Thoreau, *Walden*, "Where I Lived, and What I Lived For," 1st para.

24. See "The Collector and His Circle," in *Essays on Art and Literature*, by J. W. Goethe, trans. Ellen von Nardroff and Ernest von Nardroff (New York: Suhrkamp, 1986), 124.

25. In this respect, Thoreau anticipates Heidegger's definition of the human being (or "Dasein") in *Being and Time* (§41) in terms of *Sorge*, or "care."

26. Explaining the origins of the theoretical attitude in the opening lines of *Metaphysics*, book 1 (Alpha), Aristotle remarks that "all human beings naturally reach out for understanding." As the most basic evidence of this complex cognitive longing, he cites the delight that we take in visual phenomena.

27. See, e.g., Harry G. Frankfurt, *The Importance of What We Care About* (Cambridge: Cambridge University Press, 1988), 80.

28. Thoreau, *Walden*, "Economy," 10th para.

2. THOREAU AND EMERSONIAN PERFECTIONISM
Stanley Bates

1. Stanley Cavell, in *Emerson's Transcendental Etudes* (Stanford, Calif.: Stanford University Press, 2003), 2, considers Heidegger's distinction in relation to Emerson. Hereafter, *ETE*.

2. Henry David Thoreau, *Walden and Civil Disobedience* (New York: Norton, 1966), 9.

3. I discuss this at some length in "Cavell and Ethics," in *Stanley Cavell*, ed. Richard Eldridge (Cambridge: Cambridge University Press, 2003).

4. Stanley Cavell, *The Senses of Walden*, exp. ed. (Chicago: University of Chicago Press, 1992). Hereafter, *SW*. Cavell's writing on Emerson is now conveniently available in the book cited in note 1. I hope that it will be clear how generally indebted to Cavell's work I am. And I'm further interested in why his interventions in what is called moral philosophy have also not become a part of academic moral philosophy.

5. Thomas Hurka (*Perfectionism* [Oxford: Oxford University Press, 1993], 3) mentions all of these names, among others, as perfectionist thinkers.

6. The best historical treatment of seventeenth- and eighteenth-century perfectionism that I know is Jerome Schneewind's magisterial *The Invention of Autonomy* (Cambridge: Cambridge University Press, 1998), part 2.

7. Ibid., 169.

8. Susan James, "Kant through the Glass of History," *Times Literary Supplement*, no. 4994, 18 December 1998, 9.

9. For example, see Immanuel Kant, *Grounding for the Metaphysics of Morals* (Indianapolis: Hackett, 1993), 46–47; and Kant, *Critique of Practical Reason* (New York: Library of Liberal Arts, 1956), 40–42.

10. Guyer's analysis appears in *Perfecting Virtue: New Essays on Kantian Ethics and Virtue Ethics*, ed. Julian Wuerth and Lawrence Yost (Cambridge University Press, 2011). Guyer points out that in the fourfold division of modern moral theories that Kant uses in the *Critique of Practical Reason*, the place of an internal but intellectual principle is occupied by Wolff's principle of perfection—which is severely criticized. In relying on the same fourfold division in the *Lectures on Ethics*, however, Kant presents his own, different principle of perfection as an internal but intellectual principle.

11. I have discussed these matters at some length in "Critical Notice of Barbara Herman, *Moral Literacy*," *Philosophical Books* 49 (October 2008): 363–71.

12. Again, I have discussed this history in more detail in "Cavell and Ethics."

13. Hurka, *Perfectionism*, 3.

14. Immanuel Kant, *Critique of Practical Reason*, trans. Lewis White Beck (New York: Library of Liberal Arts, 1956), 127–28.

15. Ibid.

16. Immanuel Kant, *The Metaphysical Principles of Virtue*, trans. James Ellington (New York: Library of Liberal Arts, 1964), 43. Kant's conception of these "obligatory ends" and their significance for his moral philosophy are persuasively explicated in Barbara Herman's "Obligatory Ends," in her *Moral Literacy* (Cambridge, Mass.: Harvard University Press, 2007).

17. Stanley Cavell, *Conditions Handsome and Unhandsome* (Chicago: University of Chicago Press, 1990), xxxi. Hereafter *CHU*. Hence, Cavell's account differs from the more specific kind of perfectionism that is a moral theory discussed by Hurka, in *Perfectionism*.

18. Ralph Waldo Emerson, "History," in *The Selected Writings of Ralph Waldo Emerson*, ed. Brooks Atkinson (New York: Modern Library, 1968), 125.

19. M. H. Abrams used this phrase for the title of *Natural Supernaturalism: Tradition and Revolution in Romantic Literature* (New York: W.W. Norton, 1973).

20. I use here the formulation of Timothy Gould (personal communication). The best analysis of Romantic literature as an attempt to construct a substitute for the Christian salvational narrative is Abrams, *Natural Supernaturalism*.

21. Cavell, *SW*, 95.

22. *CHU*, xx.

23. See for example, Richard Eldridge, "Cavell and American Philosophy and the Idea of America," in *Stanley Cavell*, ed. Eldridge; Simon Critchley, "Cavell's 'Romanticism' and Cavell's Romanticism," and Russell B. Goodman, "Cavell and American Philosophy," in *Contending with Stanley Cavell*, ed. Goodman (New York: Oxford University Press, 2005); and James Conant, "The Recovery of Greece and the Discovery of America," in *Reading Cavell*, ed. Alice Crary and Sanford Shieh (London: Routledge, 2006).

24. I have attempted to describe the core of this situation in "The Mind's Horizon," in *Beyond Representation*, ed. Richard Eldridge (Cambridge: Cambridge University Press, 1996).

25. For Cavell's relating of Emerson and Thoreau to the Kantian background, see *SW* 94–95, and *ETE* 11–12.

26. *ETE* 2.

27. An exception can be found in Stanley Cavell, *SW* 93.

28. Thoreau, *Walden and Civil Disobedience*, 5.

29. Karl Marx, in *The Marx-Engels Reader*, ed. Robert C. Tucker (New York: W. W. Norton, 1978), esp. 70–81. Marx is, of course, adapting and revising Hegel's term.

30. Ibid., 149.

31. Ibid., 155–156.

32. Thoreau, *Walden and Civil Disobedience*, 7–8.

33. *The Portable Karl Marx*, ed. Eugene Kamenka (New York: Penguin, 1981), 404.

34. Thoreau, *Walden and Civil Disobedience,* 20.

35. Marx, in *The Marx-Engels Reader,* 151.

36. Thoreau, *Walden and Civil Disobedience,* 31.

37. Ibid., 43.

38. Marx discusses this at length in *Capital,* vol. 3, but he sketches an account of it as early as his "Contribution to a Critique of Hegel's *Philosophy of Right*: Introduction." See *Marx-Engels Reader,* 62–65.

39. Thoreau, *Walden and Civil Disobedience,* 23.

40. Marx, *Marx-Engels Reader,* 50.

41. Ibid., 105.

42. Thoreau, *Walden and Civil Disobedience,* 217.

43. Marx, *Marx-Engels Reader,* 74.

44. Emerson's elegy for Thoreau is reprinted in Thoreau, *Walden and Other Writings,* with an introduction by Ralph Waldo Emerson (New York: Modern Library, 2000), xiv.

45. See Robert B. Richardson Jr., *Henry Thoreau: A Life of the Mind* (Berkeley: University of California Press, 1986), 298–300, for a brief sketch of some of the difficulties of their relationship.

46. Quoted ibid., 299.

47. *Selections from Ralph Waldo Emerson,* ed. Stephen E. Whicher (Boston: Houghton Mifflin, 1960), 327.

48. Quoted in Richardson, *Henry Thoreau,* 299.

49. Cavell's essay is "Thinking of Emerson," published first in the expanded edition of *The Senses of Walden,* and now included as the first chapter of *Emerson's Transcendental Etudes.* The comparison to which I refer in the text can found in *ETE,* 11–14.

50. To see an instance of Thoreau's "rewriting" of Emerson (to adopt Cavell's term about Nietzsche's use of Emerson) compare their remarks on charity: Emerson, "Self-Reliance," in *Selections from Ralph Waldo Emerson,* 150; and Thoreau in *Walden,* 49.

51. Thoreau, *Walden and Civil Disobedience,* 61.

52. Ibid., 214.

53. Ibid., 57. Cavell reflects on this passage in *SW,* 7–8.

54. Cavell, *SW,* xiii.

55. Thoreau, *Walden and Civil Disobedience,* 1.

56. Ibid., 108.

57. Ibid., 110.

58. Richardson, in *Henry Thoreau: A Life of the Mind,* discusses this topic under the heading "Self-Culture," 54–57.

59. Thoreau, *Walden and Civil Disobedience,* 48.

60. Marx, *Marx-Engels Reader,* 144.

61. Cavell takes Thoreau's beginning his residence at Walden on the Fourth of July to be a reenactment of the original colonial settlement of New England "in order this time to do it right, or to prove that it is impossible." Cavell, *SW*, 8. I take this to be an aspect of the redoing of the foundationalist project that I find in *Walden*. One should also compare Cavell's essay, "Finding as Founding: Taking Steps in Emerson's 'Experience'," now in *ETE*, as chapter 6.

62. Russell Goodman in "Thoreau and the Body" (in this volume) presents a beautifully detailed account of how Thoreau emphasizes the embodied side of human living.

63. Quoted in Richardson, *Henry Thoreau*, 188.

64. Thoreau, *Walden and Civil Disobedience*, 213.

65. Ibid., 221.

3. THOREAU AND THE BODY
Russell B. Goodman

1. Henry David Thoreau, *Walden* (Princeton: Princeton University Press, 1971), 129. Henceforth cited parenthetically as *W*.

2. S. T. Coleridge, *Poems* (New York: Knopf, 1963), 52–53.

3. Samuel Todes, *Body and World* (Cambridge, Mass.: MIT Press, 2001), 81–83. Henceforth cited parenthetically as T.

4. See Hubert L. Dreyfus, *Being-in-the-World* (Cambridge, Mass.: MIT Press, 1991), 69–72.

5. Thoreau, "Walking," in *Walden and Other Writings*, ed. Brooks Atkinson (New York: Modern Library, 1965). Henceforth cited parenthetically as Wa.

4. SPEAKING EXTRAVAGANTLY: PHILOSOPHICAL TERRITORY AND ECCENTRICITY IN *WALDEN*
James D. Reid

1. "Philosophy is a Greek word by good rights, and it stands almost for a Greek thing" (Thoreau's *Journal*, 15 December 1859). Thoreau's *Journal* is cited by date of entry: see *The Journal of Henry D. Thoreau*, ed. Bradford Torrey and F. H. Allen (New York: Dover, 1962). For the idea of philosophy as a way of life in antiquity, see Hadot's *Philosophy as a Way of Life* (Cambridge, Mass.: Harvard University Press, 1995) and Foucault's multivolume *History of Sexuality*. Martha Nussbaum's account of Hellenistic ethics in *The Therapy of Desire* (Princeton, N.J.: Princeton University Press, 1996) is also helpful on this score, with special emphasis on the medical paradigm in ancient philosophy. A wide-ranging discussion that begins with Socrates and includes Nietzsche and Foucault is provided in Alexander Nehamas's *The Art of Living* (Berkeley: University of California Press, 2000).

2. Henry Thoreau, *Walden*, ed. J. Shanley (Princeton, N.J.: Princeton University Press, 2004), 14. See also *I to Myself: An Annotated Selection from the Journal of Henry D. Thoreau*, ed. J. Cramer (New Haven, Conn.: Yale University Press, 2007).

3. Thoreau, *Walden*, 51. As usual, Emerson gets to the heart of the matter in his tribute to Thoreau, published in the *Atlantic Monthly*, 1862: "He declined to give up his large ambition of knowledge and action for any narrow craft or profession, aiming at a much more comprehensive calling, the art of living well." Introduction to *Walden and Other Writings* (New York: Modern Library, 2000), xii.

4. It seems to be taken for granted that Aristotle was right when he praised the merely contemplative way of life as the best in the last book of the *Nicomachean Ethics*. But Aristotle at least felt the need to argue for this position on the best of all conceivable and attainable lives.

5. See Albert Camus, *The Myth of Sisyphus* (New York: Vintage, 1991).

6. Thoreau, *Walden*, 91.

7. As Plato's Socrates announces in the *Gorgias*, it is no small question the philosopher struggles to answer but "How should one live?"

8. Plato, *Republic* 490e.

9. Walt Whitman, "Song of Myself," lines 1–3 in *Leaves of Grass* (New York: Norton, 1973), 28.

10. Kant's motto, borrowed from Bacon's *Instauratio Magna*, added to the second edition of the *Critique of Pure Reason*, ed. and trans. P. Guyer and A. Wood (Cambridge: Cambridge University Press, 1999).

11. Thoreau, *Walden*, 3.

12. Plato, *Euthyphro* and *Lysis*. Of course, there's a large body of commentary on Plato's dialogues that takes their "literary" character seriously.

13. Harry Frankfurt, *The Importance of What We Care About* (Princeton, N.J.: Princeton University Press, 1988).

14. Heidegger makes this point in his own somewhat cumbersome way in a lecture course delivered in the summer semester of 1923. See *Ontology: The Hermeneutics of Facticity*, trans. J. van Buren (Bloomington: Indiana University Press, 1999), 12–13. According to Kant, concepts (he means the a priori concepts of possible thought about the world) that are neither contained in the possibility of experience (as its conditions) nor built up out of the elements of a possible human experience are altogether impossible or at least meaningless to us. See *Critique of Pure Reason*, A95.

15. One could probably write an alternative history of modern philosophy from this point of view, one that would explain, perhaps, why figures such as Jacobi, Kierkegaard, Nietzsche, and even Heidegger are often consigned to the sidelines of our intellectual history. Thoreau is certainly not alone in being dismissed. The American pragmatists should also perhaps be included here, despite

the efforts of respectable philosophers such as Hilary Putnam to show their enduring relevance.

16. Thoreau, *Walden*, 3.

17. Ibid., 4. One might accuse Thoreau of inconsistency here; but whether you find it so or not will, I think, depend on what you believe it is to give an account of your own life. If a life cannot be altogether detached from the "infinite extent of your relations" to other things, then part of what it is to render an account of your life is to talk about the lives of others, in this case, the lives (or *forms* and ways of life) of those in Concord you've left at least temporarily behind, call them your former associates. If Thoreau can be said to be in search of the "eternal" (as some have suggested), he seems to think that there's no fitting way to get there save through what surrounds you here and now.

18. Ibid., 64. Thanks to Rick Furtak for pointing out the possible scatological meaning in this passage.

19. Ibid., 325.

20. Friedrich Nietzsche, *The Will to Power*, trans. W. Kaufmann and R. J. Hollingdale (New York: Vintage, 1968), §853.

21. Robert Nozick, "The Holiness of Everyday Life," in *The Examined Life: Philosophical Meditations* (New York: Simon and Schuster, 1990), 57.

22. Thoreau comes close to affirming this in the journal: "A true description growing out of the perception and appreciation of [something] is itself a new fact" (13 October 1860). But it is nonetheless a peculiar fact, "never to be daguerreotyped, indicating the highest quality of the [thing],—its relation to man."

23. Nelson Goodman uses the expression "ready-made world" as a way of capturing the conception of reality underlying the correspondence theory of truth in his *Ways of Worldmaking* (Indianapolis: Hackett, 1978), 94. John Dewey employs the phrase "readymade," mostly disparagingly, in a variety of works meant to defend a more open and "pragmatist" conception of truth in the *making* and ever revisable.

24. " . . . a man of settled views, whose thoughts are few and hardened like his bones, is truly mortal, and his only resource is to say his prayers" (19 December 1859).

25. Thoreau, *Walden*, 28. Thoreau's most extensive description of the unsettling face of nature is probably "Ktaadn," the first of three pieces first published in 1864 as *The Maine Woods* (New York: Penguin, 1988). But we should also place *Cape Cod*'s depiction of nature's indifferent, life-devouring ocean here as well (Princeton, N.J.: Princeton University Press, 2004). Rilke, too, recognized the importance of finding ourselves unsettled in an alien landscape. See his remarkable sketch of the uncanny in nature in the short piece on "Worpswede" in *Where Silence Reigns*. Thoreau would, I suspect, heartily agree with the following statement of the task and worth of art: "It is not the least and is, perhaps, the peculiar

value of art, that it is the medium in which man and landscape, form and world, meet and find one another" (*Where Silence Reigns: Selected Prose* [New York: New Directions, 1978], 9). There are more than a few noteworthy similarities between these two otherwise very different sorts of poet, each struggling to find in poetry and poetic experience resources for the affirmation of the world, in spite of suffering, disappointment, and despair. For more on Rilke, see my introduction to *Rilke's* Duino Elegies: *A New Translation with Philosophical Commentary* (Northwestern University Press, forthcoming).

26. Laura D. Walls grapples with Thoreau's project from the standpoint of the world as something we can see variously, depending on how we are disposed to take it up, in *Seeing New Worlds: Henry David Thoreau and Nineteenth-Century Natural Science* (Madison: University of Wisconsin Press, 1995). Her work is also worth mentioning for having drawn attention to the *scientific* significance of the naturalist's endeavors.

27. Thoreau, *Walden*, 8. But in a late journal entry, Thoreau describes approvingly an encounter with an old farmer, fresh from gathering apples and cheerful: "This old man's cheeriness was worth a thousand of the church's sacraments and *memento mori*'s. It was better than a prayerful mood. It proves to me old age as tolerable, as happy, as infancy" (20 October 1857).

28. Thoreau, *Walden*, 9. The cynical reader is ready to remind us that Thoreau squatted on land purchased by Emerson, that he was educated at Harvard and had access to its library in later years, that he read widely, and that he wrote in a "mother tongue" not of his own making.

29. Or more straightforwardly in the journal: "I think it will be found that he who speaks with most authority on a given subject is not ignorant of what has been said by his predecessors. He will take his place in a regular order, and substantially add his own knowledge to the knowledge of previous generations" (31 December 1859).

30. Thoreau, *Walden*, 41.

31. The allusion here is, of course, to "Economy"; but I have Nietzsche in mind here as well: "Thus men ... plunge into wild nature, not to find themselves in it but to lose and forget themselves in it. 'To be outside oneself' [is] the desire of all the weak and the self-discontented" (*The Will to Power*, §941). In §829, Nietzsche criticizes the search for "the charm of exoticism (strange times, customs, passions)" as a symptom of sentimentalism and romantic decadence, "a makeshift substitute for a defective 'reality.'"

32. Thoreau, *Walden*, 107. As Thoreau puts it in the journal, "Think of the consummate folly of attempting to go away from *here*! When the constant endeavor should be to get nearer and nearer *here*. . . . Foolish people imagine that what they imagine is somewhere else. That stuff is not made in any factory but their own" (1 November 1858).

33. For the idea of *Walden* as a newer testament or "sacred text" see Stanley Cavell, *The Senses of Walden: An Expanded Edition* (Chicago: University of Chicago Press, 1992), 14–16. Thoreau uses the expression "newer testament" in "Walking" (*Walden and Other Writings*, 662), and speaks of "*my* New Testament" in a journal entry dated 16 October 1859.

34. Thoreau, *Walden*, 11.

35. Ibid., 175.

36. These are the words Thoreau is rumored to have uttered to Pillsbury on his deathbed. See Robert D. Richardson's *Henry Thoreau: A Life of the Mind* (Berkeley: University of California Press, 1988), 389.

37. Henry David Thoreau, *A Week on the Concord and Merrimack Rivers*, in *Walden and Other Writings*, 454.

38. Thoreau, *Walden*, 136.

39. I don't mean to dismiss biographical approaches to Thoreau. But every good biography of a *thinker* is going to have to be *thoughtful*; and if the thinker is philosophically motivated, as I'm arguing Thoreau was, then the work is going to have to delve into the philosophical issues its subject took to heart.

40. See Perry Miller's "Thoreau in the Context of International Romanticism," *New England Quarterly* 34 (June 1961): 147–59.

41. See my "Ethical Criticism in Heidegger's Early Freiburg Lectures," *Review of Metaphysics* 59, no. 1 (2005): 54.

42. We have early Heidegger, and more distantly Dilthey, to thank for insisting that the world is a context of *Bedeutsamkeit*. See my essays "Dilthey's Epistemology of the *Geisteswissenschaften*," *Journal of the History of Philosophy* 39 (July 2001): 407–36, and "Ethical Criticism in Heidegger's Early Freiburg Lectures." It's hardly surprising that some of Heidegger's best later work deals with poetry as a distinctive way of disclosing the world. I discuss Heidegger's "ethical ontology" of the work of art, as a way of bringing the world of human significance to light, in the second chapter of *Heidegger's Moral Ontology* (forthcoming).

43. Thoreau, *Walden*, 94.

44. Thoreau, *Journal*, 8 December 1859.

45. Thoreau, *Walden*, 96.

46. Thoreau, *Journal*, 10 May 1853. For an interesting discussion of degrees of reality (depth and meaning), and degrees of focus, attention, and creativity, see Nozick's "Being More Real," in *Examined Life*.

47. On New Year's Day 1858, after a stint of surveying the Walden woods, Thoreau worries that "this particular dry knowledge may affect my imagination and fancy, that it will not be easy to see so much wildness and native vigor there as formerly" (1 January 1858). Thoreau, it should be said, is not hostile to fact and the scientific classification and explanation of fact; but like the pragmatists in

America, he tends to see the worth of knowledge in practical and poetic terms. The Indian's knowledge of a certain species of tree involves "a more practical and vital science" than our official botanical science (5 March 1858). In this respect, Thoreau's stance resembles Rousseau's. Both worry about the tendency of some scientific accounts to drain the phenomena of their significance. "Science," in a characteristic passage from the journal, "is inhuman. Things seen with a microscope begin to be insignificant" (1 May 1858). "Modern botanical descriptions approach ever nearer to the dryness of an algebraic formula, as if x + y were = to a love-letter" (16 December 1859).

48. See Descartes's fascinating discussion of what moved him to search for a method of inquiry in the *Discourse on Method*.

49. Thoreau, *Journal*, 5 November 1839.

50. Ibid., 9 November 1851.

51. Thoreau, *Walden*, 124.

52. Thoreau, *Journal*, 10 May 1853.

53. Ibid., 7 September 1851.

54. Richardson suggests, plausibly, that Thoreau's work confronts, under the influence of Carlyle, "the problem of how to lead a heroic life in the busy modern nineteenth century" (*Henry Thoreau*, 165). But unlike Carlyle's, Thoreau's vision of heroism is removed from elitism. Thoreau delivered a public lecture on Carlyle in February 1846, centered on *Cromwell* and *Heroes, Hero-Worship and the Heroic in History*. Whether Thoreau inclined toward elitism is hard to say, and probably will depend on what we mean by the term. His frequent diatribes against common sense and the common way of speaking tells in favor of it; but he also insists that every life, however poor and mean, can be lived well, provided the individual owns up to who she is. "However mean your life is, meet it and live it; do not shun it and call it hard names. It is not so bad as you are" (*Walden*, 328). "This is the only way, we say; but there are as many ways as there can be drawn radii from one centre" (*Walden*, 11).

55. In a lecture delivered in 1843 and subsequently published in one of the last issues of the *Dial*, Thoreau praised Homer as the very voice of nature and his tropes as both the earliest and the latest productions of the poetic mind. See *Henry Thoreau*, 141–43. Richardson points out that this piece announces one of Thoreau's abiding themes, i.e. how to reconcile the savage, the primitive, the wild, on the one hand, with the cultivated and civilized, on the other.

56. Thoreau read widely about Native Americans and compiled thousands of pages of notes on Indian subjects. The longest stretch of *The Maine Woods*, dealing with his trip with Joe Polis, a leading figure in the Penobscot tribe, is, in Richardson's apt characterization, "the culmination of all his years of Indian reading" (*Henry Thoreau*, 355). Writing a few months after the trip, Thoreau asks, "Why . . . make so great ado about the Roman and the Greek, and neglect

the Indian?" (22 October 1857). For a full account of Thoreau and Native Americans, see Robert F. Sayre's *Thoreau and the American Indians* (Princeton, N.J.: Princeton University Press, 1977).

57. One of the few passages in *Walden* speaking of worship elaborates on morning hours and awakening in the figure of Aurora (*Walden*, 88–90). Throughout the journal, Thoreau praises the religious sentiments and stances of the Greeks, who worshipped natural phenomena unashamedly. If Thoreau's stance is religious, his religiosity is nothing provincial and partial (see *Walden*, 109). In "Reading," for instance, he complains that most of us don't realize "that any nation but the Hebrews have had a scripture" (*Walden*, 106). Perhaps we'd do well to speak of Thoreau's efforts to preserve the "mysterious and unexplorable" sense and being of things (*Walden*, 317). Or we might situate Thoreau's religious leanings in the tradition of Stoicism, with its accent on the divine element within each individual: "We check and repress the divinity that stirs within us, to fall down and worship the divinity that is dead without us" (*Journal*, 16 November 1851). Cf. Seneca's 41st Letter to Lucilius in *The Stoic Philosophy of Seneca: Essays and Letters*, trans. M. Hadas (New York: Norton, 1958).

58. Thoreau, *Walden*, 228.

59. Ibid.

60. Ibid., 229.

61. Ibid.

62. Ibid., 230.

63. Ibid., 231.

64. Ibid., 161. I don't mean to deny that passages like this have something playful about them, that Thoreau might be seen as adopting a mock-heroic attitude. As Charles Larmore, among many others, reminds us, irony is one central strand in the romantic legacy. As Larmore puts it, "We cannot honestly profess a wholehearted identification with any . . . form of life. Something . . . always urges us . . . to stand back, if only just a bit" (*The Romantic Legacy* [New York: Columbia University Press, 1996], 69). Thoreau gives expression to this in his own way in an important passage in "Solitude": "We are not wholly involved in Nature." A few lines later, Thoreau speaks of "a certain doubleness" in himself and an awareness of "the presence and criticism of a part of me, which, as it were, is not a part of me, but spectator, sharing no experience, but taking note of it" (*Walden*, 135).

65. Thoreau, *Walden*, 162. It's worth noting that shortly after this scene, Thoreau gives an itemized list of expenditures and income, as if to set in sharp contrast the work of mythmaking and the labor of the accountant. Which of the two accounts does greater justice to what it means to farm and to reckon the worth of husbandry is pretty clear.

66. Thoreau returns to this theme in the late essay "Life without Principle," in *The Higher Law* (Princeton, N.J.: Princeton University Press, 2004). H. Daniel Peck makes some similar observations in *Thoreau's Morning Work* (New Haven, Conn.: Yale University Press, 1994).

67. Thoreau, *Walden*, 325.

68. Emerson, "Spiritual Laws," in *The Essays of Ralph Waldo Emerson* (Cambridge, Mass.: Harvard University Press, 2006), 77.

69. "Understanding one another," as John Dewey reminds us, "means that objects, including sounds, have the same value for both with respect to carrying on a common pursuit" (*Democracy and Education* [New York: Free Press, 1944], 15).

70. Thoreau, *Walden*, 10.

71. It's at least worth mentioning here that Thoreau is often equally happy to describe *human* conduct in terms more commonly applied to the behavior of animals. See especially the account of the ways of the Canadian woodchopper (Alex Therien) in "Visitors," and the opening paragraph of "Higher Laws," where Thoreau tells of his own savage delight aroused in the woods by the sight of a woodchuck: "I found myself ranging in the woods, like a half-starved hound, with strange abandonment, seeking some kind of venison which I might devour" (*Walden*, 210). At times he's even willing to assimilate human life to the vegetable: "I grew in those seasons like corn in the night, and they were far better than any work of the hands would have been" (*Walden*, 111). The passage discussed at length below on thawing sand and clay in spring is, perhaps, the best known and most suggestive of these assimilations and blendings of human, animal, and plant life.

72. "I believe that the mind can be permanently profaned by the habit of attending to trivial things, so that all our thoughts shall be tinged with triviality" (Thoreau, "Life without Principle," 173).

73. What about a figure such as Don Quixote? Is he a hero worthy of our admiration or someone to be dismissed as a madman? Or is he just someone worth poking fun at? It's worth noting that Descartes, in the *Meditations*, marginalizes certain cases of "insanity" as unworthy of serious philosophical consideration for no better reason than *because* they strike the reasonable person as insane, although the line of argument he's developing, at least initially, has struck some philosophers as unsound. Thoreau, by contrast, seems anxious to convince us that we dismiss *Walden* as the product of insanity because we are ourselves more than a little insane.

74. Thoreau, *Walden*, 136.

75. Ibid., 111.

76. Ibid., 162. As Thoreau makes the point in the journal, "Natural objects and phenomena are the original symbols or types which express our thoughts

and feelings, and yet American scholars, having little or no root in the soil, commonly strive with all their might to confine themselves to the imported symbols alone" (16 October 1859).

77. "It is remarkable that the highest intellectual mood which the world tolerates is the perception of the truth of the most ancient revelations, now in some respects out of date; but any direct revelation, any original thoughts, it hates like virtue" (*Journal*, 16 November 1851).

78. Thoreau, *Walden*, 88.

79. Ibid., 97.

80. For those who may be tempted to see in *Walden* something like Rousseau's contempt for modern European civilization and celebration of the savage life in *The Discourse on the Arts and Sciences*, it's worth recalling that Thoreau's life of simplicity is in the service of a poet's (newly civilized) life. In "Economy" he scorns the "savage taste of men and women for new patterns" (*Walden*, 26); and, in a crucial passage, Thoreau grants with heavy qualification that "civilization is a real advance in the condition of man" (*Walden*, 31). Those who are still mired in the coarse labor of survival cannot pluck the finer fruits of life. "Actually, the laboring man has not leisure for a true integrity day by day; he cannot afford to sustain the manliest relations to men" (*Walden*, 6).

81. Thoreau, *Journal*, 24 April 1859.

82. Thoreau, *Walden*, 308.

83. Cf. Nietzsche, *Will to Power*, §826.

84. Thoreau, *Walden*, 323.

85. Ralph Waldo Emerson, "The American Scholar," in *The Essential Writings*, ed. Brooks Atkinson (New York: Modern Library, 2000), 57. Heidegger's coinage (*es weltet*) comes in a lecture course delivered in the War Emergency Semester of 1919, *Zur Bestimmung der Philosophie* (Frankfurt am Main: Klostermann, 1987), *Gesamtausgabe* 56–57, p. 73.

86. One might read Proust in the same spirit, as Joshua Landy does in his admirable study *Philosophy as Fiction: Self, Deception, and Knowledge in Proust* (New York: Oxford University Press, 2004).

87. For the concept of the "unpredictable landing," see Jean-Luc Marion's *Being Given*, trans. Jeffrey L. Kosky (Stanford, Calif.: Stanford University Press, 2002).

88. Larmore, *Romantic Legacy*, 35. As Dewey notes in *Democracy and Education*, "Only a personal response involving imagination can possibly procure realization even of pure 'facts.'" (236)

89. The world, Thoreau suggests in the journal, would be an "experience repeated a certain number of times" fruitlessly and drearily "were it not for the faculty of imagination" (13 February 1859).

90. See *Critique of Pure Reason*, A405–567/B432–595. Whether Kant would be receptive to the idea that we "world" comes to expression in the work of great poets is a separate question. But see the account of genius in sections 46–50 of the *Critique of Judgment*, and the discussion of this material in Tim Gould's "The Audience of Originality: Kant and Wordsworth on the Reception of Genius," in *Essays in Kant's Aesthetics*, ed. T. Cohen and P. Guyer (Chicago: University of Chicago Press, 1985).

91. See Nietzsche's early, unpublished essay on language, "Truth and Lies in a Non-Moral Sense," for the development of a similar train of thought. This is, in fact, an old view. We can trace it back to Herder, and possibly to Vico. It was made popular during the Romantic era in Germany and England, and it was echoed more recently by, among others, Richard Rorty.

92. This was, of course, the alternative in the early days of the Romantic Movement; and it's fair to say that Thoreau inherits it and takes what resembles a "romantic" stand in the very passage under consideration: "The earth is not a mere fragment of dead history . . . but a living earth" (*Walden*, 309). Kant himself appears to give the mechanical world of the first *Critique* an organic makeover in the *Critique of Judgment*; and part of what grounds the "teleological" turn is, arguably, Kant's growing sense of the need for a more compelling *moral* worldview.

93. Thoreau, *Walden*, 225. See Peck's interesting discussion of this passage in "The Wording of Walden," in *Thoreau's Morning Work*, 117–33.

94. It is, perhaps, worth noting here that, according to Richardson, Thoreau's observations were made in February, *before* the onset of spring proper. The phenomenon is, then, something more like a herald of spring in winter, an anticipation of what's to come.

95. See Thoreau's own early entry on spring in the *Journal*, 29 September 1843.

96. Thoreau, *Walden*, 304–5.

97. Thoreau, *Journal*, 18 February 1860.

98. Thoreau, *Walden*, 307.

99. Ibid., 308.

100. Ibid.

101. Ibid., 302. As I suggested above, Thoreau's vision of the primacy of organic form places *Walden* in the tradition of romantic *Naturphilosophie*, and reminds us of Schelling's opposition to those who, like Fichte, see in nature nothing more than the "not-I"; and it's worth mentioning as well that this seems to place Thoreau in subtle opposition to Emerson who, despite a certain feeling for nature and wilderness, tends to speak of natural form as an emblem of a higher spiritual reality, and who, in his first published work, had used the

Fichtean expression "NOT ME" to designate Nature. See "Nature," in *Essential Writings*, 4. In the opening paragraph of his address to the senior class of Harvard's Divinity School, Emerson paints a moving picture of nature in summer, only to say, in the second paragraph, that "when the mind opens and reveals the laws which traverse the universe and make things what they are, then shrinks the great world at once into a mere illustration and table of this mind" (*Essential Writings*, 63). But the issue is clearly more complicated than this; and Thoreau, after all, is as eager as Emerson is to restore the rights of the experiencing subject and the *significance* of the natural fact *für mich*, for the alert, deliberate perceiver. This more blatantly "spiritualizing" perspective comes out clearly in the "Conclusion" to *Walden*, where Thoreau takes leave of his beloved pond and his prose takes an "inward" turn toward "the private sea" (*Walden*, 322). Or rather, a return to the perspective of "Where I Lived, and What I Lived For": "Wherever I sat, there I might live, and the landscape radiated from me accordingly" (*Walden*, 81). Schelling, too, was anxious to preserve the truth of the first-person point of view that emerges within the natural world; and so he wrote a *System of Transcendental Idealism* as well as a series of contributions to the philosophy of unconscious nature, aspiring at higher levels to achieve organization and, eventually, self-consciousness. Perhaps under the influence of Spinoza, the German philosopher saw what we call "nature" and "spirit" or "consciousness" as two sides of a single, underlying reality, united in an admittedly mysterious "point of indifference or identity." What we discover in and about ourselves as thinking beings has its organic precedent in preconscious appearances in nature. In the terms we're developing here, there is a subtle correspondence between natural and spiritual phenomena, each fruitfully mirroring the other. Whether you think this lineage discredits Thoreau or not will, I suspect, depend on whether you think Schelling and his followers were responding with intelligence to a genuine problem or not; on the view I favor, *Naturphilosophie* is an attempt to offer a nonreductive naturalism that makes room for the language of human experience and meaning without placing the subject outside of nature's order. In a sense, I take it that this is Thoreau's ambition as well.

102. "Who would have suspected so large and cold and thick-skinned a thing to be so sensitive? Yet it has its law to which it thunders obedience when it should as surely as the buds expand in the spring" (Thoreau, *Walden*, 302).

103. Ibid., 162. This is, perhaps, the passage that brings into the sharpest focus the poetic import of Thoreau's various experiments; and combined with the chapter titled "Reading"and a few remarks in "Economy," it speaks most clearly and tellingly against any reading of *Walden* that pits its author against civilization.

104. Ibid., 308.

105. Ibid., 309.

106. Ibid., 308.

107. I don't think we should read this in the light of the traditional argument for God's existence from design. But it would take up too much space to spell out why in detail here. We'd have to deal at length with Thoreau's view of the *source* of our being and the power that shapes our world (Thoreau, *Walden*, 134); and this may prove to have little or nothing in common with orthodox conceptions of God, which seem to underwrite the traditional argument from the apparent order of the world. It may prove just as well to read passages like this in the light of Emerson's rather heterodox views on the "Over-Soul" presented in a famous essay by that name, even if we rightly wonder whether Emerson's eccentric Platonism was acceptable to Thoreau. And we'd have to consider Thoreau's remarks on the importance of keeping the cosmos somewhat mysterious (*Walden*, 317–18); the argument from design seems to make the world a bit too (theologically) intelligible, making it over in the image of a superintelligent watchmaker whose workings are not so inscrutable, after all, and seem a bit too easily reassuring, and reading the "evidence" in a questionable spirit of *literalness*. There's more than a little reason to doubt the testimony of "the men of routine, the men of *sense*; in whom a literal obedience to facts has extinguished every spark of that light by which man is truly man" (Emerson, "History," in *Essays of Ralph Waldo Emerson*, 18–19). But perhaps the greatest testimony of all, carrying us beyond the scope of *Walden*'s argument, is to be sought in Thoreau's well-documented siding with Darwin against the scientific "creationist" Agassiz. When Thoreau speaks of the Maker and, more generally, the divine, I take it that he's using ancient words to call attention to the *worth* of something he thinks we ought to care about, in a language that's familiar. And of course it's always possible that he is simply being playful and making sport with traditional theological argument: If God is a highly skilled watchmaker, as William Paley and his followers in all seriousness argued, why shouldn't he be entitled to seek out a *patent* for his brilliant design.

108. As Heidegger argues in his well-known essay on the origin of the work of art, perhaps more radically even than Thoreau, things come to *be* what they are in the poetic disclosure: The ancient Greek temple, for instance, *reveals* something about earth and sky, animal and plant, and their being in relation to mortal life. I've argued elsewhere that this claim doesn't amount to the silly suggestion that works of art literally bring crickets and tables and people into being in the way that God, in our religious traditions, brings things into being out of nothing (or by giving shape to preexisting matter). It means, rather, that art brings existing things into a space of *meaning* and helps us assign to things their *weight*

(the weight of importance, value, significance). Heidegger also seems to have thought that traditional philosophy, under some description, has accomplished this sort of thing as well. This is, perhaps, why he insists that the poet and the thinker are neighbors. For the phenomenological concept of a "space of meaning," see Steven G. Crowell's valuable study *Husserl, Heidegger, and the Space of Meaning* (Evanston, Ill.: Northwestern University Press, 2001).

109. Thoreau, *Walden*, 171. I've argued elsewhere that the most essential aspects of our existence don't behave like "facts" and mere "things" in the usual sense. See my "Owning Up to Life and Death: A Heideggerian Account" (forthcoming). A longer version of this essay forms a chapter of *Heidegger's Individuals.*

110. Thoreau does not seem to incline toward the view that the poet ought to disclose a world for all of us or, as Heidegger seems to have thought, for a particular *Volk*. If anything, he seems to be calling upon each of us to live up to the poetic potential in every human life.

111. Emerson, "American Scholar," 57.

112. Percy Bysshe Shelley, "A Defence of Poetry," in *The Norton Anthology of English Literature*, ed. M. H. Abrams et al. (New York: Norton, 1993), 2:755. The standard criticism of poetry as a way of disclosing the world can probably be traced back to the tenth book of Plato's *Republic*, 595b: "I think all such poetry [Socrates has the tragic poets in mind] is likely to corrupt the mind of those of its hearers who do not have knowledge of what [things are] really like as a drug to counteract it." On this view, poetry is, at best, an imitation of an imitation that offers a feeble copy of ultimate reality; at its worst, it is a finespun distortion of the truth that leads the mind astray and, for all its charms, alienates us from the good.

113. William Wordsworth, *The Prelude* (1805), book 11, 123–28, in *The Prelude: The Four Texts* (New York: Penguin, 1995), 470.

114. Emerson, "The Transcendentalist," in *Essential Writings*, first published in 1843 in the *Dial*, 82.

115. See Rick Furtak's fine essay "Skepticism and Perceptual Faith: Henry David Thoreau and Stanley Cavell on Seeing and Believing," in *Transactions of the Charles S. Peirce Society* 43.3 (2007): 542–61; and his earlier "Thoreau's Emotional Stoicism," in the *Journal of Speculative Philosophy* 17.2 (2003): 122–32.

116. Thoreau, *Walden*, 327. In a late entry in the journal, Thoreau goes as far as to say, in at least superficial opposition to the stance developed above, that the "real facts" of the life of a poet "would be of more value to us than any work of his art." "Shakespeare," he goes on to lament, "has left us his fancies and imaginings, but the truth of his life, with its becoming circumstances, we know nothing about" (27 October 1857).

117. Thoreau, *Walden*, 287.

118. Ibid., 9.

119. Ibid., 90.

120. See Heidegger's *Being and Time*, sec. 43, where the problem of the reality and *Beweisbarkeit* [verifiability] of the *Außenwelt* [external world] is dismissed as a pseudo-problem, in favor of the fuller idea of reality as a correlate of *Sorge* [care].

121. It is, at least, worth noting that Thoreau read Darwin's work carefully and largely agreed with its account of biological descent by natural selection. And it is well known that Thoreau did important field work for Agassiz, although he sided with Darwin against the theory of special creation advanced by the Harvard professor of zoology and geological science. In 1861, Thoreau dismisses as a "vulgar prejudice" the view that some species of plant are "spontaneously generated." (*Journal*, 14 January 1861). See also Richardson's *Henry Thoreau*, chaps. 96 and 98.

122. One might point out here that *Walden* has had an impact on the environmental movement.

123. Thanks to Patricia Churchland for pointing out this fact in her talk, "Neuroethics in Perspective," on morality and the biological basis of human behavior, at "The Study of the Human Self," a conference held at the College of William and Mary in September 2008.

124. Thoreau, *Journal*, 13 October 1860. It would be instructive, I think, to read Thoreau's journal in the light of the phenomenological concept, deployed in late writings by Husserl and made popular by Heidegger, of the *Lebenswelt* as the rich prescientific soil or basis of scientific thought. See in particular Husserl's *Crisis of European Sciences and Transcendental Phenomenology*, and the account of everydayness and being-in-the-world in the first division of *Being and Time*.

125. Heidegger, *Introduction to the Phenomenology of Religion*, *Gesamtausgabe* 60:11.

126. In Emerson's way of speaking, "Each word was at first a stroke of genius, and obtained currency, because for the moment it symbolized the world to the first speaker and to the hearer. The etymologist finds the deadest word to have been once a brilliant picture. Language is fossil poetry" This is from "The Poet," in *Essays of Ralph Waldo Emerson*, 231.

127. Thoreau, *Walden*, 97.

128. See Emerson, "Transcendentalist," for a short statement of the Kantian roots of the American movement, and Cavell's "Thinking of Emerson" in *Senses of Walden*. In one of several similar journal entries, Thoreau notes that the scientist and layperson alike mistakenly believe that the captivating phenomenon is

something independent and not essentially related to the perceiver. "The important fact is its effect on me" (5 November 1857).

129. Adam Smith's work on moral sentiments is a classic statement of this position. What he calls sympathy is largely the result of an imaginative effort to place ourselves concretely in the otherwise inaccessible life of another.

130. As I noted earlier, so many of Thoreau's descriptions of animal behavior in *Walden* involve seeing something analogous to human conduct in the movements of a brute; or, alternatively, seeing in our own conduct something resembling the behavior of an animal.

131. For the role of poetic and literary imagination in moral experience, see Martha Nussbaum, *Poetic Justice* (Boston, Mass.: Beacon Press, 1995) and the essays collected in *Love's Knowledge* (New York: Oxford University Press, 1990).

132. For details concerning the far-reaching consequences of Copernicus's *De Revolutionibus*, see Thomas Kuhn, *The Copernican Revolution: Planetary Astronomy in the Development of Western Thought* (Cambridge, Mass.: Harvard University Press, 1957).

133. Charles Darwin, *On the Origin of Species*, quoted by Robert J. Richards in "Darwin on Mind, Morals and Emotions," in *The Cambridge Companion to Darwin*, ed. J. Hodge and G. Radick (Cambridge: Cambridge University Press, 2003), 100. Darwin's often overlooked indebtedness to the romantic tradition is the subject of Richards's fine work on the origins of evolutionary theory in the nineteenth century.

134. Richard Rorty has argued for this thesis in his own playful way in a variety of essays, and in his book *Contingency, Irony, and Solidarity* (Cambridge: Cambridge University Press, 1989). I should say, for what it's worth, that I'm not prepared to embrace relativism in the philosophy of science (or, for that matter, in ethics), as the drift of thought just sketched seems to imply, for reasons I cannot begin to spell out here. For a useful critique of the relativistic implications of several figures in the philosophy of science, broadly construed (including Quine, Goodman, Kuhn, and Gadamer), see James F. Harris, *Against Relativism* (Peru, Ill.: Open Court, 1992).

135. Historians of Plato's thought often distinguish too sharply between the strictly philosophical and conceptual stretch of a Platonic dialogue and the explicitly imaginative, allegorical, and mythmaking component (the image of the sun, the divided line, the allegory of the cave, the myth of Er), forgetting that Plato's arguments are often built around pictures. The same is likely to prove true of every great philosophical innovator. For Kant, thinking is like *bundling or binding things together* (*Verbindung*); in Fichte and Schelling, it's again most fundamentally like *seeing* (*Anschauung*); in Hegel, it seems to be a matter of returning to yourself, *unfolding* yourself in a common world of spirit, and sporting

with an evolving repertoire of *Begriffe* (which are themselves *graspings*, ways of getting the things of this world *in grip*) in a progressive series of more satisfying *uplifts* (*Aufhebungen*). For Husserl, consciousness of material reality involves the *shadowing forth* of the object in partial perspectives (*Abschattungen*) of the perceived thing. The list could easily be extended. So basic is this "metaphorical" way of dealing with fundamental things that we are almost left to wonder whether talk of "metaphor" is even useful any longer, except, perhaps, when we are talking about quantities. And this seems to be even more obviously true when we turn to the language of the moral life.

136. Thoreau, *Walden*, 17.

137. Ibid., 324.

138. Even Kant, as everyone who's read the first *Critique* even casually knows, assigns a central *cognitive* role to the productive imagination. I discuss the unifying function of *Einbildungskraft* in Kant's account of human subjectivity and the life of reason in the first part of "On the Unity of Theoretical Subjectivity in Kant and Fichte," *Review of Metaphysics* 57, no. 2 (2003): 243–77.

139. Thoreau, *Walden*, 88.

140. Ibid., 333. I owe many thanks to Rick Furtak and Jonathan Ellsworth, for asking me to contribute to this volume and getting me involved in the editorial work, for comments on an early draft, and for more than a decade of fruitful conversation on topics directly addressed in and indirectly related to this essay (some of my thoughts on Thoreau's philosophical significance first began to crystallize during a long and memorable discussion on *Walden* with Rick in Colorado Springs during, fittingly enough, the *spring* of 2005, while I was teaching Thoreau for the first time in a course on environmental ethics); to Rick more particularly for several helpful references; to the lively participants in a talk on Thoreau I gave at Colorado College in the fall of 2008; to Patricia Kandle for a lovely and secluded cottage in the woods in Virginia, where the bulk of this was written during a period of unusual and short-lived tranquility; to the Department of Philosophy at the College of William and Mary for a happy year of teaching and writing in one of the cradles of American culture; to the landscape in Colorado for helping me realize more acutely how important it is to attend to what surrounds us and to think and write more carefully and reverently about it; to my former students in Denver who allowed me to work out most of the thoughts developed more systematically here, both in the classroom and in private conversations; to brute companions T. and B., and to K., whom I still remember and, barring dementia, will not forget; and to Candace Craig for countless conversations on our beloved Transcendentalists, going back more than a happy decade now, and, just as important, for the makings of a better world in almost every sense.

5. IN WILDNESS IS THE PRESERVATION OF THE WORLD:
THOREAU'S ENVIRONMENTAL ETHICS
Philip J. Cafaro

1. Holmes Rolston III, *Environmental Ethics: Duties to and Values in the Natural World* (Philadelphia: Temple University Press, 1988).

2. Philip J. Cafaro, *Thoreau's Living Ethics:* Walden *and the Pursuit of Virtue* (Athens: University of Georgia Press, 2004).

3. Good recent philosophical discussions of environmental virtue ethics include Louke van Wensveen, *Dirty Virtues: The Emergence of Ecological Virtue Ethics* (Amherst, N.Y.: Humanity Press, 2000); Philip Cafaro, "Thoreau, Leopold, and Carson: Toward an Environmental Virtue Ethics," *Environmental Ethics* 23 (Spring 2001): 3–17; and Ronald Sandler, *Character and Environment: A Virtue-Oriented Approach to Environmental Ethics* (New York: Columbia University Press, 2007).

4. Cited by Walter Harding, *The Days of Henry Thoreau: A Biography* (Princeton, N.J.: Princeton University Press, 1992), 250–51.

5. Henry David Thoreau, *A Week on the Concord and Merrimack Rivers* (Princeton, N.J.: Princeton University Press, 1980), 26–27, 30–33.

6. Ibid., 26, 29, 37.

7. Cf. Cafaro, *Thoreau's Living Ethics*, 140–44.

8. Rolston, *Environmental Ethics*; Paul Taylor, *Respect for Nature* (Princeton, N.J.: Princeton University Press, 1986).

9. Thoreau, *A Week*, 37.

10. Parenthetical citations within the text all refer to Henry Thoreau, *Walden* (Princeton, N.J.: Princeton University Press, 1971).

11. Thoreau, *A Week*, 37–38.

12. The quarrel is recounted in Harding, *Days of Thoreau*, 392–95, which also quotes Thoreau's unanswered letter of protest to Lowell.

13. John Locke, *Two Treatises of Civil Government* (Cambridge: Cambridge University Press, 1988), 296.

14. Not only does Locke make human use all-important, he slights higher, nonconsumptive human uses and the basic ecosystem services such as clean air and water on which human life depends. Recent scientific calculations put nature's contributions to human economic productivity much higher.

15. Philip Cafaro, "The Naturalist's Virtues," *Philosophy in the Contemporary World* 8, no. 2 (2001): 85–99.

16. See, for example, Henry David Thoreau, *Journal*, ed. Robert Sattelmeyer et al. (Princeton, N.J.: Princeton University Press, 1991), 3:217 (5/6/51), and 305–6 (7/12–16/51); Henry David Thoreau, *Journal* (Princeton, N.J.: Princeton University Press, 1992), 4:415–20 (4/2/52); Henry David Thoreau, *The Journals of Henry D. Thoreau* (New York: Dover Press, 1962), 9:296–98 (11/8/58). In the first of

these entries, Thoreau writes: "How important is a constant intercourse with nature and the contemplation of natural phenomena to the preservation of moral and intellectual health! . . . The ethical philosopher needs the discipline of the natural philosopher. He approaches the study of mankind with great advantages who is accustomed to the study of nature."

17. Henry David Thoreau, *Journal* (Princeton: Princeton University Press, 1981), 1:338 (11/30/41).

18. "The Ponds" suggests that a correct environmental ethics must be holistic: valuing wholes as well as individuals, ponds as well as woodchucks. Contemporary environmental ethicists such as Holmes Rolston III and J. Baird Callicott have tried to affirm such holism (see Holmes Rolston III, *Conserving Natural Value* [New York: Columbia University Press, 1994]; J. Baird Callicott, *In Defense of the Land Ethic: Essays in Environmental Philosophy* [Albany: State University of New York Press, 1989]). But it has proven easier for philosophers to extend attention and concern to nonhuman individuals than to comprehend and appreciate non-human or more-than-human wholes, such as species or ecosystems. Such wholes are "looser" and more difficult to demarcate. It is not clear that a forest or a pond can have "interests" that may be harmed. Perhaps most important, modern ethicists are more used to valuing individuals than collective entities (in this they differ significantly from ancient ethicists, who usually placed the civic or collective good above the good of individuals). For better and for worse, we live in an individualistic age. Still, I believe Thoreau is right to suggest that ethical holism is a necessary part of getting right with nature. Perhaps one way to meet the difficulty here is to temporarily set aside the theoretical effort to ethically value wholes, and to ask instead how we might value them concretely and actually. We may then see *Walden* as a veritable how-to manual for appreciating natural wholes, from woodchucks and trees to ponds and forests. *Walden* suggests that even partial success in such ethical appreciation may make us better people: more knowledgeable, more aware, more alive.

19. Plato, *Symposium*, 194E–201C.

20. See the chapter "Economy," in Cafaro, *Thoreau's Living Ethics*.

21. Henry Thoreau, *Wild Fruits*, ed. Bradley Dean (New York: W. W. Norton, 2000), 37–59.

22. Henry Thoreau, "Walking," in *Natural History Essays* (Salt Lake City: Peregrine Smith, 1980), 112.

23. Ibid., 112, 114, 117. See also Henry David Thoreau, *Journal* (Princeton, N.J.: Princeton University Press, 2000), 6:197–98 (6/13/53).

24. See, for example, Daniel Botkin, *No Man's Garden: Thoreau and a New Vision for Civilization and Nature* (Washington, D.C.: Island Press, 2000), 23. Botkin also presents the venerable "Do you want us all to live in caves?" argument (40).

6. ARTICULATING A HUCKLEBERRY COSMOS: THOREAU'S MORAL ECOLOGY OF KNOWLEDGE

Laura Dassow Walls

1. Ralph Waldo Emerson, *Journals and Miscellaneous Notebooks*, ed. William Gilman et al., 16 vols. (Cambridge, Mass.: Harvard University Press, 1960–82), 11:218. Hereafter cited parenthetically as *JMN*.

2. Ralph Waldo Emerson, *Collected Works*, ed. Alfred R. Ferguson et al., 6 vols. to date (Cambridge, Mass.: Harvard University Press, 1971–), 6:17. Hereafter cited parenthetically as *CW*.

3. Henry David Thoreau, *Excursions* (Princeton, N.J.: Princeton University Press, 2007), 204, hereafter cited parenthetically as *E*; Thoreau, *Wild Fruits* (New York: Norton, 2000), 121, hereafter cited parenthetically as *WF*. In Concord dialect, "meadow" refers to land that is generally under water.

4. Ralph Waldo Emerson, *Complete Works*, ed. Edward Waldo Emerson, 12 vols. (Boston: Houghton Mifflin, 1903–4), 10:480.

5. Henry David Thoreau, *The Journal of Henry David Thoreau*, 14 vols., ed. Bradford Torrey and Francis Allen (Boston: Houghton Mifflin, 1906), 10:165. Hereafter cited parenthetically as *J*.

6. Henry D. Thoreau, *Faith in a Seed: The First Publication of Thoreau's Last Manuscript*, ed. Bradley P. Dean (Washington, D.C.: Island Press, 1993); Henry D. Thoreau, *Wild Fruits: Thoreau's Rediscovered Last Manuscript*, ed. Bradley P. Dean (New York: Norton, 2000).

7. Henry David Thoreau, *Reform Papers* (Princeton: Princeton University Press, 1973), 90. Hereafter cited parenthetically as *RP*.

8. Thoreau, *The Writings of Henry David Thoreau: Journal*, ed. John C. Broderick et al., 7 vols. to date (Princeton, N.J.: Princeton University Press, 1981–), 1:19. Hereafter cited parenthetically as *PJ*.

9. Henry David Thoreau, *Walden* (Princeton, N.J.: Princeton University Press, 1971), 79. Hereafter cited parenthetically as *W*.

10. Henry David Thoreau, *The Maine Woods* (Princeton: Princeton University Press, 1972), 71.

11. Emerson knew this quite well, which is why this statement, for the sake of brevity, oversimplifies his thought, in which trickster figures are an essential element. I have pursued this line of Emerson's thinking at length in *Emerson's Life in Science: The Culture of Truth* (Ithaca, N.Y.: Cornell University Press, 2003).

12. See Bruno Latour, *The Politics of Nature* (Cambridge, Mass: Harvard University Press, 2004), 125: "The outside is no longer fixed, no longer inert; it is no longer either a reserve or a court of appeal or a dumping ground, but it is what has constituted the object of an explicit procedure of externalization."

13. Philip Cafaro, *Thoreau's Living Ethics: Walden and the Pursuit of Virtue* (Athens: University of Georgia Press, 2004), 181, 186.

14. Latour, *Politics of Nature*, 8.

15. Alexander von Humboldt, *Cosmos*, trans. Elizabeth C. Otté, 5 vols. (New York: Harper and Brothers, 1850–70), 1:68. Facsimile ed., vols. 1–2 (Baltimore: Johns Hopkins University Press, 1997).

16. Ibid., 3:7.

17. Ibid., 1:79.

18. Immanuel Kant, "Eternal Peace" (1795), in *The Philosophy of Kant*, ed. Carl J. Friedrich (New York: Modern Library, 1949), 448.

19. Walter D. Mignolo, "The Many Faces of Cosmo-polis: Border Thinking and Critical Cosmopolitanism," in *Cosmopolitanism*, ed. Carol A. Breckenridge et al. (Durham, N.C.: Duke University Press, 2002), 181, quoting Slavoj Žižek.

20. I have told this story at length in *The Passage to Cosmos: Alexander von Humboldt and the Shaping of America* (Chicago: University of Chicago Press, 2009).

21. Wilhem von Humboldt, "On the Historian's Task" (1821), in *The Theory and Practice of History: Leopold von Ranke*, ed. Georg G. Iggers and Konrad von Moltke (Indianapolis, Ind.: Bobbs-Merrill, 1973), 7.

22. According to Bradley Dean, Thoreau is referencing recurrent place-names from Bernardin de Saint Pierre's *Studies of Nature* (1796), locations critical to the economy of the Moluccas, Indonesia, or the "Spice Islands" (*WF*, 288).

23. Humboldt, *Cosmos*, 2:68.

24. This account is inspired by Latour, *Politics of Nature*, 84–85.

25. This is the same plant that Whitman, under the name "Calamus," takes for the title of his poems on adhesive love in *Song of Myself*.

26. Wilhelm von Humboldt, "On the Comparative Study of Language and Its Relation to the Different Periods of Language Development" (1820), in *Wilhelm von Humboldt: Essays on Language*, ed. T. Harden and D. Farrelly (Frankfurt: Peter Lang, 1997), 18.

27. The linkages between linguistic, cultural, and biological diversity are a growing international field of study affecting national and world policy. For an introduction see Luisa Maffi, "Linguistic, Cultural, and Biological Diversity," *Annual Review of Anthropology* 34 (October 2005): 599–617.

28. In this light it is interesting to recall that when Thoreau turned down the invitation to join the American Association for the Advancement of Science, he listed his scientific interest as "The Manners & Customs of the Indians of the Algonquin Group previous to contact with the civilized man." See *The Correspondence of Henry David Thoreau*, ed. Walter Harding and Carl Bode (New York: New York University Press, 1958), 309–10.

29. Mss. letter to John Pickering, 24 February 1821; collection of the Boston Public Library Rare Book Room. Wilhelm von Humboldt was working on a massive study of Native American languages, which he argued were as sophisticated

and expressive as any in Europe; he died before he could finish this study, and the scattered manuscripts are only now turning up in European libraries. His correspondence with the pioneering American linguist John Pickering was part of this project. The work and philosophy of the Brothers Humboldt was ultimately taken up by Franz Boas, who used it to found modern anthropology. In the United States, Albert Gallatin took up the study of Native American languages at the same time as Pickering, and under Alexander von Humboldt's encouragement, founded the American Ethnological Society, still in existence today; Gallatin's work, also little known today, was taken up by John Wesley Powell. I have covered this story in some detail in *Passage to Cosmos,* chap. 4, but the larger story remains to be told.

30. Earl Shorris, "The Last Word," *Harper's,* August 2000, 43.

7. THE VALUE OF BEING: THOREAU ON APPRECIATING THE BEAUTY OF THE WORLD
Rick Anthony Furtak

1. Alfred North Whitehead, *Science and the Modern World* (New York: Free Press, 1967), 54. Cf. Susan Bordo, *The Flight to Objectivity* (Albany: State University of New York Press, 1987), 37–38.

2. Bernard Williams defends this notion in *Descartes: The Project of Pure Enquiry* (New York: Penguin Books, 1978), 230–42, 300–301.

3. C. S. Peirce, "A Critical Review of Berkeley's Idealism," in *Selected Writings* (New York: Dover, 1966), 82.

4. John McDowell, "Aesthetic Value, Objectivity, and the Fabric of the World," in *Mind, Value, and Reality* (Cambridge, Mass.: Harvard University Press, 1998), 119.

5. J. S. Mill, *Early Essays* (London: George Bell & Sons, 1897), 206–7. On "secondary" qualities, see also John Locke, *An Essay concerning Human Understanding* (1689; Oxford University Press, 1979).

6. All references to Thoreau's *Journal* are cited by date of entry. Unless otherwise noted, I refer to *The Journal of Henry D. Thoreau,* ed. Bradford Torrey and F. H. Allen (New York: Dover Publications, 1962).

7. Henry David Thoreau, "Natural History of Massachusetts," in *Collected Essays and Poems,* ed. Elizabeth Witherell (New York: Library of America, 2001), 41.

8. Alfred I. Tauber, *Henry David Thoreau and the Moral Agency of Knowing* (Berkeley: University of California Press, 2001), 18. Laura Dassow Walls remarks that Thoreau's "quest for meaning" led him to seek "a new form of science," one that would be defined by "relational knowing." Facts, on this view, are not "objective givens," uncontaminated by subjectivity; they are, rather, "*made* by the interaction of mind with external nature" (Laura Dassow Walls, *Seeing New Worlds: Henry David Thoreau and Nineteenth-Century Natural Science* [Madison: University of Wisconsin Press, 1995], 86, 147).

9. Henry David Thoreau, *Walden; or, Life in the Woods*, ed. Jeffrey S. Cramer (New Haven, Conn.: Yale University Press, 2004), 88–95. All parenthetical citations of *Walden* refer to this edition.

10. Henry David Thoreau, *Faith in a Seed*, ed. Bradley Dean (Washington, D.C.: Island Press, 1993), 144.

11. Stanley Cavell, "Night and Day: Heidegger and Thoreau," in *Appropriating Heidegger*, ed. James Faulconer and Mark Wrathall (Cambridge: Cambridge University Press, 2000), 44. "The transformation would be of our relation to our language," he adds; this would bring about "a transformation in our relation to the world."

12. Douglas Anderson, "Awakening in the Everyday," in *Pragmatism and Religion*, ed. Stuart Rosenbaum (Urbana: University of Illinois Press, 2003), 145–47. On the seriousness of Thoreau's highly unconventional religious language, see Paul Friedrich, *The Gita within Walden* (Albany: State University of New York Press, 2008), 7–10.

13. John Dewey, *The Quest for Certainty* (New York: G. P. Putnam's Sons, 1960), 302–6.

14. Tauber, *Henry David Thoreau and the Moral Agency of Knowing*, 152. See also page 174: for Thoreau, "the world indeed exists independent, real, and knowable," and yet there is a "dialectic" between subject and object.

15. Cf. Stephen R. L. Clark, *God's World and the Great Awakening* (Oxford: Oxford University Press, 1991), 220. On coming to know the divine by refining one's power of sight, see Plotinus, *Enneads* 1.6. See also Pierre Hadot, *Plotinus*, trans. Michael Chase (Chicago: University of Chicago Press, 1993), 56–65. If God is absent from the world, then nothing in life will matter very much, as Plotinus claims in *Enneads* 2.9.

16. Henry David Thoreau, *A Week on the Concord and Merrimack Rivers* (Princeton, N.J.: Princeton University Press, 1980), 382.

17. Henry David Thoreau, "Autumnal Tints," in *Collected Essays and Poems*, ed. Elizabeth Hall Witherell (New York: Library of America, 2001), 390. Italics added.

18. Henry David Thoreau, "Life without Principle," in *Collected Essays and Poems*, 349.

19. Henry David Thoreau, "Walking," in *Collected Essays and Poems*, 229. The phrase "to be met with," in the next sentence, is from Immanuel Kant, *Critique of Pure Reason*, trans. Norman Kemp Smith (New York: St. Martin's Press, 1965), note "a" to B70: the redness of a rose is there "to be met with" in the object's "relation to the subject."

20. Thoreau, "Autumnal Tints," 391. Making a similar point in connection with another example, William C. Johnson comments: "It is a reality born in the

conjunction of the light source and the right use of the eye" (William C. Johnson, *What Thoreau Said* [Moscow: University of Idaho Press, 1991], 43).

21. See Hilary Putnam, *The Collapse of the Fact-Value Dichotomy and Other Essays* (Cambridge, Mass.: Harvard University Press, 2002). On page 135, Putnam adds that value pertains to all of our experience, not only a small portion of it.

22. Cf. Kant, *Critique of Pure Reason*, note "a" to A120: "Imagination is a necessary ingredient of perception itself." This implies that "worlds are 'made' by the interaction ... of the creative self and the world" (H. Daniel Peck, *Thoreau's Morning Work* [New Haven, Conn.: Yale University Press, 1990], 122–23).

23. John Gatta, *Making Nature Sacred* (Oxford: Oxford University Press, 2004), 131, 137–38. On "the way in which the play of our imagination makes possible the disclosure of reality or truth," see also Colin Falck, *Myth, Truth, and Literature* (Cambridge: Cambridge University Press, 1989), 127–38. When William Blake proposed that all deities reside in the human breast, Falck observes, "he was not thereby denying the sense in which they might also be disclosures or revelations of the true nature of the world in which we live."

24. Thoreau, *A Week on the Concord and Merrimack Rivers*, 325–26. Goethe is the "great poet" to whom Thoreau refers in this passage.

25. This assumption is attacked by Martin Heidegger. See "Remembrance of the Poet," in *Existence and Being*, trans. Douglas Scott (Chicago: University of Chicago Press, 1949), 275. Cf. Martin Heidegger, *Being and Time*, trans. Joan Stambaugh (Albany: State University of New York Press, 1996), p. 130 [§29], on the mood of theoretical observation.

26. Stanley Cavell, *The Senses of Walden*, exp. ed. (Chicago: University of Chicago Press, 1992), 104. Cf. McDowell, "Aesthetic Value, Objectivity, and the Fabric of the World," 130: "How can a mere *feeling* constitute an experience in which the world reveals itself to us?" Unlike Kant, McDowell does not wish to conclude that feeling lies outside our faculty of knowlege altogether: see, e.g., *Critique of Pure Reason*, A802/B830.

27. See also Loren Eiseley, *The Star Thrower* (New York: Harcourt Brace Jovanovich, 1979), 237.

28. As Philip Cafaro points out in *Thoreau's Living Ethics* (Athens: University of Georgia Press, 2004), 132.

29. See, e.g., Martin Heidegger, *Poetry, Language, Thought*, trans. Albert Hofstadter (New York: Harper and Row, 1971), 94–111.

30. Max Scheler, "Phenomenology and the Theory of Cognition," in *Selected Philosophical Essays*, trans. David R. Lachterman (Evanston, Ill.: Northwestern University Press, 1973), 137–38.

31. Thoreau, *A Week on the Concord and Merrimack Rivers*, 382–83.

32. Henry D. Thoreau, "Wild Apples," in *Wild Apples and Other Natural History Essays*, ed. William Rossi (Athens,: University of Georgia Press, 2002), 144.

33. Cf. William James, "Is Life Worth Living?" in *James and Dewey on Belief and Experience*, ed. John M. Capps and Donald Capps (Urbana: University of Illinois Press, 2005), 91–93. Dewey agrees that our "so-called means of verification" are "constituent parts of the object," and not only in exceptional cases. See David Hildebrand, *Beyond Realism and Antirealism* (Nashville: Vanderbilt University Press, 2003), 52.

34. Thoreau, "Autumnal Tints," 393.

35. Ibid., 393–94.

36. William James, "The Will to Believe," in *Selected Writings*, ed. G. H. Bird (London: Everyman, 1995), 268.

37. William James, "On a Certain Blindness in Human Beings," in *Selected Writings*, 326–34. When the poet "opens up to receive, in a flood of emotion, the being of the thing he sees," then he or she has arrived at the "way of seeing" that is "the origin of poetry" (J. Hillis Miller, *The Disappearance of God* [Urbana: University of Illinois Press, 2000], 321).

38. Cavell, *Senses of Walden*, 145. See also Stéphane Mosès, *System and Revelation*, trans. Catherine Tihanyi (Detroit: Wayne State University Press, 1992), 91: "Our primordial certitude of the reality of the world, the certitude underlying all our experiences, is of the realm of values." I am grateful to Karin Nisenbaum for pointing out this reference.

39. Tauber, *Henry David Thoreau and the Moral Agency of Knowing*, 20.

40. Cf. Marcel Proust, *Time Regained*, trans. Andreas Mayor and Terence Kilmartin (New York: Modern Library, 1993), 325–26. See also Clark, *God's World and the Great Awakening*, 69: the "thing we think of existed before we thought of it, and exists even while we think of it in ways that we do not know."

41. Henry David Thoreau, *The Maine Woods* (New York: Penguin Books, 1988), 93–95. If there is ever a real abhorrence of Nature to be found in Thoreau's writings, it is when he considers what the "vast and wild" sea is able to "vomit" onshore after a shipwreck: see Henry David Thoreau, *Cape Cod* (Princeton, N.J.: Princeton University Press, 1988), 5–6, 90.

42. Cf. James, "On a Certain Blindness in Human Beings," 337: "Neither the whole of truth nor the whole of good is revealed to any single observer, although each observer gains a partial superiority of insight from the peculiar position in which he stands."

43. Robert Kuhn McGregor, *A Wider View of the Universe: Thoreau's Study of Nature* (Urbana: University of Illinois Press, 1997), 113. On this point, James is again in harmony with Thoreau: "The *fons et origo* of all reality," he writes, "is *ourselves* . . . as thinkers with emotional reaction." See William James, "The Psychology of Belief," in *James and Dewey on Belief and Experience*, 67.

44. Thoreau, "Autumnal Tints," 391. As Peter Blakemore notes, "An actual rainbow requires an actual perceiver" in order "to be seen and, more importantly, [to be] significant." See Blakemore, "Reading Home," in *Thoreau's Sense of Place*, ed. Richard Schneider (Iowa City: University of Iowa Press, 2000), 117.

45. Immanuel Kant, *Critique of Pure Reason*, trans. Werner Pluhar (Indianapolis: Hackett, 1996), A45–46/B63.

46. Max Oelschlaeger, *The Idea of Wilderness* (New Haven, Conn.: Yale University Press, 1991), 136.

47. Tauber, *Henry David Thoreau and the Moral Agency of Knowing*, 4–5. See also Walls, *Seeing New Worlds*, 212–13.

48. As René Descartes does in part 3 of his *Discourse on Method* (1637; Chicago: Open Court, 1962), adding that he will have to live somewhere else during the renovation.

49. Michel Foucault, *Ethics: Subjectivity and Truth*, trans. Paul Rabinow (New York: New Press, 1997), 278–79. Thanks to Jonathan Ellsworth for making me aware of this quotation.

50. *Walden*, 250; see also *Walden*, 172–73. 273, on the "evil genius" hypothesis and on the possibility that one might be dreaming, respectively. I also discuss Thoreau's relation to Cartesian skepticism in Furtak, "Thoreau's Emotional Stoicism," *Journal of Speculative Philosophy* 17, no. 2 (2003): 123.

51. Cavell, *Senses of Walden*, 51. See also Stanley Cavell, *In Quest of the Ordinary* (Chicago: University of Chicago Press, 1988), 84: "Epistemology is obliged to keep aesthetics under control, as if to guard against the thought that there is something more (and better) seeing can be, or provide, than evidence for claims to know, especially claims that particular objects exist."

52. William James also observes that we "feel things differently" in different moods and states of awareness. See Russell Goodman, *American Philosophy and the Romantic Tradition* (Cambridge: Cambridge University Press, 1990), 63.

53. David M. Robinson, *Natural Life* (Ithaca, N.Y.: Cornell University Press, 2004), 100–101. On the "synthesis of poetic, scientific, and ethical perception" that Thoreau aims to achieve, see Robert Milder, *Reimagining Thoreau* (Cambridge: Cambridge University Press, 1995), 175.

54. Cf. "Walking," 250. In Kant's terminology, the imagination expands our thoughts to include more "than what can be apprehended and made distinct" (*Critique of Judgment*, trans. Werner Pluhar (Indianapolis: Hackett, 1987), p. 183 [§49]. I am indebted to James Reid for noting the relevance of this passage, and for many suggestions that have improved this essay. For helpful comments in response to earlier drafts, I also thank Gail Baker, Stanley Bates, Jonathan Ellsworth, Russell Goodman, Marion Hourdequin, Ed Mooney, and Karin Nisenbaum.

8. THOREAU'S MORAL EPISTEMOLOGY AND ITS
CONTEMPORARY RELEVANCE
Alfred I. Tauber

1. See Francis O. Matthiessen, *American Renaissance* (Oxford: Oxford University Press, 1941).

2. Joel Porte, *Emerson and Thoreau: Transcendentalists in Conflict* (Middlebury, Vt.: Wesleyan University Press, 1966).

3. James McIntosh, *Thoreau as Romantic Naturalist* (Ithaca, N.Y.: Cornell University Press, 1974).

4. See, e.g., H. Daniel Peck, *Thoreau's Morning Work* (New Haven, Conn.: Yale University Press, 1990).

5. Sharon Cameron, *Writing Nature: Henry David Thoreau's* Journal (New York: Oxford University Press, 1985).

6. Laura D. Walls, *Seeing New Worlds* (Madison: University of Wisconsin Press, 1995).

7. Robert K. McGregor, *A Wider View of the Universe* (Urbana: University of Illinois Press, 1997).

8. Philip Cafaro, *Thoreau's Living Ethics* (Athens: University of Georgia Press, 2004).

9. See Alfred I. Tauber, *Henry David Thoreau and the Moral Agency of Knowing* (Berkeley: University of California Press, 2001). In what follows, I have also adapted some material from Tauber, *Science and the Quest for Meaning* (Waco, Tex.: Baylor University Press, 2009).

10. Hugo A. Meynell, *Redirecting Philosophy: Reflections on the Nature of Knowledge from Plato to Lonergan* (Toronto: University of Toronto Press, 1998), p. ix.

11. Cf. Susan Nieman, *The Unity of Reason: Rereading Kant* (New York: Oxford University Press, 1994).

12. See also Frederick Beiser, *German Idealism* (Cambridge, Mass.: Harvard University Press, 2002); Beiser, *Schiller as Philosopher* (Oxford: Oxford University Press, 2005).

13. See, e.g., John H. Zammito, *A Nice Derangement of Epistemes: Postpositivism in the Study of Science from Quine to Latour* (Chicago: University of Chicago Press, 2004).

14. To borrow a phrase from Evelyn Fox Keller, "The Paradox of Scientific Subjectivity," in *Rethinking Objectivity*, ed. by Allan Megill (Durham, N.C.: Duke University Press, 1994), 313–31.

15. I discuss this line of thought in *The Elusive Synthesis: Aesthetics and Science* (Dordrecht: Kluwer Academic, 1996). Especially relevant works by the philosophers I have just listed include Goethe's essay "The Experiment as Mediator between Object and Subject," trans. by Douglas E. Miller in Goethe's *Scientific Studies* (New York: Suhrkamp, 1998), 11–17; and Heidegger's essays "The Age of

the World Picture" and "Science and Reflection," both included in *The Question concerning Technology and Other Essays*, ed. William Lovitt (New York: Harper, 1977). See also Schiller's *Letters on the Aesthetic Education of Man*, Husserl's *Crisis of European Sciences and Transcendental Phenomenology*, and Dewey's *The Quest for Certainty.*

16. Debates revolving around deep ecology, the environmentalism emerging from American Transcendentalism, and the various critics of scientism—e.g., Paul Feyerabend, *Science in a Free Society* (London: NLB, 1978) and Theodore Roszak, *Where the Wasteland Ends* (Garden City, N.Y.: Doubleday, 1972)—have brought these philosophical issues to bear in public discourses in various guises. Most recently, in the so-called Science Wars, this resistance took the form of rejecting the claims for science's unique standing in the academy and even its claim to a hegemonic reason. For further discussion see Tauber, *Science and the Quest for Meaning.*

17. Henry David Thoreau, *Journal*, vol. 3: *1848–1851*, ed. Robert Sattelmeyer et al. (Princeton, N.J.: Princeton University Press, 1990), 380.

18. Cf. Stephen Toulmin, *Return to Reason* (Cambridge, Mass.: Harvard University Press, 2001).

19. Again, see Tauber, *Henry David Thoreau and the Moral Agency of Knowing.*

20. See, e.g., Hilary Putnam, *The Collapse of the Fact/Value Dichotomy and Other Essays* (Cambridge, Mass.: Harvard University Press, 2002).

21. Ernan McMullin, "Values in Science," *PSA: Proceedings of the Biennial Meeting of the Philosophy of Science Association* 2, no. 1 (1983): 3–28.

22. The blurring of the fact/value dichotomy, both within the laboratory and outside, represents the overriding characteristic of postpositivist science. This position argues that a relaxation of the rigid fact/value dichotomy recognizes that science continually evolves diverse value judgments regarding its own practice that are never steadfast but always changing in response to new demands and contexts. Chosen and developed, they hardly stand stable. No formal, final method exists to define fact/value relationships. The notion of an insular "fact" belies how facts are so commingled with the values and theories in which they are embedded that to disentangle the relative roles of these supports becomes a highly convoluted, and sometimes an irresolvable, endeavor.

If values seem a bit suspect from a narrowly scientific point of view, they have, at the very least, a lot of "companions in the guilt": justification, coherence, simplicity, reference, truth, and so on, all exhibit the *same* problems that goodness and kindness do, from an epistemological point of view. None of them is reducible to physical notions; none of them is governed by syntactically precise rules. Rather than give then give up all of them . . . and rather than do what we are doing, which is to reject some—the ones which do not fit in with a narrow instrumentalist conception of rationality which itself lacks all intellectual justification—we should recognize that *all* values, including the cognitive ones, derive their authority from our idea of human flourishing and our idea of reason. These two ideas are interconnected: our image of an ideal theoretical intelligence is simply part of our ideal of total human flourishing, and makes no sense wrenched out of the total ideal, as Plato and Aristotle saw.

This is from Hilary Putnam's *Realism with a Human Face* (Cambridge, Mass.: Harvard University Press, 1990), 141. So-called value-free science adopts three basic claims concerning the construction and use of facts (see H. Kincaid, J. Dupré, and A. Wylie, Introduction to *Value-Free Science?: Ideals and Illusions*, ed. Harold Kincaid, John Dupré, and Alison Wylie [Oxford: Oxford University Press, 2007], 13). Objective science never presupposes nonepistemic values (1) in determining what the evidence is or how strong it is; (2) in providing and assessing the epistemic status of explanation; nor (3) in determining the problems scientists address. Each of those assertions, over a wide spectrum of arguments, has been challenged repeatedly: See, e.g., Robert Proctor, *Value-Free Science?: Purity and Power in Modern Knowledge* (Cambridge, Mass.: Harvard University Press, 1991). When theory and fact conflict, sometimes one is given up, sometimes the other, and the choice as often as not is made "aesthetically," by adopting what appears to be the simplest, the most parsimonious, or elegant, or coherent—qualities which themselves are *values.* These are what Hilary Putnam calls *action-guiding* terms, the vocabulary of justification, also historically conditioned and subject to the same debates concerning the conception of rationality. The attempt to restrict coherence and simplicity to predictive theories is self-refuting, for the very logic required even to argue such a case depends on intellectual interests unrelated to prediction as such. In short, by dispelling the intellectual hubris of the scientific attitude we are left with a more dynamic, albeit less formal, understanding.

23. Henry David Thoreau, *Journal*, vol. 4: *1851–1852*, ed. L. N. Neufeldt and N. C. Simmons (Princeton, N.J.: Princeton University Press, 1992), 356. On Goethe, see Alfred I. Tauber, "Goethe's Philosophy of Science," *Perspectives in Biology and Medicine* 36, no. 2 (1993): 244–57.

24. McIntosh, *Thoreau as Romantic Naturalist*, 156. My emphasis.

25. Henry David Thoreau, *Journal*, vol. 1: *1837–1844*, ed. E. H. Witherell et al. (Princeton, N.J.: Princeton University Press, 1981), 69.

26. "Ordinary philosophers"—represented by Richard Rorty, Stanley Cavell, and Stanley Rosen—attempt to replace a deconstructive skepticism with a

constructive understanding of pretheoretical, everyday experience. They obviously differ as to how this goal might be achieved, but the movement against philosophical formalisms is shared by each. Further, the key for a philosopher such as Rosen is to see that ordinary experience is saturated with the extraordinary (Stanley Rosen, *The Elusiveness of the Ordinary* [New Haven, Conn.: Yale University Press, 2002], 10) and that philosophy's present task is to recover "the origins of human experience, that is, to remove the sediment deposited by traditional rationalism" (Rosen, *Elusiveness of the Ordinary*, 6–10). Rorty, in reviewing Cavell's *In Quest of the Ordinary*, succinctly captures this sentiment.

> [Certain philosophical] problems could only be stated in a particular jargon, in Philosopher's Talk. They cannot arise if we speak Ordinary Language. Descartes and Ayer had discussed, for example, whether the external world was real. Real? Austin asked. As opposed to what? A plywood stage set? A hallucination? A computer simulation? In the ordinary, human world these are the sorts of alternatives that give the word "real" its use and its force. In the philosophers' world, there is nothing to do the same job. That is what Wittgenstein meant when he said that Philosopher's Talk is language "on holiday."

This review, titled "The Philosophy of the Oddball," appears in the *New Republic*, 19 June 1989, 38–41. (This footnote has been adapted from Alfred I. Tauber, *Patient Autonomy and the Ethics of Integrity* [Cambridge, Mass.: MIT Press, 2005], 235–37.)

27. Henry David Thoreau, *Journal*, vol. 5: *1852–1853*, ed. P. F. O'Connell (Princeton, N.J.: Princeton University Press, 1997), 120.

28. Henry David Thoreau, *Walden*, ed. J. L. Shanley (Princeton, N.J.: Princeton University Press, 1971), 218.

29. Thoreau, *Journal*, vol. 1: *1837–1844*, 466–67.

30. Ibid., 187. From an entry dated 11 October 1840.

31. Ralph Waldo Emerson, *Nature*, in *The Collected Works of Ralph Waldo Emerson*, (Cambridge, Mass.: Harvard University Press, 1971), 1:44–45.

32. John Dewey, *Human Nature and Conduct* (New York: Henry Holt, 1922), 296.

33. Ibid., 278–79.

34. Alasdair MacIntyre, "Objectivity in Morals and Objectivity in Science," in *Morals, Science, and Sociality*, ed. H. T. Engelhardt Jr. and D. Callahan (Hastings-on-Hudson, N.Y.: Hastings Center, Institute of Society, Ethics, and the Life Sciences, 1978), 37. See also Alasdair MacIntyre, *After Virtue* (Notre Dame, Ind.: University of Notre Dame Press, 1984), 56–60. Putnam also notes this interplay of values in discovering reality, which hardly means that anything goes. "I do not see reality as morally indifferent: reality, as Dewey saw, makes

demands on us. Values may be created by human beings and human cultures, but I see them as made in response to demands that we do not create. It is reality that determines whether our responses are adequate or inadequate" (Hilary Putnam, *Jewish Philosophy as a Guide to Life* [Bloomington: Indiana University Press, 2008], 6).

35. Dewey, *The Quest for Certainty*, 204.

36. John Dewey, *Philosophy and Civilization* (New York: Capricorn Books, 1931), 4.

37. See note 26 above. See also John R. Shook, *Dewey's Empirical Theory of Knowledge and Reality* (Nashville, Tenn.: Vanderbilt University Press, 2000).

38. In *The Grace and Severity of the Ideal: John Dewey and the Transcendent* (Chicago: University of Chicago Press, 2002), 24, Victor Kestenbaum quotes Charles Tomlinson's poem, "Ode to Arnold Schoenberg" ("Meshed in meaning / by what is natural / we are discontented / for what is more"), and then observes,

> We are not meshed in society, history, or language but rather in the meanings—tangible and intangible—which they institute and sustain. Further, we are meshed in meaning "by what is natural." The ranges of "natural" here exceed the specifications, themselves inexact, of philosophical naturalism, including Dewey's naturalism. It is not difficult to see, however, that our discontent does not arise from the state of being "meshed in meaning" but from being "meshed in"—as in "hemmed in"—by meaning which is restricted to the natural. We are discontented [desirous] "for what is more."

39. Here, I have avoided an important characterization of Thoreau the metaphysician. If the line demarcating the moral from the epistemological seems faint, the line separating metaphysics from these other concerns is similarly obscure, for not until one journeys well within each territory does the landscape more clearly reveal its terrain. After all, did not Thoreau himself describe himself as a transcendentalist? Given his mystical reveries, spiritual pursuits of various kinds, and the larger quest for personal meaning that mark all of his literary works, we must account for his metaphysics. Unfortunately, the sketch offered here can offer only a promissory note of a fuller description in which Thoreau's epistemology would be shown to "drive" his metaphysics.

40. Michael Polanyi, *Personal Knowledge: Towards a Post-critical Philosophy* (Chicago: University of Chicago Press, 1962).

41. Simply, the values of science allow investigative findings to find their rightful place as scientific data and theory development. Typically, philosophers of science see that exercise as placing facts within broader conceptual theories or models. See note 22 above, and the texts cited there.

42. Again, see Tauber, *Science and the Quest for Meaning*. From this under-standing, an orientation toward science's political posture and personal signifi-cance take form. Politically, two strategies follow: The first is an "integrative" approach. Better to openly bring science into its full moral context, and by reci-procity, apply science to its full social potential, e.g., let ecology support environ-mental ethics and the corresponding social policy directed toward "saving" the environment. The alternative view, the "separatist" position, maintains that while the fact/value distinction is hardly rigid, and in many respects collapses, it is best to acknowledge the difference between the *identification* of a scientific fact and its *application* in a social policy argument. Science thus remains maximally neutral and its social and political uses then become *derivative* functions. Accordingly, scientific fact and social value, legitimate in their own domain, should optimally remain discrete and separate. Another aspect of science and its ethics concerns the application of scientific findings to human problems. What is the appropriate pos-ture a scientist might assume in juxtaposing her identity as scientist with that as expert citizen? Where does science end and ideology begin? Such questions have no ready answers, as history has amply shown, but it seems self-evident that given the authority science brings to questions of social policy, the ethics of engage-ment require scrutiny. See Tauber, "Ecology and the Claims for a Science-based Ethics," in *Philosophies of Nature: The Human Dimension,* vol. 195 of Boston Studies in the Philosophy of Science, ed. R. S. Cohen and A. I. Tauber (Dordrecht: Kluwer Academic, 1998), 185–206. See also Max Weber, "Science as a Vocation," in *From Max Weber: Essays in Sociology,* trans. and ed. H. H. Gerth and C. W. Mills (New York: Oxford University Press, 1946), 137–56; and Daniel S. Greenberg, *The Politics of Pure Science* (New York: New American Library, 1967).

9. HOW *WALDEN* WORKS: THOREAU AND THE SOCRATIC ART OF PROVOCATION
Jonathan Ellsworth

1. If so, then Kant's first *Critique* is a work of philosophy, but Boethius' *Consolations of Philosophy* is less clearly so.

2. All references to *Walden* will refer to chapter and paragraph rather than page numbers.

3. Plato, *Apology*, trans. G. M. A. Grube, in *Plato: Complete Works*, ed. John M. Cooper (Indianapolis: Hackett, 1997), 36c. All translations from Plato are from this edition unless otherwise indicated.

4. Diogenes Laertius, *Lives of Eminent Philosophers*, 2.7, trans. R. D. Hicks (Cambridge, Mass.: Harvard University Press, 2000).

5. Stanley Cavell, *The Senses of Walden* (Chicago: University of Chicago Press, 1992), 31.

6. Henry David Thoreau, "Life without Principle," in *Walden and Other Writings*, ed. Brooks Atkinson (New York: Modern Library, 2000), 643.

7. Cavell, *Senses of Walden*, 12.

8. In his journal entry of 21 October 1857, Thoreau writes, "Is not the poet bound to write his own biography? Is there any other work for him but a good journal? We do not wish to know how his imaginary hero, but how he, the actual hero, lived from day to day."

9. Thoreau, *Walden and Other Writings*, 638.

10. Thoreau's remark here, "yet *I* never read them," clearly ought not to be taken at face value. For *Walden* itself contains a number of allusions to various Platonic works, including not only the *Apology*, but also the *Timaeus*, *Critias*, and *Republic*. So this might be an insignificant rhetorical quip, or a false modesty. Or perhaps, given what he has said about the exceedingly difficult and heroic task of reading well, that in the strong sense, he cannot claim to have read—fully reckoned with—Plato's Dialogues.

11. Pierre Hadot, *Philosophy as a Way of Life* (Oxford: Blackwell, 1995), 267.

12. Ludwig Wittgenstein, *Philosophical Investigations*, trans. G. E. M. Anscombe (Malden, Mass.: Blackwell, 2001), §123.

13. "I confess, that practically speaking, when I have learned a man's real disposition, I have no hopes of changing it for the better or worse in this state of existence" (*Walden*, 4.12). See too 7.15.

14. Twenty years after the publication of *Walden*, Nietzsche would wrestle with similar concerns in his essay *Schopenhauer as Educator*, and later in *Thus Spoke Zarathustra*. In "Nietzsche's Perfectionism: A Reading of *Schopenhauer as Educator*," James Conant writes, "In order for an exemplar to play an educative role in our lives, he must know how to defeat our tendency to want to mimic, rather than be provoked by, his example." See *Nietzsche's Postmoralism*, ed. Richard Schacht (Cambridge: Cambridge University Press, 2000), 36.

10. WONDER AND AFFLICTION: THOREAU'S DIONYSIAN WORLD
Edward F. Mooney

1. Henry David Thoreau, *A Week on the Concord and Merrimack Rivers*, ed. Carl F. Hovde, William L. Howarth, and Elizabeth Hall Witherell (Princeton, N.J.: Princeton University Press, 1980), 67. Henceforth *Week*. From the *Journals*: "What a pity if the part of Hamlet be left out" (21 March 1840, 1st paragraph). "The whole of life is seen by some through this darker medium,—partakes of the tragic,—and its bright and splendid lights become thus lurid" (1 September 1852); "It is the . . . wild thinking in Hamlet—in the Iliad—and in all the scriptures and mythologies that delights us" (16 November 1850). Henry D. Thoreau,

Journal, vols. 1–8, ed. John C. Broderick et al. (Princeton, N.J.: Princeton University Press, 1981–2008). I thank Lyman Mower for compiling these passages.

2. Henry David Thoreau, *Cape Cod* (New York: Thomas Y. Crowell, 1961), chapter 6, 123–24. In 1850 Thoreau traveled from Concord to the site of the shipwreck to search for Fuller's remains, but did not find a body he could identify as hers. In his *Journal*, 31 October 1850, he records walking a beach in search of remains; later he inserts that evocation with slight changes, in *Cape Cod*. See below in the section titled "Redemptive Writing and Reading" regarding his inability to identify the body.

3. "A Plea for Captain John Brown," and "The Last Days of John Brown," in *The Essays of Henry D. Thoreau*, selected and ed. Lewis Hyde (New York: North Point Press, 2002). Henceforth *Essays*.

4. In "Silence and the Night" (unpublished), Lyman Mower discusses the contention of Levinas that although tragic drama can succeed in bringing suffering to a partial relief through catharsis, there is raw suffering from which there is no release, escape, or mitigation through art or any other means: pointless, useless, insufferable. He calls this "the tragic." See Emmanuel Levinas, *Time and The Other*, trans. Alphonso Lingis (Pittsburgh: Duquesne University Press, 1987), 73. Thoreau starts his *Journal*, noting the trouble (if not outright suffering) of the always recurring human need, his need, "to escape myself" (*Journal*, 22 October 1837).

5. Both Thoreau and Levinas can be seen to endorse "ethics as first philosophy," the idea of a call or demand or "appearance" ("ethics") that exceeds our most heroic metaphysical reach. Alfred I. Tauber begins this discussion in *Henry David Thoreau and the Moral Agency of Knowing* (Berkeley: University of California Press, 2001); he acknowledges an encompassing debt to Levinas (xi, 231). See also Diane Perpich, *The Ethics of Emmanuel Levinas* (Stanford, Calif.: Stanford University Press, 2008), especially chap. 5, "Scarce Resources? Levinas, Animals, and the Environment."

6. Frederick Beiser, "*Schiller as Philosopher*: A Reply to my Critics," *Inquiry* 51, no. 1 (2008): 69. "The personal suffering or sacrifice involved in performing some moral actions is the result of tragic circumstances as much as the weakness of human nature. Gods, angels, or titans, which have much more robust constitutions, could do all their duties with grace simply because they are never prone to suffering. Dignity indeed arises because of the great weakness of human nature; but that weakness reveals itself only under tragic circumstances." Of course not all suffering is tragic suffering. Suffering through a traffic jam is hardly tragic.

7. Friedrich Nietzsche, *The Birth of Tragedy from the Spirit of Music*, ed. and trans. Douglas Smith (New York: Oxford University Press, 2000), 27. Henceforth *Birth*.

8. Ibid., 28.

9. See "Slavery in Massachusetts," in *Essays*, 193.

10. Thoreau, *Journal*, 31 October 1850, 3:127; see also *Cape Cod*, 123–24.

11. On the possibility that some tragic moments are beyond redemption, see note 4, above.

12. "In wildness is the preservation of the world," which becomes an environmentalist banner, comes from "Walking," in *Essays*, 162: "The West of which I speak is but another name for the Wild, and what I have been preparing to say is, that in Wildness is the preservation of the World. Every tree sends its fibers forth in search of the Wild. The cities import it at any price. Men plow and sail for it. From the forest and wilderness come the tonics and barks which brace mankind." Note that "the wild" is something cities import and tree roots seek: Even trees in wilderness forest preserves long for the wild. In the city, we want tree-lined streets and city parks but also medicines and salves derived from wild plants and trees.

13. Thoreau transfigures Brown's execution into a deserved immortality. That "translation" into heaven might be a harbinger of life after apocalypse: Brown would "return" to reign, following the carnage and fires of a great Civil War. See "The Last Days of John Brown," in *Essays*. I discuss Thoreau's transfiguration of Brown in "Thoreau's Translations: John Brown, Apples, Lilies," chap. 12 of *Lost Intimacy in American Thought* (New York: Continuum, 2009).

14. Thoreau, "Wild Apples," in *Essays*, 312; "Walking," 168.

15. Thoreau, "Walking," 166; see also *Journals*, 16 November 1850, 3rd para.

16. See Thoreau, *Week*, 337. The Corybantes were children of Apollo and Thalia (the rustic muse of comedy). Revelers enacted deaths and rebirths through nonlinguistic vehicles not unlike Thoreau's reveling rituals of walking, tasting, beholding, and climbing, each of which follows a pattern of death-and-rebirth.

17. Thoreau, "Walking," 173.

18. Ibid., 164.

19. Thoreau, *Walden*, "Higher Laws," opening paragraph. Within the opening pages we are given the wildly comic picture of Thoreau wanting to devour a woodchuck, to ingest wildness itself, as if incorporating wild flesh makes one even *more* wild. Eating the wild also (or alternatively) might *tame* or *deflect* it. Further on in "Higher Laws," the wild seems less reverenced, and the Apollonian ("higher"), more. Thoreau plays out both instincts, neither one unnerving the other. He tilts *Walden* toward the Apollonian and "Wild Apples" or "Ktaadn" (for instance) toward the Dionysian. Nietzsche has tragic drama require the reign of *both* divinities.

20. John Winthrop's 1630 sermon to New Englanders warned them that the world was watching their experiment in holiness, citing Matthew 5:14: "You are the light of the world. A city that is set on a hill cannot be hidden."

21. *Phaedo*, 64a–c. Plato also lets Socrates say, in this context, that he has had a recurrent dream wherein a voice instructs him to "make music and compose"—or, as J. Hillis Miller translates, "O Socrates, make music and work at it." See *Phaedo*, 60e. As translated by J. Hillis Miller in his *Theory Now and Then* (Durham, N.C.: Duke University Press, 1991), 117.

22. On John Thoreau's death, see *Henry Thoreau: A Life of the Mind*, by Robert D. Richardson Jr. (Berkeley University of California Press, 1986), 113–14, and Wai Chee Dimock's brilliant account of the "symbiosis" between brothers through which Henry took on John's bodily symptoms ("Global Civil Society: Thoreau on Three Continents," in *Through Other Continents* [Princeton, N.J.: Princeton University Press, 2006], chap. 1). The somatic-psychic border is porous within any single person, but also between persons and across time. Henry's body is porous to John's and Henry's psychic borders are porous enough to receive the Gita, allowing it to link humankind globally and through time. Her account of the "travel" of the Gita's account of death, life, and violence from Thoreau to Gandhi to King inspires my essay "For Love of the World: Thoreau's Translations." For the transmutation of Duston's saga into a myth of American Fall from Innocence, see Linck C. Johnson's invaluable *Thoreau's Complex Weave: The Writing of* A Week on the Concord and Merrimack Rivers (Charlottesville: University Press of Virginia, 1986), 122–62. I am grateful for the provocation of her essay, and to Clark West for passing it on. On Thoreau's use of the Gita, see Paul Friedrich, *The Gita within Walden* (Albany: State University of New York Press, 2008).

23. See Henry David Thoreau, *The Maine Woods*, ed. Joseph J. Moldenhauer (Princeton, N.J.: Princeton University Press, 1972). See also "Ktaadn," in *Essays*, 69–71.

24. We could say that philosophy's concern is to raise what is best from the dead—raise the "friend"—or brother—evoked in a *Week*, or the Fuller who reigns over the beach, or the good or just Plato finds buried in memory's graves, or the "ordinary' (our finiteness) that Wittgenstein finds forgotten. We have every reason to raise what can be retained as the love or smile or enlivening power of the dead, and no need to redeem what is better split off and discarded, buried, as *appropriately* decaying waste or flesh. To distinguish what is best left buried and what is worthy lifting up from the grave is the accomplishment of wise perception. The raising of the dead is an achievement of perception and equally of wise and eloquent words that deliver that perception to others. See sections below titled "Sensing Heaven in Hell," "Achieving Perception and Affinity," and "Wonder-wounded Hearing."

25. Thoreau writes, "A glorious lurid sunset tonight, accompanied with many somber clouds. . . . Pale saffron skies with faint fishes of rosy clouds dissolving in them. A bloodstained sky." See Richardson, *Henry Thoreau*, 215.

26. Holy Saturday commemorates the Harrowing of Hades, Christ's descent into Hell to raise those deserving better. Clark West suggests this possibility. I thank him for countless insights into the religious dimension of Thoreau's writing.

27. "Falling in love with the world" is a "blindness" permissible in the face of dismal skepticism. See Stanley Cavell, *The Claim of Reason* (New York: Oxford University Press, 1979), 431. See my "Acknowledgement, Suffering and Praise: Stanley Cavell as Religious Continental Thinker," in *Soundings, an Interdisciplinary Journal* 88 (Summer 2005): 393–411.

28. Thoreau, *Cape Cod*, 123.

29. Lacking a definitively identified body, no grave was ever erected for Fuller or for her husband. Their son's body was found. I thank Steve Webb for detective work.

30. Søren Kierkegaard, *Papers and Journals: A Selection*, ed. and trans. Alastair Hannay (New York: Penguin Books, 1996), 101. He raises a toast: "To genius, beauty, art, and the whole glorious world: . . . May it live a transfigured life here or hereafter" (*Early Polemical Writings*, trans. and ed. Julia Watkin [Princeton, N.J.: Princeton University Press, 1990], 66–67). See Joseph Westfall, *The Kierkegaardian Author: Authorship and Performance in Kierkegaard's Literary and Dramatic Criticism* (Berlin: Walter de Gruyter, 2007), 51, 216–17. See also my review of Westfall's book, "What Is a Kierkegaardian Author?," *Philosophy and Social Criticism* 35, no. 7 (2009): 867–80.

31. Thoreau, *Cape Cod*, 123.

32. See Ian Hacking on "deflection" in *Philosophy and Animal Life*, by Stanley Cavell, Cora Diamond, John McDowell, Ian Hacking, and Cary Wolfe (New York: Columbia University Press, 2008). Cavell sees philosophical skepticism about other minds as a deflection of deep, and often tragic, loneliness and separation. Hacking reminds us that deflection is not always an unhealthy defense.

33. See my essay "Thoreau's Translations."

34. Thoreau, *Week*, 186–88.

35. Joel Porte sees the upriver trip as a search for "the source of the Concord and Merrimack rivers," and the source "of all seas and mountains, indeed of primal daylight" (*Consciousness and Culture: Emerson and Thoreau Reviewed* [New Haven, Conn.: Yale University Press, 2004], 131).

36. Thoreau, "Slavery in Massachusetts," 192.

37. Ibid., my italics. This mimics Kant's moral imperative, "*So act that the maxim of your action can be made universal law.*"

38. For Thoreau there is life even in flowing sand. He works out this perception of living sand over visits and revisits to a sandbank, cut to make way for a railbed. The "sandcut" is described in *Walden*, "Spring."

39. Thoreau, *Week*, 382, my italics.

40. E. A. Ch. Wasianski, *Immanuel Kant in seinen letzten lebensjahren* [Kant's Last Years], quoted in W. R. Washington Sullivan, *Morality as a Religion* (New York: Macmillan, 1898), 50.

41. Thoreau, *Week*, 235–36. Joel Porte notes this passage, and relates it to Bachelard's discussions of Thales (water) and Heraclitus (a hearth's fire) in *Consciousness in Concord* (New Haven: Yale University Press, 2004), 132. Among Parisian philosophers, Bachelard was a great reader of Thoreau, as was Pierre Hadot. See Timothy Stock, "The Waters of Metaphysics," http://alphabet-city .org/issues/water/articles/the-waters-of-metaphysics.

42. Thoreau, *Week*, 382.

43. A group of Concord intellectuals became "transcendentalists" in tribute to what they knew of Kant's "transcendental philosophy." "Transcendentalists" was an adopted identity for Emerson, Fuller, and others—but it meant many things. When Thoreau calls John Brown a "true transcendentalist," he means a man who lives high ideals, someone who transcends moral mediocrity. In contrast, "the transcendental club" of Boston accepted the moniker bcause they saw themselves as following the "transcendental" spirit of German philosophy— Kant, but also his romantic and idealistic successors. Frederick Hedge returned from Germany fired up about Kant, Herder, Fichte, Schiller, Kant, Coleridge, and others who offered a lofty moral philosophy that put emphasis, in Kant's phrase, on "coming into one's maturity" through critical reason that would undermine illiberal, authoritarian, and clerical conservatism. Allied with imagination, reason could provide *intuitions* about the role of regulative ideals like morality and freedom. How much emphasis the transcendentalists (or Thoreau) put on Kant's epistemology (as opposed to his moral philosophy) is uncertain. The "productive imagination"—an anti-Lockean idea of an *active, world-shaping* mind, sometimes linked to the idea of genius—would be of more interest than the bare-bones empiricism of Locke or Hume. Kant denied access to "the thing-in-itself." Decoupled from accountability to "the thing-in-itself," imagination and poetry were set free (or so one could argue). See Phillip Gura, *American Transcendentalism: A History* (New York: Hill and Wang, 2007). Thoreau makes a claim that seems to transcend Kant's First Critique position. "*The boundaries of the actual are no more fixed and rigid than the elasticity of our imagination*" (*Journal*, 5:203). The question of Kant aside, Thoreau's claim might be interpreted along the lines of Cavell's moral perfectionism, first voiced in *The Senses of Walden* (New York: Viking, 1972), and continued in a number of later writings, including *Cities of Words: Pedagogical Letters on a Register of the Moral Life* (Cambridge, Mass.: Harvard University Press, 2005). Imagination might let us become the actual persons we can be, let the actual be as elastic as the imagination. We find a person, a writer, continually transcending his or her latest version of their worlds and the selves they can be. It is imagination that reveals that

we are not "beyond reproach" morally, and thus that there is always an improved self to make actual. Our imagination thus expands the bounds of the actual. Thoreau took philosophy to be as unfinished as the self, and devoted to the care of the self. One enlists imagination in the effort to bring the best to light through transfiguration of the soul and of social life. Imagination takes Thoreau to Concord's jail; his transfiguring experience there travels to Gandhi and King, remaking the world.

44. J. M. Bernstein, *The Fate of Art* (University Park: Penn State Press, 1992), 96.

45. Again, see my "Thoreau's Translations."

46. For an account of the education of the senses and perception in the never-ending achievements of moral sensibility, see Sabina Lovibond, *Ethical Formation* (Cambridge, Mass.: Harvard University Press, 2002).

47. See Wayne M. Martin, "Conscience and Confession in Rousseau's Naturalistic Moral Psychology," available at http://privatewww.essex.ac .uk/~wmartin/MartinRousseauPaper.pdf.

48. An echo endorses perceptual affinity as a call into nature is returned in kind. Thoreau writes, "Of what significance is any sound if Nature does not echo it"; and "woodland lungs . . . seemed particularly sound to day," seeming "to mouth" the answer they give (*Journal*, 31 October 1850, 129).

49. Cavell, *Claim of Reason*, 431, and see also my "Acknowledgement, Suffering and Praise." Cavell's *Claim of Reason* does not exclude the heart. I consider his defense of "passionate utterances" that "improvise in the disorders of desire" (as contrasted with performative utterances) in my *On Søren Kierkegaard* (Aldershot: Ashgate, 2007), 52–53. And see the section below titled "Thoreau and Philosophy."

50. See Lovibond, *Ethical Formation*, on McDowell's and Aristotle's second nature.

51. Lyman Mower points out that here Thoreau expands the Heidegger of *Being and Time*: for Heidegger things can appear as instruments-in-use ("at hand") or as "mere occurrences" (looked at with detachment), but as Thoreau insists, they also appear as things to enjoy, take delight in, be repelled by, or love.

52. Thoreau, *Journal*, 7 December 1838.

53. As the gap between perceiver and perceived closes—as it does in Thoreau's romp with a fox, or as, in a famous passage, in the second walk in Rousseau's *Reveries of a Solitary Walker*—directionality of impact seems to recede in significance, disappear as a meaningful distinction. Rousseau recounts a moment of rebirth after having been felled by a racing Great Dane: "Night was beginning to fall. I perceived the sky, some stars, and green leaves. This first sensation was a delicious moment. I was conscious of myself only through this. I was being born

into life in that instant, and it seemed to me as if *all I perceived was filled with my frail existence*" (my italics). Rousseau chooses the idiom of the perceiver flowing out, reaching out to the world. The perceiver envelops the perceived. But we might reverse the directionality of gap-closing. We might invoke an idiom that places initiative out in the world, the world (as it were) flowing in to flood the perceiving self. Drenched by an onset of significance, the self disappears, leaving *only* the world. Perhaps there is a perspective that erases directionality, makes the choice—inside out or outside in—unnecessary. From a third perspective we have a seamless interconnectedness, with inside-out being the other side of outside in. The coldness of the stream into which one plunges one's hand becomes the coldness of the hand enveloped by a freezing stream. Coldness, hand, and stream then become an experientially undifferentiated plenum. Some aspects of Emerson's famous passage toward becoming a "transparent eyeball"—where he is what appears and what appears is he—can be understood along similar lines. See Barbara Packer, *Emerson's Fall* (New York: Continuum, 1982), 79–82.

54. Shakespeare, *Hamlet*, 3.1. Here, the stars themselves "stand as wonder-wounded hearers" before the wails of Laertes; but the irony is that his wails would not catch the interest of a toad. Hamlet is sarcastic. When the stars *do* stand still in wonder, we know that eloquence stops in its tracks everything on earth and in heaven. I will call this "the dance of perception."

55. Henry David Thoreau, "The Landlord," in *Excursions*, ed. Joseph J. Moldenhauer (Princeton, N.J.: Princeton University Press, 2007), 47.

56. Rick Anthony Furtak, "Skepticism and Perceptual Faith: Henry David Thoreau and Stanley Cavell on Seeing and Believing," *Transactions of the Charles S. Peirce Society* 43 (Summer 2007): 552. My italics.

57. Thoreau, *Journal*, 25 July 1839.

58. For a defense of moral thinking as engaging imagination in a register quite other than moral judgment and forensic argumentation, see Alice Crary, *Beyond Moral Judgment* (Cambridge, Mass.: Harvard University Press, 2007).

59. Stanley Cavell, *Philosophy the Day after Tomorrow* (Cambridge, Mass.: Harvard University Press, 2005), 185; see also my discussion in *On Søren Kierkegaard*, 52–54.

60. Writers can transform selves through enactments of convention and law, but also through intimate intervention in the lives and souls of readers. When I participate in conventions or activate formal procedures to effect a change in my world—say as I apologize and promise to return your tool now resting in my garage (thus participating in those practices), or as I vote to change the bylaws of my association (activating a formal procedure)—my words and gestures have what philosophers of language would call "performative force." The force of Thoreau's writing has its effect at a more intimate level, the level Cavell calls "passionate utterance." See his discussion in "Passionate and

Performative Utterance," *Contending with Stanley Cavell*, ed. Russell Goodman (New York: Oxford University Press, 2005), 192–93.

61. For Socrates as far more than an intellectual interrogator, see *On Søren Kierkegaard*, chaps. 1–4.

62. See Mooney, *Lost Intimacy*, especially chaps. 7, 11.

63. See Paul Friedlander's neglected study, *Plato, an Introduction* (Princeton, N.J.: Princeton University Press, 1958), for Plato as a poet who wants *his* (philosophical) poetry to set the standard. In the final chapter of *Cities of Words*, Cavell suggests that Plato's aim (in the *Republic)* is not to banish all poetry but to let philosophical poetry show its claim to be heard.

64. See Frederick Garber's short remarks on the resonances between Rousseau's fifth walk and Thoreau's seeking "immediate presentness" (Frederick Garber, *Thoreau's Redemptive Imagination* [New York: New York University Press, 1977], 153–54).

65. Immanuel Kant, "Conjectural Beginning of History," in *On History*, ed. Lewis White Beck (Indianapolis: Bobbs-Merrill, 1963), 55. Instinctual responses of animals are expressions (for Kant) of obedience. Their *actions* voice compliance. Creatures who can hear the will of another, showing their obedience in action, also *judge*: The cat judges that she has to run faster to catch her prey, or that instead she should rest in the shade.

66. In a set of *Discourses* from 1849, Kierkegaard has the lily and the bird obey the voice of God who asks them to be themselves; they respond "instinctually" and affirmatively. I thank Marcia Robinson for noting this resonance. The year 1849 also marks Thoreau's first walk on Cape Cod and of his essay on resistance to civil government.

67. Ludwig Wittgenstein, *Philosophical Investigations* (Oxford: Blackwell, 1958), 223.

68. Perhaps we would not understand lions because they don't have an *inaccessible* "inner life" of dialogue with themselves, which they could report on if only they had speech. Perhaps we *don't share a way of life*, and so *couldn't* understand a speaking lion. My amendment need not imply that Wittgenstein has made a mistake. His claim is open-ended enough to support more than one reading and, to my ear, invites elaborations that go contrary to its apparent point. It provokes as much as it declares, and that may be enough for his immediate purposes.

69. Cavell et al., *Philosophy and Animal Life* is close at hand, and no doubt tilts my formulations.

70. Wittgenstein holds that thinking runs astray when "a picture holds us captive." We might think of pictures as playing a role in static representations, as in picture galleries, where we can take in the whole scene in a glance. Images, in contrast, might be seen as shifting, indefinite, "spectral" items in narrative or

poetry, things inchoate and hard to pin down, even while having dreamlike power. See Thoreau, "Autumnal Tints," in *Excursions*. See also Bence Nanay, "Narrative Pictures," *Journal of Aesthetics and Art Criticism* 67, no. 1 (2009): 119–29.

71. He belongs shelved with philosophy, as do Henry James, Dostoevsky, and Proust (to name just a few whose identities are wider than any single disciplinary or cultural classification).

72. Cora Diamond, "The Difficulty of Reality and the Difficulty of Philosophy," in Cavell et al., *Philosophy and Animal Life*, chap. 1. Some of the trouble or trembling we undergo is not only the sign of a vagrant, flawed, or ill-formed subjectivity. Troubles also afflict the most unflawed, since there are dark troubles rooted in objective realities.

73. Thoreau, *Journal*, 21 March 1840.

74. Thoreau, *Cape Cod*, 123.

75. Thoreau, *Journal*, 7 December 1838.

76. Søren Kierkegaard, *Papers and Journals*, ed. and trans. Howard V. Hong and Edna H. Hong (Bloomington: Indiana University Press, 1978), 5:116.

77. I thank Rick Furtak, who suggested the proximity of Kierkegaard and Thoreau in *The Stanford Encyclopedia of Philosophy*, which inspired my comparison here. I also thank him for suggestions greatly improving this essay.

78. Parallel lives? Thoreau lived from 1817 to 1862; Kierkegaard, from 1813 to 1855. Thoreau starts his journal in 1837; Kierkegaard starts his in 1834. Thoreau's first essay appears in 1842, the year of John's death. Kierkegaard publishes *Either/Or, Fear and Trembling*, and *Repetition* in 1843. In 1846, Thoreau writes "Ktaadn," and in 1849 "Civil Resistance" and *A Week on the Concord*. He retrieves Fuller's body in 1850 and publishes *Walden* in 1854. "Slavery in Massachusetts" appears in 1854, and in 1857 he meets John Brown. In 1859, he delivers "A Plea for John Brown." After Thoreau and others arranged a memorial service in Concord on the day of his hanging, outraged Concord citizens hanged Brown in effigy. Kierkegaard was not martyred, but church dignitaries shunned his funeral, and student supporters disrupted the graveside service, protesting church rites they were sure he would have despised.

79. Søren Kierkegaard, *Papers and Journals, A Selection*, ed. and trans. Alastair Hannay (New York: Penguin Books, 1996), 109.

80. Thoreau, *Journal*, 30 January 1841.

81. See *Kierkegaard's* Repetition *and* Philosophical Crumbs, ed., intro., and notes Edward F. Mooney, trans. Marilyn Piety (New York: Oxford University Press, 2009), and my "*Repetition*: Getting the World Back," in *The Cambridge Companion to Kierkegaard*, ed. Marino and Hannay (Cambridge: Cambridge University Press, 1998), 282–306.

82. See Charles Larmore, *The Romantic Legacy* (New York: Columbia University Press, 1996), for the move from the epistemological goal of neutral cognition to the broadly ethical goal of "subjective" responsibility.

83. Thoreau, "Ktaadn," 113.

84. See Søren Kierkegaard, *The Concept of Anxiety*, trans. Reidar Thomte (Princeton, N.J.: Princeton University Press, 1980).

85. Stanley Bates, "Stanley Cavell and Ethics," in *Stanley Cavell*, ed. Richard Eldridge (Cambridge: Cambridge University Press, 2003), chap. 2.

86. Ibid., 39.

87. Philosophers have much to learn from Robert Pogue Harrison's *Forests: The Shadow of Civilization* (Chicago: University of Chicago Press, 1993), *The Dominion of the Dead* (Chicago: University of Chicago Press, 2005), and *Gardens: An Essay on the Human Condition* (Chicago: University of Chicago Press, 2009). These explorations in moral philosophy emerge from the academic precincts not of philosophy but of comparative literature, confirming Bates's thesis.

88. Bates, "Stanley Cavell and Ethics," 39.

89. Diamond, "The Difficulty of Reality and the Difficulty of Philosophy," in Cavell et al., *Philosophy and Animal Life*, 74–78.

90. Stanley Cavell, *Conditions Handsome and Unhandsome* (Chicago: University of Chicago Press, 1990), 2.

11. AN EMERSON GONE MAD: THOREAU'S AMERICAN CYNICISM
Douglas R. Anderson

1. Ralph Waldo Emerson, *The Portable Emerson*, ed. C. Bode (New York: Penguin Books, 1981), 297.

2. See, e.g., Pierre Hadot, "There Are Nowadays Professors of Philosophy, But Not Philosophers," *Journal of Speculative Philosophy* 19, no. 3 (2005): 229–37.

3. Antisthenes, according to Paul A. Vander Waerdt, "was the spiritual father of the Cynics and apparently the most influential of the Socratics during the first fifteen years after Socrates' death." See *The Socratic Movement* (Ithaca, N.Y.: Cornell University Press, 1994), 7. And although he may not have had a master-pupil relationship with Diogenes, Antisthenes is named the originator of Cynicism by a number of Hellenistic authors, including Epictetus, Dio Chyrsostom, and Diogenes Laertius. Furthermore, as A. A. Long notes, "Antisthenes' writings and his interpretation of Socrates were probably the most potent influences on Diogenes' philosophical development." See A. A. Long, *The Cynics* (Berkeley: University of California Press, 1996), 32. So although Antisthenes did not have a direct influence on Diogenes and subsequent Cynics, he does share the Cynics' basic orientation, which explains why he came to be viewed as a founding figure. See D. R. Dudley, *A History of Cynicism* (London: Methuen, 1937), 1–16.

4. Jeffrey Henderson, ed., *Diogenes Laertius II*, trans. R. D. Hicks (Cambridge, Mass.: Harvard University Press, 2000), 27. Modified translation.

5. Ibid., 21.

6. Julie Piering, "Cynics," in *The Internet Encyclopedia of Philosophy*, http://www.iep.utm.edu/c/cynics.htm.

7. R. F. Nash, *Wilderness and the American Mind* (New Haven, Conn.: Yale University Press, 1967).

8. Piering, "Cynics," 3.

9. Henry David Thoreau, *The Portable Thoreau*, ed. C. Bode (New York: Penguin Books, 1982), 566.

10. Piering, "Cynics," 4.

11. William Desmond, *Cynics* (Stocksfield: Acumen, 2008), 153.

12. Henry David Thoreau, *The Works of Thoreau*, ed. H. S. Canby (Boston: Houghton Mifflin, 1946), 21.

13. Thoreau, *Portable Thoreau*, 632.

14. Henderson, *Diogenes Laertius II*, 29.

15. Thoreau, *Portable Thoreau*, 590.

16. Ibid., 591.

17. Ibid., 566.

18. Ibid., 457.

19. Ibid., 613.

20. Piering, "Cynics," 2.

21. Thoreau, *Portable Thoreau*, 306.

22. Henderson, *Diogenes Laertius II*, 107.

23. Ibid.

24. The same mistaken prejudice pervades our American education system where we honor mathematicians and scientists over humanists. Often, high school "honors" courses in mathematics are strictly exclusionary, whereas honors English or literature courses are open to anyone who wants to join.

25. Henderson, *Diogenes Laertius II*, 107.

26. Thoreau, *Portable Thoreau*, 623.

27. Ibid., 638.

28. Thoreau, *Works*, 22.

29. Thoreau, *The Portable Thoreau*, 636.

30. See Piering, "Cynics," for a brief discussion of these three. See also Desmond, *Cynics*, 49.

31. Thoreau, *Portable Thoreau*, 325.

32. Thoreau, *Works*, 8.

33. Henderson, *Diogenes Laertius II*, 25.

34. Thoreau, *Works*, 12.

35. Thoreau, *Portable Thoreau*, 335.

36. Thoreau, *Portable Thoreau*, 567.
37. Desmond, *Cynics*, 158.
38. Thoreau, *Works*, 9.
39. Henderson, *Diogenes Laertius II*, 53.
40. Thoreau, *Works*, 8.
41. Ibid., 9.
42. Piering, "Cynics," 5.
43. Thoreau, *Portable Thoreau*, 343.
44. Henderson, *Diogenes Laertius II*, 109. See also 33.
45. Thoreau, *Portable Thoreau*, 469.
46. Ibid., 270.
47. Ibid., 562.
48. Foucault, 1983 lecture on Cynicism, http://foucault.info/documents/parrhesiasts/foucault.diogenes.en.html, p. 2.
49. Thoreau, *Portable Thoreau*, 632.
50. Henderson, *Diogenes Laertius II*, 49.
51. Foucault, 1983 lecture, 2.
52. Thoreau, *Portable Thoreau*, 259.
53. Ibid., 270.
54. Dudley, *History of Cynicism*, 45.
55. Thoreau, *Portable Thoreau*, 270.
56. Thoreau, *Works*, 21.
57. Thoreau, *Portable Thoreau*, 630.

12. HENRY DAVID THOREAU: THE ASIAN THREAD
Robert Kuhn McGregor

1. For an elaboration of my interpretation on any points of Thoreau's biography, please consult Robert Kuhn McGregor, *A Wider View of the Universe: Henry Thoreau's Study of Nature* (Urbana: University of Illinois Press, 1997). I have drawn freely from my own book, especially for the last third of this essay.
2. Robert D. Richardson Jr., *Emerson: The Mind on Fire* (Berkeley: University of California Press, 1995), 114–17; Ralph Waldo Emerson, *Nature: A Facsimile of the First Edition* (Boston: Beacon Press, 1985).
3. Emerson, *Nature*; John McAleer, *Ralph Waldo Emerson: Days of Encounter* (Boston: Little, Brown, 1984), 149–69; Walter Harding, *The Days of Henry David Thoreau* (New York: Dover, 1982), 52–157; Alan D. Hodder, "'Ex Oriente Lux': Thoreau's Ecstasies and the Hindu Texts," *Harvard Theological Review* 86, no. 4 (1993): 403–38; Ralph Waldo Emerson, "The Over-Soul," in *Essays: First and Second Series* (New York: Vintage Books, 1990), 153–70.
4. Hodder, "Ex Oriente Lux." Hodder expands his discussion in *Thoreau's Ecstatic Witness* (New Haven, Conn.: Yale University Press, 2001).

5. Ibid.; Arthur Christy, *The Orient in American Transcendentalism* (New York: Octagon Books, 1969); F. I. Carpenter, *Emerson and Asia* (Cambridge: Harvard University Press, 1930); Beongcheon Yu, *The Great Circle: American Writers and the Orient* (Detroit: Wayne State University Press, 1983); Rick Fields, *How the Swans Came to the Lake: A Narrative History of Buddhism in America* (Boston: Shambhala Press, 1986).

6. *Mahabharata, Harivansa, ou Histoire de la Famille de Hari*, 2 vols., trans. M. A. Langlois (Paris: Oriental Translation Fund of Great Britain and Ireland, 1834–35).

7. Harding, *Days of Henry Thoreau*, 113–57; Robert D. Richardson Jr., *Henry Thoreau: A Life of the Mind* (Los Angeles: University of California Press, 1986), 89–90; Richardson, *Emerson*; Hodder, "Ex Oriente Lux."

8. Scholars have cast some doubt on whether the effort was primarily Thoreau's work, though most analysts continue to accept his authorship. We can safely say that Thoreau took considerable interest in the Buddhist texts, adapting the images found in the *Dial* translations for his own uses in *A Week on the Concord and Merrimack Rivers*. See Hodder, "Ex Oriente Lux," and K. P. Van Anglen, Introduction to Henry David Thoreau, *Translations* (Princeton, N.J.: Princeton University Press, 1986), 160. Burnouf's translation is entitled *Sassharmapundarika, Le Lotus de la bonne loi*, trans. M. Eugene Burnouf (Paris: Asiatic Society of Paris, n.d.).

9. Thoreau's most direct contributions to the "Ethnical Scriptures" series in the *Dial* were "The Laws of Manu" (January 1843); "The Chinese Four Books" (October 1843), and "The Preaching of the Buddha" (January 1844). The significance of Thoreau's translation of the Lotus Sutra is discussed in Fields, *How the Swans Came to the Lake*, 59–65.

10. "The Preaching of the Buddha," *Dial*, January 1844, 391–401.

11. *The Lotus Sutra*, trans. Burton Watson (New York: Columbia University Press, 1993), 97–106.

12. Linck C. Johnson, *Thoreau's Complex Weave: The Writing of* A Week on the Concord and Merrimack Rivers (Charlottesville: Bibliographical Society of the University of Virginia, 1986); Henry David Thoreau, *A Week on the Concord and Merrimack Rivers* (Princeton, N.J.: Princeton University Press, 1980).

13. Thoreau, *Week*, 66–67, 71.

14. Ibid., 135–43; Arthur L. Herman, *A Brief Introduction to Hinduism* (Boulder, Colo.: Westview Press, 1991).

15. Emerson, *Nature*; Johnson, *Thoreau's Complex Weave*, 202–60.

16. Henry David Thoreau, "Ktaadn and the Maine Woods," *Union Magazine* 3, five installments (July–November, 1848): 29–33,73–79, 132–37, 177–82, 216–20; Thoreau, *Week*, 382.

17. James Elliot Cabot, "The Philosophy of the Ancient Hindoos," *Massachusetts Quarterly Review* 4 (September 1848): 26–47.

18. J. Lyndon Shanley, *The Making of Walden* (Chicago: University of Chicago Press, 1957); Richardson, *Thoreau*, pp. 204–5.

19. Henry David Thoreau, *The Writings of Henry David Thoreau: Journal*, 8 vols. to date (Princeton, N.J.: Princeton University Press, 1981–2002) 3:21–22, 29; *Mahabharata, Harivansa*; Thoreau, "The Transmigration of the Seven Brahmins," in *Translations*, ed. K. P. Van Anglen (Princeton, N.J.: Princeton University Press, 1986), 135–44.

20. *Puranas. Vishnupurana. The Vishnu Purana, a System of Hindu Mythology and Tradition* (London: J. Murray, 1840); Isvarakrsna, *The Sankhya Karika*, trans. Henry Thomas Colebrooke (Oxford: Oriental Translation Fund, 1837); *Vedas. Samaveda. Translation of the Sanhita of the Sama Veda*, trans. Rev. J. Stevenson (London: Oriental Translation Fund, 1842); Kalidasa, *Sakoontala; or The Lost Ring*, trans. Sir William Jones (London: Rivingtons and Cochrane, 1825); Asiatic Society of Bengal, *Bibliotheca Indica: A Collection of Oriental Works*, vol. 14 (Calcutta: East India Company, 1853); David Collie, *The Chinese Classical Work, Commonly Called The Four Books* (Malacca: Mission Press, 1828); Confucius, *The Works of Confucius*, vol. 1, trans. J. Marshman (Serampore: Mission Press, 1809); Thoreau, *Journal*, 3:61.

21. Sankhya Karika; Thoreau, *Journal*, 3:216–17.

22. Thoreau, "Transmigration of the Seven Brahmins."

23. Manu, *Institutes of Hindu Law*, trans. Sir William Jones (London: Rivingtons and Cochrane, 1825), chapter 1, verses 10–50; Thoreau, "Literary Notebook," extracts published by Kenneth Walter Cameron, *Transcendental Apprenticeship: Notes on Young Henry Thoreau's Reading* (Hartford, Conn.: Transcendental Books, 1976), 189–90.

24. Vishnu Purana, chaps. 1, 2, 5.

25. Mahabharata; Harivansa; Thoreau, *Journal*, 3:215.

26. *Bhagvat-Geeta*, trans. Charles Wilkins (London: C. Nourse, 1785), 37, 52–54, 62–64, 75.

27. For discussions of the place of nature in traditional Western thought, see Carolyn Merchant, *Ecological Revolutions* (Chapel Hill: University of North Carolina Press, 1989, and Merchant, *The Death of Nature: Women, Ecology, and the Scientific Revolution* (San Francisco: Harper and Row, 1980); Clarence Glacken, *Traces on the Rhodian Shore: Nature and Culture in Western Thought to the End of the Eighteenth Century* (Berkeley: University of California Press, 1967); Anna L. Peterson, *Being Human: Ethics, Environment, and Our Place in the World* (Berkeley: University of California Press, 2001).

28. Loren Eiseley, "Thoreau's Vision of the Natural World," in *The Star Thrower* (New York: Harcourt, Brace, Jovanovich, 1978), 229; see also H. Daniel Peck, "Better Mythology: Perception and Emergence in Thoreau's Journal," in

Thoreau's World and Ours, ed. E. A. Schofield and R. C. Baron (Golden, Colo.: North American Press, 1993), 304–15.

29. Thoreau, "Walking," in *The Major Essays of Henry David Thoreau*, ed. Richard Dillman (New York: Whitson, 2001), 180; Shanley, *Making of Walden*, 29; Henry David Thoreau, *Walden* (Princeton, N.J.: Princeton University Press, 1971), 57, 85, 96, 106–7, 270, 298.

30. Hodder, "Ex Oriente Lux"; Fields, *How the Swans Came to the Lake*, 59–65.

31. Lotus Sutra, 151.

32. Thoreau, *Walden*, 17–18, 84.

33. Ibid., 89–90.

34. Ibid., 90.

35. Ibid., 333.

36. Harding, *Days of Henry Thoreau*, 346–50; Richardson, *Thoreau*, 336–38.

13. THE IMPACT OF THOREAU'S POLITICAL ACTIVISM
Paul Friedrich

1. For instance: "In the morning I bathe my intellect in the stupendous and cosmogonal philosophy of the Bhagavat-Geeta . . . in comparison with which our modern world and its literature seem puny and trivial, and I doubt if that philosophy is not to be referred to a previous state of existence, so remote is its sublimity from our conceptions" (Henry David Thoreau, "The Pond in Winter," in *Walden*, ed. Jeffrey S. Cramer [New Haven, Conn.: Yale University Press, 2004], 287–88).

2. See, e.g., The Bhagavad-Gita, trans. R. C. Zaehner (Oxford: Oxford University Press, 1973), 10.10.

3. Len Gougeon, *Virtue's Hero: Emerson, Antislavery, and Reform* (Athens: University of Georgia Press, 1990), p. 152.

4. Thoreau, *Walden*, 166.

5. Ibid., 198.

6. Walter Harding, *The Days of Henry Thoreau* (New York: Alfred A. Knopf, 1965), 346–50.

7. Henry David Thoreau, "Resistance to Civil Government," in *Walden and "Resistance to Civil Government,"* ed. William Rossi (New York: W. W. Norton, 1992), 233.

8. Henry David Thoreau, "Slavery in Massachusetts," in *The Essays of Henry D. Thoreau*, ed. Lewis Hyde (New York: North Point Press, 2002), 193.

9. Robert D. Richardson, *Henry Thoreau: A Life of the Mind* (Berkeley: University of California Press, 1986), 372.

10. Harding, *Days of Henry Thoreau*, 418.

11. Henry David Thoreau, "A Plea for Captain John Brown," in *The Essays of Henry D. Thoreau*, 137. On Thoreau's strategy, also employed throughout

Walden, of assailing the complacencies of his fellow Americans with reference to their own religious ideals, see also Michael West, *Transcendental Wordplay* (Athens: Ohio University Press, 2000), 436–37.

12. David S. Reynolds, *Beneath the American Renaissance: The Subversive Imagination in the Age of Emerson and Melville* (New Haven, Conn.: Yale University Press, 1988).

13. *The Mind of Mahatma Gandhi*, ed. R. K. Prabhu and U. R. Rau (Ahmedabad: Navajivan Publishing House, 1968).

14. Mahatma Gandhi, as quoted by Webb Miller in *I Found No Peace* (New York: Garden City, 1938), 238–39.

15. Henry S. Salt, *The Life of Henry David Thoreau* (Urbana: University of Illinois Press, 1993), 100–101.

16. George Hendrick, "The Influence of Thoreau's 'Civil Disobedience' on Gandhi's *Satyagraha*," *New England Quarterly* 29, no. 4 (1956): 471.

17. P. V. Narasimha Rao, "Speech to a Joint Meeting of the House and Senate." Manuscript delivered in 2000. For further information see Paul Friedrich, *The Gita within Walden* (Albany: State University of New York Press, 2008), 140. Some of the material in this chapter can also be found in a list of biographical examples on pages 134–37 of *The Gita within Walden*.

14. *WALDEN* REVISITED: AN INTERVIEW WITH STANLEY CAVELL
Interviewed by Rick Anthony Furtak

1. Henry David Thoreau, *Walden; or, Life in the Woods* (New Haven, Conn.: Yale University Press, 2004), 172–73, 273.

2. Stanley Cavell, *The Senses of Walden: An Expanded Edition* (Chicago: University of Chicago Press, 1992), 51.

3. In the email exchange, Cavell uses "nb" (nota bene, or note well) to call attention to an echo in Descartes of a phrase used by Thoreau.

4. Cf. René Descartes, *Meditations on First Philosophy*, trans. Donald A. Cress (Indianapolis: Hackett, 1993), 13–15.

5. Thoreau, *Walden*, 1–2.

6. Ludwig Wittgenstein, *Philosophical Investigations*, trans. G. E. M. Anscombe (Oxford: Blackwell, 1953), cited parenthetically in the main text of this interview.

7. Stanley Cavell, *The Claim of Reason*, 2nd ed. (New York: Oxford University Press, 1999), 496: "But can philosophy become literature and still know itself?"

8. Stanley Cavell, "Night and Day: Heidegger and Thoreau," in *Appropriating Heidegger*, ed. James Faulconer and Mark Wrathall (Cambridge: Cambridge University Press, 2000), 40. Cf. Thoreau, *Walden*, 95: "God himself culminates in the present moment, and will never be more divine in all the ages. And we are

enabled to apprehend at all what is sublime and noble only by the perpetual instilling and drenching of the reality that surrounds us."

9. Thoreau, *Walden*, 95: "The universe constantly and obediently answers to our conceptions." Cavell portrays this as "an elegant summary of the *Critique of Pure Reason*" in *Senses of Walden*, 125.

10. Cavell, *Senses of Walden*, 103–4. On Emerson's epistemology, or logic, of moods, see *Senses of Walden*, 126.

11. The word "prompts" occurred in a follow-up email message.

12. Stanley Cavell, *This New Yet Unapproachable America* (Albuquerque: Living Batch Press, 1989).

13. Most notably, Alfred Tauber, in *Henry David Thoreau and the Moral Agency of Knowing* (Berkeley: University of California Press, 2001). See also the essays in this volume by Stanley Bates, Russell Goodman, James Reid, Laura Dassow Walls, Rick Anthony Furtak, Alfred Tauber, and Edward Mooney.

14. Stanley Cavell, *In Quest of the Ordinary* (Chicago: University of Chicago Press, 1988), 14–21.

Contributors

Douglas R. Anderson is Professor of Philosophy at Southern Illinois University, Carbondale. He works on the history of philosophy and American philosophy especially, and is interested in philosophy's relationship with other dimensions of culture. He is the author of *Philosophy Americana* (2006) and of two books about the philosophy of Peirce, in addition to numerous other publications.

Stanley Bates is Professor Emeritus of Philosophy at Middlebury College, where he continues to teach in his retirement. He has written on ethical themes in the work of Cavell, Emerson, and Wittgenstein, and on various topics in the philosophy of art. At present, he is working on a book about moral perfectionism.

Philip J. Cafaro is Associate Professor of Philosophy at Colorado State University. His scholarly interests center on environmental ethics, virtue ethics, wild lands preservation, and population and consumption issues. He is the author of *Thoreau's Living Ethics* (2004) and has contributed to various philosophical journals and edited collections.

Stanley Cavell is Walter M. Cabot Professor, Emeritus, of Aesthetics and the General Theory of Value, in the Department of Philosophy at Harvard University, and former President of the American Philosophical Association. He is one of the most illustrious philosophers of recent times, having earned wide acclaim for his work, which centers on the intersection of American, continental, and analytic philosophy, psychoanalytic thought, and the arts. He is the author of eighteen books, including

Must We Mean What We Say? (1969), *The Senses of Walden* (1972), *The Claim of Reason* (1979), *Pursuits of Happiness* (1981), *Disowning Knowledge* (1987), *Conditions Handsome and Unhandsome* (1990), *A Pitch of Philosophy* (1994), *Philosophy the Day After Tomorrow* (2005), and a philosophical memoir titled *Little Did I Know* (2010).

Jonathan Ellsworth is an independent scholar who lives in Santa Fe, New Mexico. During his time as a graduate student at the University of Chicago, he also taught in the Philosophy Department at Wheaton College. His publications include "Apophasis and Askêsis in Mystical Theology," in *Rethinking Philosophy of Religion*, edited by Philip Goodchild (2004), along with other articles and book reviews.

Paul Friedrich is Professor Emeritus of Social Thought, Anthropology, and Linguistics at the University of Chicago, where he is still actively teaching. His many books include *The Meaning of Aphrodite* (1978), *The Language Parallax: Linguistic Relativism and Poetic Indeterminacy* (1986), and *Harmony in Babel: Selected Poems and Translations* (2007).

Rick Anthony Furtak is Associate Professor of Philosophy at Colorado College. He is author of *Wisdom in Love* (2005) and editor of *Kierkegaard's* Concluding Unscientific Postscript: *A Critical Guide* (2010), in addition to other literary and philosophical publications. He teaches widely in the history of philosophy, moral psychology, and existential thought, and is currently working on a book about emotion and cognition.

Russell B. Goodman is Regents Professor in the Department of Philosophy at the University of New Mexico. His books include *American Philosophy and the Romantic Tradition* (1990) and *Wittgenstein and William James* (2002), and he is currently at work on a history of American philosophy. He has written on a variety of figures and themes in the history of ideas—European, Asian, and Anglo-American—ranging from Neoplatonism to pragmatism.

Robert Kuhn McGregor is Professor of History at the University of Illinois, Springfield. His scholarship is focused on American and environmental history, as well as modern English literature, and he is the author of *A Wider View of the Universe: Henry Thoreau's Study of Nature* (1997).

Edward F. Mooney is Professor of Philosophy and Religion at Syracuse University. The titles of two of his recent books convey the range of his interests: *On Søren Kierkegaard* (2007) and *Lost Intimacy in American Thought* (2009). He writes and teaches on a number of thinkers whose work lies at the intersection of philosophy, religion, poetry, and literature.

James D. Reid has previously taught at the University of Chicago, Colorado College, and the College of William of Mary, in addition to the United States Air Force Academy. He is currently Assistant Professor of Philosophy at Metropolitan State College of Denver. He has written on the philosophical legacy of Kant, Fichte, Heidegger, and Dilthey, among others, and his essays have appeared in the *Review of Metaphysics*, the *Kantian Review*, and the *Journal of the History of Philosophy*. His forthcoming book is called *Heidegger's Moral Ontology*.

Alfred I. Tauber is Professor of Philosophy and Zoltan Kohn Professor of Medicine at Boston University, where he directed the Center for Philosophy and History of Science from 1993 to 2010. He has written extensively on how scientific knowledge rests on a complex array of epistemic and nonepistemic values. His books include *Henry David Thoreau and the Moral Agency of Knowing* (2001), *Science and the Quest for Meaning* (2009), and *Freud, the Reluctant Philosopher* (2010).

Laura Dassow Walls is William P. and Hazel B. White Professor of English at the University of Notre Dame, where she is also affiliated with the graduate program in the history and philosophy of science. She has published widely on Thoreau, Emerson, and related figures, and she is the editor of *The Concord Saunterer: A Journal of Thoreau Studies*. Her most recent book, *Passage to Cosmos: Alexander von Humboldt and the Shaping of America* (2009), won the Merle Curti Award for intellectual history from the Organization of American Historians, and she has received a Guggenheim Fellowship for her next book project, *Writing the Cosmos: The Life of Henry David Thoreau*.

Index

AMERICAN PHILOSOPHY

Douglas R. Anderson and Jude Jones, series editors

Kenneth Laine Ketner, ed., *Peirce and Contemporary Thought: Philosophical Inquiries.*

Max H. Fisch, ed., *Classic American Philosophers: Peirce, James, Royce, Santayana, Dewey, Whitehead, second edition.* Introduction by Nathan Houser.

John E. Smith, *Experience and God, second edition.*

Vincent G. Potter, *Peirce's Philosophical Perspectives.* Ed. by Vincent Colapietro.

Richard E. Hart and Douglas R. Anderson, eds., *Philosophy in Experience: American Philosophy in Transition.*

Vincent G. Potter, *Charles S. Peirce: On Norms and Ideals, second edition.* Introduction by Stanley M. Harrison.

Vincent M. Colapietro, ed., *Reason, Experience, and God: John E. Smith in Dialogue.* Introduction by Merold Westphal.

Robert J. O'Connell, S.J., *William James on the Courage to Believe, second edition.*

Elizabeth M. Kraus, *The Metaphysics of Experience: A Companion to Whitehead's "Process and Reality," second edition.* Introduction by Robert C. Neville.

Kenneth Westphal, ed., *Pragmatism, Reason, and Norms: A Realistic Assessment—Essays in Critical Appreciation of Frederick L. Will.*

Beth J. Singer, *Pragmatism, Rights, and Democracy.*

Eugene Fontinell, *Self, God, and Immorality: A Jamesian Investigation.*

Roger Ward, *Conversion in American Philosophy: Exploring the Practice of Transformation.*

Michael Epperson, *Quantum Mechanics and the Philosophy of Alfred North Whitehead.*

Kory Sorrell, *Representative Practices: Peirce, Pragmatism, and Feminist Epistemology.*

Naoko Saito, *The Gleam of Light: Moral Perfectionism and Education in Dewey and Emerson.*

Josiah Royce, *The Basic Writings of Josiah Royce.*

Douglas R. Anderson, *Philosophy Americana: Making Philosophy at Home in American Culture.*

James Campbell and Richard E. Hart, eds., *Experience as Philosophy: On the World of John J. McDermott.*

John J. McDermott, *The Drama of Possibility: Experience as Philosophy of Culture.* Edited by Douglas R. Anderson.

Larry A. Hickman, *Pragmatism as Post-Postmodernism: Lessons from John Dewey.*

Larry A. Hickman, Stefan Neubert, and Kersten Reich, eds., *John Dewey Between Pragmatism and Constructivism.*

Dwayne A. Tunstall, *Yes, But Not Quite: Encountering Josiah Royce's Ethico-Religious Insight.*

Josiah Royce, *Race Questions, Provincialism, and Other American Problems, Expanded Edition.* Edited by Scott L. Pratt and Shannon Sullivan.

Lara Trout, *The Politics of Survival: Peirce, Affectivity, and Social Criticism.*

John R. Shook and James A. Good, *John Dewey's Philosophy of Spirit, with the 1897 Lecture on Hegel.*

Gregory Fernando Pappas, ed., *Pragmatism in the Americas.*

Donald J. Morse, *Faith in Life: John Dewey's Early Philosophy.*

Douglas R. Anderson and Carl R. Hausman, *Conversations on Peirce: Reals and Ideals.*